IMAGINING
WORLD
POLITICS

Steven L. Schweizer

Benedictine College

Prentice Hall, Upper Saddle River, New Jersey 07458

Library of Congress Cataloging-in-Publication Data

Schweizer, Steven L. (Steven Laurence), (date)
    Imagining world politics / Steven L. Schweizer.
        p.   cm.
    Includes bibliographical references and index.
    ISBN 0-13-241761-8
    1. World politics—1989–   I. Title.
D860.S38   1997   96-11411
327.1'01—dc20   CIP

Editorial director : Charlyce Jones Owen
Acquisitions editor: Michael Bickerstaff
Editorial assistant: Anita Castro
Editorial/production supervision: Linda Pawelchak
Marketing manager: Chaunfayta Hightower
Cover design: Jayne Conte
Copy editing: Valerie Havas
Proofreading: Maine Proofreading Services
Manufacturing buyer: Robert Anderson

This book was set in 10/12 Palatino by NK Graphics
and was printed and bound by RR Donnelley & Sons.
The cover was printed by Phoenix Color Corp.

 © 1997 by Prentice-Hall, Inc.
Simon & Schuster/A Viacom Company
Upper Saddle River, New Jersey 07458

Printed in the United States of America
10   9   8   7   6   5   4   3   2   1

ISBN 0-13-241761-8

Prentice-Hall International (UK) Limited, *London*
Prentice-Hall of Australia Pty. Limited, *Sydney*
Prentice-Hall Canada Inc., *Toronto*
Prentice-Hall Hispanoamericana, S.A., *Mexico*
Prentice-Hall of India Private Limited, *New Delhi*
Prentice-Hall of Japan, Inc., *Tokyo*
Simon & Schuster Asia Pte. Ltd., *Singapore*
Editora Prentice-Hall do Brasil, Ltda., *Rio de Janeiro*

To My Parents
Robin Brown Schweizer
and
Ralph G. Schweizer

CONTENTS

ACKNOWLEDGMENTS

I would like to thank the colleagues and students who have made this book possible. I am particularly grateful for the wise guidance given by Herbert Tillema (University of Missouri—Columbia), James McCormick (Iowa State University), Mariusz Dobek (Benedictine College), and T.H. Baughman (Benedictine College), all of whom helped me to conceptualize this project. I am also appreciative of the comments that the reviewers made; their suggestions and criticisms enabled me to hone my arguments. These reviewers were Peter G. Howse, American River College; William E. Kelly, Auburn University; and George S. Masannet, Western Kentucky University.

I want to thank Roger Siau (Benedictine College) for his translations of Nikolai Danilevski's darker passages. I am grateful to Katherine Immel (University of Kansas) for the editorial suggestions that have given greater clarity to my prose. I am appreciative of the help professors Douglas McKenzie and Michael O'Hare (Benedictine College) gave me in solving various software problems that arose in the course of this project. I want to thank two of my students at Benedictine College, Marcela Keim and Darren Samson, for reading and commenting on an early draft of this text. Their comments and criticisms helped me keep this book relevant to contemporary students' concerns and interests. I also wish to express my gratitude to the students in my world politics classes who have challenged and shaped my thinking about many of the ideas that are offered here.

I am particularly appreciative of the support I received from Benedictine College and Cornell College. I owe a debt of gratitude to Benedictine College and particularly to R. L. Cook, dean of the college, for providing me with a leave of absence and a timely sabbatical to complete this project. At Cornell College, I am indebted to the Department of Politics (colleagues Craig Allin, David Loebsack, and Robert Sutherland) and the dean of the college, Dennis Damon Moore, for providing the intellectual stimulation, financial support, and the leisure that allowed me to do most of the research that made this book possible.

I would also like to thank the following resource people: the interlibrary loan personnel at the Atchison (Kansas) Public Library and at Cornell and Benedictine College made my research much easier than it would have otherwise been. I particularly want to commend Sue Lifson of Cornell College, Claudia Bosshammer of the Atchison Public Library, and Florine Muhlenbruck of Benedictine College for the efforts they made to track down particularly elusive books. I want to thank one of my students, Micki Beermann, for the bibliographic work she did for me.

Finally, I owe a debt of gratitude to the fine Prentice Hall staff with whom I worked so closely. I appreciate the support of Political Science Editor Mike Bickerstaff and Editorial Assistant Anita Castro in making this book a part of Prentice Hall's offerings in political science and in securing the reviewers who helped me think more critically about the text. I want to particularly thank Production Editor Linda B. Pawelchak and Copy Editor Valarie Havas for the editorial guidance that has made this book much better than it would have otherwise been.

Although all these individuals and institutions contributed to this book's strengths, I am ultimately responsible for the arguments that are presented herein. Any errors in fact, interpretation, and judgment rest solely with me.

Steven L. Schweizer
Atchison, Kansas

INTRODUCTION

Dead Poets Society was and still is a popular film. Two of the film's themes are shared by this book: making the most of opportunities and wondering about the more important things in life. As you may recall, the film is about the adventures of a group of boys attending an eastern prep school. The opening minutes of the film give us a picture of a traditional, stuffy campus where the boys, under the lash of perhaps overly strict Latin, mathematics, and chemistry teachers, suddenly encounter a wonderfully refreshing literature teacher named John Keating. A graduate of the school, Keating seeks to inspire his students to develop an understanding of themselves and to value the things that are most important in life. In one memorable scene, Keating ushers the boys from the classroom to the hallway, where a trophy case displays photographs of former students. Keating urges the boys to lean forward and to listen to the whispered advice of these bygone students: "Carpe diem. Seize the day, boys. Make your lives extraordinary."[1] The point is made: each boy has the potential to do something exceptional with his life. But one question remains: will he seize the day, discover his talents, and commit himself to becoming extraordinary?

How is this related to world politics? We are living in a most interesting time—a time of uncertainty but one that promises all the hope and opportunity that Keating lays before his students. On the one hand, conflict in southeast Europe shows us that modern politics is strongly affected by historical forces that seem to defy control. Humans, it seems, are unable to create a peaceful, just world order. On the other hand, Niccolò Machiavelli, the sixteenth-century Italian political thinker, reminds us that life is not without hope. For Machiavelli, humans have control over half their actions; the other half is subject to "fate." We can argue about the proportion of our actions that can meaningfully affect world events; nevertheless, it is clear that we are far from being hemmed in by a world we did not make, cannot control, and have no hope of influencing. If Keating and Machiavelli teach us anything, it is that humans can be effective partners in change; they can bring about a much better world. The opportunities are there; we must simply make the most of them.

Are there greater opportunities today than there were ten years ago for bringing about a better world? Yes, but taking advantage of these opportunities will require rethinking what we want to achieve through world politics. Within the last decade, historical changes in international politics have created a whole new world of opportunities. The bipolar international system—a system dominated by two superpowers, the United States and the Soviet Union—has evaporated before our eyes and has given way to a new, evolving world order. In this new order, peace appears to be closer in the Middle East; more people are being fed than in the history of humankind; international support for solving environmental problems is increasing; the awareness of basic human rights is growing; and democratic regimes are beginning to take hold in Eastern Europe and, it is hoped, in Russia as well. However, the international political landscape is still littered with the remnants of the cold war: armed conflicts in the Persian Gulf, South America, and Africa; civil war in Liberia; ethnic "cleansing" in Bosnia; the resurgence of nationalism in Russia; and stagnant economics in so-called less developed countries. One senses that the way we have thought about world politics in the last fifty years cannot provide us with reliable guideposts for thinking about the problems bequeathed to us by the cold war or about the opportunities presented by its ending. By freeing ourselves from the cold war's intellectual straightjacket that has framed our recent thinking about world politics, we will have the opportunity to conceive of another way of handling the problems and aspirations of the world's people. Re-asking the fundamental questions that have helped us make sense of world politics can aid us in our quest for creating a just world order. To successfully address the challenges that we will face in the next fifty years, we will need to engage in broader conversations than we have in the past.

All of us have a personal interest in the great sea changes that are taking place in world politics. Nevertheless, it is not easy to see how world politics impacts our daily lives. By looking back at the cold war from our present vantage point, we can see its probable impact on our lives. In the last thirty years, how many Russians and Americans were aware of the debilitating effects that the cold war had on the economic well-being of each nation? Clearly, the cold war (and especially the nuclear arms race) was a major factor in the economic and political collapse of the Soviet Union, and many believe that it helped weaken the national and international economic position of the United States. The spread of communism led to America's involvement in the Vietnam War, an involvement that would ultimately increase Americans' skepticism about their government and about the effectiveness of citizen participation in politics. The cold war affected defense policies, which in turn impacted the lives of the American people. In the 1980s, heavy military spending without corresponding spending cuts or tax increases compounded the U.S. debt. By most accounts, the debt threatens the economic viability of the country and with that the standard of living of and economic opportunities for most of the American people. In the future, evolving world political and economic systems will have an impact on the lives of every person in the world. Economically, the fortunes of each citizen will be tied in some measure to the strengths and weaknesses of the world economy. In imperceptible and subtle ways, the world economy will help sort out the winners and losers in the game of life. The direction in which world political structures develop in the next decade or two will have an important, if invisible, impact on your life. A more threatening world would increase defense expenditures in ways that could hamper attempts to solve national social and economic problems. It is especially important for citizens of democratic nations to develop an understanding of the choices that lay before them. With that understanding, they can be part of a dialogue that will help structure the future world order—an order under which they will certainly live and from which they will not escape.

Given the great changes that have recently taken place in the world, there is a real need to engage each other in a revitalized, expanded dialogue about the nature and ends of world politics. This raises several questions. First, are there hidden questions that need to surface in this discussion—questions we have not asked because traditional approaches to world politics have discouraged them from being raised? Second, to what extent would the conversation benefit from an expanded knowledge of competing visions of world politics? Finally, what can serve to spark the human imagination in ways that can help us all think more seriously about world politics?

The first question is most intriguing because it suggests that some important issues remain outside the typical daily dialogue on world politics. For example, much of the conversation on the Gulf War centered on how the United States and its allies could persuade Saddam Hussein to leave Kuwait peacefully. Conversations focused on marshaling world public opinion, applying economic sanctions, and using the threat of a multinational force to persuade the Iraqi leader to leave Kuwait. Little attention centered on whether the economic sanctions were just, especially because the brunt of the economic hardships wrought by the sanctions fell most heavily on the people of Iraq. Beyond the Gulf War, there are myriad other concerns that are not typically found in public discussions of world politics. What moral responsibility, if any, do richer nations have toward people starving in poorer countries? What is the best form of international political organization and what should be its ends or goals? What are the rights of humankind, if any, and are some forms of international political organization more effective than others in securing these rights?

Moreover, one often forgets that actions taken by actors on the world political scene often have moral implications. Take an oversimplified issue in foreign trade: protective tariffs. Protective tariffs are taxes on imported goods that increase the price of foreign goods to the point that they are not competitive with domestic goods. Tariffs erected to protect manufacturers in one country may have the effect of restricting the ability of another country to sell its products abroad. In many cases, the tariffs perpetuate existing economic inequalities among nations. When rich nations erect tariffs to protect their own manufacturers and producers from less expensive products of poor nations, less developed countries find it difficult to sell their products to rich nations; and economic development in poor countries levels off or declines relative to rich nations. Thus, protective tariffs perpetuate or increase economic inequalities between the rich and poor nations. Beneath a seemingly straightforward trade policy, then, is the value of equality or inequality. Let us take a second example: justice and the international political system. Some suggest that world politics is a competitive struggle between nations for world power and influence. The victor in this struggle for power determines who is "rewarded" and who is "punished" in world politics; the strongest nation determines what is due to weaker ones. But what *is* due to the weaker nations of the world? Are we to believe the Greek historian Thucydides who reports the Athenians making the argument that the strong will do what they can, and the weak must suffer as they must? As these examples suggest, any serious thinking about world politics needs to include questions of value.

Because values and hidden questions exist in discussions of world politics, one purpose of this book is to raise twenty-one thematic areas, or issues, that will help the serious observer of world politics begin to think about them. Beginning with discussions about human nature and ending with a dialogue on a liberal international political and economic order, this book takes the reader through a series of issues that have occupied the minds of those who have thought seriously about world politics. Issues are raised concerning war, international law, power, freedom, equality, imperialism, the environment, empire, and world federalism. These and other issues are ordered in a way that will allow the reader to develop an integrated view of world politics.

Let us address the second question: how could an understanding of competing visions of world politics revitalize a conversation about world politics? As the world communication network expands and as nations become more dependent upon one another for their material well-being, discussions about world politics would benefit from a broader understanding of Western and non-Western ideas. Even though it is important to understand orthodox views of Western international relations theory (classicism, realism, liberalism, and Marxism), a number of alternative approaches deserve attention—including feminist, Islamic fundamentalist, and Russian nationalist and anarchist political theory. The Western canon—classicism, realism, liberalism, and Marxism—has inspired the way we think about ourselves, other cultures, politics in general, and world politics in particular. To disregard the canon is to strip us of those ideas that help us understand the meaning of life and to deny those of us in the West an understanding of how these ideas have developed over time. However, as the world, in all its diversity, enters an era in which international political power is to be more broadly shared, it is also important to consider the contributions that feminist, Islamic, and Russian nationalist and anarchist theories can bring to the conversation. The ideas embodied by these contending theories of world politics will be important in framing future discourses on world politics.

Let us return to a second point made in the *Dead Poets Society* in answering the third question: what can serve to spark the human imagination in ways that can help us all think more seriously about world politics? Mr. Keating—eager to get his students to think more critically about the world in which they live—mounts his desk. Towering over the class, he suggests that one's position in life defines how one perceives that life. In world politics, no two nations will perceive the international order in the same way. To understand how others view the world order requires an act of imagination and wonder on our part. Thus, the third and final purpose of this book is to encourage the reader to "wonder" about world politics. The Greek philosopher Aristotle once remarked that all knowledge begins in wonder. Wondering is an integral part of the human psyche. From the day that we first ask "why," we have embarked on a quest to understand the world in which we live. In trying to understand or even transform that world, humankind has made use of its imagination (and its sense of wonder) to arrive at the fundamental principles that serve as the wellspring of knowledge. As the human world changes before our eyes, presenting new challenges and new opportunities to build a better world, it is more important than ever to be able to sever ourselves from outmoded habits of thought. Now is the time to dare to imagine a different world, to wonder about alternative visions of the international order that could light the way at the dawn of this new day. We *should* wonder about world politics, because some kind of future world order will inevitably close in on us. But we have a choice. Each of us can develop a vision of a world order that will allow us to be partners in creating a better world for ourselves and our children. Or, we can let others, perhaps with more sinister plans, create that future world for us.

On Using This Book

As suggested earlier, my primary goal in writing this book is to expand the discourse on world politics. In so doing, I have written a book that will expose the reader to a wide variety of opinions on these twenty-one issues: human nature, human equality, the origin of the state, the ends of the state, and the best form of government (the foundation of world political thinking, Chapter 2); the actors in world politics; the equality of those actors; power; international anarchy, society, and law; war and peace; and the just war (Chapter 3); power, equality and liberty, justice, imperialism, preserving the environment, and human rights (the goals of actors in world politics, Chapter 4); the balance of power, world monarchy, world federation, and a liberal international political and economic order (alternative international orders, Chapter 5). This is not to say that there are only twenty-one issues that have been of perennial interest to political thinkers; there are more. Today, these issues appear to be some of the most important questions facing those who are interested in thinking about world politics. It is my hope that your discussion of these issues will go far beyond the classroom, and that the ideas contained in these pages will be discussed in dorms and apartments, in cafeterias and at dinner tables, in study sessions, and in organized or random conversations. I would hope that the knowledge gained from this book and the questions raised by it will become a part of a lifelong conversation on world politics. As a way of framing a dialogue on world political issues, I discuss how classicists, realists, liberals, and Marxists have posed and answered questions about each issue. Then I show how feminists, Russian nationalists, and Islamic fundamentalists have reacted to the canon. In the ensuing discourse, you will be able to use these ideas to think about, analyze, and debate the value of the answers provided by these political thinkers. Perhaps more important, this book will encourage you to raise other questions as you ponder these ideas.

I have organized this book in a way that will allow you to develop your own thoughts on world politics. I have written and structured the twenty-one issues so that how you think about one issue will help you think about subsequent issues. For example, how you conceive human nature will help structure the way you think about the best form of world political organization or about the causes of war and peace. In Chapter 2, I discuss fundamental concepts that serve as a foundation for developing your own world political views. You will be introduced to contending views on human nature, equality, the state, the best form of government, and the ends of government. I start with these ideas because you are most familiar with them. You probably have some opinions on the best form of government and some idea that governments are created for the purpose of securing, protecting, or promoting certain ends—perhaps life, liberty, and the pursuit of happiness, as Thomas Jefferson put it in the Declaration of Independence.[2] As you will see, many of the domestic arguments about the ends of government or best form of government can be applied to international politics. For example, arguments favoring a federal form of national government are often used to support a world federal form of government. Chapters 3 through 5 focus on issues in world politics. By developing an opinion on each issue with a view toward relating one issue to another, you will create a way of looking at and judging world politics, and you will walk away from this book with something of enduring value—your own theory of world politics. As a practical suggestion, you might wish to keep a journal of your responses to the twenty-one issues addressed in this book. Placing your evolving ideas on paper is often the best way to sort out where you stand on each issue.

Finally, it is my hope that this book will help you begin to "wonder" about the critical issues in world politics. In this era of political change, it is more important than ever for us to think seriously about the future world order. To create a mental image of a world that may be significantly different from the one you currently know requires an active imagination and a sense of wonder. I hope that this book will stimulate your imagination. To this end, I encourage you to read this text with the intention of developing your own view of world politics. Put the book down often, imaginatively reflect about what you have read, jot down responses to questions that the book raises in your mind, and discuss your thoughts with others. If you do these things, I believe that you will develop a deeper understanding of world politics, your place in it, and the contributions you can make to change it.

Finally, I would encourage you to e-mail constructive suggestions, comments, and criticisms about this text to me at sls@raven.benedictine.edu. Although I may not be able to incorporate all suggestions e-mailed to me into the next edition, I will give careful consideration to all correspondence. Let me thank those of you who take the time to write me.

NOTES

1. Steven Haft, Tony Thomas, and Paul Junger Witt, *Dead Poets Society* (Burbank: Touchstone Pictures, 1989).
2. "Declaration of Independence," *The Struggle for Democracy*, Edward S. Greenberg and Benjamin I. Page, 2d ed. (New York: HarperCollins College Pub., 1995), A17.

CHAPTER *1*

WONDERING ABOUT WORLD POLITICS

Many of us have heard John Lennon's popular song "Imagine," have read Reverend Martin Luther King's "I Have a Dream" speech, or have seen the Disney film *Beauty and the Beast*. Lennon asks the listener to conjure up a picture of a world where people live in peace and harmony. Martin Luther King asks us to dream of a time in which a universal brotherhood of humankind will arise. And in *Beauty and the Beast*, Belle—born into a community that is vastly smaller than her ambitions—longs for a chance to see a much larger world.[1] The thread that runs through these examples is simply the process of "wondering."

Wondering involves curiosity, intellectual speculation, thought, doubt, awe, amazement, admiration, spiritual elation, and surprise. Being naturally curious and inclined to intellectual speculation, humans wonder about the origins of the universe, the good life, solutions to the problem of racism, or why people voted for a particular presidential candidate. Wonder can also express a sense of doubt: we wonder if peace on earth will ever become a reality. Beyond what appears to be the intellectual side of wonder is the affective dimension. In speculating on the complexity of the human being, one might wonder—in amazement or awe—whether such an organism could be simply a random creation of a nondivine nature. Wonder may result in a spiritual elevation of the human soul. Wondering about God's plan for humankind brings believers into closer contact with the meaning of life and spiritually ennobles them. And wonder might also imply astonishment. One might wonder why someone behaved in a way that was simply out of character. Taken as a whole, wondering seems to be both affective and intel-

1

lectual. The intellectual vision of a world filled with diverse people walking hand in hand in peace, justice, and universal kinship is also awe-inspiring, emotionally captivating, and spiritually uplifting.

THE NATURE OF WONDERING

Put down this book and take several minutes to wonder about something in some detail. Once you have done this, think about the nature of wonderment. Undoubtedly, some of you wondered about what you would do for the weekend; others thought about what you would do next; others thought about their girlfriend or boyfriend; still others may have wondered about how to deal with some issue raised in class; and some may have even wondered about wondering! When you think about the wondering process, about what do you think? Two things seem to be involved in wonderment: first, the process of wondering and second, the object of wonder—the thing about which you are wondering. The process of wonderment involves what goes on in the intellect that allows each of us to wonder. The object of wonder, in contrast, refers to the subject matter that is the focus of the wondering.

Wondering seems to be a process; it suggests the existence of a world of ideas or images about which we wonder; and it implies a certain liberation. The process of wondering has many properties and dimensions. It seems to have a beginning and an end: we move from one kind of thought process into that of wonderment and then back again. Wondering appears to be something that we can control: we seem to be able to start and stop it at will. Wondering appears to be separated from the immediate world around us: we seem to be able to walk back and forth between the world in which we live and an "imaginary" world—a world of ideas or images. Wondering appears to be either a creative process or a discovery process: through wonderment we are able to discover something that is hidden from view or we are able to take ideas or images and put them in interesting new combinations. As a discovery process, wondering might involve conjuring up some idea that helps us make sense of why humans behave the way they do. As a creative process, wondering helps us imagine a gold- and diamond-studded mountain. Let us look at several of these features prior to turning to the object of imagination.

First, the process of wondering allows us to move out of the immediate world of consciousness and into a different state or level of consciousness. In the process of reading a book, you have no doubt put it down and begun to wonder about something substantially different. Something in the text may have inspired the departure; some personal problem may have suddenly popped into your mind; or perhaps you just needed a break. In wondering, you transport yourself to a seemingly different world—one that is much different from the world in which you live. It may be a world of ideas with which you are toying; a world of personal pain and anguish or one of love, peace, and inner harmony; a world of enchant-ment or of vexing devils and ghouls; or a world of sensual images—flowing streams, babbling brooks, chirping birds, and small animals scampering through rustling leaves. What is the nature of this imaginary world? Is it merely a fantasy land or is it in some mysterious way more "real" than the world we encounter each minute of our lives?

There are no simple answers to these questions; however, an argument can be made that this imaginary world of ideas is in fact more "real" than the world in which we live. To make such an argument, one would have to hold that the mate-rial, temporal world in which we live is but a distortion of the ideal world of ideas and spirit. If humans can know this perfect, eternal world of ideas, why is it that the world in which we live is riddled with murder, hatred, racism, war, and injus-tice? One answer is that humans have chosen to live mistakenly, valuing material objects above spiritual matters. They have created social, economic, political, reli-gious, and educational institutions that perpetuate values and patterns of social life that are destructive to genuine human association. Faced with pervasive in-equalities and philosophies that trivialize the spiritual dimension of life, human beings find it difficult to develop themselves and their personal relationships in ways that lead to true happiness.

A life lacking the proper social contexts that allow us to fulfill what it means to be truly human is "unreal." This assumption is illustrated by both Belle and the Beast in *Beauty and the Beast*. For Belle to achieve personal fulfillment, she must move beyond the confines of a parochial town that seemingly offers only an ego-centric, chauvinistic, demented hunter for a potential husband. Similarly, the Beast (a formerly handsome prince whose spiritual shortcomings were responsi-ble for his transformation into a physically grotesque creature) was doomed to re-main a "monster" until such time as the spark and pulse of love, eventually shared with Belle, allowed him to become human in the true sense of the word.[2] The point, of course, is that humans do not become truly and fully human until they join the web of humanity, a web of social relationships, joys, and responsibil-ities. A good society organizes the hearts and minds of all community members to encourage and support each person's pursuit of a fulfilling life. When eyes burn with hatred, souls seethe with vengeance, hearts seek in vain for lasting love or friendship, and minds remain ignorant of the knowledge or faith that makes sense of human existence, then the community has failed and human life has been de-graded. In contrast, a "good" society meets the physical needs of all its members, enabling them to unite in love and friendship and to create a community commit-ted to giving reality to the eternal ideal of justice.

This leads to the second point. The world of wonder is a world of ideas or images that are discovered by, or are creatures of, a creative mind. Given a real world of rationally ordered ideas that are accessible to human reason, the task of the intellect is simply to "discover" those ideas, not to "create" them. Discovery differs from creation in that discovery involves a process of making known that which exists but is temporarily unknown to the thinker; thus, it assumes that what is to be known exists beyond the immediate perception of the human mind. Thus, when one thinks of the discovery of America, one conjures up the existence of a landmass that is unknown to the explorers, a landmass made known through the discovery and exploration process. The creative process is much different, because it is based upon the bringing into existence of new ideas or things that did not previously exist in that form. One might argue that the computer, for example, is not found in some natural state but is a product of an active, inventive mind. That mind used an understanding of nature, matter, and mechanical and electrical processes to unite them into a new combination that takes the form and function of a computer. No doubt creativity and discovery are related to one another. Discovery of ideas that exist beyond human experience—ideas that exist in the mind of God, for example—may involve combining or generating ideas that are divine ideas. One can argue that Albert Einstein's theories of the universe were simply creative ideas that disclosed, however imperfectly, part of the mind of God. His novel theories were acts of discovery. On the other hand, there are those who would argue that creation need not involve the divine at all; in their view, creative ideas or inventions such as the lightbulb are merely examples of how the human intellect can be utilized in ingenious ways to produce new thoughts or objects.

Arguing that the wondering process focuses on the discovery of a body of rationally ordered ideas accessible to the human intellect, these ideas aim to structure and direct human life in a way that brings about its perfection. Wondering allows each person to gain access to ideas such as justice, peace, and freedom, and by understanding those ideas to create an economic, social, and political order that could serve as a model for improving life on earth. Thus, one of the beauties of wondering is that it allows us to contrast the life we live on earth with a life that, if we choose to live it, will bring goodness and human happiness in its wake.

This draws attention to the third component of wonder: liberation. Liberation releases something or someone from bondage. It is simultaneously a release "from" as well as a release "to" something. Lincoln's "Emancipation Proclamation," for example, liberated the nation from the moral, physical, economic, social, and political shackles of slavery. At the same time, it freed all Americans to live a life guided by justice and equality. Thus, wondering liberates humans from the social, economic, political, and theological shackles placed on them by life in a world that is too often marred by acts and philosophies of violence and injustice. Wondering leads us to an unfettered realm of ideas where goodness, truth, and social justice exist in all their splendor. The liberating effect of wonder is not dissimilar to the process of setting free a hot air balloon. As it is filled with hot air, the balloon strains against the moorings and the bags of ballast that prevent it from rising to its place in the heavens. After being released from these restraining influences, the balloon rises into a world of peace, tranquillity, and freedom—a world beyond the reach of humankind's injustices.

Now let us apply the concept of wondering to world politics. In the minds of many political scientists, wondering about world politics takes two fundamentally different forms: (1) thinking about political matters encountered in the everyday life of those people and nations involved in international relations and (2) developing thoughts on what constitutes a good, just international order and what policies actors on the world stage should pursue to make that order a reality. In the first case, wondering centers on subjects that we experience through our senses—things that we read in newspapers and magazines, hear on the radio, see on television, and discuss in everyday conversations about the international environment. Such wondering involves following the actions and interactions of the various "players," including nations; organized religious groups; the United Nations; the World Bank; terrorist groups; multinational corporations (MNCs), corporations with operations in more than one country; and international labor or business organizations. These actors may interact in any number of ways. They may, for example, engage in diplomacy, impose economic sanctions, wage wars, conduct arms races, or forge treaties. When political scientists wonder about everyday world politics, they are often—though not exclusively—looking for theories that explain why actors in world politics behave the way they do. For example, countless scholars have tried to develop theories explaining the causes of war. Some have created economic theories, suggesting that nations wage war because they need new markets or expanded access to natural resources. Others argue that males are more aggressive than females, and that males, who have created and controlled power in world politics, have developed an international system that condones and justifies war.

The second way of thinking about world politics centers on thinking about the "good" and just international order. This is referred to as the normative approach and is the domain of normative political theorists. Those involved in world political theory may not be so much interested in the everyday events of world politics as they are in identifying those values that should guide the thinking and policies of actors in world politics. They think about these types of questions: What is the best international political order? What is justice and what constitutes a just world order? What is equality and to what extent should nations be economically, politically, and legally equal? Is a war ever just and if so, what criteria should be used to determine the justness of a war? What are the nature and origin of international law? Are there such things as human rights and if so, what are the specific rights granted to humans? What are the causes of war and peace? What is freedom and should it be a goal of the international community to promote the freedom of individuals and states? What is sovereignty and are nations sovereign? These and many more questions are posed by international relations theorists.

As discussed in the Introduction, it is the position of this text that thinking about world politics suffers if the normative dimension is excluded from consideration. This is so for two reasons. First, thinking about politics is grounded in a greater world of value. Take something familiar to you: the American two-party system. When political scientists study the party system, they usually claim that their study is "value free"—free, in other words, from the influence of personal values. Although these political scientists bring such terms as "parties" and "competition" to the study, these terms are viewed as neither good nor bad, but rather as part of the world of political fact. There is, however, a contrary view. According to this perspective, any study of the American party system is laden with value judgments. The concepts of competition and parties are embedded in a greater normative theory of politics that presents competition as a good to be pursued. Competition, according to this way of thinking, brings out the good and the bad in people and situations. If we allow two candidates to compete for public office, the ensuing debate will reveal the strengths and weaknesses of the candidates, and the public will be better informed on the issues of the day. A lack of competition between political parties is not in the public interest; too much cooperation may discourage voting records from being discussed, may cause issues to be left unexplored, and may cause problems to remain unexamined. Regarding parties, the root of parties is "part." Many Americans believe that the diversity of the nation's population implies that our society is simply a whole divided into many parts, each of which deserves representation. Believing that one political party cannot represent everyone, they favor a political system comprised of at least two parties. This theory of a competitive party system is part of the Western liberal tradition that values diversity and competition. Thus, the very terms that we use to describe the operation of the American two-party system have a normative foundation in a broader philosophy of life.

Similarly, wondering about world politics can take the form of trying to come to a deeper understanding of the everyday events of world politics, or trying to discover which structures, norms, and values could best be used to bring about a good and just world order. This book focuses on the normative dimension of international relations, in an effort to help expand the dialogue about world politics. There are three reasons for focusing on the normative dimension of world politics. First, the most valued things in life center on questions of freedom, peace, justice, order, happiness, friendship, and human equality. Without these values that inspire and shape our lives, life would scarcely be worth living. Second, developing an understanding of a right and just world political order provides us with a way of judging the policies of nations and other world political actors. Finally, to the extent that the real world of justice and freedom differs from the world in which we live, the realm of justice and freedom serves to spark the imagination and the wondering process that are a natural part of the human intellect.

HOW TO WONDER ABOUT WORLD POLITICS

If wondering is natural to human beings, it might seem trivial to discuss the topic, "How to Wonder." In fact, whereas there is clearly an inclination to wonder, the wondering process takes different forms at different points in one's life and needs to be cultivated. Many psychologists, for example, believe that the objects of wonder change as intellectual growth occurs. The Swiss psychologist Jean Piaget argues that the human intellect evolves through four stages: sensorimotor, pre-operational, concrete operational, and formal operational. Sensorimotor and pre-operational thinking takes place within the material world that surrounds the child. The small child wonders about the concrete, visible, everyday things that he or she encounters: Mom, Dad, and toys, for example. By early adolescence, the child's mind begins to handle abstract ideas that have no visible referent to reality: equality, justice, rights, energy, and atoms, for example. These ideas are "unseen" and require the individual to be able to think of pure ideas. Thus, the object of wonder can change with changing intellectual abilities: although the young child wonders about the world of concrete experience, the adolescent is able to transcend this world and imagine a world of abstract ideas. One suspects that the "idealism" of youth, to the extent that it exists, is in part a function of the evolution of the thought processes that give the adolescent glimpses into a world filled with justice, peace, and harmony. Regarding the cultivation of the reasoning and wondering process, there is plenty of evidence that one's academic environment is associated with the development of this ability to think abstractly: mathematics, philosophy, and science are all strongly correlated with the development of the ability to conceive and manipulate abstract ideas. Not surprisingly, as adolescents develop the ability to think abstractly, this thought process is honed by courses in mathematics that encourage students to think abstractly. In summary, whereas there is a natural inclination to wonder about abstract ideas, the ability to do so is influenced by external or environmental factors.[3]

If one of the preconditions for wondering about world politics is the ability to do so, a second precondition concerns the object of the wondering process: a world of abstract ideas such as justice, equality, law, empire, rights, freedom, and power. As argued previously, an understanding and ordering of a just world order are accessible to creatures of reason. This history of international relations theory is replete with various attempts to determine the "best" ordering of international life. These contending theories provide the human imagination with a well of provocative ideas and theoretical frameworks that can be drawn upon to develop a more adequate theory of world politics. The Western political tradition has been remarkably flexible in developing alternative conceptions of international relations. As you will discover, there are classical, realist, classical liberal, and radical theories of world politics. However, there are important voices—some contemporary and others more historically remote—that provide different perspectives on world political theory. Challenges to traditional Western political thought have come from feminists, Islamic fundamentalists, and Russian nationalist political theorists, among others; such challenges have the virtue of providing alternative ways of thinking about the nature, ends, and organization of world politics. Beyond this, they can provide a critique of the orthodox, Western approach to thinking about international relations, thereby serving to spark the wondering process.

Although we are all capable of wondering about world politics, it is another matter to begin to clarify or develop our own theory of world politics. Developing a theory of international relations requires integrating many facets of the world of politics into a single, coherent whole. Coherence suggests that a variety of ideas are related to one another. For example, some theorists hold that nations, like humans, are self-regarding. As such, they pursue their own interests, regardless of the well-being of other nations. A world of self-regarding nations, without an international authority to settle disputes between nations bent on pursuing their own interests at the expense of another's interests, will lead to war. In this case, a belief about the wellsprings of national behavior is linked to war. Developing a coherent theory of world politics seems to suggest five things. First, wondering should be purposive—directed to some purpose; second, this wondering will require an understanding of some basic ideas of world politics; third, wondering should be directed at integrating those ideas into a greater whole; fourth, wondering should liberate you from preconceptions, biases, and prejudices; and fifth, wondering will require time for reflection.

To say that wondering is purposive suggests that one makes a conscious effort to accomplish some intellectual goal or purpose through the wondering process. Although daydreaming is a form of wonder, it tends to lack purpose. In contrast, the wondering you are about to do is more intellectually rigorous and requires that you undertake the activity with a keen desire to gain a clearer understanding of the object of your thought. In achieving a better understanding of the object of wonder, you might be interested in the nature of the idea and how it relates to other ideas. For example, in thinking about justice, you might be interested in its definition and its relationship to human rights or war. To help focus your thinking, this book discusses twenty-one issues that bear on world politics. In wondering about these issues and relating them to one another, you will be able to develop a more coherent way of thinking about world politics. This moves us to the second point. In order to wonder about world politics, you will need some ideas about which to think. The following chapters introduce you to ideas that have excited the minds of political thinkers: justice, equality, human nature, human rights, the environment, unity, power, authority, legitimacy, law, order, rights, imperialism, empire, world federalism, world monarchy, the world economy, and war, for example. There are other ideas, but the ones discussed here are historically or currently relevant. In discussing these ideas, the book presents a broad palette from which you can paint your own vision of world politics. Indeed, these ideas might best be described as points of departure, not final destinations: they can help you begin or continue the wondering process. Your task is to add your imagination to these ideas and develop your own view of world politics. Third, to think comprehensively about world politics means that you will need to relate these ideas to one another. Make a concerted effort to find connections between justice and equality, war and human nature, or peace and world federalism. To help you do this, the book discusses how various thinkers have integrated these ideas to form elegant theories of world politics. The book is organized to help you integrate these ideas. For example, how you perceive human nature will help you think about human equality; how you view human nature and human equality will help you think about the best form of government, and so on. If you approach each of the twenty-one issue areas by asking yourself how your opinions about previously examined issues can help you think about the one you are currently considering, then you will continue to develop an integrated view of world politics.

Fourth, when wondering about world politics, you must free yourself from unproductive prejudices and biases that shackle your ability to think creatively about international relations. Take the opportunity to try on different ideas, to test those ideas as well as the beliefs you currently hold, and to engage your friends in lively discussions of the issues this book raises. Finally, wonder presupposes leisure and reflection. In a world where the clock seems to determine what and where we do things, take the opportunity to dictate to the clock how you are going to spend your time: budget time for leisurely reflection and time to wonder. As you read through each of the twenty-one issues in this book, periodically stop, put the book down, and wonder about the topic about which you are reading. Come to some tentative conclusions regarding that topic. Then jot down your ideas at the bottom of the page, on a separate piece of paper, or in a journal. As you read through this book and slowly build a theory of world politics, refer back to what you have written and make an attempt to relate earlier ideas to later ones. Should you do this, by the time you have completed this book, you will have developed a theory of international politics.

In summary, here are some practical suggestions for how to begin to wonder about world politics:

1. Budget your time so that you have an opportunity to wonder about what you read.
2. Put your book down often while reading and wonder about what you have read.
3. Intend to develop your own point of view after reading each issue area.
4. Relate your view of one issue area to another.

5. Jot down in your book or on paper your ideas about each issue area.

6. Make a point of discussing your ideas with others.

7. Use these discussions to clarify, amend, and defend your ideas.

If you do these things, you will walk away from this book with a better understanding of yourself and your beliefs about world politics.

SYSTEMS OF WONDER IN WORLD POLITICS

In many ways, world politics is a natural subject matter for wonder. Because it appears so complicated and so far removed from people's everyday lives, world politics seems to be unknown territory awaiting discovery. Given 185 nations and other actors interacting in seemingly incomprehensible ways on the world political stage, it is not surprising that people find world politics to be complicated, confusing, and even mysterious. But it is precisely because the world political scene is so far removed from the everyday life of most people that it is open to wonder. Political thinkers, captivated by international relations, have tried to come to some understanding of how world politics ought to be structured and conducted.

Wondering about world politics is a serious, purposive endeavor. This book looks at those systems of wonder that are part of the Western political tradition and considers other perspectives that serve as challenges to this Western tradition. As described earlier, these frameworks for thinking about international politics are classicist, realist, liberal, and Marxist theories of the Western tradition, with the challenges to this canon coming from feminist, Islamic, and Russian political thinkers. In addition to providing the reader with a wealth of stimulating ideas about the nature, goals, and structure of world politics, these systems of thought also have the advantage of demonstrating how thinkers in these traditions have (1) wondered about world political matters; (2) woven their ideas of politics into a comprehensive theory; and (3) stimulated the imagination to think about world politics.

In the first place, these traditions of political thought provide readers with a body of concepts and assumptions that can help structure their thinking about the international order. Take what is referred to as realism. Realists begin with the assumption that human nature and nations—which are collectives of individuals—are prone to be selfish and self-interested. With no international authority to compel the obedience of these nations, states exist in an international environment of anarchy. Driven by self-interest and operating amidst anarchy, nations become concerned with amassing power that will help them to defend themselves from the machinations of other nations and to pursue their own world political and economic interests. Because nations fear the thought of being subordinated to another nation, realists pursue a balance of power policy. In so doing, they believe that nations will form alliances and leagues for the purpose of preventing one nation, or an alliance of nations, from dominating them politically. In this way, realists make some essential assumptions about human nature, motivation, anarchy, and the balance of power to create a particular way to organize their thinking about world politics.

Second, these systems of thinking about world politics provide opportunities to weave these ideas together into a comprehensive theory of world politics. In this way, a variety of issues and concepts in world politics are united into a single theory that is capable of providing a way of thinking about international relations. Take realists and the problem of war, for example. Because humans are inclined toward aggression, because international relations are in a state of anarchy, and because nations pursue their own interests, nations will inevitably run afoul of one another and, diplomacy failing, may choose war to achieve their national objectives. However, the balance of power can prevent war, according to some realists. If one nation considers pursuing its interests by resorting to war, other nations in the international system will array themselves against the aggressing state. Realizing that these nations are powerful enough to prevent it from achieving its objectives, the potential aggressor will be deterred from going to war. In this example, issues of war and peace are integrated into the broader framework of the realist's approach to thinking about world politics.

Whereas these theories constitute a particular way of thinking about the international political environment, they also serve a third function: to stimulate thinking and wondering about world politics. Take the case of classicism. The classicist approach to international relations is rooted in ancient Greek and Roman political thought—notably Stoicism—and medieval Scholasticism, and it has modern referents in Catholic social thought. Classicists believe that a divine power created the physical, animal, and vegetable worlds and with it, human beings. This power gave humans the ability to reason and to recognize their individual and common good and inclined them toward goodness. Humans are political animals in the sense that they are inclined by nature to form associations, including states, for the purposes of achieving individual and common goods. World politics is characterized by nations jointly pursuing the common good, including the protection of human rights. To do this, some classicists believe the best form of international government is a republican, federal form that has the power to settle disputes between nations, to secure human rights for all persons, and to provide for a more equitable distribution of technology and economic prosperity. For classicists, peace among people of the world is the norm, while war is clearly the exception. Peace is the norm in an international society because people are inclined to cooperate, because greater international social and economic equality among nations removes incentives to go to war, and because the international political system that amasses military power in a world federal government is more capable of deterring nations from going to war. For classicists, war is simply an irrational response of nations that really do not see that it is in their interest to work within a world society that benefits humankind as a whole.

Clearly, realism and classicism provide widely different perspectives on the international political order. A debate between these two schools of thought can lead to imaginative discussions on world politics. The basic assumptions of each school are virtually diametrically opposed: classicism holds that humans are inclined to know and do good, the international society of states is actively pursuing the common good, and cooperation and peace mark the relations between nations. Realists believe that humans are inclined toward selfishness, that there is a state of anarchy that exists between states in international relations, and that competition and war characterize the interaction between states. The differing ideas of the classicists and realists serve to spark debate and the human imagination on the nature, ends, and conduct of world politics.

Realism and classicism represent two approaches to world politics; this text will introduce you to five other perspectives: liberalism, Marxism, feminism, Islamic fundamentalism, and Russian nationalism. Traditionally, the canon of international relations theory has centered on classicist, realist, liberal, and Marxist theories. These approaches to thinking about world politics have inspired and will continue to inspire ways of thinking about world politics. Collectively, these four approaches represent orthodox ways of thinking about world politics and reflect dominant trends in Western political thought that have helped the West make sense of international relations. The feminist, Islamic fundamentalist, and Russian nationalist perspectives challenge this canon. The more radical feminist theories of international relations—theories to the "left" of liberal feminism—have been developing over the last fifteen years, and they constitute a critique of the canon. While Western feminist critiques of world politics have grown out of some women's displeasure with the theories within the canon, Islamic fundamentalism provides a non-Western critique of the canon. The religious roots are Islamic; however, some of the ideas that drive fundamentalist political theory are derived from Aristotle and Plato, two Western sources. Nevertheless, this book includes Islamic fundamentalism (and excludes many other Islamic theories of organizing politics nationally and internationally) for two reasons. First, it is rich in political thought. Second, from a practical standpoint, Islamic fundamentalism is active in the world today. To appreciate the variety of thinking in world politics requires us to understand Islamic fundamentalism. Finally, the book includes Russian nationalism and anarchism because they provide additional non-Western perspectives on world politics. At the time this book was written, it was unclear whether the Russian experiment with capitalism and Western liberal political institutions would succeed. If this experiment fails, one possible alternative is a form of Russian nationalism that is rooted in nineteenth-century Russian nationalism. Thus, some appreciation for Russian nationalist thought is particularly helpful if the "Westernization" of

Russia collapses. Collectively, these seven approaches to world politics should provide you with not only food for thought but also a more cross-cultural understanding of the ideas that have, do, may, or will form the way we think about world politics.

SUMMARY

This chapter discusses the nature of the wondering process, describes how people wonder, and suggests that an ongoing dialogue between various systems of world political thought can serve to spark the wondering process in ways that will allow participants of that conversation to develop their own approaches to thinking about world politics. First, this book is presented and organized with a view toward encouraging the reader to wonder about world politics. The work is organized around twenty-one issues or concepts that are critical to thinking about world politics. How one stands on issues discussed relatively early in the book has implications for how one will think about issues discussed later. Therefore, coming to some sense of closure on the earlier issues will help you to draw conclusions on the later ones. Although readers should actively attempt to reach some degree of closure, they should also realize that gaining closure, if it occurs at all on some issues, is a lifetime process. Second, this book attempts to stimulate the wondering process by discussing each of the twenty-one issue areas from the standpoint of the four orthodox, Western world political perspectives (classicism, realism, liberalism, and Marxism). These ideas are then put in "relief" through comparisons with feminism, Islamic fundamentalism, and Russian political thought. Ideally, the reader should come away from this book with a greater understanding about what he or she considers to be the proper ordering and conduct of world politics.

NOTES

1. Don Hahn, *Beauty and the Beast* (Burbank: Walt Disney Co., 1991).
2. Ibid.
3. Jean Piaget, "Intellectual Evolution from Adolescence to Adulthood," *Human Development* 15 (1972): 4–6; also see B. Inhelder and J. Piaget, *The Growth of Logical Thinking* (New York: Basic Books, 1958).

CHAPTER 2

HUMAN NATURE, EQUALITY, GOVERNMENT, AND THE STATE

This chapter discusses the assumptions that shape the way we think about politics. Assumptions refer to those basic ideas or principles that we hold to be truths. For example, we often hear people say that they are optimistic or pessimistic. If we could look into the minds of optimists, we might discover that they have a rosy view of human nature that colors their view of the world. If humans are naturally good and cooperative, war would be seen as abnormal and capable of being substantially or wholly eliminated. On the other hand, pessimists might believe that humans are naturally selfish and inclined toward competition and even violence. Given this picture of human nature, war would be considered a fact of life. Because war flows in the veins of humankind, we would be better advised to find methods to minimize the occurrence and intensity of war rather than trying to eliminate it. The 1995 film *Legends of the Fall* is a case in point. *Legends* is probably considered by most viewers to be a pessimistic, or realistic, film. That is because the story line is based on some rather bleak assumptions. In *Legends*, a young man named Samuel Ludlow enlists in the army, having been caught up in the irrational fervor of war in 1914. His brothers, Tristan and Alfred, enlist with him, determined to bring their younger brother home alive to his fiancée and to their father. However, despite their best efforts to rationally calculate how to keep their brother alive, Tristan and Alfred are unable to prevent his death at the hands of the machine gun. The director makes his point: humans are more creatures of passion than reason, and rational people in an irrational world find it virtually impossible to bring about much good.

The assumptions that one makes about human nature, human equality, the origin and ends of the state, and the best form of government shape one's view of the nature of politics and of world politics in particular. This chapter focuses on these five political ideas and demonstrates how they form the foundation of one's political thought. It begins with a discussion of human nature, which is one of the fundamental elements of a solid political theory.

How humans view themselves is reflected by the institutions they create, their social and political ideals, and the way they conduct their politics. Take President Ronald Reagan. Early in his presidency, he addressed a group of police officers and complimented them on the contributions they were making to an ordered society. Betraying his view of human nature, he said that there was a fine line between civilization and the jungle, and the police formed that line. The president was suggesting that in the absence of any authority in society, humans displayed a tendency to revert to the status of an animal: a creature of passion, largely devoid of human reason and temperance (self-control). Not unlike Edgar Allan Poe's poetry—which suggests that there is a nearly unimaginable perverseness to human nature—President Reagan's belief that humans were capable of terrible evil at any minute led him to support law and order, the death penalty, a strengthened police force, restrictions on civil liberties, and a strong national defense. All this was necessary because human beings could not be trusted to order their lives in a way that promoted social and political order. Let us turn now to human nature, which is the foundation upon which political thinking rests.

On Human Nature

In its broadest connotation, human nature consists of those characteristics of human life that are unique to human beings and those that are shared with the animate and inanimate worlds. Put down this book and wonder about the following question: what makes human beings different from or similar to rocks and dogs? Like rocks, humans are composed of elements and compounds. Like dogs, they have the ability to move; the need for food, water, and shelter; and an ability to sense the world around them by smell, touch, taste, sight, and sound. What distinguishes humans from dogs and rocks is their reasoning ability, which enables them to comprehend sophisticated concepts, to create and manipulate abstract ideas, and to choose between good and evil. What about a human soul? A human soul gives form to the physical and spiritual character of humans. To use an analogy, the potter is the soul or fundamental principle of the vase. By combining clay with the idea of what the vase should look like, the potter uses his or her hands to give shape to the vase. The human soul is the formative principle that allows human beings to develop in the full glory of their humanity. The soul, in other words, enables people to become rational and needful beings capable of choosing between good and evil. When looking back at twenty-five hundred years of Western thought about human nature, it is not surprising to find that so many political thinkers have concluded that there are three fundamental properties of human nature: an intellect or reasoning ability, a soul, and the appetites. Let us turn to your view of human nature.

Continue to wonder about human nature for a moment. Put down this book again, and consciously step outside yourself so that you are now looking at yourself as others see you. Look at your body; what do you see? Imagine watching yourself going through a day's activities. What human needs do you seek to satisfy? If you are like many, your first impression of yourself is that of a material being with needs and appetites: you need love and friendship and possess appetites for knowledge, food, sex, and water. You might believe that you have an intellect or rational capacity that involves the five senses, the ability to remember and make judgments, the capacity to think and wonder about abstract ideas such as justice and equality, and the ability to create new ideas. Going beyond the body, you might conclude that you have a soul, if you define it rather broadly as a moral or spiritual condition that encompasses an understanding or appreciation of goodness, truth, and beauty. Although some may see these three components of human nature—reason, soul, and appetites—as relatively distinct, others might see them as being integrated. For example, a person suffering from some physical ailment may not feel that his or her ability to reason is adversely affected. The unimpaired reasoning ability may be taken as proof that there is a degree of separation between the body and the intellect. On the other hand, some might argue that the ability to reason is directly affected by conditions of the body: if one does not get enough sleep, the ability to reason may be impaired. In this case, reason and the body appear to be more closely linked. Finally, in comparing yourself to others, you might conclude that one person might have a qualitatively greater intellect, a deeper spiritual disposition, or stronger appetites than another person. This might lead you to the conclusion that some people are intellectually gifted, others are more spiritually inclined, and still others are dominated by their appetites for food or sex.

There are other questions that a discussion of human nature inevitably raises: is human nature a settled condition or is it reflective of the culture in which one lives? What is the origin of human life? How do we come to know what human nature really is? Let us turn to the first question. If human nature is a settled condition and humans possess an intellect, a soul, and appetites, then this might suggest that these qualities are fixed and universal. By fixed I mean that humans have reason, appetites, and a soul that is similar to and different from other things. This fixed nature may be universal if one believes that all humans—regardless of race, ethnic background, or nationality—possess these qualities. If you believe that human nature is fixed and universal, you might conclude that the reasoning ability of the Chinese would be no different from that of Americans,

Haitians, or Indians. Furthermore, you might believe that all people aspire to some type of spiritual life, and that the appetites for food and water are just as necessary for South Africans and Brazilians as they are for Canadians and Koreans. On the other hand, you might believe that all life is socially constructed, which suggests that although each of us is born with appetites and the ability to reason, our social environment determines both the specific content of those appetites and the way in which we reason. How one reasons, the content of one's spiritual life, and the specific things that one desires may differ from culture to culture or they may be dependent upon gender, class, or ethnic background. For example, in an industrial society dependent upon readily available transportation, some might have an appetite for cars, an appetite missing in an ancient agrarian society that does not need them. Or take the intellect. According to some, one's intellectual ability is a function of social class: those from the upper classes have access to the best education, which enables them to develop their intellects in ways that those of lower socioeconomic status cannot. Whether intellectual differences are due to heredity, the environment, or some combination of both is another question.

In your ruminations about human nature, you may have raised other questions. These might involve the origin of human life and how we come to know human nature. What is the origin of the human being? Does human life arise through a natural, evolutionary process that involves no divine intervention? Or are humans a specific and special creation of God? Can human nature be a combination of both—an evolutionary process directed by God? Beyond questions about the origin of life there are those focusing on how we can come to know the components of human nature. How do we know what human nature actually is? This book has previously asked you to observe yourself. But what are you observing? Are you observing what you *are* or are you watching what you have been socialized to be? Take aggression. Some have argued that humans are naturally aggressive. Others believe that the aggressiveness of humankind is simply a reflection of social norms that have inclined an otherwise cooperative being toward a life of aggression. Here is the problem: how does one sort out whether the aggressiveness that is often observed in everyday life is due to nature or nurture? If we say that humans are naturally aggressive, how do we know that the aggression we see is not really due to the influence of families that promote aggression? Do we ultimately have to rely on science or religion to provide an answer? These are difficult questions, which are addressed in the following paragraphs.

This book aims to engage you in a thought experiment, the purpose of which is to try to get you to arrive at some conception of human nature by stripping away the effect that society has upon human nature. Stop reading for a moment and wonder about how you would answer the following question: if you were to suddenly abolish the police, military, and all forms of authority in this country, what would life be like? In answering this question, be specific about the mental image that you produce—how are people acting, what are their goals, and what are they saying?

What you are doing is not too different from what William Golding does in his novel *Lord of the Flies*. If you read the book or saw the movie, you know that a group of young boys is marooned on an island, distant from the civilizing effects of human society. As the story progresses, Golding slowly strips away the veneer of civilization that brings order to everyday life. As this occurs, most of the boys become more and more barbaric: greed and aggression replace the restraining influences of reason and conscience. The image of the innocence of youth gives way to a vision of youth as irrational and aggressive. The implications of this are truly frightening. Young people are shackled with the same nature as their parents. They cannot set the world right and are doomed to live the life their parents wish them to avoid—one filled with violence, hatred, and irrationality.[1]

Golding's view of human nature resembles the realist perspective. Like Golding, the seventeenth-century English philosopher Thomas Hobbes draws a terrifying portrait of human nature in his book, *Leviathan*. Abolish the police, military, and government, he argues, and humans will revert back to a state of nature, the natural condition of humankind. In that condition, humans are driven by their appetites and desires. Reason and willpower, in Hobbes's view, do not serve the function of controlling human appetites; rather, reason is a servant of the appetites. In other words, whatever a human desires, reason finds the means to obtain. Yet humans realize that reason is not sufficient to obtain all the goals in life that they desire. They need power, the ability to obtain some future apparent good. Indeed, life is a "perpetual and restless desire of power after power, that ceaseth only in death."[2] This philosophy should not sound unfamiliar to many of you. If asked why a person might go to college, many might respond that a college degree will enable them to obtain the things in life they desire. They might argue that the educational process simply shapes the ability to reason in ways that will allow people to make those decisions that will enable them to get what they desire: money, a nice car or home, or social status. Finally, they might say that an undergraduate degree (that may lead to a professional degree) would increase one's power in the marketplace. With education comes the ability to wrest a coveted job away from a less educated competitor. Once out of college, however, people will have to continue to increase their power relative to others or risk falling behind their competitors. For Hobbes, life is a continual struggle for power, as each person seeks to augment and increase the power he or she already possesses.[3]

Hobbes goes on to describe the state of nature to which humans revert. Humans, fundamentally equal in their ability to get the things they desire and without any governing authority to restrain their desires or the methods they use to gratify them, will come into serious and even deadly conflicts with others. It is a "war of every man, against every man."[4] In this state of nature, there is no agriculture (because whatever would be painstakingly grown would be stolen), no education or art (because the scramble to protect one's life would leave no time for leisurely thought and creative activity), and no form of social organization such as the family or friendship (because humans are more concerned with their own interests than those of others). In this war of everyone against everyone, nothing is just or unjust; nothing is right or wrong. Force and fraud are the two cardinal virtues that are necessary to make one's way in the world. And worst of all, Hobbes concludes, there is "continual fear, and danger of violent death; and the life of man [is] solitary, poor, nasty, brutish, and short."[5] Posing the question again, how would you imagine life without any authority? Hobbes would reply, "Ask the police who stood by and watched the south central Los Angeles riots."

Others draw a much different picture. Classicists cut in the mold of Aristotle, the fourth-century B.C. Athenian philosopher, or Saint Thomas Aquinas, a thirteenth-century Christian philosopher and theologian, believe that humans are naturally political animals. By this they mean that humans are inclined by nature to form associations for the purpose of achieving their goals in life. These associations include the family, the village, and the state. In stripping away civilization from the individual, you find a person who has a body characterized by processes of growth, development, and maintenance; the appetites for sex, food, and water; and a rational capacity that allows all humans to manage their appetites and life in a way that can lead to a life of virtue—a life of happiness. To achieve a happy life, humans form social and political associations. Aristotle reasons that humans are not as self-sufficient as Hobbes later suggests. In Aristotle's view, only through the cooperative efforts of male and female, farmer and merchant, and governor and governed can the spiritual and material things that make life worth living be secured. Thus, cooperative human effort, not radical individualism, is necessary for achieving the good life.[6] Saint Thomas Aquinas accepts Aristotle's proposition that humans are political animals. As special beings in God's creation, humans are inclined by God to seek, know, and do what is good and avoid what is evil. Human reason, reflecting on human nature, would conclude that the appetites inclined each to self-preservation—a good that is readily understood by all people who rightly think about human nature. Although much of the knowledge of what we ought to do can be understood by any human being reflecting on human nature, Saint Thomas believes that there are times when humans are unable to correctly exercise their reason and they find it difficult to discover the moral principles that ought to be followed. To solve this problem, Saint Thomas holds that God has revealed what is right and wrong through divine law—the Ten Commandments, for example. Revealed, divine law has the advantage of making unmistakably clear that moral law that might not be perfectly understood by reason.[7]

Aristotle and Saint Thomas present one foil to Hobbes's rather dreary picture of humankind. Abolish all authority and these classicists would suggest that life would go on, for the most part, as it had previously been led. Some individuals, tempted by their appetites, would rape, pillage, and plunder; most, however, would continue to follow the laws and norms they were socialized to observe. At the earliest possible moment, humans would move to re-create the family, economic relations, and the state; and these associations would guide all humans toward a happy life. What is at issue here is a fundamentally and radically different way of looking at the nature of human beings. Hobbes draws a picture of human beings as being essentially appetitive with a rational capacity that allows them to prudentially calculate how they can obtain the things in life they value. He depicts a highly individualistic, egocentric world of competition and striving. Love and compassion do not enter his thoughts as important components of human life. On the other hand, Aristotle and Saint Thomas are inclined to see human beings as social beings—bound up in a web of social relationships directed toward a virtuous life. Being essentially rational creatures, humans know those moral principles that they should follow if they desire to lead a "good" life. Even though they may be tempted to follow their appetites and veer off the path of virtue, humans have the ability to restrain their appetites and resist temptation. Aristotle and Saint Thomas believe that human beings prefer to be united by social, economic, and political bonds and a sense of community (suffocating to some) that replace the individualism that Hobbes professes.

The liberal school, as represented by the late seventeenth-century English philosopher John Locke, attempts to tread a middle ground between the realist and classicist conceptions of human nature. With the classicists, Locke shares the view that humans are capable of leading a life of reason. The ability to reason is a capacity that has to be cultivated until it is fully developed—at some point in one's twenties. Prior to that, parents have the responsibility for developing the intellectual and moral reasoning capabilities of their children. Upon reaching intellectual maturity—their "majority"—young people can assume their position in society as citizens who possess the rights to life, liberty, and property. Reason and law provide them with the guidance necessary to secure these rights for themselves and to avoid trampling on the rights of others. However, Locke shares the realist view that humans have needs and appetites that often push them beyond the limits prescribed by reason. The desire or appetite for material well-being might push humans into a life of crime. Human life would always be concerned with balancing the rational and appetitive dimensions of the soul in a way that serves personal interests while giving due respect to the rights of others. Given this view of human nature, what would happen if all authority were abolished? Locke believes that civilized life would be a mixture of cooperative and conflictual behavior. Although most humans would see the personal advantage of obeying existing laws, a few would believe that a life of crime would be the quickest avenue to satisfying their desires.[8]

Radicals such as Karl Marx and Friedrich Engels, nineteenth-century economists and social thinkers, present the greatest challenge to more orthodox ways of thinking about human nature: they suggest that a person's being is shaped by the economic classes to which he or she belongs. Humans are material beings: self-conscious, thinking, feeling, breathing, and needful creatures. Yet, their existence depends upon an outside world of nature and human society. Humans create economic systems to satisfy their basic needs. Economic forces—and secondarily religion, education, and politics—shape the needs and consciousness of the individual. Who they are, how they feel, what they believe, what they value, and how they think are simply a reflection of the class or social condition in which they are raised.[9] Take something of a Marxist reading of Charles Dickens's *A Christmas Carol.* Ebenezer Scrooge—his values, his attitudes toward his employee Bob Cratchit, his goals in life, and his needs—is determined by the bourgeois class of which he is a part. Driven to succeed as a money lender, Scrooge devotes great parts of the day to "the counting," denies himself personal pleasures, and develops a moral value system to justify his exploitation of Cratchit. The capitalist system "requires" Scrooge to adopt a way of life and personal philosophy that allow him to succeed in business. Scrooge's character, according to this interpretation, is but a creation of greater economic forces.

The feminist criticism of traditional views of human nature is similar to the Marxist critique in some ways. In their book *Global Gender Issues,* V. Spike Peterson and Anne S. Runyan assert that what is commonly known as human nature is largely a result of socialization. In their view, humans live in a society dominated by males, who have erected political, social, religious, and economic institutions to structure the lives of women. Men create elaborate ideologies to justify relegating women to an unequal and inferior position. At the root of these ideologies are theories of human nature that serve to justify the political, economic, social, and reproductive subordination of women. These ideologies are based on a faulty assumption that there are some "natural" differences between males and females that justify the unequal treatment of women. As part of these ideologies, women have been socialized into believing that they have a nature that is somehow different from that of men. The dominant actors in patriarchal culture have persuaded them to believe that women are naturally more nurturing, that they have a natural desire for children, that they are more emotional than men, and that they tend to accept the authority of others, especially men. While acknowledging some biological differences associated with the reproductive processes, the authors argue that such differences do not materially affect a woman's ability to accomplish those things that can be accomplished by men.[10]

Marxist and feminist positions on human nature are characterized by the belief that either economic or gender-related forces in society are responsible for defining the nature and value of life of each individual. Stripping away existing economic and gender-related power structures and ideologies that serve to perpetuate the rule of the powerful does two things. First, it ends relations of oppression between rich and poor or male and female. In other words, materially transforming or destroying existing oppressive power structures is a precondition for human liberation. Second, Marxists believe that humans have concrete needs that are not being met by existing social and cultural norms that support capitalism. These needs—for a creative, communal life, for example—will flourish once the existing norms have been replaced by ones created by the people themselves. For some feminists, such as J. Ann Tickner, razing the barriers to women's participation in the real centers of economic and political power would permit women to humanize an otherwise individualistic, conflictual, sexist world. The "ennobling" characteristics associated with women—their concern for others, their desire to resolve conflicts peacefully, and their aptitude for nurturing, for example—could be extended into the sphere of economics and politics. The incorporation of these feminine traits would serve to humanize society.[11]

The basis of the Marxist and feminist critique of human nature is the belief that there is nothing that can be called "human nature." What we believe, what we desire, how we think, and who we are result from the processes of socialization. Parents, religion, teachers, peers, the media, politics, and the workplace shape our ability to reason, lead us to desire the things we do, and determine what we consider to be the good things in life. To many classicists, this is all wrongheaded. Regardless of culture, class, and socialization, there is something in the nature of humans that is constant: the ability to reason, appetites and needs that require satisfaction, and an inclination to do good and avoid evil, for example. For classicists, social institutions such as the family, schools, and economic and political systems are built by humans so that human beings can realize in practice what they were meant to be. Thus, families arise because there is a need for procreation "written" into the bodies of all human beings. Economic systems are established because humans have to find some way to satisfy their needs for food, water, and shelter. And political systems are created so that humans can organize themselves in a way that allows them to lead a good life. In thinking about politics, one question that must be answered is "What, if anything, is human nature?"

Being conservative in nature, Islamic fundamentalism and Russian nationalism share a more realist understanding of human nature. Sayyid Ruhollah al-Musawi al-Khumayni, or Ayatollah Khomeini as he is known in the West, was born in 1900, was the spiritual leader of the 1979 Iranian Revolution, and died in 1989. Khomeini believed that Allah—or God—created mankind from clay and endowed him with a soul composed of reason, spirit, and appetites. Oriented toward goodness by Allah, the soul possesses the reasoning ability to pursue and know what is good. However, humans also have appetites, which attempt to divert their attention from the pursuit of goodness. These appetites for food, water, sex, and all sensual delights lead humans along a path of self-gratification and self-love. If humans allow themselves to be tempted by Satan and the sins of this world, their reason will be covered with a veil of darkness and their appetites will run virtually untethered. According to Khomeini, "man is like an animal, even worse than the other animals. Left to his own devices, he will always be inferior to the animals, for he surpasses them in passion, evil, and rapacity."[12] Despite this dreary picture of human nature, humans have a desire to know and live by Allah's law. The challenge is for humans to order their souls in a way that the appetites may be guided by divine law known by reason and disciplined or controlled by the human spirit. Thus, humans have a choice: they can choose a divinely inspired life or one of sin. If they choose the former, they can create a perfect human society, one governed by guardians who would direct humankind toward a rightly ordered society.[13]

The Russian Orthodox church claims to be the truest form of Christianity. Many members of this church believe that humans are created in the image of God, and as such are given the ability to reason and a free will, both of which separate them from the animal world. Through reason, humans can come to know God as well as good and evil. With a free will, humans are able to choose between good and evil—to turn their lives toward God and goodness or toward themselves and sin. Humans are created with bodily appetites that serve to perpetuate earthly life. In the Garden of Eden, the appetites of Adam and Eve were tempted, and they chose the path of evil, substituting their own will and view of goodness in the place of God's. In opposing themselves to God, they created a sinful world which they built to their own glory. To make matters worse, the corruption of their souls was so deep that this sin was shared with all those born after them. Therefore, humankind—the descendants of Adam and Eve—live under the domination of sin. All are born into a world pervaded by sin; their wills are weakened by the desires and appetites for ungodly things of this world. According to this view, only through the helping hand of God's grace can humans—themselves striving for a godly life—achieve fellowship with God.[14]

Whereas Russian Orthodoxy emphasizes the more sordid aspects of human nature, Islamic fundamentalism displays realistic and classicist strains of thought. Clearly, Russian Orthodoxy is similar to the realist school, because it emphasizes the corrupted nature of humankind. In both philosophies, human beings are egotistical, self-centered beings not prone to cooperation. Both are critical of Marxist and feminist conceptions of human nature, because Marxism and feminism, to a lesser degree, presuppose the eventual perfectibility of human nature. If the surrounding economic, social, political, and educational institutions that shape human behavior could be made more just, an era of peace, justice, and freedom would follow in its wake. In the eyes of Ayatollah Khomeini, humans have strayed from the path of righteousness and have chosen to live in wickedness. However, whereas Russian Orthodox thinkers believe that sinfulness is an irremediable condition of human life and society, Khomeini argues that the rational and more spiritual part of human nature is capable of exercising control over the appetitive. One consequence of this optimistic view of human nature is that humans may be led to a perfect society on earth if guardians, in control of the state, enforce God's law with the aim of orienting all souls toward goodness. While Khomeini would be classified by many as conservative or even reactionary, his teachings are revolutionary. Under the guidance of those inspired by Allah, a good society can be built upon the ruins of this earthly life. Social, economic, and political upheaval may result; however, the vision of a good society serves to guide the struggle toward its fulfillment.[15]

Let us return to the beginning of this chapter for a moment. Put down your book again, and rethink your view of human nature. To what extent are the notions of reason, soul, and the appetites important components of your view of human nature? Are love and compassion part of our nature? Is there a human nature at all? To what extent is human nature capable of being transformed into something it currently is not? Are humans capable of self-control, and if so what is the controlling element and what is controlled? Are humans innately good or evil? How does your view of human nature help you think about social change? These are among the questions that have been raised in discussions of human nature. Let us now turn to how one's view of human nature structures one's understanding of equality.

ON THE QUESTION OF HUMAN EQUALITY

Imagine for a minute a political system in which those who were to govern were selected by lots. In this system, the names of all citizens over 18 years of age would be put into a huge barrel. The barrel would be shaken, and names drawn to fill legislative, executive, and judicial positions. What would politics be like? What would be the advantages of this system of political recruitment? What would be the disadvantages? The advantage is that the selection process would be blind to social, racial, ethnic, economic, educational, political, and gender-related inequalities and biases. Color, religion, ethnicity, wealth, gender, and possession of political power would neither qualify nor disqualify a person from holding office. The legislature would more likely reflect the socioeconomic, sexual, racial, ethnic, and religious composition of the community, and to the extent that group diversity is good, the process would produce governments that would be more broadly representative of those communities than they are currently. Political and economic power would not become entrenched, as frequent lotteries would most likely replace existing governing authorities with new ones. The pulse of the country would be felt in the legislative body, because no intervening party structures or interest groups would obscure the problems, concerns, hopes, and dreams of the people.

Despite this, most of us would not favor a "lottery" for public office. Although some might point to the fact that the American political system has worked well enough to make the United States the world's oldest democracy, others would be concerned about losing the benefits that political parties bring to the governing process, and still others would express reservations about the quality of people who would secure public office. This last concern goes to the heart of the question of equality. How do your thoughts on the lottery reveal your view of human nature in general and of human equality in particular? Those who favor the lottery might say that humans are fundamentally equal in their intellectual abilities to understand social, economic, and political issues. Some might add that these people will bring with them a conventional morality and understanding of the public good that will serve deliberative bodies well. On the other hand, there would be those who would argue that the government would not be well served because many of those selected by the lottery would not have the intellect that is required to understand the complex, technical issues that frame modern political discourse. They would conclude that like it or not, there are some who are superior in character or intellect, and the lottery would not necessarily select these people for political office. The fundamental question that is being raised is simply whether humans are equal in those capacities relating to the ability to govern.

When discussing equality, there is a potential pitfall to be avoided. The history of political thought is strewn with questions about equality. Nowhere are these questions more often raised than in democratic societies. As they did in ancient Greece, equality and liberty still appear to be the cardinal values of a democratic society. If democracy is defined most broadly as "the rule of the people," then political equality, a concept that implies the participation of all in the political process, is required. If people are excluded from the political process, then only "part" of the people will be involved in politics. But some would argue that political equality is dependent upon other equalities. For example, studies in Western democracies suggest that education and economic status are important determinants of political participation.[16] Those with more education and higher incomes tend to participate in greater numbers than those with less education and wealth. Hence, if all people were given similar educational opportunities and similar chances to earn high incomes, one would expect political participation to increase. This line of thinking has led some to argue that democracy must cherish not only political equality but also other forms of equality, including equality in the educational, social, and economic spheres.

As political thinkers, all of us in democratic societies must be aware of the social and political pressures that have persuaded us that equality is a value worth honoring. In fact, many political thinkers have held that social, economic, and political inequality are to be valued over social, economic, and political equality. They argue that humans are unequal in possession of some of the very characteristics that make them human: some people have naturally greater intellects that give them access to truths that those less gifted are unable to reach. This access to the truth grants them the authority to rule; after all, who wants to be governed by fools?

There are a number of issues and problems associated with equality. First, when one speaks of equality, one must ask, "equality of what?" To say that humans are equal tells us little; they must be equal in some capacity or quality. This capacity or quality might refer to something in their nature such as the ability to reason, or it might refer to some outward characteristic such as the possession of wealth. Regarding equality and innate human characteristics, humans might be equal in reasoning ability or in the potential to reason. Perhaps they are equal in the possession of the right to life, liberty, and the pursuit of happiness. Maybe they are equal in the ability to make moral judgments or equal in the possession of bodily health. Humans might be equal in human dignity. Concerning acquired characteristics, humans might be equal (or unequal) in the possession of wealth, educational attainment, or social prestige. In other words, when one speaks of equality, it must be with reference to some quality or capability that is inherent in the nature of humans or is acquired in some way.

The second issue relating to the equal or unequal possession of some human trait concerns the relation of "sameness" to "equality." It is possible to think that all human beings are the same in the sense that all possess a capacity or ability to reason, a soul, and appetites. In this case, "sameness" simply refers to a property commonly shared by all humans. Despite this sameness, do all humans have equal abilities to reason? Do some humans have stronger appetites than others? And are some people more spiritually inclined than others? If so, then humans are unequal in the amount, level, or quality of some capacity that is inherent to human nature. Yet equality and sameness could be equivalent, too. The Stoics of ancient Greece and Rome believed that humans were not only the same in the sense that all humans possessed the ability to reason, but that humans also possessed equal capacities to reason—no one person was significantly superior to another in his or her ability to reason regardless of the fact that some people tend to be quicker than others. Given any practical problem of life, all people could reason their way to a solution.

A third issue concerns questions about whether observed natural inequalities authorize humans to treat others differently or unequally. Take natural inequalities as an example. If women are more inclined to be caring and nurturing, shouldn't they be the primary caregivers? Shouldn't those children who are intellectually challenged or gifted be placed in learning environments commensurate with their intellectual development and preparation? Shouldn't those individuals whose moral conduct is contrary to the norms of the community be treated differently than those who obey the community norms? On the other hand, if humans are considered equal in some capacity or quality, shouldn't they be treated equally? If men and women are equal in their capacity to reason, shouldn't they be treated equally in educational and other matters where reason comes into play?

The fourth issue regarding equality centers on what is commonly called the nature and convention, or the nature and nurture, argument. Here the question is whether the observed equalities and inequalities that exist among human beings are due to nature, nurture, or a combination of both. On the one hand, there are those who argue that perceived equalities and inequalities are due to nature or heredity. Reasoning ability, aggressiveness or passivity, height, weight, emotional strength, and artistic or athletic talent are largely a function of one's genetic endowment. These differences play out in the social world: those with greater physical prowess are more likely to achieve greater success in professional athletics than the proverbial ninety-eight-pound weakling. Those with the greatest musical talent such as singer Whitney Houston, violinist Anne Sophie Mutter, or timpanists Cloyd Duff and Paul Yancich of the Cleveland Orchestra find their way to the top of their profession, while those with less musical talent find themselves in less prestigious musical settings. Thus, the physical and musical inequalities and equalities that one observes in society are simply a reflection of the natural inequalities rooted in human nature. On the other hand, those who argue that all equalities or inequalities are purely conventional believe that humans are not born with a genetic blueprint for what they are likely to do and achieve in life. Rather, families, schooling, religion, work, the media, and the entertainment industry shape the abilities and interests of individuals in ways that are responsible for the equalities and inequalities one observes in life. Intellectual or athletic differences are due not to heredity, but to the effect of the environment in which one was raised. Families with educated, middle-class backgrounds who provide their children with proper prenatal and postnatal nutrition and care and who emphasize the importance of education will sharpen their children's intellects to levels above those of children who are nutritionally and educationally neglected. These thinkers might argue that all social institutions are creations of humans that can be changed and manipulated in ways to achieve certain ends. If one wishes to increase intellectual equality, then families would need to be strengthened, quality educational experiences would need to be made available to all, and adequate nourishment would need to be provided to all children. If these things were available to all children, greater intellectual equality would result.

Finally, there are those who take the middle position, arguing that although some of the inequalities that are observed between humans can be ascribed to nature, others are due to convention. Many radical feminists believe that heredity is the cause of biological differences between men and women; however, they attribute inequalities in wealth to a patriarchal cultural, economic, and political system that produces job stratification and associated economic inequalities.

The following discussion of equality demonstrates how human nature is related to equality. In the previous section, you developed a conception of human nature by a process of thinking about what human nature would be like in the absence of social life. As you read through the following discussion on equality, be mindful of your view of human nature and take particular care in relating your view of equality to it. For purposes of discussion, it would be useful to focus on two primary aspects of equality: issues centering on sameness and equality and nature and convention.

Classicists, who are inclined to argue that there is a definable human nature, regularly face the issue of sameness and equality. Plato's "Myth of the Metals" articulates this position well. Plato, living in the shadow of Periclean democracy in which the value of political equality was hotly contested, faced the problem of trying to persuade people to accept the rule of an intellectual elite: philosopher-rulers. Plato believed that a good society could only be built by philosophers whose superior intellect gave them access to the truth that was necessary to rule well. Plato developed the myth of the metals as a way to persuade citizens to accept the rule of the philosopher-rulers. The myth begins with an allusion to heredity. Plato argues that deep in the earth, each individual is created of gold, silver, iron, and brass. Gold represents the capacity to reason; silver, willpower and assertiveness; and brass and iron, the appetites. Since all human beings are born with reason, spirit, and appetite, all humans are the "same." But does this mean that humans are equal in the ability to reason, for example? No. A very small number of people, the philosopher-rulers, are given superior intellects with which to explore and know what is socially, economically, morally, and politically good for the people. Blessed with superior intellectual ability, these men and women also possess appetites and willpower. Appetites are needed to sustain the life of the body, and willpower is the faculty that permits one to control one's appetites. However, the willpower and appetites do not stand out as defining characteristics of these philosopher-rulers. A somewhat larger group of people, the guardians, who serve as soldiers and the police, are endowed with a greater aggressiveness and willpower. Like the stereotypical football player, they are aggressive but lack strong intellectual abilities and appetite. Finally, the vast majority of the population is less intelligent and is dominated by strong appetites. On the intellectual dimension of life, Plato believes that there are a small number of individuals, male and female, who are naturally gifted with higher intellectual abilities, something that the rest of humanity lacks. This inequality of intellectual abilities produces real differences between humans: only those with higher thought skills have access to the knowledge that the philosopher-rulers could use to produce a rightly ordered state. Only these philosopher-rulers could rule in Plato's *Republic*. Turning the political system over to those who are ignorant of how to rule correctly (the appetitive masses or the more aggressive military) would ultimately lead to anarchy and tyranny. Therefore, humans are in essence unequal in certain characteristics, namely reason, spirit, and the appetites, and these inequalities have important implications for who ought to rule.[17]

The Stoics, a group of Greek Hellenistic and Roman philosophers, accepted the idea that humans were equipped by the gods with a fixed nature. However, they departed from Plato on the question of inequality. Cicero, a Roman statesman and philosopher who lived from 106 B.C. to his assassination in 43 B.C., argues that the soul is composed of reason and the appetites, and that in a rightly ordered soul, the appetites should be directed to express themselves in a way that is commensurate with moral principles discovered by reason. The revolutionary concept that the Stoics and Cicero brought to political thought was that all humans possess the ability to understand the greater truths about the divine, natural, and human worlds. Not only do all humans have a rational capacity (and in this sense they are the same), but ordinary differences in intellectual acuity are not important for political life. Some might be a little quicker than others, but all are capable of using their reason to understand those moral laws that ought to direct human behavior, collectively and individually. Thus, Cicero argues that humans are essentially equal in their ability to reason.[18]

This essential equality of human beings found its way into the Christian tradition. Sarah Grimke, an antebellum abolitionist and feminist, developed a notion of the essential equality of humans. Rejecting the belief that males and females had different souls that inclined women to the private world of the home and men to the public world of productive labor and politics, Grimke argues that God created Adam and Eve with similar souls. Made in the image of God, males and females possess the ability to reason, to understand, and to transmit the teachings of Christ and the Old Testament to others. In this creation, each possesses a special dignity in the eyes of God. Therefore, conventional inequalities—inequalities in wealth, social status, and political influence—that depreciate the status of women and rob them of their dignity should be abolished.[19]

Plato, Cicero, and Grimke hold that there is some essential nature that humans possess, and in this way, humans are the same. They believe that humans possess an intellect, a will, and appetites. These components are common to all humans; however, it is reason that differentiates humans from other life forms in the animal and plant worlds. While acknowledging reason to be an essential part of human nature, these thinkers do not come to the conclusion that all humans have an equal capacity to reason. Plato believes that there are real inequalities in intellectual abilities, and these natural inequalities make individuals qualitatively different from one another. Cicero and Grimke choose to differ. Because Cicero believes that all humans have the equal ability to reason and to understand political matters, he asserts that politics should be open to a greater number of people. And Grimke, believing in the dignity of the individual and in the essential equality of men and women, became a critic of a social system that, she believed, threatened the essential dignity of women (and men) and stifled the intellectual and social development of women.

Russian nationalist thought on human equality is grounded in the Orthodox view of human nature. Like Grimke, Russian nationalists argue that humans are spiritually equal in the eyes of God. The nineteenth-century Russian novelist and nationalist Fyodor Dostoevsky believed that individuals are captains of their own souls and can freely choose to live a righteous or unrighteous life following the commandments of God and the teachings of Christ. Being children of God, all humans are brothers to one another, and because humans have the reasoning ability to know and will God's law, there is a possibility of a brotherhood of man that transcends the divisions that occur in the temporal world.[20] Although humans may be equal in the eyes of God, they are given different talents. And though some might be more talented than others, each individual is able to contribute something to the well-being of the social order. For many Russian nationalists, the best social order is one that assigns each person to some social class based on the talents that he or she could contribute to society. In nineteenth-century Russia, the landed nobility, the peasantry, the Orthodox hierarchy, and the czar represented the major components of Russian society. However, political inequality characterized the political system. Russian nationalists favored the autocratic rule of the czar and the submission of the people to the ruler's authority. Thus, while there was a spiritual equality of all humans in the eyes of God, the "reality" of this world was that innate differences in human nature led to a society that was politically unequal.[21]

The twentieth-century Islamic political philosopher Sayyed Abul A'la Maududi holds that humans are not created equally by God. Humans are the same in the sense that all have been given a physical nature with needs for food, water, shelter, and clothing. In addition to being naturally social, humans have an intellect; and as spiritual beings, humans have the ability to choose between good and evil. Socially, men and women are created by God to serve different purposes in society. The gift of childbearing and nurture, for example, was given to women; thus, women make their greatest contribution to society by maintaining a home and raising children. A man, after impregnating his wife, was free to pursue an occupation, defend his country, and participate in politics. The natural differences between males and females produced patterns of social interaction in which women served society by raising and nurturing their children, and men provided economic support for their families and managed the political affairs of their nation. Thus in any society that was properly ordered, the natural differences that characterized the sexes would be reflected in the roles each sex exercised in society.[22]

Russian nationalist and Islamic fundamentalist political thinking on human nature and equality present a fundamentally different way of conceiving political reality. Whereas both are inclined to argue that humans have a body with appetites and desires, an intellect, and the ability to lead a spiritual life, they believe that some are superior to others in the possession of these qualities. These natural differences produce real differences in social living patterns—making women more fit for raising children, some men more inclined to philosophic or scientific thinking, and other men better equipped for political life. Real differences in human abilities lead to differing degrees of social, economic, and political inequalities. Societies that strive for greater equality among those who are naturally unequal work against the natural order of human society. What can be worse than a society in which those least capable of performing critical tasks such as governing or child rearing are placed in those positions? Where those who are unequal are made equal by social convention, social institutions can become dysfunctional and counterproductive.

In these cases, the concern about the equality or inequality of human beings was examined from the standpoint of those who believe that human beings had been granted a special nature by God. However, there are those who argue that human equalities and inequalities are reflections of existing social, economic, and political conditions. The eighteenth-century French philosopher Jean-Jacques Rousseau and radical or cultural feminists are representative of this school of thought. According to Rousseau, humans are inclined by nature to be good and compassionate. While some are stronger, more intelligent, or taller than others, these differences are of little importance. As Rousseau suggests, human society is the result of years of anthropological development; there was a time when people were socially and economically equal.[23] The 1984 film *The Gods Must Be Crazy* describes this idyllic state. In this film, a tribe of African bushmen depicted as living in harmony with nature and with themselves. The fruits of nature provide for the satisfaction of all the bushmen's physical needs. However, problems arise when a soda bottle, dropped from an airplane, makes its way into the lives of the tribe. Since all have a use for the bottle and wish to take the bottle as their own property, fights break out in the heretofore peaceful community. One point made by the film is that the introduction of private property is the source of division among people who would otherwise live in peace. Rousseau makes the same argument. At some point in the anthropological development of humankind, some humans began to acquire and amass more property than others. Rich and poor classes evolved out of the economic equality that characterized a more primitive life. Political inequalities were introduced when rich people were able to persuade poor people that it was in their interest to create a political system that placed the rich in positions of political power over the poor. Thus, the history of the human race is dominated by conventional economic and political inequalities. Rousseau became incensed at these inequalities. The conventional inequality that existed between human beings was inconsistent with the natural equality that characterized human nature. Humans by nature were equal in their capacities as humans: they were equally capable of exercising independent judgment; they had similar basic needs and similar abilities to fulfill those needs. Thus, there could be no natural justification for permitting the rich, politically powerful, socially preferred members of society to create and perpetuate inequalities that resulted in death, starvation, political disenfranchisement, and slavery.[24]

Rousseau's moral outrage against conventional inequalities is understandable if one believes that humans are in some sense equal in their capacities as humans. It is this same outrage that motivates cultural and radical feminists in their criticism of human society. Beyond biological differences that bear on the reproductive natures of women and men, humans are fundamentally equal in their rational capacities for reason and in their ability to live a moral life. V. Spike Peterson and Anne Sisson Runyan argue that biological differences do not have profound impacts on other dimensions of human life such as intellectual ability or child rearing. Thus, biological differences between the sexes notwithstanding, there is no reason to believe that humans are unequal in any other human capacity. In fact, social, political, and economic inequalities are the result of familial, educational, religious, and political socialization. Historically, males have dominated the public world of philosophy, art, work, and politics. They have placed themselves in positions of power and influence, and they have been able to structure the social, economic, political, and religious life of the community in a way that benefits them at the expense of women. The culture that men have developed defines women as emotional, weak, dependent, passive, and soft-headed; women, according to this cultural mindset, are best suited to private, home-based lives. Men define themselves as strong, assertive, rational, autonomous, and capable of managing the social, economic, political, and religious institutions of society. As a result, men have captured and maintain a stranglehold on power and cultural influence that serves to create and reinforce inequalities that have arisen in contemporary societies. The society in which we live is patriarchal.[25]

According to Peterson and Runyan, humans are born with equal capacities for a rational and moral life. All observed differences between males and females are due to the lingering effects of patriarchy. Females' lower math scores; less self-confidence and assertiveness; limited access to elective politics, corporate boardrooms, and positions of religious authority; and lower income are reflections of a society that uses the power of government, law, the job market, and mental and physical coercion to perpetuate these gender-based inequalities. How are these inequalities justified? Peterson and Runyan believe that a gendered ideology develops to legitimize these inequalities. This ideology is rooted in a religious belief that males and females have specific natures that direct them into different social roles. Thus, philosophers like Aristotle are excoriated for their views that women are born with diminished abilities to reason and because of this are less capable of managing public, and even domestic, affairs. Peterson and Runyan believe that limiting women to the home restricts their ability to gain access to the wealth, social prestige, and political power that is necessary for changing the social environment that perpetuates inequalities of the kind discussed earlier.[26]

For Rousseau and Peterson and Runyan (and contrary to the classicists), all social institutions, norms, and inequalities are creations of human beings; they are not reflections of significant differences in the essential nature of human beings that, when played out in the game of life, produce significant inequalities in social class, wealth, and political power. These authors challenge those who hold positions of power and influence to justify the existence of norms, attitudes, and institutions that perpetuate grievous gendered, social, economic, and political inequalities. Their position on equality moves them toward favoring a radical reformation of society that, when complete, will bring a new day in which new vistas of freedom and democracy are open to all humankind.

Sit back and reflect for a moment on equality. What do *you* mean by equality and how is it related to sameness and difference? In what ways are humans equal, unequal, the same, or different? Does it make sense to think about inequalities or equalities that are due to heredity (height, weight, or talent) and those associated with convention (money, wealth, or social prestige)? Are differences in intellectual ability due to heredity or one's environment? Are all inequalities rooted in human nature? If not, are these inequalities conventional, that is, the result of social, economic, religious, or political forces? Do conventional equalities or inequalities reinforce natural ones? Are some inequalities or equalities more important than other inequalities or equalities? Are inequalities in wealth more important than inequalities in character or vise versa? Even if there are natural inequalities in intellect or moral rectitude between the sexes or between races, do these natural inequalities justify laws or corporate policies that would treat the sexes or races differently or unequally? On the one hand, if natural inequalities do exist between individuals or groups, is it just to pursue policies that provide for "equal treatment of unequals"? On the other hand, if humans are naturally equal in some capacity, is it just to pursue policies that treat some as unequals? Even if inequalities exist between individuals or groups, do these inequalities really make a difference in life? For example, is there really that much difference between an "A" paper and a "D" paper, or is grading pretty much a matter of splitting hairs? To what extent should we think in terms of equality? If men and women are clearly different or dissimilar (if men are from Mars and women are from Venus, as one recent bestseller puts it), is there any way to say men and women are unequal; are they just different? Can the same thing be said of individuals? These are just some of the questions that can be raised in the process of thinking about equality.

ON THE ORIGIN OF THE STATE

According to traditional theories of international relations, the state is the primary actor in world politics and if not the primary actor, certainly one of the most important actors. The existing international environment is in many ways organized around states. Members of the United Nations are states. International law grants states certain rights and expects them to behave responsibly. Beyond the legal dimensions of world politics, international political systems develop to handle the diplomatic, political, economic, and cultural intercourse between nations. Political scientists often describe international political systems as bipolar or multipolar. This refers to the number of states or blocks of states interacting with one another in some systematic fashion. Thus, when the United States and the Soviet Union were the dominant powers in world politics following World War II, world politics was said to be bipolar. Clearly, states are important components of the international system. Understanding what states are and how they rise and fall is important in the study of world politics.

What is the state? It might be defined as a body of people organized in a territory under a government. A government refers to the structures and processes associated with conducting the public's business. How does a state differ from a nation? A nation could be defined as a group of people sharing a common territory and common cultural traits. These traits might include a common language, or religion, or historical consciousness, or a similar tribal, ethnic, or racial background. A nation and a state may differ. First, a nation presupposes some consciousness of a unique cultural or linguistic bond; this is largely the case in France or Germany. However, a state may include a population that could not be characterized by religious, ethnic, or linguistic unity but by diversity. Second, a state presupposes the existence of a government, and a nation merely assumes a union of people based upon shared cultural characteristics. What is a nation-state? A nation-state would then be a group of people sharing common cultural traits, territory, and a government.

The origin of the state has been as hotly debated as the nature of human beings. Let us take several examples. Machiavelli, according to some scholars, believes that the state arises when a single prince manages to amass and exercise the power necessary to hold the obedience of the people.[27] For Aristotle, the state is a natural extension of human nature: humans as political animals create the state to achieve certain goals, values, or ends that are impossible without it.[28] Hobbes believes that the state is an artificial creation of humans to remedy the inconveniences found in the state of nature.[29] For Karl Marx, the modern democratic state evolves out of the historical and economic need to create and maintain a capitalist system.[30] Finally, Russian nationalists see the state as evolving from real historical and geographic conditions that are tied to realizing the plan that God has laid out for all humans.[31] With these contending approaches in mind, let us apply our understanding of human nature and human equality to the origin of the state.

This book's opening sections on human nature suggested that one try to imagine what life would be like in the absence of any authority. Undoubtedly, some readers went back and imagined a Hobbesian state of nature, others thought that some social order would remain substantially intact, and others might have conceived of some idyllic condition of justice, freedom, and equality. This "thought experiment" provided the reader with some insight into human nature and the nature of human equality. In the history of political thought, similar experiments have been used to arrive at conclusions about the origin of the state. If we do away with the state and return to some prepolitical state of nature, perhaps we can come to some conclusion regarding why humans chose to create or to live under a state.

Once again, put down this book and re-imagine what human life would be like if there were no authority to order the social lives of human beings. Recall your view of human nature. Given this collective picture of life and human nature, does it make sense that humans would form a state whose functions might be to secure a degree of social order, justice, human rights, or freedom, for example?

Would people prefer to live without a state? If so, why do so many people organize themselves into states? If not, are the states natural products of human association or are they purely social constructions of human beings? How does your
view of human nature help you think about why states are formed? The history of
political thought is full of theories that might help a person think about these
questions. Let us start with realism.

Both Machiavelli and Hobbes hold that the state is not natural to human beings, that is, that the fundamental unit of social organization is self-sufficient individuals. These individuals, like you and me, have the ability to meet their survival
needs without the help of others. For Machiavelli, this is a state of anarchy in
which humans not only neglect the welfare of their fellows but fall on each others'
throats as they pursue their self-interest at the expense of others. Because this condition of anarchy places all life in jeopardy, Machiavelli believes that the people
choose a prince to order the affairs of social life, and subsequently agree to obey
his commands. Machiavelli suggests that the people choose this prince for his
strength and courage, because only a prince with the strength, the courage, and
the will to force unruly opponents into obedience is capable of bringing order to a
body of people unaccustomed to authority. Once in the position to govern, the
prince uses his power to create new political institutions—such as the military and
police—to bolster his own security as well as that of the state. Machiavelli argues
that the origin of the state can be found in a "contract" between individuals and a
prince. In exchange for security, these individuals pledge their obedience to the
prince.[32] Hobbes is in fundamental agreement with Machiavelli on this point. As
you recall, Hobbes believes that if one "thought away" all forms of social control,
one would conclude that the resulting state of nature would be a war of everyone
against everyone else. However, the fear of violent death, the ability of individuals
to imagine a more peaceful life, and the discovery of a few laws that, if obeyed,
would lead to a better life, predisposes them to relinquish much of their power
over their own lives and liberties to a monarch. In exchange for protection, these
independent individuals pledge, in a "social contract," to obey the laws of this
ruler.[33] Thus, for both Machiavelli and Hobbes, the origin of government and the
state is tied to a contract that free, independent people make with a ruler. This
state is purely artificial in the sense that it does not exist by nature (it was not
found in the state of nature); it is a social construct of human beings who, for some
time in a state of nature, could exist without one.

Classicists reject this conception of the origin of the state; instead, they see
the state arising out of the natural need for humans to organize to achieve those
things in life they value. When asked to think of what life would be like if all authority were abolished, classicists would argue that the people would immediately re-create the social institutions that were necessary for a good life. Take
Aristotle, for example. He believes that humans are naturally inclined to form associations—the family, the village, and the state. The "author" of nature invests

humans with the appetites for sociality, food, water, and sex. The desire for food, water, sex, and sociality drives humans to form the family, to help ensure that these basic needs are met. The family sees to it that the young are fed and clothed, self-esteem is nurtured, and the love of others—of parent for child and child for parent—is cultivated in a way that ennobles all its members. Similarly, the state is a natural, rather than artificial, creation of humans. Humans realize that the important goals in life are achieved only by group effort. The ultimate goal of human life for Aristotle is the pursuit of a happy life. A happy life is characterized by the possession of friends, an optimal level of material wealth, a sharing of one's wealth with those in need, and a life distinguished by individual self-control (temperance), courage to meet the challenges of life, the prudence to choose well, and the just treatment of others. The state is created to secure this life. The state is responsible for not only protecting the society from outside aggression, but also for the moral education of its citizens. Strip away the state, village, and family, and individuals would immediately reconstitute these associations because the people believe they are necessary for achieving the good life.

Both the classicist and realist positions on human nature and the origins of the state may seem unduly optimistic or pessimistic. Are we really to believe with the classicists that humans are inclined to good, that politics focuses on creating a virtuous society, and that humans are inclined to political activity when the experience with human life seems to be so much to the contrary? How can the classicist explain the amount of personal and collective violence that occurs in the world? How can the classicist explain politics that seems to center on "self-serving" rather than "other-serving" motives? And how can they explain political apathy? By the same token, the realist labors under similar difficulties. If humans are preoccupied with themselves and prone to conflict, how can they explain actions whereby they selflessly help others? If the state is simply a security association to protect the lives of all in the polity, how can its beneficent activity in alleviating the burdens of poverty and helping the disadvantaged be explained? To the modern mind, neither the classicist nor the realist position corresponds to everyday experience. Modern liberalism attempts to provide answers to these questions.

To a liberal like the English philosopher John Locke, humans have the ability to exercise their reason in a way that permits them to discipline their appetites and to serve their own interests as well as the interests of others. If all human authority were abolished, Locke believes, then the world would return to a state of nature characterized by both peace and war. For the vast majority of people, life in a state of nature is nearly idyllic, he imagined. Through reason, human beings are able to come to an understanding of three God-given natural laws: the laws of life, liberty, and property. Each person has the common sense to know that if he or she keeps these laws and does not violate another's life, liberty, and property, then his or her rights to the same would be secured by others. Being social by nature, humans form families. Two functions of the family are to transmit social norms to their children and to provide for the family's basic needs. Unfortunately, there are always some who by ignorance or by design chose to disobey these laws of nature and try to deny others their life, liberty, or property. This small group of outlaws, placing themselves at war with their fellows, create enough doubt about the security of these laws of nature that all decide to create a society and then a government to protect their lives, liberties, and properties. In so doing, they establish a social contract creating a state and government whose primary function is to secure them their rights to life, liberty, and property. For Locke, government is an "umpire" in the sense that its function is to make sure that the rules of the game are enforced among all who play. This function has the added advantage of making the government responsible for enforcing the law, and leaving individuals free to pursue their own lives, liberties, and properties without having to dabble continuously in politics. Whereas Locke neither rejects the essential sociality of human beings nor denies the potential for antisocial behavior, some believe that he offers a more "realistic"—although not a more philosophically consistent—view of human life and the origin of the state.[34]

These three rather orthodox views of the origin of the state are subject to criticism from those on the political left and right. Radicals such as Karl Marx and Friedrich Engels pose one such challenge. If we were to ask them what would happen if all authority were banished, they would suggest that because humans have real needs to fulfill, they will organize themselves in economic units to provide for these needs. However, a small economic elite will arise and create a state whose purpose is to secure their interests at the expense of those who labor for this elite. In fact, the history of the world can be viewed in part as a struggle between those who own the means of production (factories, mines, and farmland, for example) and those who work for the owners (serfs, apprentices, and factory labor). Throughout history, states supported the existing economic system. Beyond that, the state exists to serve those who own the means of production at the expense of the vast majority of humankind that serves them. In the age of capitalism—the historical era that would later give way to communism—the modern state arose to serve the economically dominant class, the bourgeoisie who owned the factories and ruthlessly exploited the proletariat, those who worked for the bourgeoisie for a subsistence wage. Because capitalism produced deep economic cleavages between the bourgeoisie and the proletariat, the bourgeoisie needed the state to prevent the proletariat, alienated and fueled by anger, from physically destroying the factories and from engaging in work stoppages that threatened the viability of business. Thus, the bourgeoisie harnessed and increased the power of the state to perpetuate its control and exploitation of the proletariat, and it used the power of the state to preserve individual enterprises and the capitalistic system as a whole. The bourgeoisie also used the state to facilitate business activity

by establishing a national banking system, as well as transportation and communication networks. In summary, each historical era created a state to support
the economic interests of the ruling class over an exploited laboring class that
served them.[35]

This analysis of the origin of the state goes far beyond what Aristotle,
Hobbes, and Locke believed. Whereas these earlier writers grounded their views
of the state in human nature or in a state of nature, Marx and Engels believed that
the state is simply a creation of a society's economically dominant interests. The
origin of states and politics is associated with the rise of an economic elite. Moreover, the state is a repressive organization serving the interests of this economically advantaged segment of society. This is a far cry from Hobbes, who believed
that the state should secure one's right to life; from Locke, who added the rights of
liberty and property; and from Aristotle, who believed the state had the exalted
goal of promoting the good life. For Marx and Engels, each of these philosophers
was considered to be an apologist for the ruling class, philosophers who contributed an ideology to justify the exploitation of those who did not own the
means of production. Aristotle justified a state that served free men and sup-
pressed women and slaves; Hobbes created a state that served the interests of the
aristocracy; and Locke envisioned a state that protected the interests of the emerging English bourgeoisie. But Marx and Engels raise interesting questions about the
origin and nature of the state. Is not economics an important element in explaining the origin of the state? Does the state really serve the interests of the stronger,
more financially affluent members of society?

Like Aristotle and unlike Hobbes, Locke, Marx, and Engels, Russian nationalists and Islamic fundamentalists cannot conceive of a society devoid of a state.
The theological foundations of Russian nationalist thought on the origin of
the state can be seen in the work of such writers as Feofan Prokopovich, an early
eighteenth-century archbishop. Prokopovich believes that humans are created to
love and fear God, to protect their own lives, to treat others as they would like to
be treated, and to obey authority. Although these sentiments incline humans to a
social and moral life, their ability to do so is hampered by original sin. Born into
sin, humans do not hesitate to disobey both God's law and the inclinations toward
righteousness that were written in their nature. In the absence of any authority, society would dissolve into a ferocious anarchy that would soak the earth in blood.
A state is needed to curb the socially destructive character of human life as well as
to cultivate those inclinations that lead humans to live peacefully with one another. Beyond this, the state is necessary to organize and harmonize the social
classes that form within societies. The Russian state was unique because its Eastern Orthodox Christian religious hierarchy, the czar, the gentry, and peasants were
united into a harmonious organic body—each contributing to the well-being of
the whole state. The relation between church and state was particularly important
for many Russian nationalists.[36] Dostoevsky argued that the heart of Orthodox

Christianity was the spiritual union of all Christians in the body of Christ. As all were united in Christ, all were brothers and sisters to one another; all were parts of a single spiritual community permeated by Christian love and respect for one another. It was the obligation of the earthly state to promote the brotherhood and sisterhood of all humans by defending the church and legislating in ways that brought about a union of all Russian people. Thus, religion and the state were bound together in a common effort to bring about the harmony of all Russians.[37] Like Russian nationalists, Islamic fundamentalists rely on their religion to explain the origin of the state. Rejecting the notion that the state arises out of a social contract, Khomeini argues that the establishment of the Muslim state could be attributed to the "great man" theory, that is, one man marshals his authority or power to unite people into an enduring social and political order. In this case, Mohammed used his authority as Allah's prophet to unite Muslims under his righteous rule. As God's prophet, Mohammed revealed the divine law that served to orient the lives of all people toward doing good and avoiding evil. This law governed all social, economic, and political interactions, and it structured the relations between husband and wife, buyer and seller, and ruler and ruled. Additionally, Mohammed established norms and practices to guide public administration and foreign relations.[38]

With fervor, both Russian nationalists and Islamic fundamentalists reject the more Western notion that the state is the by-product of a contract between a group of individuals seeking to protect its members' lives, liberty, and fortunes. The source of political authority worries Islamic fundamentalists. The social contract presupposes that sovereignty, or the power to create a government, resides in the people and that the people are free to create whatever state they desire for whatever purpose. For Maududi, God, not the people, is ultimately sovereign and delegates sovereignty to the Ummah or community of Muslims to choose those who will occupy positions of public trust. These public persons are then responsible to God and not to the people; they are responsible for executing God's law, not creating arbitrary rights and legislating in a way that does not square with God's law. To allow people to create a state without any reference to God's law is anathema to Islamic fundamentalists. Yet this is what Western social contract theorists have done. In secularizing the origin of the state, Western social contract theorists have created a state that is devoid of ethical norms. Without any objective norms to define the good that ought to be pursued by the community and its individuals, injustice, ruthlessness, cruelty, brutality, fraud, treachery, and human exploitation come to characterize human relations. Without any norms guiding human behavior, the state ultimately lapses into chaos as each person, pursuing his or her own rights, refuses to accept the authority of the state. This anarchy drifts into tyranny. As people find it impossible to live with the violence that thrives in such anarchy, tyrants seize the opportunity to take charge and impose their own order. Indeed, Maududi suggests that the rise and rule of Germany's Adolf Hitler demonstrates how societies, lacking an ethical core and sense of humanity, can become devastatingly brutal.[39]

Pause for a moment and reflect on your view of human nature and the origin of the state. In what ways are they linked? Are humans political animals that require associations with others to achieve their goals in life? Or are they capable of making it through life on their own? Are humans special creations of God, capable of much good but wallowing in sin? How does your answer to the question: "What is human nature?" help you explain the origin of the state? Is the state the result of more or less cooperative human beings pursuing a common view of the good life? Does the state arise from the need of self-interested individuals to create an umpire to enforce a common law that permits each individual to pursue his or her own view of the good life within the boundaries of that law? Does the state issue from a divinely inspired person who organizes it to bring about the rule of God's law? Obviously, considering the relation of the origin of the state and human nature is important as one begins to think about politics. Let us turn now to the ends or purposes of the state.

ON THE ENDS OF THE STATE

What is meant by the phrase "ends of the state"? The ends are simply those values that the people and government of a state are committed to promote and protect. Take the Preamble to the United States Constitution. The ends it identifies include forming a more perfect union, establishing justice, ensuring domestic tranquillity, providing for the common defense, promoting the general welfare, and securing the blessings of liberty. In fulfilling the promise of the Preamble, the people entrust the government with the responsibility of promoting and defending these values. Some of these values are made even more explicit in the Bill of Rights, the first ten amendments to the Constitution. The First Amendment enumerates various types of liberty that should be granted to the people: the freedom of speech, press, assembly, petition, and religion. The Fifth, Sixth, Seventh, and Eighth Amendments speak about ensuring justice. People are guaranteed due process of the law, a public and speedy trial, and an impartial jury, for example. Thus, the U.S. Constitution specifies and elaborates on the ends that government should pursue.[40]

The ends of the state just listed are only a few of the many that have been offered by political philosophers. Other ends include, but are not limited to, the security of the rights to life, property, health care, and employment; the cultivation of virtue; community; fraternity; social, economic, and political equality; the defense or promulgation of religion; the protection of the chastity of women; and the pursuit of happiness. Why philosophers pick the ends they do has more to do with their view of human nature than anything else. If one believes that humans are relatively self-sufficient enterprisers and are responsible for meeting their own needs, there are fewer things for a state to do and therefore, the state will be given fewer ends. On the other hand, if one holds that humans need the aid or contributions of others so that their needs can be met, then government would be expected to play a greater role in providing for those needs.

This section explores the relation between the ends of the state on one hand and human nature and human equality on the other. This is important for thinking about the ends of politics within nations as well as among nations. Should nations, individuals, and associations operating in the international political system pursue justice, peace, and economic equality? Should these actors promote human rights in their dealings with one another? Should the state be guaranteed the international right to self-determination, that is, the right to conduct its internal affairs in the ways it chooses, free from interference by other nations? These and other questions are similar to the ones raised in this book's examination of the ends of the state.

The classicists are optimistic about politics and the contribution that the state makes in promoting the good life. Both Aristotle and Plato hold that humans are by nature political animals; they are born with a predisposition to form social groups for the purpose of meeting human needs and human aspirations toward a good life. As you will recall in the "Myth of the Metals," Plato argues that all humans are born into a community within the earth and are endowed with reason, spirit, and appetite. Plato argues that in a properly ordered soul, reason discerns what is right and wrong and uses the spirit's ability to exercise its willpower to control the desire for food, drink, sex, and wealth—the appetites that well up in humans in the course of their everyday lives. Justice reigns in the soul when each component part—reason, spirit, and appetite—is properly ordered in relation to one another. One of the ends of Plato's state is to provide a system of moral education that forms a just soul.[41]

As a just soul is necessary for the good life in Plato's ideal republic, so a just ordering of classes in the state is considered to be the primary concern or end of the state. As you recall, Plato believes that society consists of three social classes: philosopher-rulers, who constitute a small, intellectually gifted elite; guardians or members of the military, who are assertive and able to justly exercise the use of their power; and a large number of artisans—businesspeople and laborers interested in producing wealth. The state is just when the philosophers-rulers—the only class knowledgeable about how society should be ordered and governed— legislate in ways that permit each class of society to make its contribution to the well-being of the whole; when the guardians enforce that legislation; and when the artisans proceed to produce, distribute, and moderately consume those goods that were the fruits of their labor. It is for these reasons that Plato defines justice as minding one's own business; that is to say, each class in society should perform the function it was best qualified to perform and should not practice the function of another class. Thus, justice is the primary end of both the state and the individual.[42]

With a passing reference to the classicists, Machiavelli, a realist, writes that "many have imagined republics and principalities which have never been seen or known to exist in reality; for how we live is so far removed from how we ought to live, that he who abandons what is done for what ought to be done, will rather learn to bring about his own ruin than his preservation. A man who wishes to make a profession of goodness in everything must necessarily come to grief among so many who are not good."[43] With this one observation, Machiavelli created a great fault line between the classicists who held that humans were capable of an inspired, moral, and noble life and the realists who believed that human nature was so inclined to selfishness, greed, arrogance, volubility, hatred, gain, self-indulgence, vanity, malice, and enmity that a life of virtue was a largely unattainable earthly ideal. True to their name, the realists took human nature as they found it and preferred to think of politics in more practical, earth-bound terms.

Thomas Hobbes, also a political realist, is stamped in the same mold as Machiavelli. Hobbes believes that people are essentially creatures of appetite and passion to whom reason is purely instrumental. In other words, the function of reason is largely to find the means to satisfy the appetites and passions. Indeed, happiness consists in the continual satisfaction of one's desires and appetites. Since power is the ability to obtain the goods in life that one desires, humans pursue power relentlessly. Because each person is equal to the others in the possession of power, struggles over some scarce good would lead to unending conflict, which could not be ended by one person. Faced with the prospect of such conflict, humans choose to create a state to enforce laws that provide for safety and security. Thus, the supreme end of the state is not the good life or a life of virtue, but simply protecting life.[44]

To understand why Hobbes is so preoccupied with preserving life, one need only look at Hobbes's own life and times. Recalling that he was born in the year the Spanish Armada entered English waters and spread terror throughout England, Hobbes remarked that fear and he were born twins. Hobbes's mature years were marked by England's religious and political strife. In a time of rising parliamentary supremacy and strife between the Crown and the Parliament, Hobbes, a monarchist, feared for his life and fled England to escape persecution for his monarchist beliefs. Hobbes knew that life was indeed temporary and that human nature was such that the security of life was uncertain. He therefore believed that only an authoritarian state committed to preserving life was capable of preventing people from falling at each other's throats and littering history with the blood of patriots, thieves, and scoundrels.[45]

John Locke, a classical liberal, is less consumed by the dark forces that

Hobbes sees working their will upon human nature. Although Locke is not oblivious to the appetitive and passionate part of human nature, he professes a fundamental faith in the ability of individuals to restrain their actions so that they can live peacefully among themselves. He believes that humans have the intellect and rational capacity to understand that God has given all human beings natural laws governing life, liberty, and property; and that in everyday life, humans are able to order their lives, dreams, and passions in a way that does not violate the life, liberty, and property of others. Although all humans are subject to occasional lapses in judgment that result in placing another's property in jeopardy, Locke concludes that humans create governments whose ends are the protection of their natural rights to life, liberty, and property. By using their power to secure these rights, such governments leave individuals free to pursue the things in life that are important to them: family life, personal wealth, or a profession.[46]

In discussing the ends of the state, Locke goes beyond Hobbes in many ways. Locke is not happy with governments that simply secure the right to life; he wants them to secure liberty and property as well. On the one hand, Hobbes conceives liberty as the absence of external impediments.[47] Thus, individuals are free when nothing prevents them from obtaining the things in life they value. Because he believes that humans would break the law if they thought it was to their advantage, Hobbes asserts that the ruler should be given almost unlimited power to check the freedom of his or her subjects for the preservation of order and life. Thus, Hobbes is not strongly committed to freedom. On the other hand, Locke seeks to secure the right of individuals to pursue the things in life that they want, as long as the pursuit of these goods does not violate the lives, liberties, or property of others. Locke defines freedom as choosing in a way that does not violate the freedom of others. Who might attempt to deny people their freedom? Locke is concerned that both individuals and governments may violate their freedoms. To protect themselves from a rogue government that thoughtlessly tramples on the freedom of its citizens, people, in Locke's view, have the right to change the government—by revolution if necessary. Thus, on the issue of freedom, Locke differs from Hobbes. Locke is willing to extend more freedom to the people than is Hobbes, and this willingness is based in part on Locke's more optimistic view of the human capacity to control one's life and to live voluntarily within the boundaries of a minimal number of laws set by the state.[48] Locke also argues that the acquisition, maintenance, and disposition of private property is an additional right the government ought to protect. In so doing, Locke provides a philosophical justification for capitalism. He gives individuals the right to acquire and dispose of property as long as they do not deny others the right to do so. This justifies the possession of great wealth, as long as the benefits of an expanding economic system allow all people to pursue their desire for wealth. It also creates a picture of society as being one directed toward the self-interested pursuit of wealth, where the good society is measured not in terms of moral goodness and virtue, but in terms of wealth and freedom.[49]

The great critique of Locke and Hobbes comes from Marx and other radicals. In Marx's view, classical liberals such as Locke and the eighteenth-century Scottish economist Adam Smith create an economic and political system that justifies the concentration of the means of production in the hands of a few individuals. For Marx, the right to private property in capitalistic societies legitimizes the "right" of owners to use their property in ways that exploit labor. Owners create factory systems that pay a subsistence wage, employ workers for up to thirty-six hours a "day," and, in some cases, use unsafe machinery that results in amputations and death. Even though workers possess the right to private property, the vast majority of humankind, living at subsistence wages, cannot afford to save the money that would allow them to go into business. The possession of the right to liberty is also denied to the working class in practice. Workers have little time, energy, or money to do what they like. Finally, who could say that one had a right to life when the average age of death in heavily industrial areas of England was nineteen years of age? Thus, Marx and Engels argue that while the rights to life, liberty, and property are formally guaranteed to everyone by liberals such as John Locke, the reality is that only a small elite are able to exercise those rights.[50]

Islamic fundamentalists are also critical of unfettered capitalism—a system that is not structured by social norms that prevent the exploitation of individuals. Maududi argues that humans are born with inclinations for food, water, the need to regulate body heat (shelter and clothing), sex, and the exercise of reason. Created by God to do what is good and avoid what is evil, humans are nevertheless inclined to self-gain or selfishness. To prevent humans from being ravished by the selfish motives of others, God, by divine command, has given all of mankind the rights to life, property, freedom, and justice. They also possess the right to meet their basic needs and to be essentially equal regardless of race, color, or nationality. And women are given the right to chastity. As members of a state, humans have civil rights such as the right to property; to protect one's honor from defamation; to enjoy freedom of expression, association, and conscience; and to avoid sin, for example. God has granted these rights to humans so they can live a life filled with beauty, purity, goodness, virtue, success, and prosperity.[51]

Maududi recognizes that there are responsibilities associated with these rights, and that these rights ought to be exercised in a way to bring about a just society. A person with the right to life should recognize the right of others to live, too. Therefore, one should not take the life of another.[52] Second, the right to life implies that others have the obligation to provide assistance to the poor, the sick, and others unable to satisfy their basic needs. While humans have the right to property, they have an obligation to use that property in a manner that benefits not only themselves but others too. Thus, Maududi tells us that the wealthy have the responsibility to share their wealth with the poor.[53] The right to freedom of expression is counterbalanced by the obligation to use that freedom correctly. Thus, one should not use the freedom of speech to slander another, and expression should be used to promote virtue and truth rather than to spread evil and wickedness. In Maududi's view, Muslims should try to stomp out evil by force, by speaking out against it, and if neither of these things can be done, by condemning it in their hearts.[54] In summary, Maududi argues that humans live in a society that is ordered to establish, maintain, and develop those virtues by which God wants human life to be enriched and to prevent those evils that cheapen it. Humans are given natural and political rights that should be used to promote virtue and avoid vice.

Maududi believes that Western and Marxist societies have not secured individuals their rights in practice, and he thinks that Western capitalism has severed economics from religious ethics. Without norms controlling the production, acquisition, distribution, and use of wealth, humans pursue their lives without regard to the economic well-being of others. The rich use surplus wealth for their own material comfort, and employers exploit others by reducing wages to subsistence levels. The wealthy, who control the means of production, buy superfluous goods that go beyond the necessities of life rather than help the poor. The rich, controlling the means of production, constitute a segment of society that is living in moral and spiritual degradation. Western capitalism, separated from religious foundation, lacks a human face and becomes increasingly economically oppressive, according to Maududi.[55]

Nineteenth-century Russians such as Ivan Kireevski and Konstantin Aksakov were part of the Slavophil school of social and political thought. As a group, the Slavophils were unhappy with the Westernization that took place in Russia during and after the rule of Peter the Great. They opposed the rationalism of the Enlightenment, the individualism inherent in Western culture, and the preference for representative government. The Slavophils saw the development of Russian life as being temporarily stifled by Westernization, and their writings focused on bringing to light those elements of traditional Russian culture that could serve as the basis for the spiritual and political regeneration of Russian society. They were committed to supporting the autocracy of the czar, maintaining a strong Orthodox church whose spirit penetrated the hearts and minds of all Russians, and perpetuating Russian society that was conceived to be an organic unity.[56]

Kireevski and Aksakov recognized the importance that the church played in Russian life and politics. Kireevski, born in 1806 to parents of the landed gentry, believed that Russia would be best served by honoring its historical roots: the Orthodox church and traditional patterns of social life. The Orthodox church was the true heir to Christ, preserving Christian doctrine in its purity and fullness. Additionally, the authoritative position of the church in Russian society meant that it had a profound influence on the everyday lives of Russians. It shaped the religious and social values of the Russian nation, and it promoted a degree of unity among all classes of people: serf and gentry; peasant and czar. Politically, Kireevski favored the separation of church and state. As practical politics inevitably required compromise—even on important moral principles—Kireevski wanted the church to remain outside politics. Free from the corrosive nature of politics, the church could direct humankind toward the universal principles of human unity, peace, and justice. The church strongly influenced the moral character of the Russian people and exerted a positive impact upon the way social and political institutions developed in Russia. Customary law—that law that grew out of the everyday interactions of people—was inspired by the Christian norms transmitted by the church. Brimming with Christian love, the Russian family was a social unit marked by an unselfish, mutual love between parents and children. Both parents were committed to the family unit; they did not pursue their own selfish ends at the expense of the family. Thus, the Russian Orthodox church played an important role in ennobling and spiritualizing Russian family and social life.[57] To this social ideal, Aksakov (1817–1860) added a political component. Rejecting representative government, Aksakov was committed to the autocracy of the czar. He saw the czar as the embodiment of the unity of the people. The ends of the state were to safeguard and protect life, to provide a degree of material security for all, and to permit the moral development of its citizens by defending the role that the Orthodox church played in Russian life. The state had limited power to intervene in the private lives of the people. Since daily Russian life was built around the commune and the church, Aksakov believed that the state should leave Russians free to order their spiritual and social life in ways that suited themselves. In return, Aksakov argued that the Russian people had renounced their claim to enter politics and to political rights. Their duty to the state was simply to carry out its commands, give support to the actions of the czar, and supply the state with men and money as needed.[58]

Kireevski, along with the contemporary writer Alexandr Solzhenitsyn, is sharply critical of Western life. Kireevski, focusing on Western culture, suggests that the greatest failing of the West is its sole reliance on human reason (without divine assistance) to provide meaning to human life. The problems arising from this are particularly evident in Western social and political thought. First, the French philosophes of the Enlightenment reject the belief that God is the fountainhead of morality. Without a moral core of values to give meaning to life, Western civilization is drained of the ideals that permit people to make sense of their lives. To compensate for the loss of a spiritual dimension, the West turns to crass materialism; however, this fails because what is most meaningful in life is spiritual. Second, a destructive individualism runs rampant through European life, transforming the family. Parents, Kireevski argues, sacrifice the well-being of their children to the pursuit of wealth or social prestige. Instead of raising their children themselves, parents choose to send their offspring to be raised by boarding schools and nannies so they can spend their time in the pursuit of wealth, social prestige, and pleasure.[59] On the eve of the fall of the U.S.S.R. in 1991, Solzhenitsyn offered his thoughts in *Rebuilding Russia* and in so doing extended this critical analysis of Western politics. Similar to Kireevski and Aksakov, both of whom believed that despite attempts at Westernization the Russian peasant retained those Orthodox values that permitted the regeneration of a traditional society, Solzhenitsyn believes that communism has possibly rooted out all that was good in the Russian character and that rebuilding Russia will require a moral revolution in the souls of the Russian people. This moral rejuvenation could take place with the church, separated from the state, leading the way. The church would be the vanguard for re-Christianizing a secular Russian culture by Christianizing the Russian people. The Russians would be pious, able to control their desires and passions, committed to the welfare of others, and just. Contemporary Western culture could not be a model that Russia could imitate. Solzhenitsyn believes that European democracy was originally imbued with a sense of Christian responsibility and self-control.[60] However, the spiritual values inherent in Christianity have been replaced by selfishness promoted by "the dictatorship of self-satisfied vulgarity, of latest fads, and of group interests."[61] This decadent culture has been exported into non-Western countries. The Iron Curtain could not prevent the "continuous seepage of liquid manure—self-indulgent and squalid 'popular mass culture,' the utterly vulgar fashions, and the by-products of immoderate publicity—all of which our deprived young people have greedily absorbed."[62]

Western politics, in Solzhenitsyn's opinion, is spiritually unhealthy. As Western society loses its Christian, moral girders, its political systems are becoming less concerned with the welfare of all its members. Solzhenitsyn especially is critical of universal suffrage (the right of all qualified citizens to vote), elections, parties, and public officials in Western democracies. He criticizes universal suffrage because it does not discriminate between those few persons whose talents, contributions to society, age, and life experience provide them with deep insights into politics and the many who have little interest in, or knowledge about, politics. Giving the more politically competent and the less politically astute the same vote results in the triumph of quantity (the greatest number of votes) over substance. Furthermore, elections contribute to a politically ignorant electorate. Election campaigns dwell on frivolous issues; by focusing on such trifles, they degrade the political discourse that is necessary for voters seeking to cast an informed vote; and elections are conducted in a way that those who "appear to be the best" win, even though they may not have the necessary skills to govern a nation. Finally, parties pursue not the public interest, but their own interest in getting elected, and they therefore serve the narrow interests of their members at the expense of the common good. A small cadre of professional party politicians dominates Western politics. They have a greater commitment to the agendas of their respective parties and to their desire to get reelected than to the greater public interest.[63]

In summary, Islamic fundamentalists and Russian nationalists writing in the

Slavophil tradition share similar criticisms of Western society and politics. For both Muslims and Slavophils, world politics should be guided by moral values. Both believe that Western society is better served when its religious values are broadly shared and when it orients social, economic, and political actions toward the public good. However, the growing secularization of society and politics leads to a selfish, aggressive form of economics and politics. Religious values are purged from the capitalist economic system and divorced from politics. In the absence of any moral values that could guide the interactions of people in the marketplace, those owning the means of production feel no moral constraint in exploiting labor and marginalizing vast segments of industrial populations. Also, capitalism nurtures an acquisitive public that cares little about things beyond its own private home and work life. When citizens do become active, they use the political system not to promote the well-being of all people, but to protect their own selfish interests.

The Islamic and Russian alternatives to and critiques of Western society raise as many questions about their own worldviews as they do about the West's. On the one hand, both Russian and Islamic conceptions of politics do not separate religion from politics, and one must wonder if Western pluralistic societies can or should return to politics grounded in religious values. Both Russian and Islamic conceptions of the good society attempt to preserve their societies' values, traditions, and institutions. But again, one must wonder if what is being preserved is helpful in negotiating the problems and pitfalls of modern life. On the other hand, is there something to be learned from these two worldviews? Is there in fact a spiritual crisis that threatens the quality of life and politics in the West? Should governments use their powers to promote spiritual values—values such as sharing, the respect for the dignity of the individual, for the family, for truth, and beauty? Could the West benefit from Islamic fundamentalists who argue that where there are rights, there are corresponding obligations? If one has the right to vote, is it not reasonable to expect that voters educate themselves on the day's issues? Are both these traditions correct in suggesting that individuals in a more or less capitalistic economic system would benefit from norms that would guide the economic interactions among people in the marketplace? These are just a few of the questions that are raised by more conservative Russian and Islamic writers.

ON THE BEST FORM OF GOVERNMENT

A state is a body of people organized in a territory under a government. A government could be defined as the governing body of citizens in a state or community. Who constitutes this governing body determines the form of government. For example, if the government is a direct democracy, then all those who are citi-

tion because of age restrictions actu-
will enforce it, and name those who
blican form of government is one in
and judicial positions are nominated
ermitted to make that selection. The
nited States are typically representa-
ve and executive officials, but judges

oday, that question seems rhetorical.
ment of choice seems to be a repre-
of philosopher-rulers, the military, or
he idea that another form of govern-
acy, in spite of the fact that represen-
onsiderable stress these days. Politics
nd not the common good; people feel
ed to serve them; and governments
o perpetuate their rules without any
he sometimes unthoughtful bias to-
to explore other alternatives.
political thinkers to identify and dis-
cs, Aristotle argues that governments
may generally be described in terms of the number of people who are permitted to
participate in the governing process and the ends those governments pursue. In
the following discussion, remember that Aristotle was discussing the Greek city-
state: a territorially small geographical unit whose average size was perhaps 1,000
free, male citizens. Although Athens may have had as many as 30,000 citizens, that
number excluded at least another 30,000 women, slaves, and foreign merchants.
According to Aristotle, a government could be identified by whether one person,
a few people, or all the citizens actually governed, and whether those who governed pursued their own selfish interests or the good of the whole community.
With numbers and ends as criteria for categorizing governments, Aristotle argues
that those governments that pursue the common good are monarchies (rule of
one), aristocracies (rule of the virtuous few), and constitutional democracies (rule
of the many). Those governments that pursue their own selfish ends are tyrannies
(rule of one), oligarchies (rule of the few), and democracies (rule of the many). In
discussing democracies and oligarchies, Aristotle introduces the notion of socioeconomic class. Because the vast majority of humankind is "poor" and few are
"rich," Aristotle argues that oligarchies represent the rule of the rich few, who pursue their own self-interest, and democracies represent rule by the many poor, who
also pursue their own interests.[64] Plato makes this point very clearly. Oligarchies
are governments whose ends are to pursue wealth, and in this society, the rich

control the reins of government by using wealth as the criterion to determine who shall and shall not participate in politics. Hence, the majority of citizens who possess little wealth could not participate in the governing of the state. Democracy is a form of government in which the poor, after wresting political power from the oligarchs, move society toward greater social, economic, and political equality and liberty by redistributing wealth from the rich to the poor, ensuring that all qualified citizens can participate in governing the state, securing equal rights for all, and leaving people free to define and pursue their own views of happiness.[65] With monarchy, aristocracy, constitutional democracy, democracy, oligarchy, and tyranny as the six forms of government that serve to direct the energies of people in the state, let us turn to particular forms of government and couch the discussion of each in the context of human nature and equality. Direct or participatory democracy is one form of government that rests upon the belief that humans are capable of directly conducting their own political business. Historically, direct democracy is possible in smaller geographic political units with relatively small populations. Only in areas where populations were small and where people had a relatively short distance to travel could direct democracy work. Then people could assemble, discuss ideas, and vote on measures brought before the assembly. In a direct democracy, those participating in politics could control their political destiny rather than leaving it up to kings, aristocrats, or representatives to do so.

Rousseau's theory of democracy is perhaps the most interesting and most debated conception of direct democracy. Rousseau believes that humans are innately good. By this he means that they are inclined toward compassion and justice and that they have the ability to make, weigh, and judge matters of social importance. Because of this basic goodness, humans can be entrusted with political power and thus he favors a direct democracy. This democracy is denoted by a general will: a common set of beliefs and values about the nature of the good life. Among these values are a respect for the social, economic, and political equality of all humans. A true democrat at heart, he believes that in order for democracy to be realized, wealth should be spread widely among the people and that no one should be so rich as to be able to buy the vote of another person. Because human nature is such that all humans are able to exercise their intellects and moral capacities for the common good, he believes that all should participate in government. Because each citizen is able to participate in politics on an equal basis with others, he favors political equality. Freedom, obedience to self-prescribed law, is possible only in a direct democracy. Only in direct democracies can people make the laws that they obey and thus be free by this definition.[66]

To many, it is hard to imagine that direct democracy has any viability in a world where large nation-states and multinational corporations dominate the domestic and international political landscape. Critics of direct democracy also point out that people are not nearly as good and wise as Rousseau suggests. As a matter of fact, some people are either naturally or through life experience more inclined to politics than others, and it is best that these people do the day-to-day governing, leaving others to pursue their own private family, work, and recreational interests. Finally, critics assail those who believe that human beings have the interest and time to devote to politics. To be an active citizen means spending significant chunks of one's free time in thinking and reading about politics and economics, attending meetings, and serving as local officials. Not everyone will want to give up their leisure time to pursue politics when they can otherwise be watching football, playing with their children, vacationing, or partying. Despite these reservations, the democratic ideal that people can make a difference in local politics inspires many who have become politically active.

The vision that people are best served if they have some role in the governing process was shared by those who wrote the U.S. Constitution in 1787. These men had serious misgivings about direct democracy, and they sought to find an alternative form of government that permitted popular influence in government, but not popular control over it. To this end, they created a representative government or republic that allowed the public to choose directly or indirectly those public officials who would serve in the three branches of government: the legislative, executive, and judicial departments. Many Founders were in varying degrees skeptical about human nature. Alexander Hamilton, a person who would have preferred something more like a monarchy in the new United States, once commented that the people were a great beast. The metaphor of a beast aptly describes Hamilton's view of human nature. People are animal-like: driven by passion and anger, and largely incapable of exercising reason and self-control. James Madison, a Federalist of more moderate temperament than Hamilton, believed that human nature was such that humans did not have the rational capacity to arrive at ultimate truths concerning religion, politics, and economics. Thus, society was divided into competing religious, political, and economic visions. Given the inclination of humans to act passionately and irrationally, it was best to entrust government to those whose experience, temperament, and concern for the common good were superior to those possessed by others. These politicians were more likely to rule in the best interest of society than were most people. Furthermore, although it was desirable for the people to directly elect members to the House of Representatives, it was best that other political bodies composed of experienced and wiser politicians select the Senate, the president, and the Supreme Court. Hence, senators were initially selected by state legislatures, the president by an electoral college, and justices to the Supreme Court by presidential nomination and senatorial confirmation.[67]

Because the Founders viewed human nature as basically selfish, and because they realized that those elected to the national government would not always be enlightened statesmen, they chose to separate the powers into executive, legislative, and judicial branches and to provide each branch with checks and balances. The Founders separated the powers of government because they believed that if all power were placed in the hands of one person or one body of persons, that power might be used in a way to threaten the lives and liberties of the people. Therefore, separating powers would prevent one branch from having absolute political power. If government were to act, it would require the support of the three branches of government. This requirement would reduce the possibility that government would act other than in the best interests of the people. But realizing that each branch of government would be inclined to seize more power than they envisioned, the Founders chose to give each branch of government certain checks and balances. For example, the president had a veto that could be exercised if Congress threatened the power of the presidency or of the American people. By the same token, Congress had the power of impeachment that could be exercised to hold presidents accountable to the U.S. Constitution.[68] In reflecting on the necessity of checks and balances, Madison said, "It may be a reflection on human nature that such devices should be necessary to control the abuses of government. But what is government itself but the greatest reflection on human nature? If men were angels, no government would be necessary. If angels were to govern men, neither external nor internal controls on government would be necessary."[69]

Federalism was another feature of the U.S. Constitution. Federalism is simply a division of power between a central government and regional or state governments. In the United States, power is divided between the national government and state governments. For example, the federal government in Washington, D.C., has the power to raise an army and conduct relations with other nations—two powers U.S. states do not have. On the other hand, the states have the power to educate their citizenry, a power that is not specifically given to the federal government by the U.S. Constitution. Federalism differs from a confederal form of government. A confederation is a government composed of several sovereign states, each of which gives up some powers to a central government and agrees to be ruled by that government. Generally, confederations delegate little power to the central government and retain a good deal of power to manage their own internal affairs free from the influence of a central government. However, since the states retain their power to remain or withdraw from a confederation, they can withdraw from that government any time they desire. In fact, the Articles of Confederation (1776–1789) is an example of a confederation. Many scholars believe that the Articles of Confederation failed simply because it did not give enough power to the central government: it could not regulate economic relations among the states, could not impose taxes to finance its governmental operations, and could not effectively manage international relations. Confederated and federal governments differ from a unitary government. In a unitary system, all power is given to a central government, which has the discretion to give power to, and to take power back from, regional or local governments. Of course those who wrote the U.S. Constitution were inclined to favor a federal form of government. Although they saw the need for a strong central government with the capacity to address national issues, they also believed that the states should have substantial control over their own affairs. Because many people believed that the national government's power was not sufficiently limited, the first United States Congress wrote the Tenth Amendment to the U.S. Constitution, sometimes dubbed the "federalism amendment"—powers that were not given to the national government nor denied by the U.S. Constitution to the states, should be given or reserved to the states and people of those states. Some of the many advantages of federalism were, first, that it further divided power; now no one government was able to exercise all political power; power was shared by a national government and many state governments. Thus, tyranny was less probable under a federal form of government. Second, it permitted the people of the various states to write laws that fit their local circumstances. With such a large, diverse nation, many feared that solutions to problems proposed at the federal level would not work because the natures of the problems in other states were much different. Finally, federalism secures freedom. The Federalists believed that people were free when they were able to live their lives as they pleased. Because federalism meant that the national government was limited in what it could require the people to do or prevent them from doing, it allowed individuals greater freedom to choose the life they chose to live.[70]

The popularity of representative forms of government in today's world overlooks the claims of those who would like to center power in the hands of a single person—a monarch exercising power for the common good. Of those arguing for a monarchy, Hobbes and the Russian nationalists stand out. Recalling Hobbes's view of human nature, humans are so selfish that a war of all against all constituted relations between them in the state of nature. Eventually, individuals, fearful of their lives and seeing the possibility of a better life if certain laws were obeyed, form a society and government and give up their right to exercise political power to a monarch. The primary benefit to be gained by such an agreement is peace: the monarch, by "the terror of some power," would use force if necessary to induce people to obey the laws that fell from his or her mouth.[71] And the terror of strict law is necessary to discipline a people whose first inclination is to disobey laws that they think are not in their interest to obey. Peace among humankind is purchased at a price. Hobbes argues that the people give up their power to manage their own affairs to a monarch, authorizing him to make the laws that are necessary for their well-being. In return, the people agree to obey the laws that the monarch makes. Although a society disciplined from the top by a strong ruler has the benefit of bringing a degree of tranquillity and peace among an unruly rabble, it obviously limits the freedom of the people. People are free, by Hobbes's own admission, only in those areas of life in which the monarch permits them to live as they please. In Hobbes's society, that freedom is severely circumscribed, but people can walk the streets at night without fear of losing their lives, they are able to sleep fully and safely in their own homes, they have little worry about thievery, and they are free to pursue their private lives without the burden of being actively involved in the political process.[72]

Russian nationalists such as Aksakov, Dostoevsky, and Prokopovich favored placing all political authority in the hands of a single czar. For Prokopovich, the Orthodox archbishop, the necessity of autocratic rule is required by human nature. God had created humans with the inclination to love and follow Him, to treat others as they would like to be treated, and to preserve themselves. However, the Fall had unleashed the darkest human passions, passions that could overwhelm and transfigure the goodness written in the human heart. Capable of the worst barbarities, the Russian people need to be brought to heel by a single leader. Prokopovich introduces an important argument to support the autocracy of the czar: humans are inclined by God to obey authority, the first of all the inclinations given to humans. Although people may be naturally inclined to obey authority, Prokopovich knows that humans are capable of great evil and disobedience. So he argues, like Saint Paul had done before him, that God has commanded that all obey those in positions of authority under the penalty of divine judgment. Prokopovich believes that if the natural inclination for authority and the punishment of a just God for those who disobey are not enough to secure the people's obedience to the czar, then that obedience to authority could be gained by the "terror of some power" exercised forthrightly by the czar.[73] Dostoevsky's preference for monarchy is reflected in his view of human nature. In the *Brothers Karamazov*, Dostoevksy expands on the theme that there are human processes that lead individuals to obey those in positions of authority. Christ returns and is to be judged by the Grand Inquisitor who has the power to put Christ to flame and worldly death. The Grand Inquisitor suggests that humans would willingly and happily renounce their freedom if only someone would give them bread, that is, satisfy their basic needs. Would pleading, screaming, starving people renounce their freedom for food provided by an autocratic czar? This is a chilling question, and one answer to it recalls the attachment that many people had to the Great Depression autocratic governor of Louisiana, Huey Long, or the German dictator, Adolf Hitler.[74]

There is something therapeutic about monarchies. For societies rent by political division, social chaos, and economic disorder, the appeal of a single ruler promising to restore domestic and psychic tranquillity is a powerful one. It is even more powerful when it is linked to a view of human nature suggesting that beneath the gloss of sociality lies an angry beast, chained by little more than weak bonds of morality. Here lies the possibility of unparalleled evil and disorder. If politics is turned over to professional politicians whose commitment to the public good is as shallow as their capacity to do good in their private lives, if conventional politics seems unable to solve the most important problems in our lives, if the basic physical and psychological needs of a growing number of people remain unmet by political systems seized in gridlock, and if everyday life becomes indistinguishable from our most frightening nightmares, the prospect of rule by a beneficent monarch who can set things right is enticing. Hobbes and the Russian nationalists understood this; however, in moving toward an authoritarian government to manage the infirmities of human nature, one wonders if their solution is not worse than the problem that it attempts to solve. After all, a monarch shares the same passions and emotions as the people he or she governs. Is there not the possibility that a beneficent monarch could become a *leviathan*, or monster—a tyrant—as the Federalists argued? Perhaps the problem of social and political chaos has less to do with human nature and more to do with questions of relating to social, economic, and political inequalities.

For Aristotle and Plato, aristocracies, rule by a few virtuous persons, are an alternative to either a constitutional democracy or monarchy. This elite has the moral bearing and access to a type of social, economic, and political knowledge that the rest of the population does not have: either because the latter choose not to gain that knowledge or because they are intellectually incapable of attaining it.[75] Plato argues that only a small number of men and women are born with the intellect to access the greater truths of the universe. As soon after birth as possible, he asserts, children with superior intellect should be identified and put through a rigorous academic and physical education that prepares them for military and public service. This education, extending to middle age, would not only cultivate a knowledge of the social, economic, and political truths that are necessary to build a truly just society, but would also give these chosen few the practical experience needed to administer the day-to-day affairs of the state. This political elite would create and administer a just state, and because it is just—with everyone engaging in the work for which they are best suited and from which they gain the greatest satisfaction—both the state and the individuals in the state are happy.[76]

Aristocracies are described by Aristotle as governments in which the few and most virtuous members of society rule for the common good. Ayatollah Khomeini's political theory tends to be aristocratic and bears a close resemblance to Plato's mature political theory. Khomeini argues that God is the fountain of all law and that his law was revealed most completely to his prophet, Mohammed. The totality of Islamic law centering on morality, politics, economics, and society is the Shari'a. The Shari'a should form the basis on which society is organized and life is conducted. In the absence of an imam (a religious-political leader who receives his authority to rule through previous imams) Khomeini gave the ulama, religious scholars, the authority to rule. Like Plato's philosopher-rulers, the ulama were a small body of people who had the intellect to understand divine matters, lived a thoroughly virtuous life, and were capable of providing those less knowledgeable and spiritually inclined with an understanding of how to live their lives. The ulama, who were actively involved in supervising the implementation of the Shari'a, were guardians. Being custodians of the Shari'a, the guardians were charged with the responsibility of establishing a government whose end was to usher in the rule of the Islamic law and a life of virtue. Although not participating in the government themselves, they would establish a government whose members would legislate in a way that applied Islamic law to everyday life and who would create and supervise the bureaucracy and legal system that applied Islamic law. Although Khomeini doe not express a preference for any specific form of government, a certain aristocratic bias exists in his political thinking. Ultimately, he is satisfied with any government, supervised by the ulama, that implements Islamic law.[77]

Khomeini's understanding of politics and government differs radically from Western conceptions. The most interesting distinction centers on the relation of religion and politics. First, religion cannot be separated from politics because the Shari'a, divinely revealed law, is the foundation of how Muslims relate to one another socially, economically, and politically. As this law can be very specific—the lopping off of hands for theft, for example—it provides a practical guide for how one is to live and relate to another. The Shari'a forms the very substance of life, and all political activity centers on administering the Shari'a and interpreting it in more specific situations. Thus, legislative and judicial bodies have the simple role of taking the Shari'a and applying it to the situation they face. Second, Khomeini recognizes that his political philosophy is totalitarian—but it is, is his view, a beneficent totalitarianism. Totalitarian governments attempt to control every aspect of life from the political system and the economy to the sexual relations between individuals. Khomeini's political theory is totalitarian because he envisions a government, girded by Islamic law, penetrating all facets of Islamic life to achieve a virtuous society. It is beneficent because government action is aimed at the complete spiritual and material development of the individual. Although this rule is totalitarian, it is not arbitrary. The government's exercise of political power is confined to governing in accordance with the commands of Allah; thus, the government is limited in how it can exercise political power. In Khomeini's political theory, God's justice will reign on earth, all human needs will be met, and individuals motivated by their conscience will lead a life of virtue. Finally, authority to rule comes from God and not from the people. Khomeini points out that the authority to legislate resides in God, the prime law-giver. This law is eternal and can never be changed by human artifice. Humans do not have the authority to make law that is in opposition to the Shari'a. For this reason, Khomeini attacks those Western social contract theorists who argue that the authority to make law stems from a contract in which the people give a legislature or monarch the authority to legislate in their behalf.[78]

Needless to say, the critics of Khomeini are many. They wonder whether law that is many centuries old can serve as the foundation for modern, industrial life. Even though many Westerners may believe that mixing religion and politics is inevitable or even good, they believe that Khomeini goes too far. His religious "guardians" of the law and of all legislative acts contribute to a stifling religious conformity that denies people liberty of thought and action. Many abhor the total-itarian nature of Khomeini's political theory. Whether power is exercised in the name of God, the people, or the individual, it still is an attempt to control substan-tial portions of a person's life and moves toward total control. Finally, many peo-ple in Western societies are uneasy with the idea that absolute knowledge about law and the good life exists. If it does not exist, by whose authority are a small number of clerics imposing that law on others? Shouldn't these matters be left up to the whole community to decide? Or shouldn't the individual be given great lat-itude in carving out his or her own version of the good life?

Although direct democracy, representative government, monarchy, and aris-tocracy as forms of government have enjoyed a long history in the Western politi-cal theory, there have been those who have argued that the ideal society would be one without a state and, consequently, without a government. This view was sup-ported by Karl Marx and Friedrich Engels. They believed that life in an advanced capitalistic system would become horrendous for the exploited proletariat. The proletariat—fully conscious that capitalism was the source of their poverty, per-sonal and social alienation, and exploitation—would ultimately rise up in rebel-lion against the bourgeoisie. During the revolution, the proletariat would seize control of the state and the means of production—the farms, factories, and mines, for example. Having seized state power, the proletariat would rid the state of the bourgeoisie. Since the existence of the state was predicated on the bourgeoisie using the power of the state to oppress the proletariat and to perpetuate capital-ism, and since the bourgeoisie and capitalism no longer existed, there was no need for the state. After the state had "withered away," the people would cooperatively manage their economic affairs in a way that would lead to freedom and justice. Because economic relations determined the quality of life that a person lived, con-trolling the means of production meant that the entire productive resources of so-ciety could be managed by the workers to increase their quality of life. People would be able to engage in the type of work that they enjoyed, all their physical needs would be met, and, in the absence of class exploitation, social harmony would abound. Justice reigned to the extent that each person or social group was contributing his or her talents to the well-being of the social whole and in return, was receiving enough to meet its human needs. And since freedom could occur only when people controlled the economic forces that provided them with the op-portunity to live as they desired, and since the people had seized those economic forces, only now were they free.[79]

The criticism of Western democracy comes from Marxist sources, too. Just as representative government does not in reality secure the rights to life, liberty, and property, neither does it secure democracy. Representative forms of government of necessity arise in mature capitalistic systems. However, the government admits little popular influence. The government, according to such critics, is in fact con-trolled directly or indirectly by the monied bourgeoisie. The cost of running for office prohibits the proletariat from running for office; thus, those who hold political positions are either the bourgeoisie who have the money to run for office or candidates chosen and bankrolled by the bourgeoisie. Thus, elections are largely meaningless. In the United States, the Republican and Democratic parties are essentially bourgeois parties—parties committed to promoting capitalism, the source of modern economic, social, and political problems. The electorate, allowed to choose between two capitalist parties, has no real choice: it inevitably chooses candidates who support capitalism. Even though proletarian parties succeed in surmounting legal barriers to get on the ballot, they cannot win elections because most of the electorate has been socialized into accepting the dominant values of the capitalistic system and mistakenly believe that one of the two major parties is an effective avenue for change. As a result, the bourgeoisie manages to structure politics in a way that permits it to reduce the amount of popular influence in government and to secure its rule from popular challenge. Representative governments are in reality oligarchies: rule by the rich few. Freedom, justice, and human equality will arise only when all classes and the state are abolished.

To some, this is a devastating critique of Western-style "democracies." To many, it is extreme. First, it is rather patronizing and demeaning to describe democratic citizens as ignorant and capable of infinite manipulation by wily politicians and Madison Avenue public relations specialists. Second, to say that representative governments are really oligarchies pushes the point too far. There is no doubt that money is important in electoral politics; however, it is not clear that money serves only the rich and advantaged. Large sums of money have been expended on behalf of the poor and the environment. Third, to say that there is no real choice between the two major parties in the United States misreads history. Although there have been times when the two parties have been very similar, many in the electorate see real differences between them. Additionally, minor parties can and have put up candidates for public office. A good argument can be made that minor parties fail because their messages are not mainstream.

Put down this book for a minute and reflect on how human nature, human equality, government, the state, and the ends of the state are related to one another. Are you fundamentally optimistic or realistic about human nature? How does your view of human nature relate to government? If your view of human nature is optimistic, does it incline you to think that humans are capable of managing their own private and public affairs? If so, is a democracy the best form of government? Is it better to do away with government altogether? If so, would you eliminate the state as a body of organized power to enforce law and leave it up to individuals to organize their lives in ways that permit them to pursue the things in life they most desire? Or, given your view of human nature, is some form of government and organized power necessary to secure or order the relations between individuals and groups? How does your specific view of human nature lead you to think about the ends of government? If humans are naturally free or believe that freedom is an important aspect of human life, do you believe that a government should attempt to protect individual and social freedom? In what ways are humans naturally equal? How does this help you think about the ends of government? On the other hand, if you are more realistic or pessimistic regarding human nature, how does this view lead you to think about the best form of government? Would it lead you to believe that some form of elite rule, an aristocracy, would be preferable to the outright rule by the people? If you favor some form of democracy, would you prefer a representative democracy to a direct democracy? Do you think that a strong, centralized state is necessary if we are to have a civilized life? What are the ends of government? Should the security of life take precedence over freedom or equality? As you can see, the answer to one question inevitably affects the way you answer another question, and a well-thought-out political theory will show a degree of consistency between the answers to these and other questions you pose.

Let us move to world politics proper, and you will see that your answers to these questions will help you develop a deeper view of world politics. First, you will discover that we cannot talk about world politics without thinking about domestic politics. Individuals, interest groups, and forms of government often affect the relations between world political actors in their relations with one another. The goals we pursue in domestic politics are often the same ones we pursue in world politics. Second, some of the very concepts that are used to think about domestic politics are used in world political theory. Equality, freedom, human nature, anarchy, society, law, government, and the origin of the state are often twisted and turned to help us think about world politics. The challenge this book presents to you is to take the ideas you have developed to this point and to apply them to world politics when it is relevant. To do this, let us begin with a discussion of those individuals and groups that perform on the stage of world politics.

NOTES

1. William Golding, *Lord of the Flies* (n.p.: Wideview/Perigee Books, 1954).
2. Thomas Hobbes, *Leviathan*, ed. Michael Oakeshott (New York: Collier Books, 1962), 80.
3. Ibid., 98–102.
4. Ibid., 101.
5. Ibid., 100.
6. Aristotle, *Politics*, trans. Ernest Barker (Oxford: Oxford University Press, 1958), 2–7.
7. Saint Thomas Aquinas, *The Political Ideas of St. Thomas Aquinas*, ed. Dino Bigongiari (New York: Hafner Press, 1953), 16–20, 175–176.
8. John Locke, *Two Treatises of Government*, intro. Peter Laslett (New York: The New American Library, 1965), 311–312, 319–323, 346–352, 374–375.

9. Karl Marx and Friedrich Engels, *The Marx-Engels Reader,* ed. Robert Tucker (New York: W. W. Norton and Co., 1978), 149–151, 155–159.

10. V. Spike Peterson and Anne Sisson Runyan, *Global Gender Issues* (Boulder: Westview Press, 1993), 5, 7–8, 18–25.

11. J. Ann Tickner, *Gender in International Relations* (New York: Columbia University Press, 1992), 132–138, 148.

12. Ruhollah Khomeini, *Islam and Revolution* (London: K.P.I., 1981), 330–331.

13. Ibid., 351–352.

14. Timothy Ware, *The Orthodox Church,* rev. (New York: Penguin Books, 1993), 218–225.

15. Khomeini, *Islam and Revolution,* 66, 80, 170.

16. Gabriel A. Almond and Sidney Yerba, *The Civic Culture* (Princeton: Princeton University Press, 1963), 300–322.

17. Plato, "Republic," *The Collected Dialogues of Plato,* ed. Edith Hamilton and Huntington Cairnes, trans. Paul Shorey (Princeton: Princeton University Press, 1973), 658–660, 785–794.

18. Marcus Tullius Cicero, *On the Commonwealth,* trans. George H. Sabine and Stanley Barney Smith (New York: Macmillan Publishing Co., 1976), 136–137, 144, 197–199.

19. Sarah M. Grimke, *Letters on the Equality of the Sexes and the Condition of Woman* (New York: Burt Franklin, 1970), 20, 23–24, 84–97.

20. Fyodor M. Dostoevsky, *The Diary of a Writer,* trans. Boris Brasol (New York: George Braziller, 1954), 577–582, 979–980, 1000–1001.

21. Thorton Anderson, *Russian Political Thought* (Ithaca: Cornell University Press, 1967), 178–179, 187–188, 217–218.

22. Sayyed Abul A'la Maududi, *Selected Speeches and Writings of Maulana Maududi,* trans. S. Zakir Aijaz (Karachi: International Islamic Publications, Ltd., 1981), 216, 240–241; idem, *The Economic Problem of Man and Its Islamic Solution,* 3d ed. (Delhi: Markazi Maktaba Jamaat-e-Islami Hind, 1966), 4–5, 8–9; idem, *Purdah and the Status of Woman in Islam,* trans. Al-Ash'ari (Lahore: Islamic Publications Ltd., 1972), 118–121, 141–149.

23. Jean-Jacques Rousseau, *The Social Contract and Discourses,* trans. G. D. H. Cole (London: J. M. Dent and Sons Ltd., 1973), 28, 44, 47–48, 68–69.

24. Ibid., 89–90, 106–113; Jamie Uys, *The Gods Must Be Crazy* (n.p.: Mimosa, 1980).

25. Peterson and Runyan, *Global Gender Issues,* 19–23.

26. Ibid., 26–28.

27. Niccolò Machiavelli, *The Prince and The Discourses,* intro. Max Lerner (New York: The Modern Library, 1950), 112.

28. Aristotle, *Politics,* 1, 6–7.

29. Hobbes, *Leviathan,* 132–134.

30. Marx and Engels, *Marx-Engels Reader,* 42–46, 700–701, 751–759.

31. Konstantin S. Aksakov, "On the Internal State of Russia," *Russian Intellectual History,* ed. Marc Raeff (New York: Harcourt, Brace and World, Inc., 1966), 234–236; Anderson, *Russian Political Thought,* 179.

32. Machiavelli, *Prince and Discourses,* 112–114.

33. Hobbes, *Leviathan,* 102, 132.

34. Locke, *Two Treatises,* 311–313, 319–323, 374–377.

35. Marx and Engels, *Marx-Engels Reader,* 187, 474–483, 710–712, 754–755.

36. Feofan Prokopovich, "Sermon on Royal Authority and Honor," *Russian Intellectual History,* ed. Marc Raeff (New York: Harcourt, Brace and World, Inc., 1966), 16, 19–21, 27.

37. Dostoevsky, *Diary,* 843, 979–980, 1031–1032.

38. Khomeini, *Islam and Revolution,* 36, 40–41.

39. Maududi, *First Principles of the Islamic State,* trans. Khurshid Ahmad (Lahore: Islamic Publications Ltd., 1960), 25; idem, *Unity of the Muslim World,* 4th ed. (Lahore: Islamic Publications Ltd., 1979), 8–9; idem, *The Ethical View-Point of Islam,* trans. Mazharud-Din Siddiqi, 3d ed. (Delhi: Markazi Maktaba Jamaat-e-Islami Hind, 1966), 1–3; idem, *Political Theory of Islam,* 2d ed. (Delhi: Markazi Maktaba Jamaat-e-Islami Hind, 1973), 15–16, 19–22.

40. Alexander Hamilton, James Madison, and John Jay, *The Federalist Papers,* intro. Clinton Rossiter (New York: New American Library, 1961), 529, 542–543.

41. Plato, "Republic," 658–660, 669–686.

42. Ibid., 659–660, 675.

43. Machiavelli, *Prince and Discourses,* 56.

44. Hobbes, *Leviathan,* chap. 13.

45. Richard S. Peters, "Introduction," *Leviathan,* Thomas Hobbes, ed. Michael Oakeshott (New York: Collier Books, 1962), 7–16.

46. Locke, *Two Treatises,* chaps. 2, 3, 8.

47. Hobbes, *Leviathan,* 103.

48. Locke, *Two Treatises,* 311–313, 395–399, 401–402, 454–460.

49. Ibid., 327–344, 401–409.

50. Marx and Engels, *Marx-Engels Reader,* 40–44, 93–96, 483–488.

51. Maududi, *Human Rights in Islam* (Lahore: Islamic Publications Ltd., 1977), 3, 7–8, 12, 14–34.

52. Ibid., 14.

53. Ibid., 14–15.

54. Ibid., 17, 28.

55. Ibid., 11–12; idem, *Political Theory of Islam,* 16; idem, *Unity,* 8–9.

56. Anderson, *Russian Political Thought,* 213–215; Nicholas Zernov, *Eastern Christendom* (New York: G. P. Putnam's Sons, 1961), 185–186.

57. Ivan Kireevski, "On the Nature of European Culture and Its Relation to the Culture of Russia," *Russian Intellectual History,* ed. Marc Raeff (New York: Harcourt, Brace and World, Inc., 1966), 180, 194, 196–197, 199, 204.

58. Aksakov, "Internal State of Russia," 235–241.

59. Kireevski, "European Culture," 178–180, 200–204.

60. Alexandr Solzhenitsyn, *Rebuilding Russia,* trans. Alexis Klimoff (New York: Farrar, Strauss and Giroux, 1991), 49–50, 53, 78.

61. Ibid., 78.

62. Ibid., 45.

63. Ibid., 66–78.

64. Aristotle, *Politics,* 110–116, 157, 162–167.

65. Plato, "Republic," 785–786.

66. Rousseau, *The Social Contract and Discourses*, 68–69, 173–181.

67. Hamilton and others, *The Federalist Papers*, 79, 227–229, 334–335, 350–353, 376–377, 411–414.

68. Ibid., 301–302, 308–310.

69. Ibid., 322.

70. Ibid., 76, 109–110, 244–246, 288–300.

71. Hobbes, *Leviathan*, 129.

72. Ibid., 134–141, 143–146, 159–168.

73. Prokopovich, "Sermon," 17, 19–22.

74. Dostoevsky, *The Brothers Karamazov, Great Books of the Western World*, trans. Constance Garnett, 54 vols. (Chicago: Encyclopedia Britannica, Inc., 1952), 52: 130–137.

75. Aristotle, *Politics*, 173–174.

76. Plato, "Republic," 658–661, 695–700, 751–753, 772–774.

77. Khomeini, *Islam and Revolution*, 55–56, 59–64, 72, 83–84, 246–247; Farhang Rajaee, *Islamic Values and World View: Khomeyni on Man, the State and International Politics* (Lanham: University of America Press, 1983), 55–66.

78. Khomeini, *Islam and Revolution*, 40–41, 55–56, 80, 170.

79. Marx and Engels, *Marx-Engels Reader*, 59–61, 193–200, 529–531, 711–717.

CHAPTER 3

ACTORS, POWER, ANARCHY, SOCIETY, LAW, AND WAR IN WORLD POLITICS

Enter the mysterious domain of world politics. To many, world politics is the realm of the unknown, the enigmatic, the strange, even the bizarre. Without a doubt, world politics is all of these things to the casual observer. World politics seems to be filled with the mysterious: the players are nations with cultures much different from our own, whose motives seem foreign. The way nations interact appears different from the way ordinary people relate to one another: war, secret negotiations, espionage, assassination, and terrorism mark the relations between some nations. What makes world politics seem so strange is that it takes place far from the world of everyday life. Decisions and events that take place half a world away may seem to have little effect on our lives. World politics is enigmatic to the extent that it takes a special knowledge to understand it. One must possess a knowledge of one's own country and the goals it wants to achieve in world politics. However, this knowledge is not enough to understand world politics: one must acquire an understanding of foreign governments and their goals and motives. Equally important, some knowledge of the world economic and political system is necessary.

Despite the rather distant nature of world politics, the basic ideas that help us think about it are for the most part ideas and concepts that we often use to discuss national, state, or local politics. Actors in national politics might be individuals, associations (interest groups and political parties), or corporations. The corresponding actors in world politics might be nations (for individuals) and alliances, the Islamic organization Hamas, and the Catholic church (for associations), and International Telephone and Telegraph (ITT) Company (for businesses). If politics at the domestic and international levels is concerned with acquiring power or influencing those who have it, then the sources of power become important in understanding world politics. At the domestic level, the sources of power might be numbers, wealth, and prestige; at the international level, sources of power might be population (numbers), level of economic development (wealth), and a nation's prestige in the eyes of other countries. Here the question of equality enters. Do some nations have more power than other nations given the size of their populations, their degree of economic development, and the prestige they enjoy on the global stage? That certainly seems to be the case. And isn't this the same as interest groups in domestic politics, whose power might be dependent upon the number of members, the wealth the groups amass and spend on behalf of its members, and their prestige among policymakers? Clearly not all interest groups are equal in power or the capacity to exercise it. Therefore, as this discussion suggests, we can begin to make more sense about world politics if we think about actors in domestic politics and apply the same analysis to the world political level.

Questions concerning anarchy, society, war, and law arise in both domestic and international politics. World politics has been said to be anarchic because no existing international government possesses the power to hold nations to their agreements or to enforce international norms; yet others argue that there is a society of nations that lives by generally accepted norms and laws and that international political systems develop that determine and enforce those norms and laws. Until the late 1980s or early 1990s, for example, a bipolar regime led by the Soviet Union and the United States and their respective allies structured the relations between many of the world's nations. There seem to be domestic correlates to international anarchy and society, too. In most parts of the country, there seems to be a reasonably ordered society where people live within society's norms and where these norms are enforced by a government armed with the requisite power. In some inner cities, there appears to be no effective government other than that established by gangs. Here, the struggle for power resembles world politics at its deadliest—war. War, an armed struggle between actors in the international environment, clearly has analogues in domestic politics. The clearest example centers on the struggle for wealth, power, influence, and prestige among gangs in inner cities. To the extent that gangs are free from the control exercised by local, state, or national authorities, they exist in a "Hobbesian state of nature" in which each gang competes with other gangs for wealth, power, influence, and prestige. Just as nations in a Hobbesian state of nature may revert to war to achieve their goals in world politics, so gangs may resort to gang warfare to achieve their goals. And regarding law, just as there are laws made by the U.S. Congress or British Parliament at the national level, so there is a body of international law made by nations in international politics. Just as individuals may break any domestic law passed by a legislature, nations sometimes break international laws. Thus, in many ways, politics is politics, whether it is domestic or international. This is not to say that international politics is synonymous with domestic politics; rather, one can find similarities between the politics that occur at the national and the international levels. There are many concepts that were discussed in the last chapter that will help you organize your thinking about world politics. Now is the time for you to draw upon these ideas. You may well find that thinking about world politics is not as complicated and mysterious as you initially believed.

ON ACTORS IN WORLD POLITICS

Who are the actors in world politics? This question is not hard to answer if one relates it to domestic politics and re-asks the question: who are the actors in domestic politics? In democratic countries, citizens, special interest groups, corporations, political parties, the media, and various government officials are the actors. In world politics, who are the actors? Clearly, the "cast" includes individuals, labor organizations, *multinational corporations* (MNCs), states, women's groups, Amnesty International, Greenpeace, terrorist groups, and other intergovernmental organizations such as the North Atlantic Treaty Organization (NATO), the World Bank, and the United Nations. Although most international relations theorists would not take exception to this listing, they might suggest that some are more politically important or powerful than others. Whereas some scholars see nations as the most important actors, others believe that multinational corporations exercise more influence than nations, and still others believe that multinationals play a more important role on trade issues but that states dominate the issue of war and peace. Some nations are so small and economically underdeveloped that they are not major actors in world politics; the influence of the largest multinational corporations in world politics would dwarf these smaller states.

Let us begin with the realist school to help us answer the question: who are the actors in world politics? For realists such as Hans Morgenthau and Thomas Hobbes, the state is the most important actor and the primary unit of analysis in international relations. Morgenthau believes that world politics constitutes a struggle for power, and nations are the actors that are able to amass the greatest amount of power. Compared to terrorist organizations or multinational corporations, countries have access to a greater number of citizens to serve in the military and can generate more money through taxation to provide economic assistance to other countries. The military might and economic assistance that nations can bring to bear in world politics is often greater than that exercised by other actors.[1] Hobbes understands that the resources of a nation can be harnessed to create a formidable political power. He views human nature as essentially appetitive, imprudent, and lacking self-control. Humans revel in personal glory, social prestige, power, and wealth. In Hobbes's view, if there were no government to manage the relations between people, social life would be all but impossible; constant warfare would be the norm. Social order would be possible only when the people decided to give a monarch or sovereign the power to discipline them and replace struggle, violence, and death with some degree of peace. To achieve domestic tranquillity, the sovereign would need to exercise control over all dimensions of life: political, economic, and social. This control would permit the sovereign to manage the economic life of the state (including what we today would call business and multinational corporations) so that people would be satisfied with their lot and the power necessary to protect the state from foreign adversaries could be accumulated.[2] Thus, a realist like Hobbes argues that the sovereign, and by extension, the state, is the primary actor. All other actors are subordinate to, and serve the interests of, the state.

Because the state is the primary actor in world politics, realists tend to discount the relative importance of other nonstate actors in shaping international relations. Other actors serve the interests of the state and operate under a broader state system. Hans Morgenthau argues that the United Nations was a creation of the world's superpowers and serves their essential interests; it is not an autonomous international actor capable of exercising independent political influence in world politics.[3] Take the Gulf War. The United States, seeing its access to oil and the political stability of the Middle East jeopardized by Saddam Hussein's seizure of Kuwait, used the United Nations to generate greater international support to prosecute and to "legitimize" a retaliatory war against Iraq. According to this perspective, the UN is more an instrument of the great nations of the world than a powerful actor with a will of its own. Multinational corporations are another example. To the extent that MNCs are capable of establishing successful operations abroad and transferring wealth from the client country to the home country, they serve to increase the economic power of the home country. Thus, MNCs are important because they augment the power base of a nation, not because they are independent actors capable of influencing the course of world politics.

To the liberal, the emphasis the realist places on the state as the primary actor in world politics is exaggerated. If states exercised *all* the political power in international relations, the realists would have a stronger claim. In fact, power is widely spread among states as well as many nonstate actors, including multinational corporations, the United Nations, churches, international labor organizations, terrorist groups, political parties, and economic organizations. Other examples of these nonstate actors include Hamas, the Organization of American States (OAS), the International Labour Organization (ILO), the Conference on Security and Cooperation in Europe (CSCE), the Organization of Petroleum Exporting Countries (OPEC), and the World Council of Churches. Nonstate actors impact world politics in varying degrees. On the one hand, OPEC members are primarily influential in international energy issues. The organization's ability or inability to control an important percentage of oil production can heavily influence the price of oil and through it the performance of national economies. On the other hand, states are important actors on national security issues such as nuclear proliferation, conventional weapons disarmament, and the international arms sales. When liberals step back and look at the interaction of all world actors, they see a myriad of organizations impacting on the everyday events of international relations. States might exert the greatest influence on issues centering on reducing nuclear weapons; OPEC on world oil prices; the World Health Organization (WHO) on eliminating disease; Greenpeace on ending the hunting of whales; and various multinational corporations on transferring capital, technology, and knowledge from developed to less developed countries.[4]

However, the most important function that states perform in world politics is establishing the "rules" by which actors play. This is particularly the case regarding economic and political rules. Economically, the liberal generally believes that the good of humankind is most likely to result from an international economy that resembles a domestic free enterprise system. Let us begin by briefly discussing domestic economies. In these economies, individuals should be free to pursue their talents and interests without undue interference from their governments. Government intervention into the lives of individuals and businesses should be restricted to securing basic rights to life, liberty, and property; punishing those who violate these rights; enforcing contracts made between individuals; and establishing banking, transportation, and communications systems that promote the free flow of goods between producers, distributors, and consumers. Beyond governmental intervention in these areas, individuals are free to pursue their interests and talents—free to be entrepreneurs. In some ways, each of us is an entrepreneur. All of us have some talent or interest that we can develop and market. Some of us desire to become auto mechanics or computer analysts. Others wish to become doctors, lawyers, or teachers. Despite this variety of talents, a harmony of interests inevitably arises between individuals in a free market system. Auto mechanics have an interest in pursuing a course of study that will qualify them to be successful in their trade. Auto mechanic teachers have an interest in teaching students interested in auto mechanics. The marketplace harmonizes the interests of the teacher who wishes to teach and the students who want an education. Thus, a free enterprise system promotes a harmony of interest in which everyone benefits.[5]

If we apply this liberal approach to domestic economics to international economics, the same holds true. Nations, like individuals, have some natural resources or goods that they can market better than any other nation. This advantage derives from lower labor costs, the abundance of a natural resource, or a superior technological capacity, for instance. A successful international economic system permits nations to produce and trade the same way individuals do at the national level: they produce and freely trade those goods and services that they most efficiently produce. An international harmony of interests results from this trade. For example, Saudi Arabia is flush with oil but lacks the ability to produce the range of food its people desire; the United States is the world's most efficient producer of food but has a need for inexpensive oil. When nations are free to trade with one another, Saudi Arabia is free to sell its oil to the United States. By the same token, the United States is free to sell its agricultural products to Saudi Arabia. Thus, a harmony of interests arises between Saudi Arabia and the United States, and both benefit from mutual trade. In international economics, states have the power to establish and enforce the rules under which nations trade their products. Thus, the General Agreements on Tariffs and Trade (GATT) embodies trading rules that nations establish and enforce so as to maximize the trade between countries. Liberals believe that as long as nations do not restrict trade between each other, then prosperity will spread throughout the world, as all countries will benefit from the ability to sell their products on the global market.[6]

Although states are important in establishing the economic rules by which nations trade, liberals argue that there are other important actors in world politics. Because states are more or less restricted to establishing and enforcing the economic rules under which international trade and commerce occur, they do not severely interfere with day-to-day business activity in the world economy. This economic activity is conducted by international banks and multinational corporations, for example. Developing nations can use money borrowed from banks to finance internal improvements such as roads, dams, and communication systems; to build new factories; or to increase the availability of education. Multinational corporations have a similar value in liberal theory. MNCs such as the Ford Motor Company, International Telephone and Telegraph, and Anaconda Copper provide needed resources for nations trying to modernize. MNCs are sources for capital, new technology, managerial and technical knowledge, and communications systems. In providing capital, multinationals have the capability of starting new factories, manufacturing firms, and technology for extracting natural resources. These new factories bring with them new jobs for the growing populations of less developed nations. Moreover, they often bring the most modern and efficient manufacturing technology, which permits companies in less developed countries to compete effectively in the world economy. Managerial and technical knowledge is as important as capital in many ways. The transfer of this knowledge gives third world managers the knowledge necessary to conduct their business in a competitive world economy and permits them to gain the experience in the day-to-day management of the business. Thus, MNCs are a valuable tool for developing economies. Economic modernization takes place; growing numbers of people are employed in manufacturing, extractive, and industrial firms; and managerial and technical knowledge accumulates and spreads throughout the developing economy. As a result of this economic development, less developed nations increase their international economic and political power. The multinational corporations' development of Middle East oil has enhanced those countries' exercise of regional and international political power. It permitted Saddam Hussein to create the fourth-largest army in the world, which undoubtedly gave him the confidence to invade Kuwait. Thus, multinational corporations can have an important impact on the conduct of world politics.[7]

Like nonstate actors, states play an important role in world politics. They are the primary actors in establishing the rules that govern the *political* relations between states. For example, states created the United Nations in 1945, and they make international law through custom, tradition, treaties, and international accords. To enforce this law, states create formal or informal alliances with one another. In the Gulf War, the United States organized nations from around the world to militarily expel Iraq from Kuwait. Also, modern warfare has centered on states. States are the political entities that raise militaries to protect and defend their people. International law recognizes the right of states to political independence and to defend themselves from attack. Although terrorism has been used by some nonstate actors as a means to influence the behavior of states, war has in many ways had a greater effect on the lives and fortunes of people in the twentieth century. Finally, states have important responsibilities in managing the relations of nations. They create diplomatic missions abroad, which are responsible for resolving international tensions and promoting the common interests that exist between nations.[8]

Like liberals, classicists believe that although the state is the fundamental actor in world politics, other actors are important to the conducting of international economic and political affairs. Take, for example, Pope John XXIII's 1963 encyclical, *Pacem in terris (Peace on Earth),* and the 1986 U.S. Catholic Bishops' Pastoral Message and Letter on "Economic Justice for All: Catholic Social Teaching and the U.S. Economy."[9] Developing Aristotle's view that humans are by nature political animals, Pope John and the U.S. bishops argue that as political animals, humans create the state for the purpose of leading a fully human, Christian life. Achieving a complete life requires that humans organize themselves into associations for the purpose of meeting their human and spiritual needs. The most fundamental association is the family, followed by intermediate associations such as labor unions and corporations, and culminating in the most inclusive association, the nation-state. The principle of subsidiarity requires that any human function should be carried out at the lowest level or association possible. Thus, families, and not the state, should be primarily responsible for providing for their own material needs: food, water, clothing, and shelter. On the other hand, the state, not families, has the responsibility for conducting international relations. The state is in a better position to provide for the security needs of the nation than the family.

The state has the power to formulate and execute the nation's foreign policy, and it has the ability to raise and maintain a military sufficient to match the threat of a potential aggressor.[10]

For Pope John, the state is the primary actor in world politics; however, like liberals before him, he believes that the United Nations should play an important but secondary role. Although states are important for promoting peace and justice within their borders, they also have the responsibility of promoting peace and justice for all humankind. A just world order, the pope believes, would promote the rights of each person. Among these rights are the rights to food, clothing, shelter, association (such as forming labor unions), worship, and political freedom. However, the growth of the world economy has resulted in a condition of economic interdependence between nations; the well-being of one nation is tied to the well-being of others. No longer are nations autarchic, or self-sufficient; many less developed countries are incapable of providing food, health care, education, and employment opportunities for all their citizens. Thus, wealthier states and the United Nations and its agencies (such as the United Nations Children's Fund [UNICEF] and WHO) should be active participants in international life and should attempt to promote a just world order in which people are secured their rights as nations and peoples.[11]

In their pastoral letter on the American and world economy, the U.S. Catholic bishops extend the pope's analysis of the international order. They recognize that international capitalism, left to itself, does not lead to a harmony of interests and prosperity, as claimed by classical liberals. While favoring the right to private property and free enterprise, the bishops note the growing disparity between the rich northern countries and the poor southern countries of the world. In the first draft of their pastoral, they argue that relations of dependency have developed between rich and poor countries. Like other analysts, they imply that international banking and multinational corporations are partly responsible for this gap between rich and poor. Rather than helping third world countries develop modern economic systems that benefit their nations as a whole, multinational corporations and international banks have made developing countries dependent on the great capitalistic economic powers: the United States, Japan, and West European countries, for example. Although MNCs do invest capital in other nations, much of the profit that is made goes back to the MNC and the rich or "core" country. Although MNCs produce some jobs for workers in developing countries, those jobs often pay an exploitive wage. And though MNCs transfer managerial and technical knowledge to developing countries, many of the managers come from "core" countries, and the citizens of less developed countries are not employed as managers. This inhibits the spread of managerial and technical knowledge to these countries.[12]

Responding to these concerns, the bishops argue that three sorts of actors need to be active in world politics to solve the problems facing rich and poor nations: states, intergovernmental organizations, and transnational actors. States are the primary actors, but not the only ones, in world affairs. All states, but particularly the more wealthy ones, have the responsibility to promote the economic well-being of all people. This can be accomplished in part through open and fair trade policies that do not limit third world access to markets in the United States and other industrialized nations. The United States should also commit a reasonable share of its wealth to foreign aid to help developing nations modernize and industrialize their economies. The second group of actors active in world affairs are intergovernmental organizations such as the United Nations, the World Bank, and the International Monetary Fund (IMF). The World Bank and the IMF are important sources of money for developing countries. However, the external debt burden carried by some of these countries limits their ability to industrialize: servicing this debt may require so much of a nation's resources that little is left to invest in economic development. Therefore, the bishops suggest rescheduling such debts. The money, in other words, could be paid back over a longer number of years, thereby reducing the amount of money that a country needs pay back each year. The third group of actors are transnational organizations: multinational corporations. The bishops believe that MNCs are an important source of investment for developing countries; however, MNCs should invest in a way that aids, not hinders, the modernization of developing economies.[13]

For classicists, the state remains the primary actor in international affairs. Since humans are, as Aristotle writes, political animals, they form associations—culminating in the state—to achieve their common goals. The state is the most comprehensive association that has the ability to harmonize the activities of other associations such as interest groups, political parties, and corporations to achieve the community's goals. Like liberals, many classicists recognize that there are many other actors active in international political and economic affairs, and that states are important for establishing and enforcing the international economic and political rules. Unlike the liberal, the classicist is inclined to view the state as an active force in bringing about a more just political and economic order. The world economy does not spread the benefits of worldwide production and economic development among nations in a fair way. Some states, mostly northern, developed nations, prosper to a much greater extent than do southern, poorer nations. Thus, some state intervention into the world economy is necessary if positive steps are to be made toward economic justice. To do this, states can use their power in the United Nations, in the World Bank, and with multinational corporations to ensure that their activities are not creating economic injustices but are actively promoting a fairer distribution of the world's wealth and prohibiting policies that lead to the exploitation of workers in developing nations. It is obvious from this analysis that the American bishops speaking for the Catholic church are a major player in domestic and world politics.

Immanuel Wallerstein, a contemporary radical political economist, argues that world politics is marked by three broad categories of actors: the state, global-ized entrepreneurial groups, and antisystemic movements. Wallerstein believes that the world economy determines the specific social and political institutions that exist today. As we saw in the last chapter, Marxists believe that national eco-nomic systems were instrumental in determining the art, literature, religion, polit-ical institutions, and ideologies of the people living within that state. Wallerstein agrees; however, he argues that the capitalist world economy, not the national economy per se, is responsible for creating the major international actors: the state, entrepreneurial groups like MNCs, and antisystemic movements opposing the capitalist world economy.[14]

A world economy is a network of productive processes that forms chains of economic activity around the world. The network is driven by humankind's de-sire to accumulate more capital—the wealth and machinery needed to expand production. These productive chains are global: cotton may be grown in Egypt, shipped to a major European manufacturer that turns the cotton into clothing, ex-ported via an international merchandising firm to Venezuela, and sold to Venezue-lans in a local apparel shop. The national economy of any one state is structured by the capitalist world economy. Although some larger domestic economies have a greater impact than do smaller ones on the capitalist world economy, the fact re-mains that even the strongest economies succeed or fail based on the perfor-mance of the world economy; the health of the U.S. economy is closely tied to the health of the capitalist world economy; a worldwide recession would limit the productive capacity of the U.S. economy. Because national economies are inter-woven, with their health being determined by the capitalist world economy, Wallerstein believes that the economic health of national economies is a creation of the capitalist world economy.[15]

States are the first of three actors in world politics. They are important in-ternally and externally. Internally, the state functions to secure the property of the bourgeoisie—those people who own productive resources such as factories, banks, mines, and farms. The bourgeoisie secures and uses the power of the state for the purpose of promoting its own interests. Thus, in the latter part of nineteenth-century America, the bourgeoisie used the power of the government to build railroad systems that facilitated the transportation of goods, people, and capital across the United States. Second, this capitalist class uses the government to guarantee a degree of industrial peace between the workers (the proletariat) and the capitalists. This was done by ruthlessly repressing the U.S. labor move-ment in the nineteenth century. In the twentieth century, the government guaran-tees industrial peace by promoting a bargaining and mediation process whereby labor and management can resolve their grievances without jeopardizing the very existence of the capitalist system. Externally or internationally, Wallerstein argues that the primary function of the state is to support the bourgeoisie as it continues to expand its control of the world economy. To this end, states create an international political system that is capable of promoting and securing the interests of an international bourgeoisie. Thus, the bipolar international system permitted the capitalist nations to trade among themselves and to extend their economic stranglehold over less developed countries. The relative world political stability of the bipolar world permitted the strongest capitalistic states to determine international rules of "fair" trade. Although it might appear that the international trade agreement known as GATT would promote trade and raise the living standards of the masses of people in poorer countries, it really is a tool the bourgeoisie of the world's strongest nations can use to establish trading rules that will ultimately serve its own interests, not the interests of developing countries. Therefore, world trade typically benefits the rich nations at the expense of the poor. In the twentieth century, the economically and politically dominant states—serving the interests of the bourgeoisie—include the West European countries, the United States, and more recently, Japan.[16]

Wallerstein believes that the world bourgeoisie controls the state to such an extent that it uses the state to create a world political system—the "interstate system."[17] In the latter part of the twentieth century, this interstate system took a bipolar configuration: capitalist states (at one pole) were arrayed against the Soviet bloc countries (at the other pole). In its day, this bipolar world system permitted a degree of world political stability that allowed capitalism to spread into noncommunist, developing countries. It provided enough international peace so that the world bourgeoisie was able to expand its accumulation of capital, obtain the necessary natural resources, and engage in world trade. In addition to the formal bipolar, political superstructure of the interstate system, the United Nations and alliances such as NATO were organizations that served the capitalist world. NATO, which came to life in 1949, was a defensive alliance of Western nations pledged to fight further communist encroachment in Europe. In some ways, NATO was a military wing of the world's bourgeoisie; it protected the capitalist West from the specter of the socialist East. Similarly, the United Nations served capitalist interests by legitimizing the existing world order and protecting capitalistic states. Indeed, UN participation in the Korean War—a conflict in which the northern, communist part of the country was trying to take over the noncommunist southern part of the country—provided an example of how capitalistic states used the UN to protect their own interests. When Marxist revolutionary activity or coups threatened capitalist interests in developing countries, capitalist states found ways to protect bourgeois economic and political interests. Thus the interstate system, serving the interests of the world bourgeoisie, maintained a degree of peace that was conducive to the spread of world capitalism.[18]

Just as states representing the interests of the world bourgeoisie are important actors in world politics, so too are transnational actors. Multinational corporations (or globalized, private entrepreneurial groups) fall into this category. For Wallerstein, the multinational corporation embodies the world bourgeoisie's transnational character—its never-ending drive to "capitalize" the world. These firms, headquartered in one country but doing business in other countries, are vehicles for the worldwide expansion of capitalism. Driven by the profit motive, the need to remain competitive in a world economy, and the desire to acquire additional capital, the world bourgeoisie uses multinational corporations to achieve these ends. Penetrating the underdeveloped nations, MNCs are successful in building new factories and businesses in areas where the costs of business are much less because of these nations' low labor costs and relative lack of governmental and environmental restrictions on business activities. MNCs exploit the labor pool, paying only a subsistence wage. Indeed, in some poorer, agricultural countries, MNCs pay workers less than a subsistence wage because they know that the worker's family will find other avenues, a family garden for example, to meet its needs for food and shelter. In repatriating or returning profits to the wealthy or "core" country, the developing country, a "peripheral or semiperipheral" country, fails to receive the economic benefits of the profits extracted at such a high cost to the workers and their families. Overall, MNCs are part of the predatory nature of capitalism, one that benefits the world bourgeoisie, and one that creates a world proletariat that becomes increasingly economically marginalized and exploited.[19]

The third and last actor in world politics is the antisystemic movement. Antisystemic movements are simply social or nationalistic movements that organize to destroy the capitalist world economy. These social forces, such as communist political parties, arise amidst the economic hardships suffered by the world proletariat at the hands of the world bourgeoisie. Antisystemic movements operate within the nation-state or in world politics. When a communist party has managed to gain control of the state and to socialize its economy, this opens up the first opportunity for world socialism to take root. The success of the Communist Party of the Soviet Union in establishing the first socialist country led to the rise of other communist countries in Eastern Europe and Asia. Wallerstein argues that as the capitalist world economy weakens, as the bourgeoisie loses its hold on the working classes, and as more states become socialist, socialist states will be able to jointly pursue the goal of transforming the capitalist world economy into a socialist world economy. In such an economy, the state will disappear as a repressive power and will be replaced by an administrative structure responsive to the needs of the world's people.[20]

Feminists and Islamic fundamentalists offer a much different perspective on the actors in world politics, and both are highly critical of the basic assumptions that lie at the root of world politics. Feminists such as J. Ann Tickner believe that the world political and economic systems are fundamentally male constructs. World politics has been modeled on a male conception of human nature, and this view emphasizes the male desire for autonomy, competition, power, independence, and rationality. Most males value these traits because they have been socialized by a patriarchal society into preferring these characteristics and goals to others. On the whole, males are rather singular, autonomous individuals who pursue power in a rationally calculated way to secure those things that they desire most. Projected into world politics, the world is composed of individual, politically autonomous nation-states that are not united under any form of international authority: a Hobbesian state of nature. These states are bent on accumulating power because without it, there would be nothing to protect them from the malevolent designs of other states.[21] States can increase their security and power by forming alliances that aggregate the economic and military assets (or power) of several states. Thus, NATO was formed to counter the spread of communist governments in Eastern Europe at the end of World War II. NATO nations pooled their military capabilities to create a common military force to deter an attack from the Soviet Union. But the pursuit of power creates a "security dilemma": the more power the state amasses to protect itself, the more insecure it becomes. Other nations, threatened by this more powerful state, increase their own power capability so as to increase their own security. As a result of these spiraling security efforts, however, all are rendered less secure. This gendered view of world politics suggests that the state is the primary actor in world politics; other actors such as alliances and intergovernmental organizations are of secondary importance.

Although Tickner sees international politics as being dominated by men and states as being controlled by men, she believes that world organizations and conferences that focus on women's issues can be useful vehicles in influencing world politics. She suggests that women have been historically active in world politics. In the twentieth century, she points to the International Conference of Women during World War I, the 1985 Women's International Peace Conference, and the World Conference to Review and Appraise the Achievements of the United Nations Decade for Women, also held in 1985. Tickner is unclear as to whether these conferences were able to significantly impact the patriarchal world political system; however, she does believe that they have the potential to change the world political agenda. She argues that although women and children are often the ones who suffer the worst effects of a contaminated environment, women's involvement in transnational environmental organizations has helped improve their physical environment. Such forums and organizations can, she believes, be important actors affecting the dialogue and conduct of world politics.[22]

Tickner is critical of the assumptions that gird much of the economic thinking that has occurred in the last 250 years. Like world political theories, economic theories are socially constructed by males. The dominant economic thinkers Tickner cites are Adam Smith, David Ricardo, and Karl Marx. Focusing on the national and international economic theories of Smith and Ricardo, Tickner argues that capitalism is founded on a male conception of "economic man": a rationally self-interested person desiring to use his talents in a way that permits him to pursue his own good. At this point, Tickner's discussion of capitalism agrees with the liberals, discussed earlier, who believe that a free enterprise system gives individuals the opportunity and freedom to pursue their own goals in life. However, she is critical of capitalism because she believes that it creates a public/private division of life. Public economic and political activities—pursuing a career and governing—are reserved for men, and the private activities of raising children and keeping the home are ascribed to women. Thus, capitalism is not only grounded on a male construct of human nature, but it also serves to benefit males by placing economic and political power in their hands.[23]

Discussing the capitalist world economy, Tickner believes that it, too, is gendered and that the benefits of world capitalism accrue largely to males. She is critical of liberal theorists who suggest that the capitalist world economy will bring about a more equitable distribution of global wealth, human welfare, peace, and international cooperation. Rather, Tickner believes that the expansion of capitalism into less developed countries strengthens the position of men in business and government and drives women from the public realm to the private realm of the family. In precapitalist underdeveloped economies, women bear a greater share of economic responsibility for supporting the family; but the introduction of the gendered capitalistic system gives men the obligation to become the family's sole provider and assigns women the task of managing the affairs of the house. And even when women are able to enter the workplace, they are given less prestigious jobs with lower salaries. Although not explicitly discussing multinational corporations, Tickner's feminism suggests that MNCs are instruments in the gendered international world economy and are responsible in part for helping industrialize less developed countries. In so doing, they relocate the center of work: from the home to the factory. This leaves women with the responsibility of raising children and men with the responsibilities of providing a living for the family and governing the state. It lets loose a social structure that inevitably shackles women in webs of dependence to their husbands—a dependence that is reinforced by laws that they have no part in making.[24]

The masculine state is the primary actor in world politics; however, Tickner implies that multinational corporations and alliances of nations such as NATO are important actors, too. Even alliances and multinational organizations support the masculine politics of the pursuit of power that takes place in the world political arena. Since men have shaped the world economic and political systems to their advantage, it is not surprising to find men as the dominant figures in world politics and the major beneficiaries of the struggle for world political power. Because nations live in a masculine environment in which national security is paramount, military and foreign policy budgets of states divert resources that could otherwise be used to address such social problems as hunger, homelessness, illiteracy, domestic violence, and unemployment. Even when women such as former British

Prime Minister Margaret Thatcher venture into world politics, they often possess "male" characteristics—they are independent, autonomous, competitive, and power seeking. As we shall see later, Tickner does not wish to abolish the state and the state system; rather, she wants to humanize it by bringing women into government, foreign policy bureaucracies, and multinational corporations. Women are socialized into being caring, nurturing, and cooperative; bringing these qualities into world politics can serve to make it less security conscious, less war-prone, and more responsive to social problems.[25]

For his part, Ayatollah Khomeini believes that the state, alliances, multinational corporations, the media, transnational Islamic organizations, and nongovernmental organizations such as the world Zionist movement are the major actors in world politics. It is relatively clear from his writings that he see the state and multinational corporations as the dominant actors in international relations. In many ways, Khomeini accepts the traditional Islamic division of the world into two camps: Islamic peoples and those who oppose Islam. Writing during the bipolar era, he believes that the distribution of international power rests in the hands of the United States and the Soviet Union. These superpowers are enemies of Islamic peoples because the ideologies upon which each is based, liberalism and Marxism, are opposed to Islamic culture. Since the end of World War II, these superpowers came to dominate world politics to the extent that they succeeded in placing most of the nations of the world under their political or economic control. This picture of the world allows Khomeini to view world politics as the politics of the oppressor and the oppressed. The oppressed people are not just Islamic states; they include those non-Islamic nations that have been economically exploited or politically dominated by the superpowers. Suffering under the same oppression as Iran, these nations could peacefully coexist with Islamic nations. Khomeini hopes that these oppressed nations would join Iran in the struggle to free themselves from the clutches of the United States and the Soviet Union.[26]

Khomeini believes that alliances and multinational corporations are important actors in world politics. The superpowers had created alliances with like-minded nations. NATO and the Soviet-inspired Warsaw Pact alliances, which served to protect Western and communist nations from aggression, posed a potential military threat to Islamic nations. Similarly, the United States and Israel were locked together in an alliance that promoted world Zionism. In Khomeini's view, the goal of world Zionism is more than just establishing a Jewish state in Palestine; its ultimate goal is world domination. Regarding multinational corporations, Khomeini is particularly vehement in his criticism of the imperialism of the United States. He believes that Western capitalism is exploitative. Not only does it create and tolerate widespread poverty in Western nations, but it propagates an international, secular, materialistic culture: a culture opposed to what he sees as orthodox Muslim values. This secular, materialistic culture requires vast natural resources to support the ravenous, materialistic desires of its people. Multinational corporations are the vehicles for extracting the natural resources of poorer, oppressed nations.[27]

For Khomeini, the Western media are important actors that negatively shape the culture of Islamic nations. Western culture is transmitted to Iran by television, radio, and the cinema. The Western-educated economic, cultural, and political elite that ruled Iran just prior to the Iranian revolution in 1979 had attempted to westernize Iran and in the process had begun to strip the people of their orthodox Islamic heritage. Television, radio, and the cinema were employed by this elite to spread Western values and lifestyles that ran counter to traditional Islamic values. For Khomeini, the corrupting influences of the media fell most heavily on young people, the most impressionable group in the population. Iran's youth had been drawn away from, and made indifferent to, orthodox Islamic values. Although not opposed to the modern media per se, Khomeini believes that mass communication could best serve society if it was used in a way that supported the orthodox Islamic values that had historically served Iranian Muslims so well.[28]

Finally, Khomeini views student groups, revolutionary groups, and alliances of Islamic nations as important actors in world politics. In the struggle with the superpowers and their allies, Khomeini believes that Muslims throughout the world should seek to peacefully convert non-Muslims to Islam. Because he believes that people could be easily converted to the teachings of Mohammed and an Islamic lifestyle, Islam could be spread peacefully. Peaceful religious conversion of all non-Islamic people of the world, not war, would usher in the reign of an Islamic world. Khomeini also called for all Muslim leaders in the Middle East, Asia, and Africa to put aside their national and political differences and work for the liberation of all oppressed people. By uniting into a single Islamic political front, they could free themselves from Western imperialism. However, he realizes that there are limits to what can be accomplished politically and peacefully. For instance, in the late 1970s, he argued that Muslims ruled by illegitimate political powers should overthrow Western-style governments and replace them with Islamic governments. This call to revolution was directed not only at the people of Iran, but to Muslims in Egypt, too. The Egyptian government of Anwar Sadat was particularly reprehensible in Khomeini's view, because Sadat had broken with his Islamic brothers and had opened a dialogue of peace with Israel.[29]

In summary, realism, liberalism, classicism, Marxism, Tickner's feminism, and Khomeini's Islamic fundamentalism present different pictures of the primary and secondary actors in world politics. Who are the actors in world politics? As we have seen, the answer to this question depends upon a broader understanding of the world of politics: this includes a person's view of human nature, the state, economics, and even religion. Refer back to the political philosophy that you have been developing as you have been reading this book. How do your views on human nature, human equality, the origin of the state, and the ends of the state help you think about the actors in world politics? Do you accept the realist princi-ple that nations, just like humans, are alienated from one another and are preoccu-pied with optimizing national security? If so, do you believe that nations are the primary actors that organize the economic and social life of the country in a way that guarantees its survival in the conflictual realm of world politics? Or do you take a classicist position: are not human beings naturally inclined to band together in social and political groups to promote their common good? If so, would you not expect that nations and other actors—like international labor organizations—would be inclined to join efforts to promote what is in the best interest of people worldwide? Perhaps nation-states are not the most important actors in world pol-itics. Would you agree with the radicals who think that there is an international bourgeoisie that is very important in the conduct of international politics? These are just a few of the many questions that you could ask as you begin to develop your own political theories. Put down your book for a minute, and try to come to some conclusion about the actors who are active on the world political stage.

ON POWER

Let us return to the *Dead Poets Society*, the film discussed in the Introduction to this book. As many of you remember, the film chronicles the lives of a group of boys attending a college preparatory school. Mr. Keating, a graduate of the school, had returned to the rather stuffy, traditional school with a rigid curriculum. The rela-tionship between student and teacher is traditional: the teacher dispenses the wis-dom, and the students soak it up. Mr. Keating, recently hired as a literature teacher, has a different idea. In one memorable scene, Keating has the boys rip up the introduction to their literature book—an introduction written by Professor Pritchard, Ph.D. This apparent act of vandalism is symbolic of the debunking of authority—in this case, the authority that the Ph.D. carries as a person with al-legedly deeper insights into literature. Keating, however, is less interested in au-thorities than in using literature to help his students find out what is meaningful in their own lives. He asks them to think for themselves, rather than to passively accept what has been handed down by years of tradition and authority. However, Keating's efforts to free his students to think for themselves and to help them find their own voices in life are cut short by his dismissal from the school, which finds his views too progressive. After the suicide of one of his students, the remaining boys are pressured by their parents and by their headmaster, Mr. Knowland, into signing a statement placing the blame for the death on Keating. In the last scene of the movie, the headmaster has taken charge of Keating's literature class. As Keat-ing, having packed up his belongings, leaves the classroom for the last time, a few students stand on their desks: a symbolic dramatization of their coming of age. More students follow suit. As each student, with great deliberation, mounts his desk, Knowland admonishes them, under threat of expulsion, to sit down. All remain standing. The students have learned from Keating the value of cutting their own paths in life. And we are left with the specter of the headmaster, a teacher of many years, stripped of any apparent power to control or influence the behavior of students he so wished to inspire.[30]

In this final scene of the *Dead Poets Society*, we come face to face with many dimensions of power and authority. Power and authority seem to be bound up with hierarchy, or the proper ordering of things. Let us look first at the way the movie handles the nature of authority and then turn to its depiction of power. At Keating's prep school, the teachers and administrators are in positions of authority, and the students are those over whom it is exercised. The hierarchy is clear: the teachers and administration dominate the students. The teachers at the school exercise authority over their students because they are presumed by the students to have insights into the world of knowledge that the students do not have, and because the school is renowned for its ability to assure its graduates admission to the Ivy League. As a result, for the most part, the students willingly comply with the demands of their teachers. This willful compliance with the requests of those who are acknowledged superior in some capacity epitomizes the concept of authority. In the final scene of the movie, Mr. Knowland has lost all his authority. The boys defiantly mount their desks in support of Mr. Keating, ignoring Mr. Knowland's stern exhortations to sit down. Knowland loses his authority because the students no longer recognize the legitimacy of his commands.[31]

The *Dead Poets Society* also gives us a brief glimpse of power. In the scene in which the students are forced to sign a statement against Mr. Keating, both the parents and Mr. Knowland are exercising not authority, but their power over the boys. Whereas *authority* implies willful compliance with the requests of a person acknowledged to be one's superior, *power* implies coercion against one's will. Hence, power is getting someone to do something he or she would not otherwise do. In this case, the boys did not want to sign a statement falsely implicating Keating in the student's death; but they acquiesced when faced with the threat of being forced to leave school, which would mean losing their friends and diminishing their hopes for future success. Clearly, this is a relationship that implies the use of power and not of authority. When we look at the history of thinking about world politics, relations of power and authority are a central part of that history.[32]

To some extent, this film is helpful in thinking about power in a conflictual world of international politics. If we believe that world politics is comprised of many nations with differing degrees of power, then the nation that has the ability to get another nation to do what it would not otherwise do is more powerful. A relationship of dominance and submission results. This effectively happens in the film when Mr. Knowland, with the help of the students' parents, forces the boys to falsely accuse Mr. Keating.[33] However, is it possible that the relationship between nations has less to do with power and more to do with authority or cooperation?

Often opposing nations see that it is in their best interest to voluntarily cooperate in some endeavor. For example, many nations have agreed to sign the Treaty on the Non-Proliferation of Nuclear Weapons (NPT), which attempts to limit the spread of nuclear weapons to states that do not currently possess them. This treaty could be seen as a cooperative agreement willingly signed by individual states. If this is the case, the relationship between states is based upon cooperation and authority, not power. Although relations predicated on power may be important in international relations, they are not the only relations that develop between nations. Let us focus on power.

We might define power as the ability to get someone to do something that he or she would not otherwise do. By this definition, the United States is a powerful nation because in 1994 it persuaded the ruling Haitian dictatorship to step down and to permit Jean-Bertrand Aristide, Haiti's elected but deposed president, to return to office—something that the Haitian dictatorship did not want to do. Suppose the dictatorship refused to step down and the United States deposed it by military action. Would the United States be considered powerful? By this definition, no. The United States was not able to get or persuade the dictatorship to do what the U.S. wanted it to do; thus, the United States could not be considered as powerful. But this would seem to fly in the face of empirical fact. The United States, by most accounts, is the most powerful nation in the world. Even though the United States is the most powerful nation in the world, in this one hypothetical case, that power is not translated into actuality. Perhaps power should be defined differently. Does power boil down to the ability to prevail in a conflict? If there is any conflict—social, economic, political, military, or ideological—should we consider the person or nation that prevails in that conflict as powerful? Clearly, the nations going to war against Iraq in the 1991 Gulf War are more powerful because they won the war. But by this measure, are the Vietcong, who engineered a victory over the United States in the Vietnamese civil war, more powerful than the United States? If they are not, why did the United States lose? Did the United States use the wrong military strategy? Did it neither have the political will nor commit the necessary resources to win the war? Maybe so. But doesn't the exercise of power involve political will? A smaller nation fully committed to winning a war may be more powerful than a militarily stronger nation less committed to winning it. As all this shows, power appears to be a pretty slippery term.

Regardless of the seemingly unsuccessful attempt to define power, international politics cannot be fully discussed without reference to it: international actors possess the need to accumulate power, according to some theorists. To achieve the personal things in life that we desire, we say that we need power. The same can be said for nations or multinational corporations. In times when there is conflict between nations, the nation that can apply its power most successfully will succeed in its endeavors. Similarly, in negotiating entry of a multinational corporation into a developing country, the stronger negotiating position, whether held by the MNC or the developing nation, normally will take the day. Thus, actors find that power is important in world politics. In discussing power, let us examine the nature, use, and ends of power.

Realists like Thomas Hobbes believe that the primary concern of a nation in world politics is to acquire and use power in a way that promotes the interests of that nation. In an international environment that is much like Thomas Hobbes's state of nature—a war of everyone against everyone—and in a condition wherein the national security of a nation is constantly jeopardized by the military posture and aggressiveness of other nations, states are driven by necessity to be aware of their power relative to other nation-states.[34] Hobbes defines and describes how individuals amass power in his classic book *Leviathan*. Power is the "means to obtain some future apparent good."[35] In this definition, Hobbes talks about means and goods. On a personal level, the means that people have at their disposal are innately given to humans or are acquired by some personal effort. Sources of power therefore include physical strength, the ability to make good judgments about how to live life, and native intellectual ability. Other resources of power are wealth, reputation, friends, and even good luck or fortune.[36] In what ways are these sources of power? Education is a source of power in a society in which knowledge is required to acquire the things in life that people desire. In a competitive job market, well-educated people have greater access to better paying jobs than do those with less education. With greater wealth, people are able to obtain the goods in life that they desire: this may be political office, prestige within a profession, or an expensive home. If a person acquires a reputation for being successful in life, others are more inclined to listen to that person. Clearly, a person with a positive reputation is able to influence other people: that person has power. This notion of reputation as power is behind the E. F. Hutton commercial that many of us have seen. An obviously professional crowd is seated in an elegant dining room, chatting and eating. One patron, discussing his investments, makes the comment: "E. F. Hutton says . . ." Suddenly, the clatter of knives, forks, glasses, and chatter gives way to a deafening silence as all lean forward to hear the financial advice. The announcer breaks in: "When E. F. Hutton talks, people listen." This reputation for financial success is a resource of power. Liberality, having wealth and giving it to others to get what one desires, is also power. As Hobbes comments, money used in this way procures friends: something any major donor to political campaigns understands.[37] Power can be used to produce even more power. If wealth is a source of power, investing that wealth generates more wealth and with it, greater power.

Power includes not only means, but ends as well. According to Hobbes, people desire power for two fundamental reasons: to acquire the goods that they desire and to acquire more power. One of the most fundamental goods they desire is self-preservation; beyond that, humans desire whatever satisfies their appetites. Other than self-preservation, what people desire in life depends upon the individual: some may value wealth, education, wisdom, and social prestige; others may value political success, a close family, and a luxury car. But Hobbes believes that to acquire and maintain these goods, humans must be ever ready to increase their power.[38] Take a competitive job market, for example. The reason many students go to college is to maximize their power in the marketplace. Greater education often opens the door to more prestigious, better-paying jobs. Knowledge is power, and the greater the knowledge, the greater the power. Those with more education, attained at the more prestigious schools, have greater access to desirable job opportunities than do those with comparatively poorer educations. With the first job in hand, a professional is able to generate the income and to attain the social position that permits him or her to satisfy his or her material and spiritual needs. But landing that first job does not put an end to the power game. To climb the ladder of success and to protect their job, individuals will have to increase their power in their firm or profession. They may increase their power by demonstrating superior job performance, by running in the right social circles, by increasing their technical knowledge, or by making themselves useful to their supervisors. Thus, it is not enough for employees to acquire power; if they want greater success or to avoid losing the job they already have, they must acquire additional power. Driven by their appetites to acquire what they desire in life, there is in all humans "a perpetual and restless desire of power after power, that ceaseth only in death."[39]

It is easy to apply this discussion of power to world politics, and many scholars have looked to Hobbes for inspiration. For realists, the most fundamental actor in world politics is the state. In an international environment in which no international authority can discipline nations to live by international law and norms, nations are thrown back on themselves to provide for their own security and to achieve the goals they desire for their citizens. However, as each state decides what is in its own interest, inevitably different states come into conflict. This situation is reminiscent of Hobbes's state of nature, in which everyone is at war against everyone else. Relying on themselves for self-preservation, nations must pursue policies that help them acquire and expand their power relative to nations with whom they differ. Only in so doing will a nation be able to survive and prosper in a hostile environment in which self-interest rules the day.

The twentieth-century realist Hans Morgenthau is an heir to this Hobbesian tradition. He speaks at length about power and the resources that form the foundation of a nation's power. Morgenthau believes that power is "man's control over the minds and actions of other men."[40] When reasoned diplomacy fails, the actors in world politics resort to psychological and physical coercion to achieve their ends. The threats of war, economic sanctions, and armed conflict are but a few means that statesmen have at their disposal to establish their control over others. Morgenthau recognizes that there are many forms of power: social, economic, and political. But he focuses on political power: ways of controlling those in positions of public authority. In international relations, these authorities include presidents, military leaders, diplomats, chief executive officers of multinational corporations, and foreign policymakers. What are the resources of political power for nations? Morgenthau speaks of geography, natural resources, industrial capacity, military preparedness, population, national character, national morale, the quality of diplomacy, and the quality of the government. Geographical location, he notes, has been important to the United States. Its relative, historical isolation from the European centers of power in the nineteenth and early twentieth centuries meant the United States was able to remain geographically aloof from the two world wars that decimated European power bases. This isolation allowed the United States to develop a second resource of power: its industrial capacity. Free from the burdens of empire and physically isolated from most of the destruction wrought by the world wars, the United States was able to develop its industrial capacity, which increased its national wealth. With relatively cheap, abundant natural resources (the third resource of power) within its borders, the United States was able to nurture a strong industrial economy. Its favorable geographic location, abundant natural resources, and expanding industrial base also enabled the United States to support a growing population, another determinant of natural power. The expansion of wealth and the availability of an increasing number of people also meant that the nation, if called upon, would have the financial resources and personnel to raise a large army and navy, another resource of power. Finally, Morgenthau believes that a successful government is one that can prudently combine all the resources of power in a way that increases its power capabilities and that allows it to use its power to promote its natural interest. To be sure, the mere possession of natural resources, population, or industrial capacity does not make a nation powerful. Some nations are graced with abundant natural resources but lack the industrial capacity to use them. In other states, rapid population growth stifles economic development, as increasingly larger shares of the national income must be devoted to meeting the needs of the growing population. Finally, some states possess a large industrial capacity but are dependent on other nations for natural resources. Even though resource-dependent nations may be effective actors in times of relative peace, losing their supply of natural resources in a time of war can be economically and militarily catastrophic.[41]

Whereas realists believe that nations are the dominant actors in world politics, as they seek the power to control others and bend the world to their liking, liberals believe that there is more cooperation than conflict in international affairs. Nations, according to liberals, have common interests in avoiding war and establishing free trade policies that benefit all nations. Therefore, the use of power to order the relations of states is much more limited in world politics. Reviewing John Locke's view of human nature and the state of nature will help us grasp the liberal position more easily. As you recall, John Locke believes that in abolishing government, humans would not revert to a Hobbesian state in which everyone wages war against everyone else. Rather, he believes that the vast majority of humans would cooperate with one another because they would find that it is in their own enlightened self-interest to do so. Being fundamentally rational, inclined to social intercourse, and capable of controlling their appetites, humans know that in pursuing their desire for life, liberty, and property and in respecting the desire of other humans to do the same, cooperation would mark the vast majority of their relations with others. Only a few grasping, imprudent persons would transgress these laws and make life miserable for others. Power was needed to deter these "outlaws" from violating the rights of others and to punish them for their transgressions of the law.[42]

What is the liberal definition of power and how do liberals apply this definition to international relations? Locke defines political power as the right that public authorities have to employ force for the public good: to secure each person's life, liberty, and property. This definition of power is different from the realist's conception of power. Whereas Hobbes believes that power can be employed for any reason to achieve a person's goals in the state of nature, Locke believes that power should be employed for common ends: permitting individuals to live freely, to accumulate property and wealth, and to live in personal security. The Hobbesian notion of power leads to a war of every man against every man, whereas the Lockean idea of power suggests that the human use of power for common purposes results in peace as long as all obey the law. However, Locke would agree with Hobbes that the resources of power include such things as wealth, friends, talent, and that knowledge that is necessary to make dreams and future plans a reality.[43]

This Lockean vision of power can help us understand the cooperative nature of world politics and the liberal's exercise of power in international relations. First, just as humans, left to themselves, are capable of living with one another in relative peace, each pursuing his or her own good and cooperating with others to achieve common goods, so economic and political cooperation characterizes much of the relations of nations. From the standpoint of a country's enlightened economic self-interest, its leaders know that free trade is the best policy. With no trade barriers, the products of one nation can be sold in another nation and vice versa, and all nations prosper as a result. Politically, the nations of the world know that it is in their enlightened self-interest to settle disputes peacefully, because resorting to war would most likely interrupt their trade, depress their economic productivity, and limit the economic prosperity that is so important to the liberal lifestyle. Therefore, much of the behavior of states in international economic and political relations is purely cooperative, deriving from the self-interest of all states. This cooperation does not require the use of force, or power, to bring a degree of order to international life. Second, when is power used in international relations? According to the liberal, states collectively agree on international norms and laws. These laws and norms are codified in the United Nations Charter, written into treaties, and observed in the diplomatic customs and traditions of nations. For example, the United Nations Charter prohibits naked aggression between states. Through custom and tradition, diplomatic procedures have developed that permit nations to pursue common courses and resolve conflicts. Most states have obeyed these laws and customs out of their own self-interest. For example, they have seen that war limits trade between nations and destroys the factories and businesses that are essential to modern industrial life. Thus, the nations of the world are inclined to observe international law and to promote the beneficial, peaceful interactions of nations. However, not all nations have pursued peaceful, harmonious relations. Some nations have pressed their own interests and have broken widely accepted international law. In such cases, other nations of the world community, pledged to preserving the law of nations and world peace, may jointly employ their economic and military power to uphold international law, deter aggression, and punish the rogue state. Thus, the liberal uses power for the purposes of upholding the international norms that permit uncoerced economic and political activity among nations to take place.[44]

In reflecting on power, the classicist is critical of both realist and liberal conceptions and uses of power in world politics. Classicists are troubled over the free-wheeling manner in which realists exercise power in international affairs: no norms channel the exercise of power. In the extreme, the realist use of power leads to a "might makes right" philosophy. Those nations that succeed in securing world political power define the laws and norms by which other nations should live. If Hitler had won World War II, what is considered right and just would certainly be different from the right and justice that has prevailed after the United States "won" the cold war. Classicists are concerned about the liberal's naive view that a harmony of interests banishes the outright use of power in economic affairs. To the classicist, the international economic system is dominated all too often by powerful multinational corporations that use their economic leverage in less developed countries to exploit the poverty-stricken working classes in search of a profit. The international state system, organized by the powerful northern industrialized nations, has been all too eager to allow MNCs to run amuck in the economic and political lives of less developed countries. To remedy problems flowing from realism and liberalism, the classicist desires to expand the authority of public international institutions in the international economic realm and channel the international exercise of power toward the common good of all the peoples of the world.[45]

The classicist believes that authority should be exercised for the common good of all people. Recalling for a moment the classicist view of human nature, humans are political animals; that is to say, humans are naturally inclined to create associations and nations for the purpose of achieving common purposes or goals. The most fundamental association is the family, whose end is satisfying the basic needs of all family members. Labor unions, corporations, consumer groups, and chambers of commerce are other associations promoting the good of their members. What is this good? The common good: those ends pursued by people because they are human. Because humans have a rational capacity, human needs, and a free will, they organize themselves (1) to perfect their rational capacity by creating educational systems; (2) to satisfy their human appetites for water, food, and shelter by creating economic systems; and (3) to secure liberty by writing bills of rights limiting the power of government in human life. In a word, humans form social organizations and nations that allow them to perfect themselves as free, needful, and rational beings. All power within any association should be exercised for the collective benefit of all members of the association. Corporations should employ their workers in ways that are not life threatening and they should pay them a just wage. The public authority should govern in a way that permits humans to develop themselves as free people capable of fulfilling their basic needs and gaining that knowledge that can lead them to live a good, virtuous life. This power, exercised to perfect human life, is authority.

For many classicists, the authority to rule is derived from God, not from the people. Just as an American president or a British prime minister derives his or her authority from God, so do the Hitlers and Husseins of this world. All those who exercise public authority must exercise it in accordance with the moral law that God has written into human nature and has made known through reason, by the light of conscience. To guide individuals and society toward a realization of the life that God intends them to live, public authorities (executives, legislatures, courts, and administrative offices) may use threats, fear, promises, rewards, and punishment. However, the exercise of this authority must be for the common good, to secure and harmonize the rights that each person possesses. This means that the function of elections in representative government is to elect public officials to office; once in office, these elected officials have the obligation to exercise the authority they have been given by God for the common good. Regarding tyrants, people are obliged to obey the laws of God over those of any tyrant who would seek to exercise his or her power in a way that denies people their rights.[46]

In his encyclical *Pacem in Terris,* Pope John XXIII asserts that all too often nations use the authority granted to them by God in ways that do not promote the dignity or respect the rights of each person. On the one hand, he sees international actors pursuing their own interests in ways that harm others. They begin wars of aggression or willfully neglect the poorer nations of the world whose economic plight is the greatest.[47] Extending the pope's argument to other international actors, many multinational corporations, international banks, and terrorist groups have exercised their power in ways that have brought much suffering to the poor and marginalized people of the world. World actors have a responsibility to exercise their authority for the benefit of humankind—not against it. Multinational corporations are bound, for justice's sake, to treat the nations and workers of less developed nations fairly. Even though the international labor market would support subsistence-level wages, MNCs should provide wages that permit families in less developed nations to live with dignity. On the other hand, international society is so economically and politically complex and interdependent that the well-being of one state is tied up with the well-being of other nations. The existing international political system is incapable of securing the human, economic, and political rights of all the people in the world. Therefore, the pope argues that a universal public authority, building on the work of the UN, must be created to ensure that justice and peace find a place in the hearts and minds of all peoples and nations of the world.

For many radical political economists, the realist, liberal, and classical approaches to the nature and use of power in world politics miss the point. Realism, in pursuing the ever-increasing need for power, inevitably nurtures a capitalist system, because capitalism is the most effective economic system for producing wealth. States with greater wealth are more powerful, because wealth can be tapped by the state to raise armies, carry out aggressive foreign policies, and solidify relations with allies by providing them with economic and military aid. Classicists, who favor private ownership of the means of production, are naive to believe that the richer, more powerful bourgeois nations will redistribute wealth, and thus power, to poorer nations. Finally, liberals are wrong if they believe that the power exercised by multinational corporations and states is beneficent. The liberal international economic and political systems exist for the benefit of the most powerful class: the international bourgeoisie. This class is driven by the laws and imperatives of capitalism to use its power in international economics and politics to maintain a competitive edge in international trade, even if this results in the exploitation of the working people of the world.

To the radical political economist Immanuel Wallerstein, a nation's economy is the source of power in national and international affairs. The material base of power is a productive agricultural, industrial, and commercial capitalist economy. Because it owns the means of production, exercises political influence, and has access to great wealth, the bourgeoisie is able to control national politics for its benefit. By controlling national politics, the bourgeoisie employs the power of the state to further entrench its power and position in the economic and political system, and it uses that power to discipline the proletariat in a way that props up capitalism. In international affairs, the world bourgeoisie uses the state and MNCs to further spread and strengthen capitalism in less developed countries. The bourgeoisie achieves a peaceful international environment by using the political power and military of the state to suppress attempts to thwart the relentless spread of capitalism. Core states also intervene militarily and politically in the political affairs of less developed countries, so that capitalism has a tranquil social, economic, and political environment in which to grow. Less developed nations are also penetrated by powerful MNCs. By exploiting labor in less developed, peripheral countries and then transferring multinational profits to core countries, MNCs help enhance the power of rich countries relative to developing countries. With an enhanced power base, the powerful core nations politically dominate poorer, less developed nations—a condition, argues Wallerstein, that has not changed in the history of the capitalist world economy.[48]

In thinking about power, radical feminists believe that power is a unique feature of masculine political theory, and that a truly humane social order would be based upon cooperation, not coercion. Feminists V. Spike Peterson and Anne Sisson Runyan think that power conceived as "the ability to get someone to do what you want them to do" is a classic masculine definition of power. What is noteworthy about this definition of power is that it implies separation, competition, domination, and control: the very values that a patriarchal society cultivates in its men. Since men holding these values control the political system, the masculine world of politics is one characterized by separate, autonomous individuals competing with each other to achieve what they desire. With the powerful often working at cross purposes and creating social disorder, the only remedy is a government exercising coercive power to put an end to this disorder. Thus, politics is the art of domination and control. Power must be placed in the hands of the governors who—by physical coercion, persuasion, wealth, social position, and control over the police and military—are capable of dominating and controlling those who are weaker. Of course, power in a gendered society is exercised by males in social, economic, and political institutions. In the family, economic dependency of the wife on the husband and physical coercion in the form of domestic violence enable males to ensure their social domination. Domination is characteristic of world politics, too. Given the gendered conception of international relations as one of competing states trying to maximize their power to acquire more power, to ensure their own preservation, and to give them the capability of achieving what they desire, the nations that manage to accrue the greatest amount of power are able to dominate weaker nations politically and economically. Women and minorities inevitably suffer in this gendered world of international conflict and strife, a world in which foreign policy is determined by males. The need to devote additional resources to national defense efforts means that social programs to help women and the poor are inadequately funded. Because the relations of nations exist in a primitive state of anarchy, nations need to force order upon world politics, and this leads to militarism and eventually war. And war inevitably harms women: rape and torture stalk the lives of women and children in countries where armies roam the countryside imposing "order" and exacting retribution on alien populations.[49]

The feminist solution is to create societies that are not rooted in relationships of power and domination. Peterson and Runyan and J. Ann Tickner suggest that the gendered definition of power, which implies domination and subordination, should be replaced by a nation of "empowerment." Citing philosopher Hannah Arendt's definition of power as "the human ability to act in concert or action that is taken with others who share similar concerns," Tickner seems to advocate a society in which all people work together to promote their common interests. This vision of empowerment would certainly bring all individuals and groups into the political process; to this extent, empowerment would promote political equality and democracy. Are we to suppose that conflict will end when all people are participating in the process of defining the society in which they will live? In answering this question, Peterson and Runyan suggest that societies that recognize that the life and fortune of each person are bound up with the lives and fortunes of others will eliminate conflicts of interest. If, for some reason, conflict breaks out, the members of such a society would resolve it by nonviolent interaction and mutual learning.[50]

Put down this book for a minute and reflect on power and world politics. Given your views on human nature, the motivations of the actors that are important in world politics, and the amount of conflict or cooperation that characterizes the relations of those who are active participants, what role (if any) should power play? Are we to believe with the realists that the pursuit of power is an unavoidable feature of international relations? Is an orderly world political environment predicated upon the successful management of power? Are we to believe with the liberals that there is much economic and political cooperation between world political actors and that the use of power can in fact be limited? Are classicists right in suggesting that some form of world political organization with the authority to bring about a world of peace and justice is the fundamental solution to a world in which power is often used against the interests of humankind? Are some of the more radical feminists correct in suggesting that power is a unique creation of men who need it to create a stifling social, economic, and political world order that harms the majority of humans on this earth? Can a politics of cooperation that dispenses with hierarchical power relationships be developed among the actors in world politics? As you continue to puzzle over the question of power, let us look at how power and equality are related to one another.

ON EQUALITY IN WORLD POLITICS

Recall your thoughts on equality for a moment. How would you apply the understanding of equality that you developed in the last chapter to world politics? To begin, what objects are the subject of equality or inequality in world politics? Are you thinking about states, multinational corporations, NATO, WHO, diplomats, or citizens of a country? Once we know the object of equality, you might ask yourself in what ways or in what capacities are these actors equal or unequal? If you are speaking of states, are states equal in the possession of rights such as the right to self-determination or freedom? Are all states equal in the possession of natural resources that are necessary for economic development? Are states equal in the power they exercise in world politics? Are states equal in the possession of the resources of power: a dynamic industrial capacity, population, natural resources, food, technology, unity of public opinion or purpose, weaponry, military preparedness, national resolve, financial resources, and quality of government? Let us move beyond states to nonstate actors. Are multinational corporations equal in any way? Are they equal in power? If not, what explains the inequalities: size, wealth, technology, knowledge, or the product they desire to produce? What about citizens of any nation in the world? Do they have equal rights to liberty, life, and the pursuit of happiness? Are humans of various nations equal in their standards of living? What explains the inequalities that you see: exploitive multinational corporations that benefit the corporation more than their workers, a capitalist world economy that distributes wealth inequitably, or a world political system that puts more emphasis on national security than on satisfying basic human needs? Does it make sense to think of natural and conventional equality or inequality in world politics? Are natural equalities or inequalities among states attributable to geography, natural resource allocation, and/or climate? Are conventional equalities or inequalities among states associated with human-made things: economic or political systems, a state's form of government, or religious unity or diversity? Is it possible to conceive of equality in terms of sameness *and* equality? For example, are all states the same in the sense that they possess the right to self-determination, but unequal in the extent to which they can in fact determine their own destinies? These are a few of the questions that our discussion of equality at the national level raises as we apply equality to world politics. Let us turn to the realists to continue our thinking on equality.

Realists believe that the principal actors in world politics are states, and that states are driven by the need to preserve and increase their power relative to other nations in the world. But there is a big divide between realists on the issue of whether states are equal in power. Some argue that nations are fundamentally equal, and others believe that the power of nations differs from state to state. Let us begin with Thomas Hobbes, who serves as a model for those who think that states are fundamentally equal in power. As you will recall, Hobbes imagines humans living in a state of nature: a condition devoid of any government. He describes this condition as a war of every man against every man. In this state, humans desire power, both to get the things in life they desire and to protect themselves from violent death. You may wonder why a war would result from this condition. Isn't it possible that one person might rise above all others and by sheer force compel the rest to obey? Not according to Hobbes. He believes that humans are fundamentally equal in the personal qualities that are the sources of their power. Sure, one person might be more muscular than another person, who in turn may possess a superior intellect. However, when it comes to acquiring the goods in life that one desires, the person of intellect can use that brainpower to compensate for his or her lack of strength. Thus, humans are substantially equal in the power they exercise in securing life's goods. Let us apply this to world politics. Nations, just like individuals, exist in an international environment in which they must amass power to provide for their national security and to allow them to pursue their goals. Nations are fundamentally equal in the possession of power. Although some nations are more industrially developed than others, less economically developed nations can always form alliances with stronger states to augment their power. Or they can use their natural resources as a bargaining chip in international diplomacy. Even the smallest, most economically undeveloped nation, with the backing of powerful nations, can be a major player in world politics. Because there is such remarkable equality of power among the world's nations, no one nation is so powerful that it can impose order on the world. The equality of national power condemns nations to an eternal world political struggle.[51]

Other realists disagree. Some believe that there is a hierarchy of power in the world: some nations are more powerful than others. Let us look at Thucydides's *Peloponnesian War,* an account of the war between Athens and Sparta some twenty-five hundred years ago. Transport yourself back to ancient Greece. Though the war formally commenced in 431 B.C., the seeds were sowed some fifty years earlier. After the Athenians, the Spartans, and their Greek allies (formally organized in the Hellenic League) successfully beat back an attack by the Persians, Athens assumed leadership of the league. The Spartans and their allies dropped out of the league and formed their own Peloponnesian League, leaving Athens in undisputed control of the Hellenic League. With the passage of time, the Hellenic League was renamed the Delian League, which comprised roughly one hundred city-states. These city-states were composed of a city and the surrounding farmland, and the average population was around one thousand male citizens. These city-states ringed the Aegean Sea. If you imagine a horseshoe, Sparta and its allies (Lacedomaenians) would be located on the bottom left side of the horseshoe, Athens directly above them, and most of the other city-states allied with Athens would follow the curvature of the horseshoe from above Athens to the bottom right-hand side. To the right of the right-hand side of the horseshoe was Persia, and the Aegean Sea was the expanse between each side of the horseshoe. The glue that held the Athenian-dominated Delian League together was the fear that the Persians might attack Greek city-states on the right-hand, eastern side of the horseshoe. In exchange for Athens's protection, the member states of the Delian League voluntarily contributed ships to Athens; however, as time passed, and Athenian power increased, the Athenians were able to tax their allies and reduce them to subjects of the growing Athenian empire.[52]

Thucydides describes how Athens managed to become the most powerful city-state in Greece. The Athenians exploited many of the resources of power discussed earlier. Athens had the largest population of any city-state in Greece. There were 30,000 male citizens, while the average city-state had only 1,000. This population was capable of fielding 29,000 soldiers in times of war. Imagine how a city-state with 1,000 citizen-soldiers felt when facing the Athenian army! In addition, Athens sported and manned 300 warships. To support this military force, taxes were paid to Athens by the city-states of the Delian League; thus, Athens had a source of revenue to build, man, and support the strongest navy in the Aegean. Athens's economy was dynamic and diverse: it was agricultural and commercial, which meant that Athenian life was not totally dependent on one type of economy. This economy provided Athens with a source of revenue to support a large army and navy. The national character of the Athenian people was also a source of power. Thucydides describes them as innovative, daring, quick to act, and swift to follow up success. Athenians were law-abiding, intensely patriotic and willing to die for their country. Under the leadership of the great Athenian statesman Pericles, the Athenians developed a strong democratic government. Under the wise foreign policy leadership of Pericles, Athens transformed a league of about one hundred city-states into the Athenian Empire. By the beginning of the Peloponnesian War in 431 B.C., Athens was unquestionably the greatest power in the Aegean. As Thucydides reports, the Athenians were so dynamic and powerful that "they were born into the world to take no rest and to give no rest to others."[53]

With no single city-state seemingly capable of countering the power of Athens, arrogance characterized Athenian foreign policy. Take the Athenian destruction of Melos in the sixteenth year of the war. The Melians were originally a colony of the Lacedaemonians, and they had remained neutral through most of the war. However, they became openly hostile to Athenian power after Athens had plundered their land. With the great Athenian navy as a backdrop, a diplomatic conference took place between the Melians and the Athenians. The Athenians wanted Melos to become a tributary power of the Athenian empire, and in return, the Melians would be allowed to retain their "national identity." The Melians argued that they would prefer to remain "neutral" rather than to submit to the Athenian empire. During the conference, it became apparent that Athens would stop at nothing to bring the Melians under its yoke, and the Athenians blatantly and arrogantly brandished the superiority of their power. They made no pretense of why they had come to Melos: to secure the interests of their empire. The Athenians claimed that power and their national interest, not justice, really mattered to them, and they preferred to waste no time in speaking about justice. Rather, they appealed to the Melians to submit to the empire out of simple self-interest: servitude was better than death. After all, it was the Melians who were weak and whose lives, fortunes, hopes, and fears hung "on a single turn of the scale."[54] As it goes in the world, there is one universal law: the world is filled with strong and weak nations and "the strong do what they can and the weak suffer what they must."[55] Faced with the power of an empire, the prudent thing for the Melians to do was to submit to Athens's imperial yoke.

In summary, Thucydides and Hobbes present very different vignettes of world politics. In both pictures, however, one cannot fail to see the importance of the natural and human components of state power. Thucydides believes that there are real inequalities in power that actors possess in world politics, and these inequalities have real consequences for those who, like the Melians, are less power-ful. Today, in a world in which the United States appears to be the major world po-litical power, it is hard to imagine anyone arguing that states are equal in political power. The international power of Iraq, Sri Lanka, Liberia, or Italy pales in com-parison with the power the United States wields on the world stage. Yet the Hobbesian approach to the equality of power cannot be easily dismissed. The United States did lose a war against a nation that was not, on paper at least, a world power: Vietnam. Or take the case of modern Japan. Japan is not a world military power, but it is an economic giant, possessing economic power capable of shaping U.S. international economic and foreign policy. If power is the ability to prevail in a conflict, clearly Vietnam and Japan exercise great power. If there are important power differentials between nations, it is hard to say just why these power asymmetries originate. Some asymmetries may be due to natural differ-ences rooted in climate, the fertility and abundance of arable land, and natural re-sources. Human artifice is undoubtedly another reason. To the extent that some societies have chosen to manage population growth, to acquire the technology to exploit their natural resources, to industrialize, and to govern in a way that gains the support of the public in foreign policy matters, these societies are capable of increasing their power beyond that of nations whose culture, values, and interna-tional goals do not lead them to exploit the natural resources and geographic po-sitions they have been given by nature. Obviously, in assessing the power of the state, weight must be given to the interaction of natural endowments and human artifice or convention.

Classical liberals look at equality in international relations in a much differ-ent way. Recall John Locke's view of human nature, the state of nature, and rights. Human beings, certainly appetitive and desirous of worldly goods, are, neverthe-less, fundamentally rational creatures capable of ordering their lives in a way that permits social interaction. By applying their rational capacities, humans are able to discover those laws granting them the right of life, liberty, and property. With the exception of a few troublesome individuals, humans are able to live within those laws of nature. Thus, the state of nature (in which no government exists) is one of peace, friendship, and cooperation, punctuated occasionally by actions of individuals against another person's life, liberty, or property. Because there is no government in this natural condition, no one individual has political power over others, and each is free to pursue the quest for life, liberty, and property within the laws of nature. However, each person or a group of persons has the power to en-force the laws of nature and punish those who violate those laws. For Locke and liberals following him, there are two kinds of equality. First, humans are equal in the sense that each individual is not under the political control of another person or group of people in the state of nature: there is no government to make law and to enforce it. Second, humans are equal in the rights that God conferred on them: all possess the same rights to life, liberty, and property, though some individuals might exercise their liberty in a way that allows them to acquire even greater amounts of property. So although some differences in wealth can develop, all humans have the right to pursue the acquisition of property if they so desire.[56]

Applied to world politics, the Charter of the United Nations embodies the liberal conception of equality. First, there is the principle of sovereign equality. A nation is sovereign if it acknowledges no authority superior to it. Just as Locke believes that individuals are the ultimate authority in the state of nature with no government exercising political power over them, so in international relations each nation is the ultimate authority. These nations are equal in the sense that their existence (or life as Locke puts it) should be respected by other nations. Given the right of other nations to exist as sovereign entities, even the most powerful nations should restrain themselves from using force or the threat of force against the territorial integrity of other states. Indeed, if one nation aggresses against another (as Iraq did against Kuwait), a nation has the right to individual or collective self-defense to secure its territorial integrity. Second, sovereign equality implies "equal protection of the law." Just as each individual is protected by the laws giving them the right to life, liberty, and property in Locke's state of nature, so in world affairs each nation is protected by the same laws and rights that are extended to other nations. Third, sovereign equality also implies liberty. Sovereign nations possess the right of self-determination; that is to say, each country has the authority to manage its domestic affairs in any way it chooses and to select those economic and political systems that best serves its people. As sovereign nations, all countries have the freedom to conduct themselves in international affairs in a way that does not infringe on the liberty, territorial integrity, and rights of other states, and they are free to enter into treaties, alliances, and trade agreements. Thus, the UN Charter attempts to outline those principles or laws that should be equally applied or guaranteed to each state.[57]

Liberal dogma argues that states in the international arena should be equal under the law, but it does not follow that states should be equal in power, wealth, or level of economic and political development. States differ in territorial size, in the abundance of natural resources, in population, in economic development, and in governmental effectiveness. Thus, the resources of power vary from state to state, and some states are simply more powerful than others. This is not to say that less developed countries that are overpopulated and economically undeveloped will be forever politically marginalized by the great, industrial powers of the north. Rather, all states have the responsibility for their own economic, social, and political development, and by participating in a world capitalist economy, smaller, less developed states have the best hope of increasing their power and influence in international politics. A world capitalist economy permits each nation to market the natural resources, goods, and services that it can extract, produce, and sell at a lower price than other nations. A capitalist world economy that allows multinational corporations and less developed nations to negotiate agreements that can bring capital, technology, jobs, managerial skill, and corporate knowledge to these nations will lay the foundation for future economic development and increased political power in world politics.

Classicists take issue with some realist and liberal positions on the relative equality of world political power. Classicists believe that some nations are economically and politically more powerful than others. Geographic location, natural resource endowment, and historical development have benefited some nations more than others. Thus, they reject the view of those realists who believe that states are fundamentally equal in the exercise of world political power. Classicists would also believe that liberals are too sanguine or optimistic about the ability of less developed nations to increase their power in an international economic system that is dominated by economically and politically powerful states that, for selfish reasons, use their international economic and political power to preserve and extend their control of world politics. Classicists realize that nations do have unequal and different levels of cultural, economic, social, and political development, but they believe that more economically advantaged states have a moral responsibility to promote the well-being of states struggling with poverty, human rights abuses, and racism.

In *Pacem in Terris,* Pope John XXIII addresses the question of equality. He argues that individuals were created by God with a body, free will, and intellect. The continued existence of human life on earth requires humans to fulfill the basic needs of the body: food, water, clothing, medical care, and rest. To provide individuals with an opportunity to satisfy these needs, the state should guarantee its citizens the right to have these needs met. Humans have rights to life; to the opportunity to work; to a just, living wage; and to property. Because humans are creatures endowed with intellect and free will, the state should secure each individual the right to develop his or her intellect and exercise his or her free will. Thus, governments should guarantee individuals the right to use their intellects to pursue Truth, and as people with a free will, they should be guaranteed freedom of religion, freedom of thought, and freedom of movement. Humans are equal in the sense that they each possess these rights, and it is the obligation of the state to use its authority to secure these rights for each of its citizens. Although individuals possess these rights, they also have duties: the right to work requires humans to engage in productive labor, and the right to pursue Truth requires humans to actively engage themselves in a life-long search for the truths of the human, natural, and divine worlds in which they live.[58]

In international relations, states (like humans) possess certain rights and duties correlative with those rights. All states are equal in dignity; therefore, no nation is racially or ethnically superior to another nation. Because each state has an inherent value that should be respected by other nations, the pope argues that each state possesses the fundamental rights of existence and self-development. The right to exist brings with it duties: states should respect the existence of other states. As states have the right to economic self-development, so they have duties. The right to economic development requires a state to take the initiative to ensure that its population has its basic needs met. As a result of successful economic development, the richer, industrialized nations of the north have a duty to aid less developed nations in their quest to improve the standard of living of their people. However, in providing aid to less developed nations, economically developed countries have an obligation to avoid any unsolicited interference in the affairs of those nations. Developed nations have the obligation to respect the right of each less developed state to provide for the needs of its people in light of its unique geographic and cultural conditions. Though all states have the right to engage in world politics, they are not free to act as they wish. They are bound by international law to respect the right of other nations to exist and to respect the rights of other nations to self-development. Only in guaranteeing that these rights are exercised in practice will the nations of the world move toward greater economic and political equality.[59]

Classicists make it clear that each nation should be secured the rights that have been outlined in international agreements. The 1971 Synod of Catholic Bishops' statement, *Justice in the World*, recognizes that the existence of international conflict, the lethal nature of conventional and nuclear war, and the presence of soul-wrenching poverty in a world of plenty reinforces the power of the world's more wealthy nations. The international political system has bred expensive arms races that have diverted money from economic development to military preparedness in developed and underdeveloped nations. Historical animosities between nations and ethnic groups increase the threat of war, feed spiraling arms races, and prevent humans from living in genuine solidarity and peace with one another. Only by restraining arms races; by solving international disputes through arbitration and mediation; by diverting more economic aid to the poor countries of the world; by establishing fairer prices for raw materials mined by less developed nations; by strengthening the economic systems of developing countries; and by using the United Nations more effectively in combating world poverty, disease, starvation, illiteracy, and unemployment can every nation aspire to greater economic equality and the security of their rights as outlined in international law.[60]

Radicals, Islamic fundamentalists, and feminists believe that world politics is characterized by great inequalities of political and economic power. The radical political economist Immanuel Wallerstein argues that the capitalist world system has penetrated the less developed, peripheral or semiperipheral nations and has created great economic and political inequalities. As all political power in the international state system is a function of economic development, the capitalistic core states of the Northern Hemisphere have access to wealth, natural resources, capital, and industrial development that permits them to build great state militaries capable of defending the world capitalist economic system and bourgeois economic interests that develop in peripheral countries. The vehicles for much of the wealth that core states use to amass state power are multinational or transnational corporations. These economic giants have the capability of entering peripheral countries, creating businesses that benefit the core country (not the less developed nations), and transferring the MNC's profits back to the core country. Thus the poor, peripheral states find it virtually impossible to develop, since there are no or insignificant corporate profits to be reinvested in economic development. The powerful core nations, which serve the interests of the world bourgeoisie, structure the interstate system and the capitalist world economy in a way that solidifies the dependency that the peripheral states have on the core states. Core states use their international economic power to structure the terms of international trade to benefit themselves at the expense of less developed countries, and they exercise political power to prevent antisystemic, anticapitalistic movements from upsetting the world political order that benefits the bourgeoisie. According to this line of thinking, international organizations such as the United Nations are simply front organizations for the great capitalistic powers and serve to protect international bourgeois interests. As a result, peripheral states find it virtually impossible to increase their economic and political power, to separate themselves from the capitalist world economy, and to assume the status of independent socialist nations.[61]

Feminists, agreeing with radical political economists that economic and political inequalities in world politics do exist, ascribe these inequalities to patriarchy, not economics. Feminists such as Tickner, Peterson, and Runyan argue that men and women have been socialized into believing that all social, economic, and political inequalities between men and women are due to natural differences between the sexes. In assigning women to the private realm of the house and men to the public realm of business and politics, men have been able to accrue and use their economic and political power to create barriers to women's entrance into the public realm. Whereas male control of corporations and national governments results in policies and laws that prevent women from moving into centers of public power, world politics reinforces the patriarchal control that men have over women. For Tickner, the freedom, independence, strength, assertiveness, and competitiveness that characterize men's understanding of human nature lead to a realist's view of world politics and a capitalist's view of international economics. In assuming that nations desire power, freedom, and independence from control by other nations, men have created an international system in which power is the primary goal, war is permissible in defending one's interests, military service is an asset in running for public office, and the need for increased defense expenditures is used to justify cuts in social spending for programs that help women and minorities. Political realism reinforces the patriarchal control men exercise over women and perpetuates the economic and political inequalities that exist between them. Because the electorate honors those who have distinguished themselves in war, women, who have been excluded from combat, are at an initial disadvantage before the game of politics begins. The unconscionable rape and torture of women in war further fortifies the subordination of women to men. Economically, the world capitalist system does not free women from the home. Rather than opening up opportunities for women in a modernized economy, developing nations often employ men first. And even when some jobs are made available to women, they are the ones with the least status and lowest pay.[62] The net effect of world politics and world capitalism is that they reinforce the economic and political inequalities between men and women that serve patriarchy so well.[63]

Islamic fundamentalists believe that the great political inequalities that exist between nations today are largely due to the failure to understand the Islamic values that ought to guide the life of peoples. According to the Islamic political philosopher Maududi, humans have both a bodily and a spiritual dimension. To sustain life, humans are passionately charged with the desire for food, clothing, shelter, and sex. Humans naturally differ in intellect, talent, and bodily stature. Allah, through Mohammed, has given humankind those laws that humans can exercise in leading a good life and avoiding evil. Obedience to Islamic law allows humans to order their own lives and community life in a way that permits each person to move toward spiritual perfection. Rightfully, the natural differences that exist between humans lead some to profit more than others. A degree of economic inequality is healthy and just, and Islam teaches that those who profit most have a responsibility to help those who profit the least. Societies that reject Islamic law and adopt capitalism inevitably create a selfish rich class preoccupied with the pursuit of great wealth. These selfish rich people unconscionably exploit the poor, who lapse into even greater poverty. They also capture control of the political system, bending justice to serve their own tyrannical interests. Thus, "a class of godless materialists are [*sic*] found sitting tight everywhere on the seats of power."[64]

According to this Islamic fundamentalist view, the world capitalist economy and world politics are dominated by godless tyrants who have turned their backs on the Islamic way of life, which promotes social justice. The desire of the Western capitalists to maximize their profits drives them toward imperialism to secure new markets, new sources of natural resources, and new areas of investment. Unconcerned with the material and moral well-being of those in foreign countries, these capitalistic states (and the multinational concerns that serve them) exploit the human and natural resources of developing nations. As Maududi has so passionately put it, the Western capitalistic nations have

> set upon the world pillaging it for the capture of new markets of trade, resources of raw materials, open lands for colonization and mines yielding valuable metals, so that they may procure fuel for their ever burning fire of avarice. They fight not for the cause of God but for the satisfaction of their lust and hunger.[65]

Thus, great economic inequalities develop between rich capitalist nations and poorer dependent nations. The economic inequalities between rich and poor nations result in the political domination of the world by rich nations. Capitalistic states reject the Islamic belief in the unity of all people, and they have divided humankind into squabbling nation-states. In a world where scattered, weak, nationalistic countries compete with a few rich capitalistic nations, the rich states are capable of effectively organizing and wielding their political power to keep weaker Islamic nations pitted against one another. By fanning the fires of Arab nationalism, the West prevents Islamic countries from effectively using their combined power to free themselves from the West's death grip. The UN's Universal Declaration of Human Rights, which attempts to protect the world's people from torture, economic exploitation, and political repression, is selectively followed by capitalist states when it serves their interests.[66] On the one hand, world politics is dominated by richer, more powerful nations that have created an international political system to support their imperialistic desire for greater material well-being. On the other hand, the poorer nations suffer the ignominy of economic oppression and political impotence.

Put down your book for a minute and reflect on the issue of equality in world politics. The realist, radical, feminist, and Islamic fundamentalist critiques of the international economic and political system give one pause to think about the formal equality that liberals and classicists believe characterizes world politics. Although liberals and classicists believe that there is a legal equality of states that seeks to guarantee their right to sovereignty, territorial integrity, international freedom of action, and self-determination, there are powerful actors in world politics who trample on these legal guarantees. Whether these actors are states, the people who manage the foreign policy of states, multinational or transnational organizations, the United Nations, or alliances of states, the great economic and political powers seem to work their will in the world, casting to the wind the rights of states and of the people when it suits their own interests. Yet there is plentiful evidence that the liberal and classical visions of world politics have some merit. On the whole, the sovereignty of nations is respected, human rights have a place on the foreign policy agenda of many states, and in recent years less developed countries have been able to negotiate more equitable agreements with multinational corporations. Returning to a more personal level, how much political and economic equality is there in the world today? How about social equality? Does international political power benefit some races or ethnic groups more than others? Is the exercise of international political power predominantly male and Caucasian? Who are the most and the least powerful actors in world politics? Are they states, MNCs, international banking institutions, terrorist organizations, men, women, or minorities? Do you believe that there should be greater economic and political equality between the actors in world politics? In sum, actors, power, and equality are ideas that are intricately related in world politics. These ideas have important implications for how political theorists think about world politics. Let us turn to questions about the extent to which anarchy and society characterize the relations between world political actors.

ON ANARCHY, SOCIETY, AND LAW IN WORLD POLITICS

After discussing human nature, international actors, power, and equality, we are now in the position of being able to discuss one of the most fundamental problems in international relations: anarchy and social organization in world politics. Imagine, once again, an international condition in which there is no governing authority to order the relations between actors in world politics. What would the world be like? Would you see nations and other actors organizing themselves in ways to achieve their goals? Would you see a violent condition of chaos and anarchy existing between these actors? Would you see the stronger actor(s) suddenly imposing an order on the weak? What would you see? These questions, oddly enough, are more real than hypothetical. There is no world government or governing authority that has the power to coerce nations and other actors to obey international norms or laws. World politics seems to be a mixture of peace and war, justice and injustice, lawful and unlawful behavior, and the exercise and violation of rights. How can one make sense out of this apparent set of contradictions?

The English philosopher Thomas Hobbes is often the archetype for realists who argue that in the absence of any international government with the power to enforce a common body of rules, world politics falls into a state of anarchy. Returning briefly to Hobbes's political philosophy, Hobbes believes that humans are self-interested and are fundamentally equal in their ability to get what they desire. They seek power to achieve the object of these desires (including more power), and their interests frequently bring them into opposition with others. A state in which equals in power are bent on pursuing mutually exclusive interests will ultimately be characterized by a war of everyone against everyone. Because no one individual or group of individuals possesses enough power to put an end to this anarchical condition, it can be ended only if all the individuals choose to give up most of their political power to create a government strong enough to prevail over an unruly, appetitive population.

Not surprisingly, this vignette of domestic political life has been applied to international politics. First, nations, like individuals, have their own desires and interests, which often conflict with those of other nations. In the 1990–1991 Gulf crisis, the desire of the United States for a secure, inexpensive supply of oil came into conflict with Iraq's desire to increase its oil reserve and to drive up the price of oil by manipulating supply. Second, to achieve their interests and to increase their power compared to other nations, states will strive for power. Thus, nations will do what is in their interest to preserve and increase the power that they amass.

This could be done by increasing the size and effectiveness of the military, increasing the nation's industrial production so the country can produce more weapons, and diverting more money to foreign aid with the aim of persuading a nation to adopt a particular course of action, or developing new technology to exploit the nation's natural resources. Third, the assumption that nations are equal in power suggests that no one state has the ability to control the behavior of other states, and when the irreconcilable interests of nations collide, war is the most likely outcome. Thus, world politics is very similar to Hobbes's state of nature: nations exist as independent entities that pursue their own interests, and there is no overarching power to control their behavior. Because the interests of these nations often conflict with one another, war is often the result of international contention. Although actual battle may not always accompany international struggles for power, the lack of an international government places all nations in a psychological condition of war: at any moment an international dispute may arise and drag nations into a conflict they neither desire nor are equipped to win. Without an international government to order the relations between states, international life is one of anarchy.

One might object that the international environment is not one of constant war—actual or psychological; in fact, there are extended periods of peace and cooperation, and war is by no means the normal condition of international relations. The realist might respond that nations act in their own self-interest. If the condition of anarchy threatens the independent existence of each state, nations would come to the peace table, create a body of international law that would secure the independent existence of each state, and pledge to obey this law. One might again object that states would break this law and return to a state of anarchy if they thought it was in their best interest to do so. To which a Hobbesian might reply: perhaps, but seeing the advantages that come from obeying international laws, most states would uphold those laws and restrain the unlawful designs of rogue states. Indeed, the practice of international relations today demonstrates that self-interest has served the cause of peace. Nations have developed a body of international law that guarantees the territorial integrity and existence of states. On the whole, nations have respected the right of nations to exist as independent states. Nations have agreed to this right out of self-interest: by respecting the borders of adjoining states and by forgoing the option of war when disputes arise between nations, countries no longer need to invest large sums of their wealth in providing for their self-protection. Thus, international law has served the interests of all states reasonably well.

The German philosopher Immanuel Kant lived from 1724 to 1804 and was a major thinker of the European Enlightenment. With John Locke, he represents a major strain of Western liberalism. Kant sees a certain social unsociability in human nature. Humans, he believes, are often prompted by egotism, which leads to conflict. At the same time, humans are inclined to promote sociability. The sexual appetite and the capacity to think, reason, and converse prompt humans to organize social groups like the family to promote common goals. However, it is the rational capacity that allows human beings to transcend their purely animal or bodily nature and create social, economic, and political institutions that permits the progress of the human mind and the human condition. In the absence of government, Kant believes that humans would find ways to organize themselves to satisfy their basic needs for food, clothing, and shelter. In so doing, an economic interdependence would develop with each person producing goods that could be traded or sold to others. The lives and well-being of all people would thereby become economically intertwined. However, not everyone would live in peace and mutual interdependence. Those who violated the norms of the community would create enough chaos so that the rest of the community would choose to create a government to protect the liberty, equality, and independence of each citizen.[67]

Kant extends his thoughts on human nature, economics, and the state to the international sphere. Like Rousseau before him, Kant suggests that as soon as one group of people creates a state, others will do so out of self-protection. Thus, world politics developed out of the desire of people throughout the world to organize themselves into states. These states demonstrate the principle of social unsociability that characterizes human interaction in domestic politics. On one level, states pursue their own interests at the expense of others, turning the international environment into a state of anarchy and war. In this state of nature, Kant believes that states live a lawless freedom: doing whatever they choose to do, unrestrained by any limits that would permit the freedom of other states. On another level, states are inclined to cooperate, particularly in economic matters. The economic development of one nation benefits its own workforce as well as the prosperity of other nations. International trade permits nations to sell their products to other states, increasing worldwide economic prosperity. Thus, as nations pursue their own economic well-being, Kant suggests that they are promoting the well-being of other nations, too.[68]

Kant characterizes the relations between nations as conflictual and cooperative. As long as nations exist in a state of nature and are free to do as they please, war will result. But war is not entirely evil, according to Kant. War can promote the progress of nations. For example, the cold war and the attendant nuclear arms race between the United States and the Soviet Union stimulated the development of space technology. This technology gave us new, synthetic materials that have improved our lives on earth and provided the world with satellite communications systems. However, war is also the scourge of humankind. Kant criticizes bloated defense budgets and the interruption in commerce that attends war or the threat of war. He argues that in the future, the miseries of war will lead nations to create a federation of nations (similar to the United Nations) to ensure peace, further encourage the international commerce that would improve the material life of humankind, and order the relations of states under international laws enforced by a federated world government.[69]

Hugo Grotius, the reputed founder of international law, was born in Holland in 1583 and died in 1645. *The Law of War and Peace,* published in 1625, was written during the darkest hours of Europe's Thirty Years War. Although a contemporary of Thomas Hobbes, Grotius appeals to the classicist tradition in developing his thoughts on international relations. Grotius accepts the Aristotelian conception of human nature but gives it a Christian spin. Humans are naturally political animals, who form societies to perfect their nature as social, rational creatures. Reason (and not bodily inclinations and instincts) is the defining trait of human beings and a trait they share with God. The exercise of intellect or reason allows individuals to discover those moral, natural laws that serve to correctly structure the behavior of individuals in society. The function of government is to take these natural laws and apply them to concrete, historical conditions and to adjudicate disputes between citizens. For example, all humans are created with a natural inclination to preserve themselves; however, each society is responsible for determining the form of economic organization that would allow humans to satisfy their basic needs. Given the culture, traditions, and level of economic development of a nation, one form of economic organization might be preferable to another economic form. Societies governed in accordance with the principles of natural law permit individuals to perfect their lives as social, rational creatures.[70]

Just as individuals are inclined by nature to social life under the guidance of natural law, so states form an international community that is guided by the law of nations, or *jus gentium:* law made by humans that is grounded in or derived from natural law. The law of nations is a product of usage, everyday practice, and the testimony of jurists thoroughly schooled in international law; but its legitimacy is based upon the consent of the nations to whom it applies. The law of nations promotes harmony in international society. Because no state is economically self-sufficient, and because states need to cooperate with one another politically to realize what is in the common good of all nations, a body of international law has grown up around the political and economic interactions of nations. Because no one nation is economically self-sufficient, Grotius believes that commerce between states is necessary. Trade permits all nations to benefit from that which is produced or manufactured in other nations. This promotes the common good of the state that exports goods to a second country; it also promotes the common good of citizens of other countries. Because trade is necessary for the good of all humankind, Grotius favors freedom of the seas, which eliminates barriers to trade.[71]

Radicals (as well as many feminists and Islamic fundamentalists) differ from the realists, liberals, and classicists in that they reject the ideas that world politics exists in a state of anarchy and that there are cooperative, mutually beneficial relationships that develop among nations. There is a world order, but it is a coercive, unjust ordering of international actors by some dominant interest. For radicals like Mikhail Bakunin, the nineteenth-century Russian anarchist, the international order is an artificial construction of states that serves the interests of the most powerful states and of those persons who are the most economically powerful within those nations. He arrives at this position by arguing that there is a fundamental distinction between society and state. On the one hand, humans are naturally social animals who, if left to themselves, would organize a society to satisfy their needs as material beings: humans who have basic, material needs as well as a need for cultural enlightenment. Humans, using their rational capacities, create and coordinate economic and educational systems aimed at satisfying these human needs. The members of these societies use those natural laws that are inherent in the social dispositions of humans to direct their energies in creating just social orders. On the other hand, the state is an artificial creation of humankind. It results from a people who gather and agree to form a government that reinforces inequalities in wealth and social prestige. Like Rousseau, Bakunin believes that as soon as one state is created by a social contract, people outside that state—feeling threatened by the power represented by that association—establish their own states. The rise of states divides the fundamental social unity of all people into a number of hostile nations. This mutual hostility drives each state to seek more political power, as each fears that it might be conquered, devoured, and enslaved by other states. But the need to acquire more power inevitably leads nations to imperialism. Imperialism permits nations to expand their industrial capacity and markets, provides an expanded source of raw materials, and augments their population. Finally, imperialism enslaves the weaker to the stronger nations. Thus, world politics is characterized by rule and subordination: in the struggle for state power, the stronger imperialistic states expand their rule at the expense of weaker states.[72]

The feminists we have discussed so far also believe that the structure of world politics is based on domination: it has been constructed by males and serves them at the expense of women and minorities. As you will recall, feminists Tickner, Peterson, and Runyan argue that men have used their power to create a social, economic, and political world that justifies and permits the subordination of women to men. In justifying this order with its unequal distribution of wealth, education, opportunity, and political power, men have designed ideologies or philosophies that depict women as naturally inferior to men in reasoning ability, physical and emotional strength, assertiveness or aggressiveness, and competitiveness. On the one hand, women are best left to the home, the private sphere, in which they can exercise their unique nurturing talents. On the other hand, men are best suited to handle the more aggressive and competitive world of politics and business—worlds of human activity that are in many ways foreign to and uncomfortable for women. Thus, men situate themselves in positions of social, economic, and political power, and they use that power to perpetuate the social, economic, and political inequalities between men and women. In the corporate world, males erect barriers to women's entrance into the job market. Those women who do enter the privileged domains of corporate power find that their access to the higher reaches of corporate management is restricted. Those men who hold positions of power in government are capable of using their power to prevent women from exercising reproductive choice and to limit social services that are necessary if women are to become economically and politically equal to men.[73]

Compared to domestic politics, wherein a growing number of women have gained access to positions of political power, world politics remains an almost exclusively male preserve. Projecting the male worldview that humans are aggressive, appetitive, and power seeking, males have socially constructed an essentially Hobbesian view of world politics. Assuming nations are fundamentally estranged from one another and compete for world political power to secure and extend their own interests and power, males find it necessary to commit huge amounts of money to national defense and to deprive the powerless—women and minorities—of the social programs, such as child care and reproductive services, that are necessary for their well-being and liberation. The realist approach in conceptualizing world politics serves a dual purpose: it perpetuates the perception that males, not females, have the assertiveness, hard-headedness, and determination that is needed to conduct foreign policy, and it reinforces the subordination of women and minorities by restricting access to social programs that would move them toward greater social, economic, and political equality with men. The aggressive, male vision of world politics pictures war as the greatest problem in international relations; human rights, the environment, and women's issues are secondary to the problem of war, which poses the greatest threat to the independent existence of states. Rarely are the effects of war on women given much attention. For women, war is a disaster. The harvest of death that attends war brings great personal suffering to women.[74] In the movie *Legends of the Fall*, Colonel William Ludlow drops out of the army and politics because of the government's inhumane Indian policy. In moving to the remote reaches of Montana, he chooses to raise his three sons far from the corrupting influence of politics. One of his sons, Samuel, attends an Ivy League school, falls in love with a woman named Suzanna, and brings her back to his father's ranch. However, Samuel's educational experience has drawn him into the vortex of world politics. With the barbaric Germans threatening the civilized world, Samuel and his brother Alfred announce that the "honorable" thing to do is to enlist in the army. During the course of the war, Samuel dies. Tristan, whose love for his brother leads him to enlist to protect Samuel, is psychologically disfigured by his inability to prevent the death of his brother. But it is not Samuel's death that is most tragic: it is the life of Suzanna. The war has taken from her the one she loved, and her subsequent love affair with Tristan is doomed by his inability to come to grips with Samuel's death. Still haunted by the love she has for Tristan, she marries Alfred. Unhappy in that marriage, she ultimately puts an end to the suffering, pain, and grief that reigns over her life by committing suicide. War, a by-product of the male preoccupation with domination and power in international relations, inevitably harms the people whose way of life it wishes to protect: the women, children, and families of the fallen.[75]

Islamic fundamentalists believe that world politics is an artificial creation of nations that have fallen away from the teachings of Islam. For Islamic fundamentalists such as Ayatollah Khomeini, there is an ideal ordering to world politics: one in which all peoples of the world—regardless of color, race, nationality—are united under and are obedient to Islamic law. Unfortunately, there are people who have rejected Islamic law and have chosen to live by laws of their choosing. In turning from Islamic law, the West has raised the nation-state as the primary actor in world politics. This has divided the people of the world into many nations and has led nations to believe in their superiority over other countries. Western nations, attempting to secure what is in their own interest and to provide luxurious lifestyles for their citizens, have launched out into the world, colonized it, and placed less developed nations in their service. This has created two great blocs of nations in the world: rich and poor. Rich nations, led by the United States and the former Soviet Union, extended their economic and political control over poorer nations. Economically, rich Western countries exploited these less developed nations. Multinational corporations penetrated the economies of poorer countries; extracted and sold their natural resources at unfair, low prices; and reinvested few of the profits in less developed nations. Politically, the West has established or supported authoritarian and puppet governments in developing nations to promote political stability, Western culture, and capitalism in those countries. These governments have forced their people to adopt capitalism and to reject their own cultural traditions; and wherever resistance has surfaced, these puppet governments have not refrained from exercising their power in the most tyrannical manner. The second great bloc of nations—the poor, exploited nations—have suffered the most under the developed world's tyrannical rule. Because Islam has developed a vision of a just world order and has committed itself to ending poverty among the peoples of the world, Khomeini believes that Islamic nations, and particularly Iran, are in the best position to rally the developing nations against the West. After the triumph of Islam over the United States, the Soviet Union, and their allies, the exploitation of the poor by the rich will end, and Islam will usher in a reign of justice and equality of all people under Islamic law.[76]

Islamic fundamentalists, radicals, and feminists raise disturbing questions about world politics. They claim to expose an international hierarchy that benefits some groups or nations at the expense of others. Using gender as a tool for discovering the source of social, economic, and political inequality, feminists like Peterson and Runyan believe that the patriarchal rule of men extends from the home, through the nation, and into world politics. These writers think that the world political system reinforces social, economic, and political inequalities that exist between nations. According to Bakunin, the rise of the state inevitably leads to the rise of other states. The existence of more than one state leads to the rise of an international political system that drives states to pursue power, and in pursuing power to embrace imperialism. Finally, these writers suggest that the international political system is unjust to weaker states: world politics is governed by the stronger states, which use it to their advantage to exploit less powerful nations.

Put down your book and reflect for a moment about the nature of international politics. Are we to believe with Hobbes that in the absence of a power capable of disciplining the nations of the world, states exist in a war of all against all? There seems to be so much evidence against this position. War or cold wars do not seem to plague the nations of the world; rather, peace is the normal state of affairs between the nations of the world. Are not most nations of the world law abiding? Further, Hobbes believes that nations are motivated by parochial and egotistical interests, and even the policies that promote the well-being of other nations are adopted simply because they serve their own self-interest. Is this the case? Are not many nations' foreign policies pursued without regard to the benefits or costs they bring in their wake? If so, is not Grotius's description of world politics as a society of nations grounded in a respect for international law promoting justice, economic prosperity, and peace in the world more accurate? Is there not an international law that is widely respected because it does promote peace and justice? Have not more and more nations developed "democratic" forms of government that seek to secure the fundamental rights of all human beings listed in the Universal Declaration of Human Rights? But if nations are inclined to organize and conduct their activities under international law, how can we explain the existence of war, which violates the very law that nations choose to erect against it? Also, are we to believe that nations are motivated by the sentiments of justice and peace? Is not self-interest the primary motive in the behavior of nations? Do the classical liberals like Locke and Kant have a valid point when they suggest that nations, like humans, act from mixed motives? Nations seem to create and obey international law out of enlightened self-interest, and yet we can find nations that, misperceiving what is in their interest, run afoul of international law. Finally, are we to believe that there is an international political structure that serves to benefit rich nations over poor or men over women? If there is a political hierarchy in world politics, can it not be attributed to the success of some nations in acquiring greater shares of power and influence in international relations? Is not power more dispersed among nations than is suggested by radicals? Isn't there considerable discord and conflict between the more powerful nations of the world that prohibits collusion for the purpose of exploiting less developed countries? These are some of the questions that might be raised in discussing anarchy, society, and law in world politics. War, one of the most perplexing phenomena in international relations, is fundamentally related to all of these questions.

ON WAR AND PEACE

What is war? Perhaps the simplest definition would be armed conflict between states. War presupposes the existence of states, states that have a government or public authority capable of declaring and conducting a war, and the military capability to engage in an armed conflict. Terrorism and civil war are forms of violence, but these cannot be subsumed under the concept of war because they do not involve two states. Terrorism often encompasses transnational groups based in one or more states that use acts of violence as a source of power to shape the behavior of international actors. They may operate independently of any government, or they may be financially supported and militarily trained by states that have an interest in seeing their causes succeed. Civil wars differ from war in the sense that they are internal: fought by groups within a state. The 1994 Rwandan Civil War was fought between two tribal groups: the Hutus and Tutsis. Thus, terrorism and civil war are attended by armed violence but are not wars in the strict sense of the word—they are not armed conflicts between states.

What are the causes of war? In his marvelous book *Man, the State and War*, Kenneth Waltz presents three images of the causes of war. He points to those who argue that the causes of war are written into human nature. Humans are naturally aggressive: war runs in their veins. A second group argue that war is the result of factors operating within the borders of states. Thus, a particular form of government or economic system might be responsible for war. The third image associates the cause of war with the international political system. For example, states are driven to war to protect or extend their power relative to other nations in world politics. Thus, Waltz suggests that there are several levels of analysis that writers have used to explain the causes of war: the individual, the state, and the international political system.[77] Take the 1991 Gulf War. Why did Iraq invade Kuwait? Can it be reduced to Saddam Hussein's personality: his alleged desire for power, glory, prestige, and Islamic leadership in the Middle East? If so, one might argue that the root of war rests within the individual. Perhaps the Gulf War could be explained by the form of government. Are personalist or autocratic forms of government more prone to war than democratic ones? Perhaps the autocratic Saddam Hussein, without any real constitutional checks on his domestic power, believed that he was free to go to war to push his own agenda. If so, the form of government in the state might be associated with war. Finally, is it possible that the international system was in some way responsible for the Gulf War? Is it possible that the United States, having watched Iraq acquire more and more power in the Middle East, feared for Israel's security? If so, is it conceivable that the United States intentionally misled Saddam Hussein by instructing its ambassador, April Glaspie, to tell the Iraqi leader that the United States had "no opinion on Arab-Arab conflicts," thereby luring him into invading Kuwait, with the hope of engaging him in a major war that would decimate his military and nuclear capability and establish a more favorable balance of power between Middle Eastern countries?

What is peace? It is simply the absence of war, or is it a positive condition of unity or harmony? Perhaps peace is a state of international harmony in which all nations interact with one another within international law. If peace is the simple absence of war, then the United States and the Soviet Union were at peace during the cold war. Perhaps it is possible to think of peace as a psychological condition of calm. If so, then it would be hard to say that the cold war was a state of peace, because great psychological tensions and anxieties existed between the Soviet Union and the United States. Regardless of how one conceives of peace, there is still the question of the causes of peace. Using Waltz's levels of analysis, we could deduce that peace is a function of human nature, the state, and the international political system. At the individual level, if the foreign policymakers of the world are rational and capable of coming to a consensus on laws that would allow the nations of the world to live in peace, then peace could be ascribed to the nature of human beings. Or we could conclude that peace is promoted by democratic forms of government. Because the citizens of democratic nations bear the brunt of war—physically, economically, and emotionally—people do not normally favor going to war. And because democratic governments are influenced by popular opinion, these governments will normally heed the peaceful inclinations of their citizens and refrain from war. And last, we could suggest that the structure of the international political system is responsible for peace. When one nation or an alliance of nations dominates other nations by its superior power, war is less likely: there is no incentive for a weak nation to take up arms against the majesty of a powerful nation, because the weak state would certainly lose. Let us develop a better understanding of the issue of war and peace in world politics by using Waltz's three levels of analysis.

Some writers believe that the cause of war is rooted in human nature. Saint Augustine, the bishop of Hippo who lived between A.D. 354 and 430, believed that human beings were Fallen creatures whose politics were marked by perpetual conflict, the desire for power, the lust for domination, and the inevitability of war. Saint Augustine thought that humans were suspended between the spiritual world of God and the material world of nature. They were endowed with goodness by God. Humans were given the ability to reason to know God, the free will to choose between good and evil, and the bodily appetites to provide sustenance for the body. From their Creation to their Fall in the Garden of Eden, Adam and Eve knew the law of God, kept it in their actions, and loved God as they loved each other. However, Adam and Eve possessed free will: they could choose to disobey God's laws if they so desired. And disobey they did; being tempted by the Devil in the garden, Adam and Eve chose to violate God's command not to eat from the tree of knowledge of good and evil. In so doing, they turned away from the life that God had laid out for them and began to live a life that suited their own desires. This first sin was so great that it was passed on from generation to generation down to the present day.[78]

The effect of this sin was catastrophic for humankind, because it turned people against one another. In turning from God, humans distorted their souls. No longer did reason discipline the bodily appetites; no longer were those appetites used to promote the good of others. In turning from the love of God and of their fellow humans, people turned to the love of self. They gave free rein to their appetites and lived according to the flesh: a selfish life filled with carnal pleasures, immorality, licentiousness, drunkenness, idolatry, anger, quarrels, murder, and war. People sought social, economic, and political power because that power promised the future satisfaction of their carnal passions, even at the expense of others. In pursuit of the pleasures of this world, individuals inevitably fell at each others' throats: crime, murder, friendship simply for the sake of profit, death of close friends, rape, torture, and all shades and varieties of human injustice marked the social and political lives of people. The exercise of political power permitted individuals to use the state to further their own interests at the expense of others. Thus, the state, which arose out of people's lust for domination over others, was little more than a group of bandits.[79]

The domestic conflict that plagued relations between individuals and groups was matched by the disunity of nations. One source of this disunity was depicted in the Bible's account of the attempt to build the Tower of Babel. After turning from God, humans arrogantly believed that they alone possessed the knowledge to order their own affairs. This arrogance found a parallel in their attempt to build the Tower of Babel: a tower that could connect earth and heaven. To prevent them from realizing their goal, God made each person speak a different language, thus preventing them from realizing their plan and erecting a linguistic barrier to the unity of all humankind. Future generations of humans formed nations, each with their own language. Like humans, these nations were bent on world domination.[80] In the opening chapter of *The City of God*, Saint Augustine speaks of the earthly "city [Rome] which lusts to dominate the world, and which though nations bend to its yoke, is itself dominated by its passion for domination."[81] As long as the desire for domination, the lust for power, and the greed for worldly wealth characterizes the motivations of individuals and nations, war is inevitable. Reflecting on the history of war and peace in the world, Saint Augustine argues that the "mutability of the human estate can never grant any realm an absolute security from all incursions of hostility."[82] In world politics, no state finds ultimate security from the malicious machinations of other states. The world being divided into nations, "wars, altercations, and appetites of bloody and deadly victories," subject the weaker to the stronger nations.[83] But through what carnage did stronger nations walk to build their empires and maintain their control over hostile populations? Straining against the manacles of empire and unhappy under the bloody sword, conquered peoples inevitably rebel, turning an illusory peace into the fury of human slaughter.[84] Thus, Saint Augustine argues that war is rooted in the sinful nature of humankind.

Most classical liberals did not think that war flowed in the veins of humans; they ascribed war to domestic factors. In discussing his state of nature, John Locke argues that humans are fundamentally rational creatures capable of controlling their passions. Valuing life, liberty, and property, humans believe that it is in their rational self-interest to allow others the opportunity to pursue a life lived in accordance with these values. As long as individuals do not deprive others of their natural rights to life, liberty, and property, peace and harmony prevail among them. Each person freely pursues, acquires, and enjoys the things in life he or she most desires. However, this picture of peace and tranquillity is defaced by those who choose a life of stealing, killing, and restricting the freedom of others. In such cases, Locke believes, those who obey the laws of nature will punish those who violate the laws of nature.[85] Applied to international relations, many liberals thought that the nations of the world believed that international law and international agreements should protect the territorial integrity of states; should permit states the right to determine the government, economic system, and social institutions under which they choose to live; and should allow the greatest amount of free trade. In pursuing these international norms, states were acting in their own self-interest. Free trade would benefit the well-being of all states, because economic prosperity would follow the free flow of goods. The right to self-determination permitted societies to live happily according to the laws, government, economic system, and culture they chose. Leaders who believed that their countries were not likely to be attacked by other states desiring their natural resources and productive capacities would devote fewer resources for military preparations for war. Unfortunately, some states would violate international law out of the mistaken belief that it was in their interest to do so.[86] These nations might desire the material wealth of another nation—as Iraq did in the Gulf War—or desire to politically dominate the world—as Hitler did. Whether states were headed by irrational leaders who did not know what was in their enlightened self-interest, by leaders who misperceived their self-interest, or by those who desired to impose their view of the world on the whole of humankind, all these in some way act irrationally—against their enlightened self-interest. Take Saddam Hussein. Was it in Saddam Hussein's self-interest to violate the territorial integrity of Kuwait in order to secure upwards of 25 percent of the world's oil reserves? Did he really believe that the United States and other nations, states that desire a plentiful and relatively inexpensive source of oil, would permit him to control a greater percentage of world oil, which would give him more leverage in oil markets to drive the price up? If you answered "yes" to these questions, then you could conclude that given the outcome of the war, Saddam Hussein seriously misperceived his rational self-interest in the matter of Kuwait. Indeed, nations that choose to flaunt the international law and international norms that legally permit them to be successful actors in world politics seriously misjudge their self-interest and are responsible for war.

How can the world be at peace if national leaders misperceive what is in their own enlightened self-interest? The German philosopher Immanuel Kant provides one answer: fill the world with states that are republics, and then organize these states into a world federation of states committed to enforcing international law. Kant, like Locke, believes that human beings on the whole could accurately judge their own self-interest, and war is not in the enlightened self-interest of states. The burden of war falls more heavily upon the citizens of a state. It is the citizenry who fall in battle, who pay higher taxes in preparing for and prosecuting a war, who destroy the life and properties of others, and who bear the burden of financing a national debt to maintain a standing army. Kant believes that the citizenry, when faced with the burden of preparing for and prosecuting a war, will see that it is not in its self-interest to go to war and will pressure the government to settle international disputes by peaceful means. Kant also believes that republican nations—nations governed by constitutions that protect the freedom, independence, and equality of all citizens before the law—are less inclined to go to war, because such states value the freedom, independence, and equality of all states. Therefore, international law seeks to guarantee the freedom of all states to engage in world politics and trade, to determine the shape and ends of their societies, and to be treated equally before the law of nations. Even though some renegade nations would violate international law in the mistaken belief that they would gain by it, Kant argues that the nations of the world should form a federation of states (similar to the United Nations) for the purpose of enforcing the rights of states, treaties between states, and agreements that encourage the spread of international trade and norms of civilized behavior between nations. By uniting all the nations of the world behind international law and by jointly pledging to enforce it, the peace-loving nations of the world would amass such a formidable police force that no single state would violate international law for fear of the consequences. Thus, a confederation would usher in a reign of world peace.[87]

Whereas Kant examines the domestic and political dimensions of war and peace, Vladimir Lenin, a Russian radical, argues that the internal dynamics of the domestic capitalist economic system drive nations into imperialism and war. As we have seen, Marxists argue that capitalism is a system in which the means of production (capital) concentrate in the hands of the bourgeoisie. The members of the proletariat, who sell their labor at subsistence wages and who become conscious of their exploitation, eventually revolt against the bourgeoisie and the state that uses its power to maintain the capitalist system. Although the economic and social conditions endured by workers in nineteenth-century capitalist nations were indeed oppressive, no proletarian revolution occurred. Lenin hypothesizes that the bourgeoisie discovered a way to temporarily avert this revolution: through imperialism. Imperialism, according to Lenin, is the highest stage of capitalism. A domestic capitalistic system produces more goods and creates more capital than it can consume and use. As national economies expand and produce more and more goods, they acquire an ever-growing need for natural resources. With more capital than can be used at home, the bourgeoisie and the governments that serve their interests are driven to export their capital to the underdeveloped countries of Africa and Asia, where cheap labor provides the possibility of great profits for international combines. Colonized areas open markets for domestically produced goods that cannot be sold at home, and they provide their "mother" countries with steady supplies of the natural resources necessary to produce capital and manufactured goods. In the headlong drive to colonize the world to reap these benefits, the Western capitalistic nations agreed to divide Africa and Asia into spheres of influence for the purpose of controlling colonization and preventing conflict. However, after Africa and Asia had been carved up by the imperial powers, there was no additional land available to continue the capitalistic expansion. Nevertheless, the need for new capital markets and natural resources and the need to sell domestic goods abroad continued to grow. Without additional natural resources and expanded markets for what was produced, the domestic economy would fail. The bourgeoisie feared that the proletariat, faced with the specter of a diminished standard of living, would revolt. To avoid a revolution and to secure economic prosperity, capitalistic states would therefore be driven to war to secure natural resources and markets.[88]

Mikhail Bakunin, the Russian anarchist, and Karl Marx share similar criticisms of capitalism and the state, and both believe that economic forces cause war. However, Bakunin is clearer than Marx on the image of a postcapitalist, peaceful world. Bakunin condemns the exploitive nature of the capitalist system. Capitalism, he believes, creates a propertied, leisured class—the bourgeoisie—that exploits the working people—the proletariat—by paying them subsistence wages. He agrees with Marx that the bourgeoisie relies on the power of the state to maintain its legal control of its capital and wealth and to exercise control over the ever-exploited, revolutionary working class. Only a workers' revolution that abolishes capitalism, returns the means of production to the people, eliminates social classes, ends the coercive control of the bourgeoisie over the proletariat, and abolishes the state can bring peace to the world. In abolishing the state, the revolution would abolish the military, an organ not only used by the bourgeoisie to control the proletariat, but a force that could be used to wage war on other nations. The evolving world order would be based on a hierarchical, free federation of individuals formed into communes, communes freely formed into provinces, provinces into national social groupings with no government, and nations into a federation of nations. The economic activities of each of these associations would be coordinated by larger economic groupings, for the purpose of achieving a degree of individual economic equality that would permit each individual to develop his or her own talents and potentials. A universal federation of nations founded on liberty, justice, and equality would unite the people of the world in the bonds of kinship and peace.[89]

Although Kant, Lenin, and Bakunin point to domestic politics and economics as the sources of war between nations, it is unclear that the reorganization of a nation's economic and political life would lead to peace. John J. Mearsheimer, a contemporary realist, points out that the proliferation of republican governments in the twentieth century did not prevent democracies from going to war with authoritarian nations. And although the liberals believe that war is stemmed by the respect for human rights, concerns for human rights are generally overridden by nationalism and religious fundamentalism.[90] The question of nationalism points to a potential weakness in Bakunin's argument: if humans are social creatures who freely form nations, is it not more probable that people will become more attached to their nation than to some transnational kinship of humankind?

Let us look at one last question: is an international political system with no governing authority conducive to war? Jean-Jacques Rousseau, the eighteenth-century French philosopher, believed that it is. As long as nations are the principal players in world politics, as long as nations have opposing interests, and as long as states exist in a condition of international anarchy with no ultimate authority to peacefully solve disputes between states, war is inevitable. Rousseau comes to this conclusion by discussing the origin of society, inequality, and the international state system. Rousseau believes that humans are born good; that is to say, they are born with compassion for the well-being of others and a desire to preserve themselves. In a state of nature, humans are independent: all their needs are satisfied by the gifts of nature and the fruits of their labor. Although physical inequalities exist between individuals, they are of no consequence, because all the goods in life can be readily attained by the individual. If a struggle between two or more people occurs over food, no one dies: one snatches the food and the other leaves peacefully. As long as humans retain this rustic individualistic simplicity, they are satisfied with their life. However, when humans form societies, economic and political inequalities arise. With the advent of agriculture, differences in wealth and class arise, because the stronger are able to till more land than the weak. With the natural compassion for others repressed by the desire for gain and wealth, the rich exploit the poor and the poor eventually revolt. Rather than to live in a condition in which the rich and poor could lose their lives and the rich their possessions, Rousseau suggests that the rich and the poor created a state whose existence gives new power to the rich and places new fetters on the poor. Speaking metaphorically, "men . . . banded together to cut each other's throats, and to see all the horrors of war arise from the very efforts which have been taken to prevent them."[91] Thus, the new state reinforces the existing social and economic inequalities by placing the political and legal power of the state in the hands of the rich who exercise it in their own interest.[92]

Rousseau believes that as soon as one state rises, others soon follow, and this creates an international environment with no overarching political power to order their relations with one another. Because these states are conscious of their relative inequality in political power, Rousseau argues that they all become concerned with their national security. The safety and preservation of each state requires all nations to make themselves stronger than their neighbors. Thus, nations run headlong into the struggle for world political power to secure their interests and borders. To extend their power, these nations develop industrial and commercial economies to support not only a luxurious lifestyle for the privileged but also the ever-growing need for armies, fortresses, and military equipment. The rise of international commerce between countries establishes a degree of interdependency between them. However, this interdependence does not promote peace; rather, it heightens the possibility of war. If deprived by another nation of the goods or natural resources that are essential to its national well-being and power, a state will go to war to ensure its supply. The international political system brings with it the necessity of a foreign policy and defense bureaucracy. But even these government officials are sources of war: their own jobs can be justified only by the existence of the international conflict that they can create. Rousseau has little faith that international law, without an international authority to enforce it, is capable of binding states in the cause of peace.[93]

Rousseau's view of world politics and war is perhaps more disturbing than the realist's view. The realist holds that the aggressive, appetitive nature of human beings will lead to war when conflict cannot be resolved. War is part of the human condition about which we can do little more than pile up barriers against it. Rousseau believes that war results from human choice. In Rousseau's primitive state of nature, all live in relative peace. Rather, war is a consequence of the "civilized life" that humans have chosen to create and live. As long as human civilized life centers on the state, as long as humans have the short-sightedness to pursue their own interests at the expense of all humankind, and as long as a state of international anarchy exists, humans will be unable to escape the logic that leads states to war. Rousseau challenges the Kantian belief that republican nations are most conducive to peace. Paradoxically, good states, to protect themselves in the international environment, will be dragged into war by renegade states that desire to dominate other nations or the world. The Adolf Hitlers and Saddam Husseins of this world make it impossible for peaceful and freedom-loving states to live in peace. Because states are forced to choose whether or not to go to war, the question of the justness of war arises.

Reflect for a moment on war and peace. What is war? Does terrorism qualify as war? Given your view of human nature, do you believe that war is innate in human beings? Are humans—individually or in groups—naturally aggressive? Are men more aggressive than women? If so, and since world politics is predominantly a male bastion, are males in some way the cause of war? If humans are not naturally aggressive, war must be a social phenomenon. If humans have created war, can they rid themselves of it? Are the causes of war rooted in "domestic" political dynamics? Are tyrannies more prone than democracies or military governments to war? Do political elites in any form of government go to war to unify the people behind them, particularly when public support of their regime flags? Is war largely a result of a condition of international anarchy? Is the division of the world into nation-states a precondition for war? In a world of nation-states competing for international power, prestige, and natural resources, does the absence of an international authority with the power to resolve disputes increase the chance of war? Is war the result of capitalistic economic imperialism, as Marxists claim? If so, would socialism usher in a world of peace? Are world economic inequalities between rich and poor nations a cause of war? Will the alleged scarcity of natural resources lead to resource wars in the future? Is the pursuit of international justice associated with war? Does the economic interdependence of nations lead to war rather than to peace? What is peace? Is peace simply the absence of war? Are democracies more prone to peace than other forms of government? Without doubt war is perhaps the most perplexing and vexing phenomenon of world politics. Let us now turn to a related issue: whether war can ever be considered just.

On the Just War

In an age when nuclear weapons have the potential of creating a dark and cold world, in a century that has witnessed two major European wars that have reduced towns and human lives to rubble, and in a world that has seen so many smaller but no less tragic wars, one begins to wonder if there can be any justification for war. The Disney film *The Lion King* raises the issue of the just war.[94] By various wiles, Scar, the evil brother of the good king Mufasa and uncle of Simba, is able to murder Mufasa and send Simba into exile. Scar's tyrannical rule upends the order of life of the kingdom, and the natural world becomes as dark as Scar's brooding, vengeful, calculating character. His rule leads to environmental destruction, and places the lives of all the animals in the kingdom in jeopardy. Simba eventually has a choice about whether or not to take up the mantle of justice and organize the remaining lions to fight Scar and his allies, the hyenas. Nations are often faced with the same question: should a nation go to war to right the wrongs that one nation has visited on another and bring about a just ordering of society once again? If so, what are the conditions under which a war can be justly waged?

The case for a just war can be made from two broad points of view. One position (taken by liberals, classicists, Islamic fundamentalists, and Russian national-ists) holds that by natural law or by social convention, nations form an interna-tional society that is governed by rules, and these rules specify the conditions under which nations can justly resort to the use of force. The other position (held by realists such as the fifth-century B.C. Athenian, Thucydides) holds that the in-ternational system is one of anarchy, in which there are no rules other than those based on the right of the strongest. International conflict and war permit the strongest nations to rise to the top of the international system and rule it as they choose. The mighty lay down those rules that determine what is just and unjust in the behavior of nations. Both of these approaches rely on some definition of jus-tice. In the broadest sense, justice is "rendering each one's due." Accepting this de-finition, then the question becomes: what is one's due? Is one's due based on merit: should those with superior performance be granted more benefits than a person who achieves less? Or is one's due based on need: should those with greater needs be granted more of some good than those who have fewer needs? Is one's due based upon universal rights that ought to be secure for everyone? Is one's due the goods one is able to acquire, regardless of the method by which one achieves them?

The classicist position on the just war is succinctly put in the U.S. Catholic bishops' pastoral letter, *The Challenge of Peace*.[95] As you will recall, many classicists believe that humans naturally form associations, societies, and states to realize the common good. Modern classicists are inclined to believe that the well-being of the earth's peoples cannot be attained within the boundaries of the state. Therefore, nations must organize on the international level to promote the common good of people throughout the world. In so organizing, they must frame all international law in a way that squares with the moral, higher, or natural law: the law issuing from God that determines what is due to nations and the peoples of the world. In other words, international law grounded in God's law specifies which actions are just and which are unjust among nations. To achieve the common good of all peo-ples of the world, humans should organize their international political system to ensure that the natural and international laws are enforced and observed.

Natural and international law determines which actions of nations are just and which are unjust. Recognizing that there is no international authority to en-sure peace, the American bishops argue that nations have the right and obligation to self-defense if attacked by an aggressor. They suggest, however, that seven cri-teria be met before the decision is made to go to war. First, the cause must be just. There must be a real danger that important moral and legal principles of interna-tional law have been violated. These reasons might include protecting a nation from attack, restoring human rights that have been wrongfully denied, invading a nation to restore human rights, or reestablishing a just world order and peace. Sec-ond, the intention in going to war should be related to the just cause. If a nation declares war on another nation, the intention to do it must be framed by the desire to right a wrong or to restore human rights, for example. Thus, it is forbidden to cloak wars of aggression with the mantle of justice. Third, war can be declared only by those who have the public authority to do so. In the United States, the war power is jointly exercised by the president and Congress, and unless that power is exercised rightly, a war cannot be just. Thus, duly constituted public authorities of a state, and not multinational corporations or private groups, can declare war. Fourth, in deciding to wage war, nations need to raise the issue of comparative justice. In most wars, each side of a dispute claims justice for its cause, and a nation should ask whether it is sufficiently justified in unleashing the horrors of war. Fifth, the principle of last resort imposes an obligation on all nations contemplating war to engage every effort to exhaust all peaceful alternatives before going to war. These efforts might include negotiation, mediation, and the use of sanctions and blockades. Sixth, there must be some probability that the war will be successful; to enter a war that would result in the annihilation of a nation could hardly be just.[96] Author James Childress points out that this criterion applies more to offensive wars than to defensive wars. A nation that has been unjustly invaded may offer resistance to the invader, even if it faces certain defeat. Here "success" is broader than "victory." That nation may be fighting for higher principles, which its resistance attempts to secure. If, however, a nation wages a clearly futile war of aggression, which will most probably end with the massive loss of life, then that war is patently unjust—even if the nation is attempting to reclaim an international right wrongfully denied. Finally, there is the criterion of proportionality. The "damage to be inflicted and the costs incurred by war must be proportionate to the good expected by taking up arms."[97] Thus, the consequences of some wars, nuclear wars for example, may be so destructive and grievous that they cannot be justified. This principle would hold true in conventional wars in which the delivery of ordnance and the conduct of the war would be so destructive as to make human life barely tolerable. Given these criteria, some argue that a war can be considered just if all seven criteria are met. Others believe that in the very messy world of politics, only some of these seven criteria must be met. Still others favor an ordering of the criteria. For example, a just cause is a necessary principle that must be met prior to applying the other criteria.[98]

Recall for a moment the liberal view of world politics and imagine how it relates to war. Humans, rational yet subject to moments of lawlessness, create the state for the purpose of securing certain rights: life, liberty, and property for Locke; liberty, independence, and equality before the law for Kant; and life, liberty, and the pursuit of happiness for Thomas Jefferson. In the international system, states organize themselves in a way to secure their fundamental rights. Issuing from treaties, custom, tradition, international legislative bodies, and judicial interpretation, international law identifies what is due states and the people of the world. Thus, one can look to international law as the source of what is right and just in world politics. Under what conditions is war justified for the liberal?

Many liberals believe that enlightened self-interest will lead states to obey international law; but they fear that a rogue, yahoo state will arise, violate the rights of states and peoples outlined in international law, and press wars of aggression. In that case, the liberal hopes that law-abiding states will intervene to limit additional aggression and punish that state for the violation of international law. Under what conditions is war permissible? Kant believes that in the absence of an international authority, nations will organize themselves to make and enforce international law the best they can. In international relations, nations develop those laws that will secure their rights to self-determination, to enter into agreements, and to remain neutral when their neighbors are at war, for example. In an international system with no overarching power to authoritatively mediate disputes between nations, Kant suggests that states are permitted to go to war to secure these rights. He also grants states the right to initiate a war under two conditions: if another nation began to mobilize its forces against it, or if another state had gained so much power that it threatened the rights of other states.[99] Thus, a war can be justly waged if the rights given to states by international right (law) are violated by another state or groups of states. This same principle is written into the Charter of the United Nations. Although states are pledged to pursue peaceful solutions to international problems and the Security Council may approve other measures short of force (such as sanctions and blockades), nations have the right to individual or collective self-defense. If attacked by an aggressor, a nation may defend itself by force of arms or it may ask for and use the armed help of other nations.

One realist view of the just war is outlined in Plato's *Gorgias* and applied in the Peloponnesian War by the Athenians. In *Gorgias*, Plato has Callicles—a quick, hot-tempered, irascible, haughty man—make the argument that justice is simply the advantage of the stronger. In a world where there are no higher, moral, god-given laws to guide the behavior of people and where the only "natural law" is the law of tooth and fang, survival of the fittest determines who survives and who does not; those who survive the struggle are the strongest, the most successful, and the best, and they deserve to rule. The just society is one in which the stronger rule the weaker and establish the laws that benefit the stronger.[100] Arguing that societies attempt to restrain the best people in society by emphasizing equality, Callicles explains that society's way is to "take the best and strongest among us from an early age and endeavor to mould their character as men tame lions." Continuing, he says:

> We subject them to a course of charms and spells and try to enslave them by repetition of the dogma that men ought to be equal and that equality is fine and right. But if there arises a man sufficiently endowed by nature, he will shake off and break through and escape from all these trammels; he will tread underfoot our text and spells and incantations and unnatural laws, and

by an act of revolt reveal himself our master instead of our slave, in the full blaze of the light of natural justice.[101]

To the extent that the greater, more powerful nations are able to free themselves of the trammels of international law, international public opinion, and the constraints imposed by other states, they too emerge to define the moral terms around which world politics turns.

World politics is an environment that has a natural law that determines what is just and how world political power should be used; that natural law is the survival of the fittest. In the struggle for survival—a war of every nation against every nation—the strongest state that wins the battle for power is entitled by its simple success to determine what is right and just. Thucydides chronicles the initial triumph and eventual downfall of fifth-century B.C. Athens. He often makes the point that at the height of its power, the Athenian empire, which survived the international struggle for power among all the Greek city-states, determined what was just and unjust. In discussing the fate of the people of Melos, the Athenians claim that in the absence of rules of justice to guide the actions of nations, "the strong do what they can and the weak suffer what they must."[102] Similarly, the citizens of Mitylene, people who were part of the Athenian empire but fiercely independent, chose to ally themselves with Sparta and revolted. They hoped that they would be able to escape the ever-tightening grip and weight of Athens's colossal empire. The Athenians believed that if Mitylene successfully revolted, other states would follow. Athens would lose tribute, ships, and the men they needed to carry on the war with Sparta. The Athenians therefore put down the revolt. In this zero-sum game wherein every loss for Athens would be a gain for Sparta, the Athenians debated the question of whether or not to make an example out of the Mitylenians and put the entire male population to the sword. Arguing in favor of this policy, Cleon, a demagogic democrat, reminded the Athenians never to forget that their empire was despotic and that only their military might kept the city-states in submission. He suggested that because Athens's military superiority had fashioned this empire, they had the right to determine the rules of justice by which all city-states in the empire lived. That rule of justice was simply to benefit friends and harm enemies. Since the Mitylenians were the declared enemies of Athens, the Athenians should move swiftly to execute the citizens of Mitylene "for where vengeance follows most closely upon the wrong, it best equals it and most amply requires it."[103] Thus, Cleon clearly argued that justice is defined by those who win the international struggle for power.[104] A similar argument might be made concerning the contemporary struggle for power. The cold war—the struggle for world dominance between the United States and the Soviet Union—ended with the rule of the stronger, the United States. Ruling in the splendor of its victory and power, the United States now supports its friends who support Western liberal values and institutions, and it seeks to foist its view of justice and right on those, like Saddam Hussein, who would choose to rule the world on different terms. The gentle tyranny of liberal economic and political institutions is nevertheless a tyranny.

Jihad, the exertion of power in the way of Allah, has a long history in Islamic political thinking. Historically, it developed as a way of spreading religion and of establishing an imperial world state under Islamic law. When the universal Islamic state reached its height during the Western Middle Ages, it recognized two worlds: *dar-al-Islam* (the world of Islam) and *dar-al-harb* (the world of war). Dar-al-harb consisted of the nations outside of Islam that refused the rule of Islamic law. In addition to this twofold division of the world, Islamic political theory acknowledged the existence of non-Islamic states that paid the jiza, a tax, to the Islamic empire. These nations were tolerated by dar-al-Islam. Jihad could be fought by persuasion or by armed conflict. The obligation of propagating Islam could be filled by the heart, tongue, hands, or sword. By the heart, jihad was spiritual: it was a war against the evil that lurked in the hidden recesses of one's soul. By tongue and hands, jihad provided a way of supporting right and correcting wrong. By the sword, jihad was equivalent to a war against unbelievers and the enemies of Islam. As international Islamic power waned after the tenth century and as Muslim nations lost crucial wars, jihad lost some of its crusading zeal; however, the leader of the community, the imam, could revive it whenever he thought it was necessary.[105]

The Islamic theory of the just war is grounded in the Qur'anic command for the individual and community to promote and defend Islam. For many Islamic fundamentalists, human beings were spiritually oriented toward Allah and could know His law. However, as creatures of flesh, they were also inclined to selfishness: self-gratification and self-love. As with individuals, Islamic states, while bending toward Allah, could also be consumed by the desire for power, fame, natural resources, territory, wealth, and earthly preeminence over one another. War was the inevitable consequence of this selfish turn away from Allah. Wars in the way of man, and not in the path of Allah, are condemned by the twentieth-century political theorist Maududi. Thus, jihad is the only just war. It is both offensive and defensive, and it can be waged by force of arms or by persuasion. Maududi believes that all humans are brothers and sisters to one another under Allah, and that jihad seeks to unite them under the single umbrella of Islam. In bringing them into one community, jihad is fought for the welfare of humankind and "the establishment of a just, equitable social order among human beings."[106] Maududi rejects the Western distinction between offensive and defensive wars; jihad is both offensive and defensive. On the one hand, Muslims and Islamic nations are enjoined by Allah to protect and defend Islam; thus, they are committed to fighting wars in which they are attacked. On the other hand, jihads are offensive in the sense that they are conducted to bring all peoples of the world into peace and harmony with one another under Islamic law. Although Maududi believes that there is a role for persuasion in bringing the people of the world together under one roof, he also believes that the annihilation of tyrannical regimes, oppression, mischief, strife, immorality, and exploitation in the dar-al-harb will require Muslims to resort to arms.[107]

In the eyes of Fyodor Dostoevsky, a Russian nationalist, the justness of war was tied up with Eastern Orthodox theology and contemporary European political theory and politics. Dostoevsky accepted much of the criticism of European politics and culture, which were in eclipse. The root of this decline was the Europeans' rejection of God and their faith in human reason. In exercising their reason, humans claimed the capability to know what constituted a good social and political order. With this knowledge, they would be able to refashion and reform the unjust social, economic, and political institutions of their time and usher in the good society. But in the absence of God—who provided spiritual and moral dimensions to life—European society had fallen into the endless pursuit of wealth. Sunk in the dirty world of capitalistic commercialism and self-seeking, European culture was no longer capable of sustaining the highest social value: love of one another. Additionally, international political life revolved around the nation-state, which instead of uniting the people of the world divided them into competing political units. Too often, the result of this competition was war.[108] On the other hand, the Eastern Orthodox religion had penetrated the hearts and minds of the Russian and other Slavic people such as the Serbs.[109] With Russia at its head, Dostoevsky hoped that all Slavic peoples would unite in the love of Christ. As he put it so well, this was:

> a spiritual union, of all those who believe that our great Russia, at the head of the united Slavs, will utter to the world, to the whole of European mankind and to civilization, her new, same and as yet unheard of word. That word will be uttered for the good and genuine unification of mankind as a whole in a new, brotherly, universal union whose inception is derived from the Slavic genius, pre-eminently from the spirit of the great Russian people. . . .[110]

Dostoevsky believes some wars are just: those whose ends are international peace. In his *Diary of a Writer,* he describes the justness of the Russian War with the Ottoman Empire. The empire conquered the greater portions of the Balkans and with them, the Serbs. The Eastern Orthodox Serbs of Serbia and Montenegro had been massacred and plundered under the heel and scimitar of the Islamic Ottomans. Dostoevsky believes that as long as this Balkan tyranny existed, the peace of Christ that unites all Christians could never come to fruition. To achieve this peace, he believes that Russia should join the Serbs and Montenegrins (their fellow brothers in Christ) in overthrowing the Ottoman rule. In establishing a federation of all Slavic peoples under Russian leadership, peace would be brought to all Slavandom, and with that peace, the reign of "brotherly accord of all nations abiding by the law of Christ's Gospel."[111]

The idea of the just war is rooted in both religious and secular views of world politics; however, there are those who hold that no war is ever just. From a Christian perspective, Count Leo Tolstoy—the Russian novelist—and Jonathan Dymond—a nineteenth-century American theologian—lay down serious challenges to the just war theory. Tolstoy believed that the thrust of Christianity could lead one only to the conclusion that war was unjust. He thought that all humankind was united in one great family: as God was the Father of all, so all humans were brothers and sisters to one another. This universal kinship had its roots in the Christian moral law that issued from the Old and New Testaments, and this moral law served to guide Christians in their relations with others. For example, the Ten Commandments and the teachings of Christ provided each person with the moral blueprint for how he or she should conduct his or her life relative to others. Because these laws specified the way in which humans should relate to one another, they formed the foundation upon which the actions of individuals could be considered just or unjust. People were "just" to the extent that they followed the moral law, and "unjust" to the extent that they turned from it. If justice was rendering each one's due, what was due to each of God's children? Tolstoy answered this question by saying that you should do unto others as you would have them do unto you. But this still begged the question, what was your due? In Tolstoy's view, the Ten Commandments outlined what that was. As all human life was valuable, the Ten Commandments absolutely prohibited anyone from taking the life of another person. The Old Testament commandment, "Thou shalt not kill," applied to all brothers and sisters united in God's love and care, and this law knew no exceptions. To take the life of a person in the heat of passion or in any war was still taking a life. Furthermore, Tolstoy believed that the law of God was the standard by which all human law ought to be measured, and if a conflict arose between human law and God's law, God's law ought to prevail. Thus, declarations of war that led to killing were in opposition to God's law, and they were unlawful and unjust. In addition to the prohibition on killing, the testament of Christ added much to Tolstoy's belief that war was morally wrong. Christ taught that it was wrong to kill, and he strengthened this prohibition with the law of love: one should love one's neighbors as oneself, one should love one's enemies, and one should not return injury for injury. Thus, Christians are commanded to take no lives and to love one another. The very nature of war contradicted these moral precepts. War violated the most obvious moral law: thou shalt not kill. It violated the principle of treating others as we would ourselves: as we would not want to be killed ourselves, so we should not kill others. Christ taught that one should love one's enemies, yet war begets hatred and is morally odious. Christ believed that injury ought not to be returned for injury, yet what is war but the injury of one inflicted on the other. In violating the fundamental principles of Christianity, Tolstoy believed that war was inherently unjust.[112]

Like Tolstoy, Jonathan Dymond holds that no war is just, and he offers specific refutations to those who think that there are cases in which war is justified. Dymond believes that a moral law issues from the will of God. This law is revealed to the prophets of the Old Testament and is clarified through the teachings of Christ. This law is both general and specific in nature. Where it is specific, it provides clear and distinct guidelines for human life, and where it is general and vague, it invites humans to supplement it with human law deduced from broader Christian principles. The moral law finds its way into each individual's conscience, and humans are commanded by God to obey this moral law. Government has the duty to act and legislate in a way that promotes the law of God, and if government ever acts in a way that violates that law, individuals of good conscience are obliged to disobey it. As the moral law provides the standard for the law within states, it also provides a standard for international law. On the one hand, in cases in which an international law expressly contradicts the moral law, nations are obliged to obey the moral law. On the other hand, moral principles should form the foundation upon which nations interact. The moral principles of justice, Christian charity, and peace should govern the relations of states.[113]

Dymond attacks three of the legs upon which the just war theory stands. First, he rejects the notion that nations can ever have just cause to take up a defensive war. Wars of aggression and of self-defense are contrary to Christian morality: they involve the taking of life, which is prohibited by the moral law. Dymond specifically attacks the belief that wars of self-defense are justified. He rejects the classicist's view that there is a natural inclination for self-preservation or self-defense that gives an individual or nation the right to protect itself. Although Dymond does not deny that there is an inclination for self-preservation written into the nature of humankind, he argues that inclinations should always be guided or regulated by God's moral law. If, for example, a Christian is attacked by another person, he or she is permitted to take those steps necessary to protect his or her life within the bounds of Christian morality. The Christian being attacked cannot, however, kill the attacker, because Christian morality does not permit the taking of a human life. In fact, he or she should be willing to die to uphold his or her pacifist Christian principles. The same holds true in relations between nations. Although nations have a right to defend themselves, that defense is circumscribed by the prohibition on killing. Therefore, if one nation attacks another, the aggrieved nation has no recourse to self-defense other than the protection of divine providence. Dymond finds another problem associated with self-defense: it is not clear what self-defense means. Is self-defense an army defending the lives of its soldiers? The lives of its citizens? The defense of property? Or their glory and their crimes? Though there is a difference between the defense of a soldier's life and the defense of the crimes a nation commits against another nation, Dymond believes that the distance between them is so small that once a nation employs one justification, it inevitably employs the other. The defense of the soldier will escalate to the defense of great crimes committed against other nations. A final problem of the self-defense argument concerns the problem of keeping a defensive war defensive. Although a nation may attempt to defend its people, Dymond suggests that as soon as the defender tastes victory, the war will cease to become defensive. It will become offensive: the defender will become a punishing aggressor. Thus, the justness of the war—grounded in self-defense—is lost: "Moralists may *talk* of distinctions, but soldiers will *make* none."[114]

Next, Dymond attacks the classicist's criteria of competent authority and comparative justice. Classicists argue that only the duly constituted authorities of the state can declare war. Dymond denies that the persons to whom the authority to govern the state has been given by God can ever possess the authority to make war. All authority in the state must be exercised with the consent of the people, in the interest of the people, and in accordance with God's law. Since God has forbidden the killing of people, the rulers of the state have no authority to take a nation into war. Third, Dymond raises the issue of comparative justice. Just war theorists argue that before a nation can go to war, there must be substantial evidence that justice is on their side, and the nation must have suffered blatant, obvious injustices at the hands of another nation. Dymond believes that this is virtually impossible to determine. Conflicts between nations are bound up in the web of history, and it is never clear who is in the right. The action one nation takes against the other is often a response to an earlier injustice. In cases like this, it is difficult to establish who is the aggressor.[115]

The Indian nationalist leader Mahatma Gandhi (1869–1948) was equally opposed to war and took aim at those who, like Callicles, argued that war is just if it benefits the strongest nation in world politics. Gandhi believed that humans possessed a carnal body and a spiritual soul. Reason is seated in the soul and it apprehends those higher, moral, religious laws that direct the lives of all human beings. In a rightly ordered human being, the soul directs the body along the path of divine law laid before humankind by God. This law is the center of social relationships, and Gandhi believes that the highest duty prescribed by this law is to serve humankind. All humans are brothers and sisters to one another, are of equal worth in the eyes of God, and should treat each other with love, kindness, generosity, sympathy, and justice. Nevertheless, in some people the brutish, carnal side of human nature rules the soul, causing them to pursue and glorify the body at the expense of the soul. Ultimately, a life bent toward the body results in selfishness, injustice, hatred, murder, struggles for power over others, oppression, and war. The question in Gandhi's mind is which force was the stronger: forces issuing from the body (brute force) or those from the soul (soul-force)?[116]

Gandhi's philosophy focuses on the pursuit of Truth, nonviolence, and suffering. One pillar of Gandhi's political thought rests on Truth. God is Truth and the source of all Truth. As the source of all Truth, God is also the source of the moral law that should instruct all those who turn to follow it. By applying their reason, humans are capable of discerning the moral law; however, in pursuing an understanding of that moral law, they may develop different understandings of it. Thus, Gandhi calls for toleration for those who have different beliefs; despite the relativity of Truth, he seems to suggest that the glow of Truth would grow ever-stronger in the hearts and minds of more and more humans with time. Because of the doubt that humans have about the Truth of things, Gandhi believes that humans do not have the authority to punish others. Punishment presupposes Truth—the knowledge that a person is in fact guilty of a crime. Doubt may exist regarding the guilt of the accused, and punishment cannot be meted out by the doubtful.[117]

The second and third pillars of Gandhi's philosophy center on ahimsa and suffering. Truth is nonviolence or *ahimsa*. Ahimsa has two dimensions: it prohibits acts of violence by one person on another and it promotes love of all humankind. Nonviolent people would neither harbor ill will or resentment toward others nor would they act violently toward others. In the realm of the body, Gandhi opposes war, assassination, torture, and physical violence; and in the realm of the soul, he banishes all forms of resentment, hatred, and malicious thoughts of ill will. Gandhi believes that the all-embracing power of love binds human beings together. In loving one another, humans seek to use their lives and talents to benefit all humankind. Even those who are chosen to be one's enemies will, through spiritual enlightenment, be embraced in the bosom of our love. Suffering is the third pillar of Gandhi's philosophy of life. In a world in which darker powers relentlessly prowl the earth, people committed to pursuing Truth and living nonviolently in unity with one another will inevitably face personal suffering. Those consciously committed to pursuing Truth and living by a higher moral law will often suffer at the hands of those who live by gun and knife. Truth seekers will suffer with the intention of bringing about a universal brotherhood of humankind. Truth seekers will suffer in the knowledge that they have held to their convictions in the face of death. Such suffering is a source of moral strength and internal peace.[118]

Gandhi applies his philosophy of ahimsa or nonviolence to the question of war. No war is just because war violates the basic principle of ahimsa in many ways. First, war involves violently taking the life of another, and as we have seen, no human has the right to take the life of another human being. Second, war violates Gandhi's belief in the brotherhood of humankind. Affronting the loving striving of each to promote the welfare of all, war divides humanity into friends and enemies. This violates the principle of ahimsa, because among people united in Truth with one another, there can be no room for an enemy. Third, war diminishes the integrity of the individual. Each person is a special creation of God and deserves to be respected as such. However, war denies the dignity of the individual to the extent that one person takes the life of another. Fourth, war distorts the moral nature of human beings. Ahimsa requires individuals to love one another and to harbor no uncharitable thoughts against others. Yet war promotes contrary values: it creates enemies among brothers and sisters, and it fans the flames of hatred and resentment. Fifth, ahimsa does not prohibit a nation from defending itself if it is attacked by another nation; however, it does prohibit a nation from using armed force to protect itself. Rather than taking up arms, the people of a nation should unite in nonviolent resistance to the invaders. Although an occupied people would no longer be free and independent, the invading army could expect no compliance to its attempt to rule them. Though the tyrant may slaughter the people of a nation for not bending to his rule, what is his rule but the rule of a tyrant over a graveyard? Gandhi holds out the hope that men, women, and children offering themselves in nonviolent resistance to an invading army would silence rifle, machine gun, and tank. Whether nonviolent resistance is an effective and moral response to war is one question. Nevertheless, war could never be justified, according to Gandhian principles.[119]

Whether or not to go to war is perhaps one of the most anguishing questions a nation asks itself. Indeed, the spiritual and material well-being of all nations hangs in the balance. We are often troubled with clichés that proclaim that we wage war to secure peace or to promote justice. Most of us see war as inescapable, if not inevitable. We occupy ourselves with finding ways to prevent it, minimizing its deadly fury when it occurs, and patching the world together again to minimize its reappearance. To the pacifist, this wondering does not get us very far in solving the problem of war, because it assumes that war is part of the human condition. The pacifists discussed in this book begin by assuming that division and war are not part of the human condition. They assume that there is a fundamental unity among all humankind, that there is a moral law that serves as the foundation of the intercourse of nations and peoples, and that humans and nations have the capacity to choose to live in peace and unity according to this moral law. Given the moral, social, economic, and political forces that affect the interaction of human life, pacifists generally believe that moral forces can or do exercise a greater influence than others in human life. Their practical problem is finding how to free the human spirit from the shackles that prevent it from exercising its influence. Simply put, how do peaceful people persuade their warring brothers and sisters to turn from violence when war seems so profitable and virtue brings death?

Put down this book for a minute and ask yourself this question, "Can war be justified?" How would you answer this question? To answer it you must obviously have some understanding of justice and the nature and end of war. Your answer would probably involve your view of human nature, the moral principles that you hold most dear, your understanding of international law, the relative existence or absence of an international society, and the structure of international political power. Each of the positions discussed in this section raises questions about the justness of war. Are there any universal norms acknowledged by the nations of the world that determine what is just or unjust in matters relating to war? If so, what is their origin? If not, is there any way in which a war can be just or unjust? Can *any* war be just? If not, are only defensive wars just? If so, are there some conditions that must be met for such a war to be just? Can an offensive war be just? If so, are there some criteria that make such wars just? Must their goals be just? Can a nation justly go to war to promote human rights, to achieve greater global economic equality, to advance democracy, or to prevent genocide? Although we have not talked about the behavior of nations and armies during a war, questions of justice arise here, too. Are there limits on the type of weapons and munitions that are employed in war, limits that, if violated, would make a war unjust? If it were just to enter a war, would the war continue to be just if additional fighting would lead to the loss of large numbers of noncombatant lives? If population centers were bombed for the primary purpose of reducing the will of a nation to resist, would such a war be just? Perhaps your thinking on the causes and justness of war can bring greater clarity to a world that has yet to find ways to avoid the horrors of war and is still searching for a way to ensure that peace and justice rule the hearts and minds of all people.

NOTES

1. Hans J. Morgenthau, *Politics Among Nations,* 6th ed., rev. Kenneth W. Thompson (New York: Alfred A. Knopf, 1985), 4–17.

2. Thomas Hobbes, *Leviathan,* ed. Michael Oakeshott (New York: Collier Books, 1962), 129, 185–190, chap. 13.

3. Morgenthau, *Politics Among Nations,* 503–504.

4. Michael W. Doyle, "Liberalism and World Politics Revisited," *Controversies in International Relations Theory,* ed. Charles W. Kegley Jr. (New York: St. Martin's Press, 1995), 83–106; Mark W. Zacher and Richard A. Matthew, "Liberal International Theory: Common Threads, Divergent Stands," *Controversies in International Relations Theory,* ed. 107–150; Robert O. Keohane and Joseph S. Nye, *Power and Interdependence,* 2d ed. (New York: HarperCollins Pub., 1989), 29–37.

5. Milton Friedman, *Capitalism and Freedom* (Chicago: University of Chicago Press, 1982), 7–16, 22–27.

6. Ibid., 73–74; Michael Donelan, *Elements of International Relations Theory* (Oxford: Clarendon Press, 1992), 179–181, 183–187.

7. C. Fred Bergsten, Thomas Horst, and Theodore H. Moran, *American Multinationals and American Interests* (Washington, D.C.: Brookings Institution, 1978), 3–15.

8. Donelan, *Elements,* 181–183.

9. Pope John XXIII, "Pacem in Terris," *The Gospel of Peace and Justice,* ed. Joseph Gremillion (Maryknoll, N.Y.: Orbis Books, 1976); U.S. Catholic Bishops, "Economic Justice for All: Catholic Social Teaching and the U.S. Economy," *Origins,* 16 (November 27, 1986).

10. U.S. Catholic Bishops, "Economic Justice," 411–412, 415–416; Pope John XXIII, "Pacem in Terris," 202–203.

11. Pope John XXIII, "Pacem in Terris," 213–214, 231–232.

12. U.S. Catholic Bishops, "Catholic Social Teaching and the U.S. Economy," *Origins,* 14 (November 15, 1984): 372–375. See U.S. Catholic Bishops, "Economic Justice," 436.

13. U.S. Catholic Bishops, "Catholic Social Teaching," 437–440, 443.

14. Immanuel Wallerstein, *The Politics of the World Economy* (New York: Cambridge University Press, 1984), 4, 7, 57.

15. Ibid., 2–4, 7.

16. Ibid., 4–5, 19–20, 34.

17. Ibid., 4.

18. Ibid., 32–36.

19. Ibid., 53–54.

20. Ibid., 20–22, 25, 59, 130.

21. J. Ann Tickner, *Gender in International Relations* (New York: Columbia University Press, 1992), 3–6, 32–4, 42.

22. Ibid., 52–54, 115–116.

23. Ibid., 71–73.

24. Ibid., 74–76.

25. Ibid., 6, 63, 136–137, 146.

26. Ruhollah Khomeini, *Islam and Revolution* (London: K.P.I., 1981), 185–187, 195, 210, 239–240, 275–276, 286.

27. Ibid., 27–28, 210, 276.

28. Ibid., 33, 127.

29. Ibid., 234–235, 286–287, 301, 304.

30. Steven Haft, Tony Thomas, and Paul Junger Witt, *Dead Poets Society* (Burbank: Touchstone Pictures, 1989).

31. Ibid.

32. Ibid.

33. Ibid.

34. Morgenthau, *Politics Among Nations,* 10–11, 31–37.

35. Hobbes, *Leviathan,* 72.

36. Ibid., 72–76.

37. Ibid., 75.

38. Ibid., 80, 102.

39. Ibid., 80.

40. Morgenthau, *Politics Among Nations,* 32.

41. Ibid., 41–43, 151–169.

42. John Locke, *Two Treatises of Government,* intro. Peter Laslett (New York: The New American Library, 1965), chaps. 2, 3; 361–362.

43. Ibid., 400–401, 405.

44. Morgenthau, *Politics Among Nations,* 596.

45. Pope John XXIII, "Pacem in Terris," 230.

46. Saint Thomas Aquinas, *The Political Ideas of St. Thomas Aquinas,* ed. Dino Bigongiari (New York: Hafner Press, 1953), 167–172, 190–192; Pope John XXIII, "Pacem in Terris," 211.

47. Pope John XXIII, "Pacem in Terris," 209–210, 227–228.

48. Wallerstein, *Politics*, 4–5, 29, 38, 50, 83–84.

49. V. Spike Peterson and Anne Sisson Runyan, *Global Gender Issues* (Boulder: Westview Press, 1993), 33–34, 45, 68, 79, 151–152.

50. Peterson and Runyan, *Global Gender Issues*, 152; Tickner, *Gender*, 65.

51. Hobbes, *Leviathan*, 98–100.

52. Thucydides, *The Peloponnesian War*, intro. T. E. Wick (New York: The Modern Library, 1982), 56.

53. Ibid., 40, 41, 56, 66, 95–96, 123, 125–126.

54. Ibid., 353.

55. Ibid., 351.

56. Locke, *Two Treatises*, chaps. 2, 3.

57. Morgenthau, *Politics Among Nations*, 331–334, 596.

58. Pope John XXIII, "Pacem in Terris," 202–209.

59. Ibid., 202–208, 218–228.

60. Synod of Bishops, "Justice in the World," *The Gospel of Peace and Justice*, ed. Joseph Grimillion (Maryknoll, N.Y.: Orbis Books, 1976), 289–290, 298–300.

61. Wallerstein, *Politics*, 4–6, 9–10, 14–17, 33, 50, 80.

62. Tickner, *Gender*, 6, 37–39, 71–76.

63. Peterson and Runyan, *Global Gender Issues*, 19–25, 35–37, 68, 95–98.

64. Sayyed Abul A'la Maududi, *The Economic Problem of Man and Its Islamic Solution*, 3d ed. (Delhi: Markazi Maktaba Jamaat-e-Islami Hind, 1966), 4–18, 23.

65. Idem, *Jihad in Islam*, (Lahore: Islamic Publications Ltd., 1976), 1.

66. Idem, *Unity of the Muslim World*, 4th ed. (Lahore: Islamic Publications Ltd., 1979), 1–4.

67. Immanuel Kant, *Political Writings*, intro. Hans Reiss, trans. H. B. Nisbet, 2d ed. (Cambridge: Cambridge University Press, 1991), 44–45, 221–231.

68. Ibid., 48–49, 164–167, 172–173, 106–108, 128–130.

69. Ibid., 44, 90–91, 102–105, 232.

70. Hugo Grotius, *The Law of War and Peace*, trans. Francis W. Kelsey (Indianapolis: Bobbs-Merrill, 1925), 11–12.

71. Frank Russell, *Theories of International Relations* (New York: D. Appleton-Century, 1936), 150–154.

72. Mikhail Bakunin, *Bakunin on Anarchy*, ed. and trans. Sam Dolgoff (New York: Alfred A. Knopf, 1972), 132–137; idem, *The Political Philosophy of Bakunin*, ed. G. P. Maximov (New York: Free Press, 1953), 84–92.

73. Peterson and Runyan, *Global Gender Issues*, 17–33.

74. Ibid., 81–82, 90–91; Tickner, *Gender*, 37–41.

75. Jane Bartelme and Sarah Caplan, *Legends of the Fall* (Culver City: Columbia Tristar Video, 1995).

76. Khomeini, *Islam and Revolution*, 28, 181–187, 195–197, 210, 237, 239, 257, 275–276, 286–287, 304.

77. Kenneth Waltz, *Man, the State and War* (New York: Columbia University Press, 1959), chaps. 2, 4, 6.

78. St. Augustine, *The City of God*, trans. Gerald G. Walsh and others (Garden City: Image Books, 1958), 317–319, 278–279, 262–263, 434–436.

79. Ibid., 297, 300–301, 321–322, 327–328, 392, 444–447.

80. Idem, *The City of God,* trans. J. H. 2 vols. (London: Griffith, Farran, Okeden, and Welsh, 1890), II: 221.

81. Idem, *The City of God,* 40.

82. Idem, *The City of God,* II: 150.

83. Ibid., II: 57, 162.

84. Ibid., II: 221.

85. Locke, *Two Treatises,* 311–313.

86. Donelan, *Elements,* 112–113, 143, 184–187.

87. Kant, *Political Writings,* 103–108, 160–165, 172–175.

88. V. I. Lenin, "Imperialism, the Highest Stage of Capitalism," *Selected Works,* 3 vols. (New York: International Publishers, 1967), I: 692–695, 721, 725–728, 734–742, 753.

89. Bakunin, *Political Philosophy,* 182–236, 275–300; idem, *Bakunin on Anarchy,* 85–88.

90. John J. Mearsheimer, "Why We Will Soon Miss the Cold War," *The Atlantic Monthly,* August 1990, 46–47.

91. Jean-Jacques Rousseau, *Rousseau on International Relations,* ed. Stanley Hoffmann and David P. Fidler (Oxford: Oxford University Press, 1991), 36.

92. Idem, *Social Contract and Discourses,* 47, 67–69, 88–89.

93. Idem, *International Relations,* 93.

94. Don Hahn, *The Lion King* (Burbank: Walt Disney Co., 1994).

95. National Conference of Catholic Bishops, *The Challenge of Peace: God's Promise and Our Response* (Washington, D.C.: United States Catholic Conference, 1983).

96. Ibid., 22–31.

97. Ibid., 31.

98. James Childress, "Just War Theories," *Theological Studies,* 39 (1978), 436–442.

99. Kant, *Political Writings,* 164–167.

100. Plato, *Gorgias,* trans. Walter Hamilton (New York: Penguin, 1983), 77–79.

101. Ibid., 79.

102. Thucydides, *Peloponnesian War,* 351.

103. Ibid., 173.

104. Ibid., 172–176.

105. Majid Khadduri, *War and Peace in the Law of Islam* (Baltimore: The Johns Hopkins University Press, 1955), 51–57, 64.

106. Maududi, *Jihad in Islam,* 8.

107. Ibid., 5–7, 18, 25–26.

108. Fyodor M. Dostoevsky, *The Diary of a Writer,* trans. Boris Brasol (New York: George Braziller, 1954), 761; Ivan Kireevski, "On the Nature of European Culture and Its Relation to the Culture of Russia," *Russian Intellectual History,* ed. Marc Raeff (New York: Harcourt, Brace and World, Inc., 1966), 176–178.

109. Dostoevsky, *Diary,* 424.

110. Ibid., 780.

111. Ibid., 665–671, 980.

112. Count Leo Tolstoy, "The Soldier's Memento," *Letters and Essays,* trans. Leo Wiener (Boston: Dana Estes and Co., 1905), 27, 41; idem, "Patriotism and Government," *Letters and Essays,* 159, 165–169.

113. Jonathan Dymond, *To That Small But Increasing Number Whether In This Country Or Elsewhere, Who Maintain In Principle And Illustrate By Their Practice, The Great Duty Of Conforming To The Laws Of Christian Morality Without Regard To Dangers Or Present Advantages, This Work Is Respectfully Dedicated* (New York: T. B. Smith, n.d.), 16–18, 31–32, 37, 55, 81–82, 95–98, 307–309.

114. Ibid., 556; idem, "Self-Defence Incompatible with Christianity," *War and the Christian Conscience*, ed. Albert Marrin (Chicago: Regnery Co., 1971), 164–167; idem, *Laws of Christian Morality*, 554–557.

115. Ibid., chap. 19.

116. Mahatma Gandhi, *The Selected Works of Mahatma Gandhi*, ed. Shriman Narayan (Ahmedabad: Navajivan Publishing House, 1968), IV: 8–35.

117. Ibid., IV: 213–215.

118. Ibid., IV: 216–219; Joan V. Bondurant, *Conquest of Violence*, rev. ed. (Berkeley: University of California Press, 1965), 16–32.

119. Gandhi, *Selected Works*, VI: 129–131, 223–226, 260–262.

CHAPTER 4

THE GOALS
OF WORLD POLITICS

The previous chapter examined the actors involved in world politics; the extent to which they are equally capable of influencing political processes; the nature of international society; the causes of war; and the origin and nature of international law. This chapter builds on those ideas by asking the simple question, "What do actors wish to accomplish in the world political arena?" To help us answer this question, we could pose an additional one. To what extent do the goals of actors in domestic politics help us understand the goals of actors in world politics? One could argue that domestic theories of politics can help us think about world politics. Ideas like equality, rights, freedom, order, justice, and power are believed to be ends of domestic political action. Consider for a moment the idea of equality. When one thinks about equality in domestic politics, one may think of whether individuals are inherently equal in some trait such as intellect, strength, or moral stature. Or one could think of equality in terms of whether individuals or groups are equally capable of influencing policymakers. Finally, one might think about whether social, economic, or political equality ought to be the end of political action. We can apply this thinking about equality in domestic political life to world politics. For example, we can explore the extent to which world political actors are inherently equal in their possession of the resources of power, and whether they are equally capable of influencing political action in international relations.

In examining the ends or goals of political action, this chapter explores the more distinctly normative dimension of world politics: what goals actors *ought* to pursue. We might wonder whether various forms of equality *ought* to be an end or goal pursued by actors in the international political system. For example, should equality be limited to the legal equality of states in the eyes of international law, or should the international political system guarantee all states a degree of economic equality—something that would require a massive redistribution of global wealth? Similar arguments can be made regarding liberty, human rights, justice, order, and the environment. Many states seek to guarantee the rights to life, order, and liberty for their citizens; should action in world politics attempt to promote these values internationally? If we believe that liberty is a value that actors in world politics ought to pursue, whose liberty should we promote? Are we protecting the liberty of states to conduct their internal and foreign affairs as they see fit, or should liberty be guaranteed to each individual within a state? If one chooses the latter, the power of the state to order its internal and external affairs would be restricted by international law, which, in securing the freedom of each person in the world, would limit the power of government to do as it wished with its citizens. This chapter discusses these and other values, which serve to inspire the imaginations of those who have thought about world politics.

ON THE PURSUIT OF POWER

For most realists, Machiavelli is right: "he who abandons what is done for what ought to be done, will rather learn to bring about his own ruin than his preservation. A man who wishes to make a profession of goodness in everything must necessarily come to grief among so many who are not good."[1] So it is in world politics. We can hardly plumb the depth to which nations and governments may sink in promoting their own interests at the expense of others. Whether this selfishness is rooted in the sinful condition of humanity or in the self-indulgent behavior of nations, the effect is the same: each nation pursues its own interests. Most often, these interests conflict with those of other nations, and when such conflicts cannot be adjusted by quiet diplomacy, the results are war and the harvest of death. It is little wonder that Georg W. F. Hegel, the German philosopher, refers to history as the slaughter bench of nations.[2] Into this world of international strife each of us is born, and through this world each of us must travel. Those nations that travel the path of world politics with the purpose of promoting justice, peace, liberty, human rights, and greater social and economic equality among the nations of the world will fall victim to those nations whose interest is much more practical: the pursuit of power. Although the sentiments for justice and the rest are lofty goals about which we can dream, inevitably they are pressed to the earth by the realities of power and self-interest in world politics. Generations of dutiful soldiers have paraded into battle with dreams of securing their nation's freedom; all too often, the blinding flash and deafening blast of an artillery shell have, in just one instant, separated body from soul, bearing witness to the triumph of power over dreams.

Given this rather sordid nature of human beings and the lack of any world authority to peacefully order the relations of contentious nations, power—"man's control over the minds and actions of other men"—must be the primary value and objective of those charged with the care of conducting world politics.[3] To that end, national leaders should consciously adopt policies aimed at enhancing the power of their nation. Such policies involve strengthening the economy and the military; providing the population with an adequate standard of living and education; finding, exploiting, and stockpiling the natural resources needed for the nation's security; obtaining public support for the nation's foreign policy; employing diplomacy to settle conflicts of interest; projecting power worldwide to demonstrate resolve; and arming the nation to the teeth. Nations that maximize their power capabilities and relentlessly pursue their interests in world politics will find themselves in a position to provide for their national security, to defend their vital interests around the globe, to exploit international opportunities, and to avoid international disasters that arise in the daily affairs of states.

It is not surprising that Rostislav Andreevich Fadeev, a nineteenth-century Russian nationalist, believed that a nation's leaders should take care that their state amasses power and prudently exercises that power in world politics. He believed that power, and more specifically force, is the arbiter of problems that arise between nations. Because there were no international standards for the exercise of power, Fadeev found no moral reason to justify any use of power. In world politics, great and small nations contest for political, military, and diplomatic supremacy. In this struggle, Fadeev believed that Russia should organize itself internally to exploit its human and natural resources to enhance its military strength. But there is a social dimension to Russian power. Fadeev thought that any great nation is unified by an effective government, religion, and common culture. Russia possessed two of these traits during Fadeev's lifetime: the Russian Orthodox church and the monarchical rule of the czar. The religious unity of the Russian people was promoted by the church, which transmitted a common spiritual life to the people. The rule of the autocratic czar provided a degree of political order to the Russian people. However, the ethnic and cultural diversity of Russia prevented its cultural unity. Given the balance of power in Europe, Russia needed to strengthen its military power. Prussia, France, and England were the major European powers—powers that were hostile to Russia. Given this hostility, Fadeev believed that war was inevitable between Russia and Western Europe. He thought that Russia needed a buffer zone of friendly, Slavic-speaking states in eastern and southeastern Europe; this would give Russia a front line of defense in any conflict with Europe. Since this buffer zone would project Russian power closer to Europe, he believed that Europe would go to war to prevent any form of union of Slavic-speaking peoples with Russia.[4]

There are many critics of the view that power ought to be the ultimate goal of actors in world politics. The Russian nationalist Fyodor Dostoevsky differs with Fadeev on the international use of power. Whereas Fadeev believes that no norms govern the use of power, Dostoevsky's brand of universalistic, Orthodox humanism drives him to conclude that power should be exercised in accordance with the Gospel. Unrepentant of his own Christian idealism, he writes, "There is no reason for being ashamed of one's idealism: this is the same road to the same goal. So that, in substance, idealism is as realistic as realism, and it can never vanish from the world."[5] Applying his idealism to world politics, Dostoevsky argues that the best policy of a great nation is a policy of honor, magnanimity, and justice, even if it opposes the "apparent interests" of the nation. Despite their seeming impracticality, justice, honor, and magnanimity triumph in world politics.[6] Indeed, every great people believes that it should use that power to lead other nations "in a concordant choir toward the final goal preordained for them."[7] This would be as true with Russia as it had been with Rome, France, and Germany. It is Russia's destiny to bequeath its special, universal gift to the world: to make real the brotherhood of man, not just for all Russians, but for all the world's people. Russia should be concerned with exercising its power not by the sword in its own self-interest, but by cleaving to its universal mission to bring divine justice from heaven to earth. In its world historical deeds, Russia seeks the reconciliation of all national controversies in the universal, transcendental love of all humans for one another in the gospel of Christ.[8]

The realist is not convinced by this critique of the exercise of power. He or she queries: are we to believe that God's right and truth have triumphed in the world? Are we to believe that humans have as great a love for those people in other countries as they do for their fellow citizens? Do we see our neighbors willing to live and die for the right of people in other nations to live in peace and harmony? Nay to all these questions! History paints a more sobering picture. Humans organize nations to allow individuals to pursue the good life, as it is broadly defined by their own culture. Once they have attained some measure of well-being, they find it necessary to use the power of the state in world politics to protect what is theirs from those who would take it away. Power is an end that states must pursue in the dirty world of international relations. Justice, freedom, and the brotherhood and sisterhood of humankind are fine ideas, but words do not carry the power of guns and bombs. When push comes to shove in international relations, the cries for justice and brotherhood are inevitably muffled by the roar of the cannon. The struggle for power and the exercise of power—not ideas—rule the world.

The classicist, uneasy with the freewheeling exercise of power and lack of concern for the collective well-being of humankind that the realist demonstrates, argues that the world's nations ought to and often do promote peace, justice, and freedom. Humans, the classicist claims, are by nature social animals, and they form nations to pursue the common good of all members of their society. In today's interdependent world, the common good of each nation cannot be achieved without promoting the common good of all nations. Just as nations promote domestic policies that secure peace, justice, freedom, and the dignity of the individual, so nations promote the same values internationally. According to classicists, realists do not appreciate the role that justice, peace, freedom, and the dignity of the individual play in domestic and international politics. To the classicist's way of thinking, the great political movements and major events in world politics are rooted less in self-interest, and more in achieving the common good. Actors in international politics more often than not create transnational groups and intergovernmental organizations—like the United Nations—to realize these values. To work for international peace and to reduce the level of violence in the world, states have organized the United Nations, which earnestly strives to promote peace. The World Bank, an arm of the UN, makes loans to less developed countries to help them meet the basic needs of their people by encouraging economic development. Other actions by world political actors focus on promoting the common good of all the world's people. The classicist points out that not all wars have been fought out of self-interest, the desire for power, or an interest in balancing the power of major nations; rather, many have been fought to promote or defend deep-seated values that well up in the hearts and consciences of all humans. World War II was fought to secure freedom, justice, and peace among the nations of the world that were threatened by despotic governments in Germany, Italy, and Japan. The recent revolutions that transformed Eastern Europe and the Soviet Union were motivated principally by a desire for national self-determination, justice, and freedom. No longer did these nations wish to live under the repressive yoke of the Soviet Union. Rather, they sought to reach for the freedom that all nations of the world desire: the freedom to live as they liked within the bounds of international law. In sum, to say that nations choose to promote their narrowly defined self-interests and to satisfy their desires for power is short-sighted. Much of the economic and political behavior of states is best explained by the deeply felt desire to bring about a more just, peaceful, and free world order.

To the classicist criticism that there is much cooperation in world politics and that there are overarching values that structure the foreign policy of nations, the realist responds that all this can be explained in terms of self-interest. According to the realist's perspective, the cooperation that so often occurs in the relations of nations is due to the fact that the self-interests of different nations sometimes coincide. The UN, the World Bank, and alliances exist because they serve the interests of the world's powerful nations. The Gulf War is a case in point. The UN did not send troops to the Persian Gulf; rather, the United States put together a formidable international force of nearly thirty nations to fight Saddam Hussein. The United States and other great powers used the United Nations Charter to legitimize or justify the war that was ultimately fought to secure their interest in an inexpensive supply of oil. The realist acknowledges that there are times when nations pursue freedom, justice, and the rest; however, they do so only if it is in their national self-interest. However, when it is not in their interest, nations will cast these higher values to the shifting winds of fortune and self-interest. Take the case of the former Yugoslavia. After the fall of the communist regime, the Yugoslavian provinces of Croatia, Slovenia, Bosnia-Hercegovina, and Macedonia seceded, leaving Serbia and Montenegro to form the Federal Republic of Yugoslavia. Ethnic cleansing—whereby women have been raped; men, women, and children have been forced from their homes; and civilians have been massacred, all in attempts to create ethnically "pure" states—has shocked the conscience of many a person in the Western world. Because U.S. national security interests did not seem to be at stake in Bosnia, which has borne the brunt of the war, the United States avoided military involvement. Many realists believed that there was no need for the United States to become involved in a war that could be better handled by the Europeans, in whose backyard this war was being fought. Ultimately, however, the United States did send troops to Bosnia, as part of a NATO-led peacekeeping force sent to uphold a U.S.-brokered peace agreement signed by the warring parties on December 14, 1995.

World War II followed the same principle. It was in the interest of the United States to join ranks with the Europeans against Hitler and to protect itself from the expanding power of the Japanese in the Pacific after they bombed Hawaii's Pearl Harbor. German and Japanese expansion threatened the U.S. world commercial interests and ultimately its own national security. Fighting for freedom and democracy was a fine excuse for rallying the people behind a war effort; but in actuality, World War II was fought to secure our economic and political self-interest. In sum, self-interest motivates nations.

The liberal is critical of the realist's approach to intervening in the economic affairs of a nation to create "der Machtstaat": the power state. Given the realities of the anarchic international political environment, realists believe that the state must be concerned with maximizing power. National and international economic policies should increase the nation's power capabilities by assuring the success of a vital economy. Take the issues of protective tariffs and capital investment. Realists favor trade policies ensuring that home industries vital to the nation's economic prosperity flourish. When the existence of a critical industry is jeopardized by inexpensive imports, the realist places a tariff or tax on that commodity. The tariff would have the effect of protecting the domestic industry. Because the tariff would significantly increase the price of the imported product and make the domestic product comparatively cheaper, the domestic industry would be able to survive international competition. The same holds true with capital investment.

To promote an ever-expanding economy that increases the power capabilities of a nation, the realist would develop national policies to ensure that corporations and banks would invest in the domestic economy rather than abroad. However, the liberal believes that protective tariffs and restrictive capital investment policies are detrimental to the country. Protective tariffs interfere with and restrict the free flow of goods between nations. In so doing, they limit the productive capacity of all nations. Thus, national economic expansion, so widely valued by the realist for increasing the power of the nation, is hampered by restrictive trade policies. Restrictive capital investment policies that do not permit a company to maximize its ability to make a profit by investing in less developed countries means that the nation's economic system will grow more slowly than it would under more enlightened capital investment policies.

To the realist, the liberal is wrong to believe that the international economy functions in a way that benefits all nations of the world. History proves otherwise. The near-total destruction of the European economy during World War II and the rise of the United States as a world economic and military power permitted the United States to set the terms of international trade among Western-oriented economies through the early 1970s. However, the recent weakening economic position of the United States compared to Germany and Japan proves that the world economy does not benefit all nations equally. When a nation's economic interests are threatened, free trade and capital investment policies that benefit other nations at one's own expense threaten the political power of the nation. When a state's economic well-being is placed in economic jeopardy by new international economic forces, the state must respond with economic policies that expand its power capabilities. To do otherwise is to sell the country into world political bankruptcy.

Radicals such as Rousseau and feminists such as J. Ann Tickner are concerned about the domestic problems that flow from those nations that pursue power as their primary goal in world politics. As we have seen, Rousseau hypothesizes that as soon as one population forms a state, other people—fearing the loss of their independence—do the same. The state of international anarchy in which they find themselves means that each nation has to politically and economically organize to protect itself from the malicious designs of other nations. States magnify their power capabilities by increasing their populations, cultivating science, establishing standing militaries, industrializing, and engaging in world commerce. Yet in so doing, individuals suffer unbearable burdens: the levying of increasingly intolerable taxes to support the military establishment; an industrialized economy that regiments work life around clock and machine so that maximum wealth can be produced to support the state; the evil breath of pollution spewing from factory and home; the spread of epidemics among people densely packed into tenement and factory; the exploitation of labor and the economic inequalities that flow from it; the preoccupation with the self at the expense of others; and the iron-fisted rule of the rich over the poor. The cost: the loss of life, liberty, and compassion for others.[9] J. Ann Tickner holds a similar perspective. The realist's pursuit of international power culminates in a world whose atomic weaponry raises the specter of a nuclear nightmare. Short of that, the need to maintain or increase the power of the state results in an expanding economic system that relentlessly denudes and destroys the environment in search of the natural resources that are necessary to maintain and expand the state's power capabilities. Finally, the pursuit of world political power diverts resources away from government programs that help women and the marginalized and toward the military. Realism reinforces the economic inequality of women. Thus, Rousseau and Tickner argue that the pursuit of *realpolitik,* or power politics, serves to create and reinforce many social, economic, political, and environmental problems or inequalities.[10]

The realist argues that Rousseau and Tickner make a mistake in blaming the pursuit of power for many domestic problems. The realist believes that the focus of all politics, whether domestic or international, is power. As humans are prone to assertiveness and selfishness, the only bond that permits them to live with any degree of civility is power. The pursuit and exercise of power in national or world politics bring a degree of social, political, and industrial order that makes the pursuit of the more valued things in life possible. Human nature being what it is, there will always be those who distinguish themselves economically, socially, and politically. Therefore, economic, social, and political inequalities will always be present in society. These inequalities are due more to personal characteristics of individuals than to the pursuit of power in world politics. To Tickner's criticism that the pursuit of power has created the possibility of nuclear war, encouraged environmental degradation, and reduced opportunities for women, the realist responds that the possession of nuclear weapons preserved the peace between the United States and the Soviet Union during the cold war—no small accomplishment. Problems such as humankind's damage to the environment or the inequalities facing women are largely attributable not to the pursuit of world power, but to national policies. It is too extreme to say that the race for international power is the primary or significant cause of pollution. The process of human life itself produces varying degrees of pollution and environmental degradation. The question is not how to stop the destruction of the environment, but how to manage and minimize the negative impact that human life has on it.

In summary, the realist believes that anarchic international conditions and the nature of human beings require that nations pursue power as their primary concern in world politics. Yet the realist's critics raise many troublesome questions. Is the exercise of power in international relations subject to higher values or the rule of international law? To what extent does the pursuit of international power threaten, not benefit, humankind? Do realist international economic policies lead to trade conflicts, the straining of relations with trading partners, and even to war? Is the pursuit of power a male phenomenon that serves to reinforce patriarchy? Did the struggle for power between the United States and the Soviet Union from World War II to the early 1990s diminish the economic viability of both nations? Does the pursuit of power perpetuate the status quo in world politics? How much does the conduct of world politics affect the social and political well-being of nations? Finally, are we to believe that power is the supreme value that we ought to pursue, or are there other values?

ON EQUALITY AND LIBERTY

To liberals such as John Locke and Immanuel Kant, political power should be exercised to promote equality and freedom. Although liberals may disagree with one another on whether the liberty and equality worth pursuing are those pertaining to nations, to individuals within nations, or both, they nevertheless agree that the power should be used to defend or promote these two values. Far from being an animal sunk in the fomes of sin and selfishness, liberals broadly agree that humans can live peacefully with one another within the laws prescribed by their respective communities. Indeed, the state exists to secure the freedom and equality of all citizens before the law. The government also serves to make life more convenient for individuals. Modern representative governments that admit a degree of popular influence to the decision-making process free the individual from the necessity of being involved in the everyday conduct of politics. By creating police forces to enforce the law, government also frees individuals from having to handle their everyday neighborhood security problems. Thus, government protects and frees individuals to pursue their own lives without excessive governmental interference.[11]

Many liberals believe that political power in world politics ought to be directed toward ensuring the freedom and equality of nations before the law. Nations are certainly unequal in material characteristics: population, natural resources, size, economic development, political development, military capabilities, and national unity. But these inequalities should not prevent states from guaranteeing each state the freedom to determine its own constitution, form of government, economic system, and laws. Each nation should have the right to self-determination and be free from the intervention of another state in its domestic affairs. Similarly, nations should be free to conduct their relations with other nations as they desire as long as they do not violate the norms, customs, and laws accepted by the international community. Indeed, international law must restrict the freedom of the most powerful international actors, so that the freedom of all nations can be preserved.[12]

According to the liberal viewpoint, each nation, no matter how large or small, should be guaranteed equality before international law and equality of opportunity. That is to say, international law should be applied to all states—regardless of the power they wield in world politics, their culture, their size, or their political ideology. The law being applied to all countries equally, no nation is above the laws that regulate the international economic, cultural, and political intercourse between states. The equality of nations before international law forbids discrimination against a nation because of its culture, form of government, or political ideology. Although those who break the law of nations may be punished by the international community, those who become members of the community of nations should bear no discrimination against others. Liberals also believe that the equality of nations before the law implies another form of equality: equality of opportunity. It is not the function of the international community to take nations of unequal social, economic, and political development and use its coercive power to equalize these differences. In economic matters, the international redistribution of wealth and capital between rich and poor nations is not a power that has been granted to any international body such as the UN. To do so would ultimately diminish the freedom of states to dispose of their wealth as they desire within the law of nations. Helping those countries in need of economic, political, and social development is best left to the nation-states to decide. Indeed, a capitalist world system that permits all nations to benefit from the free flow of trade and capital is the best way to remedy the economic disparities between rich and poor countries.[13]

For his part, Kant leaves the enforcement of international law to a federation of states. Where states exist in a state of nature with no power capable of ordering the relations between them, Kant believes that the enforcement of international law is problematic and war inevitable. Kant is convinced that the free, independent nations of this world will form a federation capable of enforcing that law that permits the greatest amount of freedom to coexist among the world's nations. In limiting the freedom of nations to do as they desire, Kant seeks to secure the territorial integrity and right to self-determination of each nation. He hopes that members of this federation of states, similar to the UN or League of Nations, will voluntarily agree to enforce international law and provide for the freedom and security of the member states. This federation would seek to deter any state from violating basic principles of international law. In questions of war and peace, Kant believes that no nation would start a war with another nation if the remaining states arrayed themselves against the potential aggressor. Kant is under no illusion that a federation of nations exercising its collective security will usher in an era of perpetual peace. As long as humans are inclined to disobey law and antagonize fellow humans, the risk of war remains. However, the federation of states is Kant's attempt to end the state of nature in which each nation arrogates to itself the freedom to go to war when it pleases and warring nations put "perpetual peace in the vast grave where all the horrors of violence and those responsible for them would be buried."[14]

Some realists are skeptical about the belief that states should promote the internal and external freedom of all states in the international system. In point of fact, states often pursue policies of power and domination, rather than the freedom of other nations. When one nation's power is not checked by another state or group of states, that nation will dominate other states economically, culturally, and/or militarily. As discussed earlier, Athenian power in the Aegean prior to the beginning of the Peloponnesian War in 431 B.C. surpassed that of its main rival, Sparta. Athens magnified its military power to the extent that it was able to demand tribute from the city-states that were part of its Delian League. Thus, Athens transformed the league from one that protected the free city-states from Persia to one that shackled these tributary states to Athenian imperial ambition. As one Sicilian put it, in the struggle against the Persians, the Athenians did not fight to secure the liberty of the other Greek city-states; rather, Athens sought to subject its fellow Greeks to its own empire. With that, the Greek city-states traded the mastery of the Persian Empire for that of Athens: "wiser than the first, but wiser for the evil."[15] To maintain its power over the other Greek city-states and Sparta, Athens forcibly prevented nations from defecting to Sparta's Peloponnesian League, as we saw in the case of Mitylene. Athens also intervened in the internal affairs of its neighbors. In the Corcyraean civil war that pitted the common people (democrats) against the rich (oligarchs), the Athenians intervened in such a way that supported the democratic faction.[16] Clearly, when one state becomes as hegemonic as Athens had become, the freedom of weaker states is sacrificed on the altar of power. The liberal, who argues that states should strive to secure the internal and external freedom of all states, has little understanding of the dark forces that motivate nations to secure and use power to their own advantage.

The realist preoccupation with power obscures the depth of commitment that nations have to the freedom and equality of nations before the law. The liberal thinks that nations do differ in the amount of political power they wield in world politics. The liberal also believes that powerful nations have abused their power and adopted imperialistic policies. However, two features of world politics reinforce the international commitment to freedom and equality: an international consensus that the freedom of states and equality of nations before the law are goals worth pursuing, and the spread of representative governments throughout the world. First, there is a broad consensus that nations possess the right to self-determination and that no nations should be above international law, and it follows that nations are less likely to violate the principles of freedom and equality. The invasion of Kuwait by Iraq, a violation of the principle of self-determination, was roundly criticized by the community of nations, and the Gulf War served to reinstate the legitimate government of Kuwait. Second, the spread of representative forms of government that seek to secure the right to life, liberty, and equality of all before the law has implications for world politics. Democratic nations that believe that life, liberty, and legal equality ought to be secured to all citizens are likely to believe that nations have a right to exist, that they should have the liberty to manage their own internal affairs and conduct their foreign policies as they desire within the norms permitted by international law, and that no nation should be above international law. In fact, after winning the cold war, the United States has used its international political power and influence to promote the principles of freedom and equality worldwide. Contrary to what a realist would expect, the United States has not pursued imperialist policies of world economic and political domination.

To the radical, the liberal pursuit of international freedom and equality of opportunity is simply a justification for the exploitation of weaker nations by the economically and politically stronger nations. Although the liberal believes that liberty, equality of nations before the law, and equality of opportunity should be guaranteed to the actors in the international political and economic system, the reality is much different. Successful capitalistic states manage to secure the greater share of world economic and political power, and they use that power to support a capitalist world system. Though liberals argue that less developed nations have an equality of opportunity to become wealthier through economic development, the fact remains that the poor nations of the Southern Hemisphere have not been able to do so. The radical argues that the vehicles for capitalist investment in these countries, the multinational corporation and the World Bank, develop policies that prevent these nations from becoming more prosperous. MNCs siphon off profits that are made in less developed countries and divert them to their own use, and the World Bank lends money that cannot be easily paid back without stifling economic development in the less developed nation. As a result, less developed countries have not moved toward greater economic equality with developed nations. Rather, they have become poorer and increasingly economically dependent on the core countries.[17]

Both Islamic fundamentalists and radicals agree that the freedom of less developed nations to manage their own affairs has been restrained by core nations. The liberal belief that nations have the ability to control their domestic affairs flies in the face of reality. Multinational corporations and their parent governments have penetrated less developed countries and exercised their power in ways that prevent these governments from exercising their own power to govern their countries. Ayatollah Khomeini argued that the Iranian government signed the 1961 Vienna Convention that gave foreign military advisors immunity from any crimes committed in Iran because it wanted a $200 million loan from the United States. In Khomeini's view, the Iranian government "sold our independence, [and] reduced us to a level of a colony."[18] According to Khomeini, Iran allowed its cultural, economic, military, and political affairs to be manipulated for the benefit of the United States. In placing the Shah of Iran on the Iranian throne and by fostering Western life and culture in an Islamic country, the United States and Britain violated the rights of the Iranian people to erect their own government and to live by their own customs and traditions. In this imperial environment, the UN Universal

Declaration of Human Rights was meaningless. The shah, a puppet of the United States, prohibited Iranians from fully exercising their Islamic faith: a right guaranteed by the declaration.[19] Thus, the penetration of indigenous economic and political structures by other nations deprives less developed countries of their right to self-determination.

To those who charge that liberalism does not promote equality of opportunity and freedom, the liberal responds that such critics overestimate the power that multinational corporations and nations exert in less developed nations. Multinational corporations are not the spiders of the world economic system, weaving a web to catch unsuspecting third world nations, and then sucking the lifeblood from them. Rather, the proliferation of multinationals has allowed less developed nations to choose among those MNCs that will truly benefit their country. By negotiating the percentage of profits that the MNC returns to the developing country and by arranging for the nationalization of the MNC at some future date, the less developed nation can use the multinational to spur its economic development. Thus, the less developed country is free to control its economic destiny to a greater degree than critics admit, and as an ultimate measure of freedom, less developed countries can always opt out of the world capitalistic economy and bar MNCs from entering its territory. Regarding equality of opportunity, the liberal holds that the international economic system does not promise that all the nations of the world will become wealthy, economically developed countries. Poorer nations that desire to develop modern capitalist systems can, however, use the economic resources that are available in their own country, can borrow money from the World Bank and other international banks, and can seek developmental assistance from the UN and from advanced capitalist nations. Unfortunately, successful economic development of less developed nations is stymied by corrupt political officials, according to the liberal apologist. Thus, problems of economic development lie more in the politics and culture of a nation than in the capitalist world economy.[20]

As we have seen, the classicist believes that nations should strive to work for the common good of humanity. A certain level of economic equality commensurate with the dignity of each nation should be secured to all countries. The classicist thinks that the liberal, international capitalist system cannot adequately distribute international wealth among the nations of the world. One problem is that the world capitalist system is concerned with profit, not the common good of all humankind. In the drive for profits, multinational corporations will pull their operations out of their home country and move them to a less developed country where they can take advantage of inexpensive labor and lower operating costs. In both cases, the workers are treated unjustly. Workers who lose their job in the home country often find it difficult to find other employment, especially if they live in small communities with little hope of finding other jobs. In the developing country, the multinational can pay wages so low that workers cannot adequately support their families, dooming them to poverty and malnutrition. If the multinational's profits are repatriated (sent back) to the rich countries, the developed rich nations benefit at the expense of poor nations. By putting international business in the service of profit rather than in the service of the common good of human beings, vast inequalities of wealth are produced between rich and poor nations. International business transactions must therefore always be conducted with an eye toward justice, not simply profits. Free trade raises particular problems that accentuate economic disparities between developed and less developed nations. Underdeveloped nations rely most often on their natural resources and on agricultural produce to increase their wealth. As less developed nations, they lack the large industrial and manufacturing sectors that would enable them to produce more profitable goods for sale to developed countries. Unfortunately, natural resources and agricultural produce are subject to wide swings in world supply and demand. With prices often depressed, the natural resource and agricultural trade brings in few dollars to support needed economic development efforts. Poor countries remain poor, and the rich countries become richer still. A classicist solution to this problem would be to pay a fair price for natural resources sold to developed nations: a price that may indeed be above the price set by world supply and demand for those products. In short, whether the issues are wages or the price paid for natural resources, the classicist believes that the world capitalist system should be governed by principles of justice that permit a greater degree of economic equality to exist between the rich and poor nations of the world.[21]

For the liberal, there are no international, moral norms to guide businesses and nations in international business transactions. Given the diversity of peoples, moral values, and religions in the world, the liberal doubts that any group of international actors could develop moral guidelines for the world economy. Even if one could, questions of morality are, in the liberal's view, best left to the individual actors themselves. Though there is no world community with a governing authority whose end is to define and mete out worldwide economic justice, each nation possesses the authority to determine what norms, if any, should be applied to economic transactions within states. The nation-state is guaranteed the international right of self-determination. This means that the people of that nation are the ones who can determine how much inequality of wealth constitutes a social injustice. For rich or poor nations, the best policy is to establish a government that is committed to promoting individual economic freedom. By giving individuals and groups the freedom to start their own businesses and by extending to labor the right to bargain for a decent wage, this economic freedom will permit individuals to launch into the economic world and use their talents to earn a living for themselves and their families. By admitting MNCs that will best serve the needs of their people, by encouraging internal economic development, and by securing international loans, less developed nations can become successful trading partners. By integrating themselves into the world economy, nations will find that they can successfully market their natural resources, agricultural products, manufactured items, industrial goods, and a variety of services. The great body of hard-working people will become prosperous, and this prosperity will reduce the economic gaps between individuals within each nation while diminishing worldwide economic inequalities between rich and poor countries.[22]

This discussion of liberty and equality has raised many questions. Is it clear that nations, multinational corporations, and churches pursue policies that are inclined to promote liberty and equality in world politics? Certainly the Catholic church and other religious organizations have argued in favor of protecting the freedom and equality of states in the international political system. Liberals believe that multinational corporations, in pursuing their own interest in making a profit, have increased the overall economic activity in poor nations and offered many individuals new paths to economic prosperity. Nations are broadly committed to the political principles of the freedom and equality of all nations before international law. In fact, these states have organized such bodies as the United Nations and NATO to secure the right of national self-determination. However, to some observers this picture is not as rosy as the liberal would have us believe. They ask us to wonder about a few questions. Is not the primary concern of nations and MNCs the security and enhancement of their own power? Will not any actor in world politics throw off the supposed shackles of international law and morality if it believes that it is in its best interest to do so, and if it believes it can be successful in so doing? Does the legal equality of states mean anything when faced with the existence of great powers like the United States, Japan, and Germany, which wield their economic and political power for their own advantage? Do not the powerful nations (or actors within nations) really control international economic and political life? All these questions point to another question: should international actors promote justice in world politics?

ON JUSTICE

For many classicists, justice is rooted in the human soul. A classicist might argue that human beings are political animals innately inclined by their Creator to do good and to avoid evil. The rational capacity is capable of understanding those moral or natural laws that ought to guide humans to know and do good. Many Christians also believe that the Creator has revealed divine law in the form of the Ten Commandments and the teachings of Christ. This law serves to guide humans when reason is insufficient to know with certainty what is good and what is evil. Endowed with reason, free will, and bodily appetites, humans can order their soul and body in a way that permits their intellect or reason to guide the satisfaction of their appetites. A properly ordered soul is a just soul. When individuals apply their reason to know what is moral or ethical and when they order their appetites in a way that permits them to live within that law, the soul is just and at peace with itself. However, if the appetites gain control of the soul and rebel against that moral law known by reason, then injustice reigns in the soul. It becomes plagued with guilt and is no longer at peace with itself.[23]

As humans can choose to be just or unjust, so a social ordering of human beings within a state can be just or unjust. In the broadest sense, justice is a matter of rendering each its due. But what is one's due? The classicist might argue that what is one's due is based upon those characteristics that are part of our nature. As humans we have needs for food, water, shelter, clothing, and clean air. As rational creatures we have a desire to know about the natural, divine, and human worlds in which we live. We possess a free will that permits us to choose between good and evil. As social and political animals, humans organize themselves to create states that permit individuals to freely exercise their will, to develop their rational capacities, and to fulfill their basic needs. These guarantees take the form of rights. Thus, individuals should be guaranteed the right to freedom of religion, speech, press, and migration; they should be given the right to own property, to work, to a living wage, to assembly, to political participation, to education, and to an adequate standard of living; and they should be extended the right to life, to equality before the law, and to a fair trial. Indeed, a just society would secure these rights to each individual, and it would oblige each to contribute to the good of his or her family, community, and nation.[24]

Just as humans are knit together in the common pursuit of policies that permit all people to meet their spiritual and material needs, so the international community must be ordered in a way that permits all the nations of the world to fulfill the material and spiritual needs of their citizens. But it is no longer possible for individual nations to provide for the needs of their citizens. The world has become so economically interdependent that the economic performance and actions of one nation affect the livelihoods of citizens in another nation. But the economic development that has taken place throughout the world in the last four hundred years has been extremely uneven. In this world economy, some countries have industrialized and are capable of meeting the basic needs of all their citizens. But elsewhere in the world economy, there are catastrophic pockets of poverty, disease, starvation, and death. For many people in poor countries, the world and domestic economic systems are unjust because they do not provide the food, health care, clean water and air, and educational opportunities that permit human beings to live a fully human life. Politically, there are countries throughout the world where elite rule in their own interest. They employ torture, terrorism, and fear of bodily injury to cow people into servile obedience. They deny their peoples their fundamental human rights to freedom of religion, speech, press, education, and participation in the governing process. To right the social, economic, and political injustices in the world requires the vigilance and obligation of all peoples and nations of the world to work with solidarity to promote the fundamental rights of all peoples. Justice requires that rich nations aid poor nations; that multinational corporations use their economic power to improve the economic conditions of their workers by paying a just wage; and that the nations of the world work to establish a just economic and political order.[25]

As humans form a state to secure their individual rights and join together in solidarity to secure the rights of others, so the international political order requires that nations of the world come together in solidarity to specify and secure the rights of all nations and to recognize their duty to respect and promote these rights. Among those rights that nations possess are the right to existence, self-determination or self-development, and equality and freedom under international law. Each nation possesses its own dignity and acts as a cultural unit to promote the good of its members. Regardless of a nation's culture, racial composition, or supply of natural resources, it ought to be treated with dignity and respect. Nations should enjoy the right to self-determination or self-development. The international order should secure the right of nations to determine their own social, economic, and political organization as well as their own culture. Nations should be in control of their own destiny and thus should not be subject to manipulation by other international actors, including nations, terrorist groups, labor organizations, and multinational corporations. States should also have the freedom to engage in international relations with other actors as long as that intercourse is conducted within international law and custom. States have the right to engage in diplomacy, to conduct trade fairly, to form or leave alliances, and to remain neutral in international disputes. However, these rights have corresponding duties. The right to existence brings with it the duty to recognize the legitimate existence of other states. The right to fair trade brings with it the duty to treat trading partners fairly. The right to self-determination brings with it the obligation to recognize the right of other states to chart their own destinies. However, national governments do not have the unrestricted right to self-determination. Rather, they have the obligation to respect and promote the rights of their citizens. If a nation wantonly violates the rights of its citizens, it is the duty of other states to take the necessary steps (from moral suasion to economic sanctions to war) to put an end to that violation. Thus, justice between nations is possible only if the nations of the world take the necessary actions to promote and secure those rights due to all countries.[26]

The liberal is uncomfortable with the classicist approach to justice. The liberal believes that the classicist recognizes the importance of commutative justice but goes too far in pushing for distributive and social justice. For the liberal, commutative justice is based upon the freedom of individuals to enter into and execute a contract or agreement. Take a social contract. Locke suggests that a comfortable life in a state of nature is impossible without a government to ensure greater obedience to the law. To put an end to inconveniences in the state of nature, individuals agree to a contract between themselves and between themselves and their government. All agree that in return for their obedience, the government will secure each individual's rights to life, liberty, and property. Commutative justice is achieved if the terms of the agreement are kept: as long as the government secures the rights of each individual and does not violate them, and as long as the citizen obeys the law. In international affairs, states mutually agree to create and respect the rights of nations, and international justice prevails when nations live in accordance with the rights and laws they create. Similarly, the management of a multinational corporation and the government of a less developed nation may enter into an agreement that involves paying subsistence wages. The basis for paying the subsistence wage may be an oversupply of available labor in the less developed country. Thus, as long as both the less developed country and the MNC live up to their agreement, there is no injustice in offering a subsistence wage. But the liberal believes that the classicist is wrong in abandoning commutative justice for distributive justice. Distributive justice allocates benefits and prescribes penalties on the basis of the dignity of the individual and the position that person occupies in an organization. In the case of the multinational corporation and less developed country, a subsistence wage may allow a person to earn a living but may deny the worker access to adequate health care or housing. Because a subsistence wage violates the dignity of the individual, the agreement is unjust. Similarly, the liberal sees the classicist's call for a worldwide redistribution of wealth from rich to poor countries as being wrongheaded. The classicist argues that each nation has the right to self-development. In a world where there are rich nations that have excess capacity to finance self-development and poor nations lacking capital resources for economic development, the rich nations have an obligation to contribute capital or other resources to make the right of self-development real for the poor nations. Whereas this may be justice to the classicist, to the liberal it is an injustice. According to the liberal, distributive justice prescribes taking rightly earned wealth away from a nation whose citizens have worked hard and sacrificed much to achieve their level of economic well-being. The liberal would also argue that the international economic system justly rewards nations for the sacrifices and efforts they have made to finance their own self-development and justly penalizes nations that have squandered their self-development resources. Therefore, the economic success of less developed countries rests with commutative, not distributive, justice: each state ought to enjoy equal opportunity to enter into whatever contractual agreements it believes are necessary to improve its economic and social well-being. Compared with other types of economies, a capitalist world economy is better equipped to realize the human aspiration for justice.[27]

The classicist might respond that there are serious problems with commutative justice. Two assumptions upon which the argument of commutative justice is based are, according to the classicist, of doubtful validity in application. First, commutative justice requires that the parties be equal in bargaining power. Equality is important so that the terms of the agreement represent something that equally benefits (or penalizes) each party to the contract. When parties are equal in bargaining power, one party is not likely to be in a position to take advantage of the other party. Second, commutative justice assumes that each party is *freely* entering into the agreement. An agreement signed by a person with a gun to his or her head can hardly be called an agreement. According to the classicist, commutative justice falls short in the world economy because the agreements are often made by unequals in power. As a result, such agreements are not always freely made. A relatively weak less developed country, in order to stave off mass starvation, may feel forced to make a distasteful agreement with a multinational corporation whose terms are subsistence wages rather than a just wage that allows the worker and the worker's family to meet their basic needs. Thus, commutative justice often results in real injustices against nations or individuals.[28] Similarly, alliances and other agreements between states are not, as the liberal argues, based on freedom and equality. Nations that are economically and militarily powerful structure agreements and alliances in ways that do not provide equal benefits to their less powerful partners. You may recall Thucydides' comment that right or justice is a matter for equals in power. This suggests that when there is no equality, there is no justice; the stronger can determine the nature of relations between nations with reference to their own good, not to the good of all nations.[29]

Realists and many feminists share a common concern about the classicist's belief that justice is grounded in an objective moral order rooted in God. According to feminists, the existing national and international orders are socially unjust. Men have occupied positions of economic, political, and social power over women, and men have used those positions to maintain their control over women. Socially and economically, women have been restricted to the home and are made dependent on husbands who, because they bring home paychecks, wield economic influence over women. Without income of their own, women are dependent on the income of their husband; in some cases, women are reluctant to leave abusive relationships, for fear that they will be unable to support themselves and their children. Politically, women have not had access to the political process that determines the entitlements, laws, and social programs that frame their opportunities and social condition. The justification for this, feminists often point out, is a philosophy often trotted out by classicists that argues that women and men were made naturally different by God, that women are naturally inclined to nurturing, and that the home is the natural place for women because they have so much to offer their children. Thus, a socially just order is one that reflects the natural differences between women and men: women in the home and men in the public world of business and of domestic and international politics.[30] To many feminists, this philosophy—which seeks to justify the unequal way women and men are treated—is a social construction of a patriarchal society. Many men and women have "bought into" a social myth of natural inequality that perpetuates the hegemony of men over women. A socially just society can arise only when women move into positions of economic, social, and political power; if they destroy the myth of natural differences; and if they create a society in which both men and women are empowered to pursue those things they desire in life.

The English philosopher Thomas Hobbes also rejects the classicist's view that justice is rooted in a divine order (although there are some who argue that Hobbes is not an atheist). For Hobbes, the state of nature is a war of everyone against everyone, in which there is no law to govern the relations of humans. With no law to determine what actions are just or unjust, no justice exists in the state of nature; there is no legal or moral measure to determine when people have "stepped over the line" of the law. Whereas classicists are inclined to argue that divine law exists everywhere and is eternal, Hobbes's belief that no law exists in the state of nature suggests that there is no divine, natural, or higher law to which all individuals ought to turn in the state of nature. If there is no divine or natural law, then all law and justice must be made by humans. Indeed, Hobbes argues that law and justice arise only when humans gather together to create it. The notion that law and justice are human creations applies to world politics, in which nations exist in a moral void. There is no natural, moral, or higher law governing the relations of nations. All international law and justice emanate from international actors. For example, the principle of self-determination as outlined in the UN Charter, was created by the agreement of some fifty nations. Thus, the right of self-determination is a creation of humans interested in securing states certain rights. Thus, the classicist's notion that there is a natural, moral law that ought to direct the relations of nations is a myth; all international law is human-made.[31]

Yet the classicist believes that feminists and Hobbesian realists are mistaken in arguing that all international justice and law are a social construction; there are good reasons to believe that some universal laws and rights exist. In discerning the nature of human beings, reason can abstract certain rights that ought to be guaranteed to the individual by the international community. God, the author of human nature, has inclined humans to self-preservation by giving them appetites for food and clean water, for example. The preservation of human life therefore requires nations and the international community to secure all individuals the right to food and clean water. These rights are universal, rooted in divine creation, and are in no way relative to each individual, society, or nation. Whoever and wherever they are, humans depend upon adequate nutrition and safe drinking water for their very existence. Thus, there is a divine or natural source for the fundamental laws and rights that ought to govern the relations of nations, and the international community should guarantee that these laws and rights are observed by all nations and international actors. Only when all humans are given their rights will justice be done.

Some realists argue that nations may pursue justice, but that it is not the type of justice the classicists favor. According to the realist viewpoint, the classicist does not realize that justice in international relations is simply the advantage of the stronger. In the struggle for political power, some nations will naturally rise to the top of the international political order and seek to frame the world political order to their own advantage. Backed by military and political power, these powerful nations are able to manipulate international law, economics, and political power to benefit themselves at the expense of others. Some Islamic fundamentalists believe that the Western state system is manipulated by the Western powers to benefit themselves at the expense of poorer nations. As you will recall, Ayatollah Khomeini was particularly sensitive to the economic, military, political, and cultural hegemony of the United States and Britain in Iran. Khomeini saw the Western domination of less developed countries as motivated by the need to devour an ever-increasing supply of natural resources to stoke the fires of material gain and greed.[32] In pursuit of these resources, the West had not stopped at violating some fundamental principles of Islamic law and justice. According to both Khomeini and Maududi, the West has trampled on the international right to self-determination by establishing puppet governments that give it access to inexpensive oil. Within Muslim states, these puppet governments have violated the moral sensibilities of Muslims by tolerating adultery and alcohol and have replaced Allah's law with that of human-made law. Thus, the West has used its superior political and military power in international relations to foist its own notions of justice on the less developed world. These injustices can be removed by cleansing Islamic countries of Western cultural imperialism and replacing it with Islamic culture. In laying down His law and in making it known through the teachings and actions of Mohammed, Allah gave humankind the essential laws that should frame a just social order. These laws establish the rights and duties of each individual, and they determine the relationship that exists between classes of people in the Islamic social order. Each person should be treated equally before the law, and no one should be arbitrarily denied his or her God-given rights. As women and men were created differently, women and men have different rights and responsibilities. A socially just society is one in which men and women find their natural places in the social order: men as breadwinners and authority figures, and women as mothers and homemakers.[33]

Is justice in world politics simply the interest of the stronger? The classicist may concede that there have been nations that pursued justice as if it were the rule of the stronger. However, the classicist would argue that these states have been the exception and not the rule. States that pursue policies transgressing the rights of other states and their citizens do so in the mistaken belief that this is in their interest. They rationally miscalculate that their interest is in running roughshod over the rights of other nations. This is the policy that Athens adopted and it led to its defeat in the Peloponnesian War. Hitler's invasion of France, Poland, and Czechoslovakia, and the Soviet Union's occupation of Eastern Europe, sought to benefit stronger nations at the expense of international justice, which seeks to guarantee each nation the right to sovereignty and self-determination. Those states that suffered under the rule of their captors were later vindicated. Europe ultimately rid itself of Hitler and the Soviet Union. The right to national self-determination, the equality of nations under international law, the extension of human rights to all peoples of the world, and the freedom of states to conduct their own foreign policy are concepts that were known and reaffirmed by the nations that fought Hitler and attempted to limit the expansion of the Soviet Union. Unfortunately, under a liberal international order, obedience to international law and rights will be imperfect. From time to time, nations will choose to pursue their own self-interest to the detriment of international justice. There will be periods of time in which nations of the world will serve for many years under the yoke of oppression because the world community is not sufficiently committed to rendering justice. Only in a world where some international body has the authority and coercive power to secure the rights of nations and individuals is a just international order possible.

Put down your book for a minute and reflect on what justice means to you. How would you define it? Is international justice guided by a higher law? Is justice simply a matter of consensus among nations? Is justice the advantage of the stronger? How is justice related to the rights of states and of the citizens of states? From where are these rights derived? Do they originate from God, agreements between states, or international customs and traditions? Is there a natural justice, or is justice based upon human artifice or convention? Should international law be related in some important way to justice? What motivates nations and other actors in developing the policies that they do: justice, power, equality, or freedom? These are some of the questions that have been raised in this section. Other questions center on the ends pursued by actors in world politics. Let us turn to world domination or imperialism.

ON IMPERIALISM

In the broadest sense, imperialism can be defined as the policy of extending the power or rule of one nation over other nations. History is replete with examples of imperialism. Athens, it has been argued, expanded its economic and military control over many of the Greek city-states in the Aegean. In the aftermath of the Peloponnesian War, Alexander the Great of Macedonia, who lived in northern Greece, swept down from his mountain home and conquered the squabbling Greek city-states; he subsequently extended his political control over the Middle East and northern Africa to the Western parts of India. Rome grew from a small city into an empire, as it economically, militarily, and politically incorporated the area around the Mediterranean and Western Europe under its rule. During the discovery period of European history, European nations launched out to colonize parts of the world that were heretofore unknown. Footholds were gained in North and South America, Africa, Asia, Australia, and the Antarctic. The colonization of the New

World by European countries ended in cultural, military, economic, and/or political relationships that permitted the mother countries to rule their colonies. Finally, the first half of the twentieth century was not without German, Italian, and Japanese attempts to establish their own empires. Prompted by a Marxist-Leninist ideology, the Soviet Union extended its empire over Eastern Europe at the end of World War II. Perhaps the net result of the U.S. "victory" in the cold war is that the United States has positioned itself to extend its capitalist, democratic ideology over other nations.

As realists Hans Morgenthau and Kenneth Thompson demonstrate, there are military, economic, and cultural forms of imperialism.[34] Military (or more broadly, political) imperialism is what normally comes to people's minds when they think about imperialism. Alexander the Great and Rome established much of their empires by military conquest. Nations that would not voluntarily submit to the political rule of Alexander or Rome were forced into submission by the sword. Economic imperialism focuses on the economic domination of countries by ones that are more economically powerful. Some argue that Europe's real motive in colonizing large chunks of the non-European world was economic. Beginning in the Renaissance, European mother countries created colonies in an attempt to obtain land, natural resources, labor, and markets for capital and manufactured goods. Radicals suggest that today's wealthy capitalistic countries exploit less developed nations, using less developed economies to benefit their own. Finally, cultural imperialism permits one nation to change the fundamental values of another. Morgenthau believes that this form of imperialism "aims not at the conquest of territory or at the control of economic life, but at the conquest and control of the minds of men as an instrument for changing the power relations between two nations."[35] In the mid-twentieth century, Islamic fundamentalists were particularly concerned with the spread of Western culture in traditionally Islamic states. They believed that the West was engaged in an attempt to remake the world in its own image, subverting the traditional Islamic values that gave meaning to life for so many Muslims. Through Western television, movies, music, and education, Western culture was ever-so-steadily laying hold on the Muslim mind.

In most cases, these three forms of imperialism were not analytically distinct but were mutually supporting. Whereas military imperialism led a nation to conquer another nation, governing a conquered nation—if governing is considered something beyond military rule—inevitably involved some form of "cultural imperialism." Carrying the "white man's burden" of spreading Western culture to "uncivilized" African and Asian nations, the Europeans faced a problem of how to bring non-Western peoples to the point at which they could exercise Western-style self-governance. If the inhabitants of non-Western countries were to become members of the Western state system, then they needed to be "educated" in a way that permitted them to exercise self-rule and accept the Western norms of international behavior. Similarly, cultural and economic imperialism often reinforce each other.

Dependency theorists argue that the spread of capitalism and bourgeois Western culture were closely linked. Capitalism, to be successful, rested upon a certain way of thinking about the world. The values of individualism, individual responsibility, respect for private property, freedom, competition, and materialism, for example, were necessary for capitalism to take root in a modernizing society. In promoting capitalism in parts of the world where it did not exist, the bourgeoisie of developing countries had to transform the indigenous culture to one that supported capitalist economic development.

Ayatollah Khomeini and Maududi develop an imperial theory of international politics. Culturally, Islamic fundamentalists believe that Islam is a universal religion that should be spread to all nations of the earth. Allah, the Father of all human beings, created Adam and Eve from whom the rest of human life descended, according to Maududi. Thus, all human beings on all continents are brothers and sisters, united in Allah. Allah, through Mohammed, revealed His law that should serve to direct each individual and the community toward righteousness. All who follow in the path of Mohammed are righteous and worthy of respect. Distinctions of race, color, language, and nationality form no basis on which to favor one human being over another.[36] Thus, there is a spiritual, moral community of Muslim believers that transcends all temporal distinctions that characterize the diversity of human life on earth. This view of human unity and of the dignity of the individual forms the basis of Maududi's view of equal rights. Mankind is a single race, and Allah, through Mohammed, gives all human beings equal rights, but with those rights come certain obligations.[37] Thus, Maududi believes that there is a community of Muslims who are guided by divine law. This spiritual community includes Muslims around the world—regardless of the nation in which they live, the color of their skin, the language they speak, or the amount of wealth they possess. The unity of humankind forms the basis upon which Maududi and Khomeini argue that Muslims should spread their faith to all the peoples of the earth.[38] The question that both Maududi and Khomeini pose is this: given the current political and economic condition of world politics, by what means shall Islam be spread to non-Islamic societies?

For Maududi, world politics presents certain obstacles to the spread and political triumph of Islam. Maududi believes that all people of the world descend from Adam and Eve, the father and mother of humankind, and all people are brothers and sisters to one another. Differences in race, language, physical features, and nationality are accidental, not essential, differences; and these differences are not grounds for discriminating against a person or nationality. In fact, the division of the world into nations benefits humankind. It permits each people with a common history, geographic circumstance, and language to organize its society in a way that can best promote an Islamic way of life. Collectively, Islamic nations should work together to defend Islam from those desiring to conquer them and they should jointly strive to promote Islam abroad.[39] However, those nations that have drifted from Islamic religious life and culture, or those non-Islamic nations that have refused to acknowledge the spiritual supremacy of Islam, have created a bifurcated conception of international relations based on the nations of Islam (dar-al-Islam) and the nations in the world of war (dar-al-harb). The vehemence with which Khomeini and Maududi speak against the Western nations is grounded in their belief in the spiritual supremacy of Islam compared to the spiritual depravity of the United States, the Soviet Union, and their respective allies. Both men deplore the political, cultural, and economic power that these non-Islamic nations have used against Muslim countries. Writing during the cold war, Khomeini and Maududi believed that the United States, the Soviet Union, and their allies were using their political, military, and economic power to advance their own interests at the expense of smaller, oppressed nations. Since Islam stood in its way, the West was willing to take the necessary steps to transform Islamic states into nations with a Western culture.[40]

Maududi's and Khomeini's visions of a future world political system differ. Maududi argues that the division of the world between Islamic and non-Islamic states would eventually give way to a world state ruled by Islamic law. Though national governments would not be abolished, their authority would be constrained by a world government that would orchestrate the political and economic relations between nations and would usher in a reign of peace and economic justice among the world's nations.[41] Khomeini shrugs off the idea of a universal Islamic state, but he believes that the Iranian fundamentalist revolution serves as a model for other oppressed Islamic nations seeking to rid themselves of American and Soviet influence. As the number of Islamic nations grow, they would, Khomeini believes, be united by a common commitment to pursue the well-being of their populations under the guidance of Islamic law.[42]

Both Maududi and Khomeini address the problem of how to spread Islam throughout the world. Maududi believes that this spread could be accomplished peacefully or violently. He calls upon all Muslims to propagate the faith peacefully through persuasion; but he also speaks in favor of a jihad. He believes that Islam is a revolutionary ideology and program that seek to alter the world social order and to rebuild it according to Islamic values and Islamic law. This ideology does not promote the fortunes, wealth, or glory of a particular nation. Rather, its aim is to enhance the welfare of all humankind. Maududi believes that the United States and the Soviet Union are responsible for much of the oppression that marks the human condition. He also believes that the historical evolution of world political, economic, and military power has led to the rise of capitalism and communism, both of which are aggressively hostile to Muslims. Although each has used its power and influence to penetrate Middle Eastern Muslim states, the United States and its allies have, Maududi believes, been particularly influential in the region. He sees the political, economic, military, and cultural influence of the United States and Europe as slowly perverting Islamic teaching and law in Muslim states.

Because they are a threat to the Islamic life that the Prophet called all to live, defend, and propagate, Muslims have the duty to rise against the Western powers. Maududi professes a revolutionary ideology and program whose purpose is the establishment of a just and equitable social order. Muslims must therefore wrest political power from the Western tyrants who directly or indirectly control Muslim states. But the call to annihilate Western tyranny in Muslim countries is only part of Maududi's plan for a universal Islamic state. He believes that Islam addresses itself to all oppressors of the world, regardless of whether or not they are Muslim. Threatening jihad, he calls on all nations to affirm their support of Islam and to live within a world Islamic state governed in accordance with Islamic law. He supports an international, Islamic revolutionary party whose purpose is "to destroy the hegemony of an un-Islamic system and establish in its place the rule of that social and cultural order which regulates life with balanced and humane laws."[43] Thus, Maududi believes that Islamic nations could use an international revolutionary party for the purpose of spreading Islamic faith and life throughout the world.[44]

Ayatollah Khomeini substantially agrees with Maududi on the problems Muslim peoples face at the hands of the West and the Soviet Union, the need to extend the political rule of Islam, and the necessity for war—although not a jihad. Khomeini rails at the tyranny of the West. In his view, the Jews and their allies in the West—led by the Great Satan, the United States—intend to destroy Islam. The West has attempted to root Islam from the soul of every Muslim by converting Muslims to Christianity; by stoking the fires of avarice and greed; by inflaming the desire for sex and alcohol; by disseminating a poisonous culture to corrupt Muslim youth; by erecting criminal, puppet governments supporting the plunder of the Middle East's oil by multinational corporations; and by giving military and economic support to tyrannical Middle Eastern governments. By so doing, they hope to put an end to the last barrier to their pursuit of a godless, materialistic life.[45] However, Khomeini believes that the West will fail in its effort to subvert Islam. Through propaganda and revolution, Muslims should spare no effort in spreading Islam and in overthrowing the satanic powers that seek to destroy the last best hope for peace and justice in the world: Islam. Contrary to Maududi, who favors a jihad to overthrow non-Islamic governments, Khomeini believes that Islamic nations should export revolution peacefully through propaganda and persuasion. Assuming that humans are capable of changing their beliefs and values, Khomeini exhorts all Muslims, and particularly Muslim youth, to spread the Islamic worldview to other nations. Once the teachings of Mohammed and knowledge of the Qur'an have taken root in enough countries, an unstoppable momentum would develop, further hastening Islam's spread. Like many sprouts of ivy slowly and irresistibly spreading and covering a brick house, Islam will spread and cover the world. The eventual triumph of Islam in all the countries of the world will not, however, be easy or rapid. Khomeini believes that satanic forces are at work preventing its spread. The Soviet Union and the United States had attempted to constrain the spread of the Iranian Revolution in the 1980s, because the revolution jeopardized the stability of the Soviet empire and the interests of the United States in the Middle East. With a large number of Muslims in the southern reaches of the Soviet Union, the Iranian Revolution threatened to rekindle the hopes of those Muslims to be free from the tyranny of communist rule. Similarly, the interest the United States had in the free flow of oil from the Middle East and the desire of "Muslim" governments to reap a profit from that trade led many Muslim governments to side with the United States in repressing political movements that would free them from U.S. imperialism. However, as the justness of the Islamic cause would prove superior to the material might of the United States and Soviet Union, Khomeini believes that Islam will eventually triumph. In this new millennium, the Muslim nations of the world will coordinate their efforts to achieve peace and justice for all the peoples of the earth.[46]

For the realist, the Islamic conception of a peaceful and just world state is a facade. Behind this ethical curtain, the real play is being acted out. The actors on the world stage, including Maududi and Khomeini, are engaged in gargantuan struggles for power. When the curtain is torn from the stage, all will be able to see the play for what it is: the sometimes peaceful, sometimes violent, but ever-incessant struggle for world political power. By stripping away the curtain of pretense that shrouds this play, we will be able to lay bare the true intentions of nations: the search for power. Only then will the nations of the earth be able to develop foreign policies capable of handling the international struggle for power. By recognizing the primacy of the fundamental forces of power and self-interest, nations will be able to lay the foundation for as much peace and material prosperity as are possible in a world where self-interest and the competition for power rule the day.

For a realist like Hans Morgenthau, the imperial plans of Maududi and Khomeini are means to an end, and that end is political power, not the noble sentiments of unity, justice, and peace. Power is "man's control over the minds and actions of other men," and Maududi and Khomeini make it clear that they intend to convert the minds of Christians, Hindus, Buddhists, Taoists, Marxists, Maoists, and other true believers to Islam.[47] Thus, they are in the world power game in the truest sense of the word. Acknowledging the importance of power, Maududi and Khomeini are concerned with adopting those policies that will keep, increase, or demonstrate power. In this case, they clearly desire to increase their power in world politics, and as their end *is* power, they choose to do so by a policy of imperialism. In the pursuit of power, the fundamental purpose of imperialism is to overthrow the existing balance and matrix of international political power, and to do this, Islamic states must increase their power relative to the great Western and Eastern powers: the United States, Japan, China, Western Europe, and Russia. Maududi and Khomeini do not conceal their cultural imperialism. They intend to introduce Islam into all countries in the hope that it will spread throughout the body politic, eventually consuming it in a religious frenzy. Indeed, cultural imperialism is not enough for Maududi; he is willing to extend Islam through a jihad, a holy war against all nations that refuse to willingly submit to the Islamic voice of reason, justice, and peace. As a morning mist warmed by the sun lifts and reveals the once-shrouded world for what it is, so the Islamic proclamation of international peace and justice will vanish and reveal the desire for world political power that consumes Khomeini and Maududi.[48]

According to Russian nationalists like the nineteenth-century writer Nikolai Danilevski and the twentieth-century politician Vladimir Zhirinovski—both of whom will be treated more fully in the next chapter—Russia needs to develop an imperialist policy to counter the Islamic threat to its national survival and vital interests. In rejecting Khomeini's assumption that individuals are capable of freely laying down one religion for another, these two nationalists believe that humans are intricately bound up in a historical society in which religion, society, politics, and economics mutually reinforce one another. It is, they believe, extremely difficult to peel individuals away from beliefs that are so deeply rooted in their lives. For Danilevski, the two great threats to the Russian state came from Western Europe and Turkey. Europe's Western culture had become so secularized that it spun Marxist, socialist, and nihilist philosophies that were opposed to Russian Orthodoxy. The spirit of Russian Orthodoxy was the moral glue that bound the people of Russia into one body. Theologically, Orthodoxy promoted political stability because, as the Bible teaches, all Christians were commanded to submit to the higher powers: in this case, the czar. If the influence of religion over the Russian people were diminished by the proliferation of un-Orthodox ideologies, Danilevski feared that the authority of the czar would also be diminished and Russian political life would rush headlong into anarchy. For both Danilevski and Zhirinovski see the Islamic Turkish state as threatening the national security of Russia. Not only would the spread of Islamic nations on Russia's southern border create an Islamic bloc of nations capable of challenging Russian interests in the Balkans, but a pan-Islamic movement desiring to undermine Orthodoxy and political stability would threaten Russia's very existence. The only way to counter the power of Islam and the lethal virus of Western culture was for Russia to engage in its own imperialism. Danilevski favored military expansion into eastern and southeastern Europe, thus securing a buffer zone between an increasingly hostile Europe and Russia proper. In the Balkans, in southeast Europe, Danilevski believed that a war with the Turks and Europe would be necessary to free Russia's Slavic, Orthodox citizens from European and Turkish domination. Zhirinovsky goes further. To secure the interests of Russia, he believes that Russian military forces will be forced to strike Islamic nations to the south, taking military control of Iran, Iraq, and Afghanistan.[49]

Liberals argue that the Islamic imperialism advocated by Khomeini and Maududi is a violation of the right to self-determination of nations. First, just as individuals have the right to determine how to lead their lives within the accepted laws of their society, so the nations of the world have the right to choose their own form of government, their own economic system, and their own social arrangements, within the limits of international law. As the principle of self-determination is one such law, nations should be free from the outside interference of other nations or terrorist organizations. The philosophies of Khomeini and Maududi violate the principle of the right of self-determination and nonintervention in the affairs of other nations. It is clear that these eminent Islamic political thinkers wish to encourage Islamic partisans to relocate to non-Islamic states for the sole purpose of overthrowing the existing government. Whether this is done violently or peacefully, it is nevertheless a violation of the principle of self-determination. Intervention in the political affairs of a nation for the purpose of promoting a violent or nonviolent change in that society's social, economic, religious, and political institutions is a violation of the right of nations to conduct their internal and external affairs as they see fit. Second, just as there is no common view about what is the nature of the good life for each individual, so no consensus exists among nations on what constitutes a good life. Each nation has the right to search for its own version of the good society. The diversity of the world's religions, political and economic forms, social organization, and mores suggests that each nation (conditioned by history and geography) has chosen its own path to the good life. Can one really say that the pursuit of the good life in Japan or Tibet is synonymous to that in the United States or Great Britain? Certainly not. Given the multiple roads to happiness, it is the height of moral arrogance to suppose that Islam has found the one, true path to happiness that has eluded billions of people, hundreds of nations, countless philosophers, and scores of prophets. Let this be the principle: allow the nations of the world to choose freely their own paths to the good life. Under no circumstances should a nation put war in service to their ideas: "To go to war for an idea, if the war is aggressive, not defensive, is as criminal as to go to war for territory or revenue; for it is as little justifiable to force our ideas on other people, as to compel them to submit to our will in any other respect."[50]

According to radicals and radical feminists, Khomeini and Maududi have discovered that capitalism, as legitimized by Christianity, is the source of domestic and international discord, oppression, and war. To the radical and the radical feminist, however, the Islamic solution is as horrendous as the problem. They agree that the capitalist world economy is the source of the economic exploitation of labor and of the political and economic oppression of the peripheral poor countries. They agree that the scramble, in the late twentieth century, of multinational corporations into less developed countries is an exploitive attempt to take advantage of the poorly paid workforces in those nations. Maududi, in their view, is correct in suggesting that the international state system functions to support the economic rape of less developed countries by capitalist powers. The state system enshrines the principle of self-determination or noninterference, which allows the bourgeoisie in each less developed nation to use the power of the state to create a repressive social order facilitating the exploitation of the laboring class. This principle of noninterference is used by capitalist powers to prevent state-sponsored, international socialist movements from giving financial or military assistance to the oppressed mass of less developed countries as they struggle to free themselves from the trials of economic oppression and the terror of political repression. Maududi is also correct, according to the radical feminist perspective, in wailing about the way capitalist states intervene to prop up puppet governments (or overthrow socialist governments) that serve the interests of the international bourgeoisie. However, radicals and radical feminists argue that both Maududi and Khomeini are wrong in supposing that Islamic dogma is capable of leading the world to drink from the sweet waters of justice and peace. As a religion, Islam justifies the right of private property, because it holds that Allah has given each person the right to own and acquire property. With property comes the accumulation of great wealth and the existence of heavy, oppressive poverty. To secure its citizens' right to acquire and maintain this wealth, the state is given the responsibility to protect the right of each person to own property. Acknowledging that both wealth and poverty are endemic to Islamic societies, Islam asserts that the rich should help alleviate the condition of those in poverty by paying a 10 percent income tax (the *zakat*). For his part, Maududi requires each person to obey those in positions of political authority because such is commanded by Allah. Thus, economic and political power reinforce each other in ways that continue the exploitation of the poor by the rich. Radical feminists are critical of the economic plight of Islamic women who are shackled to the home and a life of social oppression. Maududi's belief is that women's place in society is determined by their reproductive function as bearers of children and that they are better equipped to manage the affairs of the household than matters of state. This prevents women from gaining access to real centers of economic and political power that would liberate them from the travails of a patriarchal society. Khomeini also supports this traditional view of women. The political inequality of women compared to men is strengthened by the Qur'an. Although Maududi gives women the right to vote, he denies them the right to hold public office because the Prophet says that countries ruled by women would be ruined. But the feminist may well ask, "What good is the right to vote, if you have to choose between Maududi and Khomeini?" Thus for radicals and feminists, the revival of Islam will not bring about a world of freedom and equality; rather, it will perpetuate economic, social, and political repression.[51]

Islamic fundamentalists reject the charges that their views of imperialism, social change, social stagnation, the morality of economic inequalities, or the right to violate the international norm of noninterference are wrongheaded. First, to the argument that humans of various cultures are not open to changing their ideas, the Islamic fundamentalist argues that human nature suggests otherwise. All humans are rational creatures who desire to pursue and know Truth. As God has revealed the Truth to humankind through the Prophet, humans exposed to this Truth will willingly and inexorably be led to Islam. Divergent cultural barriers that have enslaved humans to the secular world will fall before the revealed Truth of Allah. Second, the realist's charge that naked empire is the goal of fundamentalist Islamic states is groundless. Although the spread of Islam would lead to a world state in the view of Maududi, Islam's ultimate goals are not imperialism and the attainment of international power. Rather, all political power would be place in service to divine law; and when the world is ruled by God's law, peace, justice, and the security of human rights will prevail among all the world's peoples. Power is only the means to an end that will usher in a new millennium of peace and justice. Third, to the Islamic fundamentalist, the international principle of the right of self-determination and noninterference in the affairs of other nations is a liberal construct that has served those capitalist countries seeking to work evil in the world. It has not prevented the capitalist powers from intervening in the internal, political affairs of less developed nations. The Reagan administration's financial and military support of the Nicaraguan Contras in the 1980s and the Bush administration's military action in Panama are but two of many such examples. Fourth, the charge that Islamic fundamentalism perpetuates economic inequality and social conformity to outdated law is misplaced. The economic norms of Islam promote greater economic equality than has been achieved in the capitalist nations, and Islamic law avoids pressing for too much economic equality at the expense of individual initiative—a problem that characterizes Marxist theory and practice. Islam provides adequate material rewards for those who utilize their God-given talents, energy, and intellects, and it secures substantial protection to the poor, aged, and indigent. Finally, Islam frees women and accords them an honor and dignity that are unknown in non-Islamic nations. For Maududi, males and females were created by God to perform certain functions in society, and Islamic law has guided and directed the activities of the sexes in ways that allow each to contribute to the well-being of society. Compared to Western or communist societies that depreciate the unique contribution women make to the family and society at large, Islam honors the contribution they make to the vitality of the family and nation. Rather than seeking absolute equality between female and male—an equality that destroys the complementary differences that exist between the sexes—Islam seeks to take advantage of the sexual differences and to use those differences to benefit the social order.

Throughout history, some nations have chosen to pursue the goal of empire. As this section suggests, empire is intertwined with other concepts that we use to think about world politics. Your view of human nature; the conflictual or cooperative nature of world politics; and the ends of political activity such as equality or inequality, justice and peace are just a few of the ideas serving to frame the value that some place on empire as an end of political action in world politics. Put down this book for a moment and consider whether you believe that empire is an end of international political activity. If not an end of political action, is it a means to some end such as justice, liberty, economic equality, or peace? Do you agree with Islamic fundamentalists when they say that empire is required to end war and political oppression? Are there advantages that an empire can bring to humankind? Can empire be liberating or does it lead to tyranny? Do you believe the radicals when they suggest that the true cause of empire is the world capitalistic system? Is the United States, by virtue of the fact that it survived the cold war, in the position to establish a world empire economically, politically, or culturally? Has it accomplished this already? Would such an empire be good? Are we to believe the liberals when they suggest that empire is a threat to the freedom of nations? If so, in what way is freedom circumscribed or limited? If freedom and order are opposite sides of the same coin, does increasing the freedom of nations and other international actors lead to disorder and war? These are some of the questions that have been raised in this section, and we explore more of them in Chapter 5 when we discuss whether or not a monarchical form of government is the best type of international government.

ON PRESERVING THE ENVIRONMENT

If one asks how a realist, classicist, classical liberal, or Marxist thinks about the goal of preserving the environment as an end of world politics, one is struck by the lack of serious thinking about the subject. Perhaps this is due largely to the fact that these perspectives on world politics are rooted in times when the impact of global environmental degradation did not have the catastrophic consequences it has today. In fact, classical liberal and realist theories of world politics have been indicted by some environmentalists as being anti-environmental. Capitalism has been criticized for promoting a consumer mentality in developed nations that leads to the ever-increasing consumption of nonrenewable natural resources such as oil and the ever-increasing pollution of our biosphere, which threatens life on earth. The realists are accused of giving power a material foundation, and this leads to environmental degradation. The power of a nation is rooted in the availability of resources, the size of its population, the level of its technological and industrial development, and the size of its military. The world's most powerful nations have harnessed these material components of power to achieve their goals in world politics. Because nations are concerned with increasing their power relative to other nations, each country is driven to expand its industrial base, to increase its consumption of natural resources, and to promote population growth. This inexorably leads to the global exploitation of the natural environment, as an ever-increasing number of nations seek international political power to secure and advance their national interests. Because many people believe that there are serious global environmental problems that need to be addressed and because the canon of international political theory has been unable to provide a way to think about serious environmental issues, it is not surprising to find that environmentalists, ecologists, and radicals have developed their own environmental/political theories. Even in the environmental movement, however, one is hard-pressed to find well-developed "green" theories of world politics. This is not to say that environmental movements do not have something to say about world politics; they certainly do, and many of these movements have views associated with the left side of the political spectrum. Rather, one could argue that there is a paucity of well-developed theories of world politics with ecological foundations.

This leaves us with two fundamental problems. First, are we to believe that the canon of international political theory has nothing to say about world environmental issues and thus is irrelevant to those who believe that there are serious environmental problems facing planet earth? Second, if these traditional approaches are irrelevant, are we to believe that we must move to the political left in order to become part of the conversation on environmental problems? To answer these questions, this book proposes two arguments. First, writers in the canon do have approaches to dealing with environmental concerns at the national level that can be adapted and projected into their theories of world politics. For example, classical liberals are inclined to believe that the domestic marketplace can solve many pollution problems. If this is the case, perhaps the international market could do the same. Second, if classicism and realism are capable of contributing to a dialogue on global environmental issues, we are not forced to turn solely to the left to address them. It is possible that a broader conversation on international environmental problems would pose alternative solutions to these problems. Let us turn to the realist perspective on global environmental issues.

Realists argue that the foundation of international political power is the availability of natural resources. Realists believe that in the absence of an international authority to order the relations of nations, nations pursuing their vital interests will search for power. The natural environment provides the raw materials of power. Morgenthau cites the availability of natural resources and the quality of a nation's arable or tillable soil as sources of national power. A nation is powerful to the extent that it possesses adequate natural resources to sustain the level of industrial production necessary to support a growing population, a defense budget to protect and advance its national interests, a diplomatic service to manage its foreign affairs, and an effective government that has the support of its people. To the extent that a nation relies on other countries for the raw materials needed to fuse economic and military power into political power, its ability to wield world political power is reduced. Take oil, for example. Morgenthau demonstrates that since the early part of the twentieth century, oil has become more and more important in determining the power of nations. Coal, once the primary source of energy for industry and manufacturing, has been largely replaced by oil. Similarly, the military, which has become increasingly mechanized, now relies more on oil and petroleum distillates than on other forms of energy to transport soldiers, supplies, and weapons. Thus, the truck, plane, and armored personnel carrier have replaced the horse, wagon, and the foot march. Battleships originally propelled by sail and wind were later moved by coal-fired steam engines and still later by oil-burning engines. The net result of these developments was that nations self-sufficient in oil production could be considered more powerful than nations that imported large quantities of oil. By realist standards, Japan, a nation that imports over 98 percent of its oil, is less politically powerful in international affairs than Russia, which is self-sufficient. Because Japan wishes to avoid upsetting its oil suppliers, it presumably has less ability to shape events in the Middle East than does Russia. Russia, in turn, presumably has more influence in world politics than does Japan, because it is unhampered by the need to take oil into consideration when framing its foreign policies. In sum, Morgenthau believes that the most powerful nations on earth are those that are largely self-sufficient in natural resources and have enough agriculturally productive land to support industrial, urban populations. In a world where the struggle for power and influence dominates the foreign and defense policies of nations and where international political power is grounded in a state's level of industrial development, countries will have to use their natural resources to provide that level of economic development that will allow them to pursue their interests in world politics.[52]

Population is another component of national power. A nation cannot be a significant power if it has a small population; in contrast, a large population can enhance a state's power status. A large population can help a country develop an industrial capacity, and provide it with the tax base to raise and maintain a military and to meet the needs and wants of its people. However, a country whose population growth rate outstrips its rate of economic development will diminish in its ability to wield power on the world stage. Populations that can neither be wholly fed nor fully employed undermine a state's power. In such cases, limited government resources may be devoured by mostly unsuccessful attempts to meet the basic needs of a burgeoning population—resources that could have otherwise been partly used to expand the country's industrial capacity and to increase employment; to invest in new technology; and to raise, equip, and maintain a military. It can therefore be argued that prudent governments must develop population policies that permit their nations to harmonize population, resource use, and economic development. Only then will their nations be effective actors in world politics. Such governments can develop policies that encourage, maintain, or discourage population growth, depending on the opportunities and challenges that the international political system lays before their nations.[53]

Is the realist oblivious to the potential environmental damage inherent in its political theory? The vision of international anarchy that drives nations to secure their national interests by increasing their power is disconcerting to many. To enhance their power, governments exploit their nation's resources to support a growing population, an expanding military, and an increased industrial capacity. The realist vision of world politics as anarchical, war-prone, and insecure depicts nations as being driven to increase their political power by exploiting the environment, expanding their industrial capacity, consuming larger quantities of nonrenewable natural resources, and increasing their population to supply armies with larger numbers of men and women. The specter of governments unleashing shovel and auger in virginal forests for the purpose of increasing their international power is frightening to many ecologists and environmentalists. What could be more frightening than the image of a dark, cold, desolate, and broken world following a nuclear holocaust? Perhaps this is the ultimate, but unintended, consequence of the realist's vision of failed politics. Even a conventional war can bring about substantial ecological destruction. Recall the burning oil fields and oil-drenched birds struggling to fly in Kuwait, and the rat-infested, blood-filled ponds of no man's land in World War I France. Such visions are enough to give one pause, should one venture into the politics of realism.

To say realism contains an ecocidal thread in its theory of world politics is too simplistic. First, it is not clear that realists are opposed to domestic efforts to protect the environment through such measures as recycling, enhancing the productivity of soil, or conserving natural resources. The natural environment is one source of national power, and a nation that recklessly expends its gifts diminishes that power. Thus, a nation's natural endowments must be shepherded, conserved, and augmented. For example, a nation should encourage efforts to recycle aluminum, to conserve its supply of a limited resource and to reduce its need to convert valuable land into garbage dumps. Their political principles would lead realists to explore the development and use of alternative forms of energy. Power generated from geothermal, solar, and wind sources could provide nations that rely on imported oil a degree of energy independence. This would free nations from their dependency on foreign oil and thus would reduce the possibility that their need for oil could be used as a weapon against them in world politics. As an ecological spin-off, the expanded use of alternative energy sources would limit the consumption of and exploration for oil and natural gas. And because the burning of fossil fuels is related to the warming of the atmosphere (known as the greenhouse effect), the global environment would be improved. Although realists are not likely to turn into organic farmers, their political principles would certainly lead them to embrace agricultural practices that minimize soil erosion. Because soil erosion inevitably diminishes agricultural productivity, it ultimately threatens a nation's ability to supply its population with food. Second, realists such as Morgenthau and Machiavelli believe that prudence ought to be one virtue of those in power, and this has ecological implications. Prudence is that worldly knowledge that allows a person to successfully achieve what he or she desires. Prudent leaders who desire to wield power effectively in international relations know when they need to erect tariffs to protect domestic industries important to their national security; they know what energy conservation policies should be developed to diminish fossil fuel energy consumption; they know what new technologies the government should financially support to ensure natural resource independence; and they know when to encourage or discourage population growth or consumer demand. In short, prudence leads the realist to be environmentally conscious. Third, some realists such as John J. Mearsheimer argue that the possession of a significant number of nuclear weapons ensures peace. The fact that neither a conventional nor nuclear war occurred between the United States and the Soviet Union or their European allies during the cold war is cited as evidence that nuclear deterrence was successful.[54] As a result of this nuclear policy, the global environment was spared the ravages of war. Fourth, realists desire an international political system in which any number of issues—including global environmental issues—can be addressed. The realist argues that a world situation with a way to manage relations between nations has environmental benefits. Worldwide and regional balances of power reduce the possibility of war and the consequent environmental destruction. Balances of power also stifle imperialism and with it the heavy consumption of natural resources, expanded industrial production, and consequent pollution that attend imperialism. In the twentieth century, nations (like Hitler's Germany) with imperial desires have increased their industrial capacity, their consumption of natural resources, their populations, their militaries, and the amount of pollution they produce. A realist's foreign policy, if successful, would check the ambitions of an imperial nation, thereby limiting global environmental damage. For these reasons, realism is not without an environmental conscience.

To many feminists, the patriarchal view of nature and science is the source of the world's environmental problems. All social, economic, political, and religious institutions that promote and maintain gender inequalities are justified by gendered social, economic, political, and religious theories. Even modern science is gendered. Science is not an objective or value-free way of understanding nature and the environment. Science is quintessentially male in its emphasis on a highly rationalized and mathematized scientific method, and it denies that the more intuitive insights into nature characteristic of some feminist approaches to science can produce reliable knowledge about nature. The male vision of science took an exceedingly destructive turn when it moved away from an organic view of the world to a mechanistic view in the seventeenth and eighteenth centuries. Organic views of the world were fundamentally classical and permeated Greek, Roman, and medieval philosophy. In viewing the world as an organism, classicists held that all parts of the world (animal, vegetable, and mineral) were inherently bound up in webs of relationships in which the survival of one part depended on the survival of all parts. For example, human life on earth depended on the well-being of the animal and vegetable worlds that provided food and shelter for humankind. Even minerals were conceived as having life.[55] However, modern science, in devitalizing nature, chose to mechanize it. The late sixteenth-century scientist Johannes Kepler hoped to "show that the celestial machine [is] to be likened not to a divine organism but to a clockwork."[56] The clock analogy implied that the universe was created of distinct parts that were united into a single system, where one part of the world helped drive another part. Humans, standing outside the world, could discover those natural laws that explained how nature ticked. This implied that the scientist was not *in* this world of nature but *outside* and *over* it. Once the scientist discovered how the world of nature worked, that knowledge could be used by humans to make a better world for themselves. Thus, an understanding of the atom would allow humans to create nuclear reactors capable of providing nuclear energy. Understanding the physical principles of the lever would allow humans to create giant earth-moving machines to mine gold and other natural resources. A knowledge of insect chemistry would allow humans the ability to make pesticides to kill insects that might otherwise eat the crops destined for human consumption. In short, the mechanized view of nature placed men and women at the summit of creation, capable of bending nature to their own ends. No longer was humankind organically rooted in nature; rather, humankind stood outside nature and viewed nature as something to be studied, analyzed, conquered, and exploited for human purposes.[57]

Feminists such as J. Ann Tickner believe that realists hold a similar view of nature—a view they believe leads to environmental destruction. The natural environment is one element of state power, and nations, these feminists believe, will exploit their natural resources to increase their power relative to the power of other nations. The anarchical condition of world politics makes national security the primary concern in international relations. Nations must remain economically productive to fund the military establishment that protects their national security. An economy without sufficient growth is a threat to national security because it is unable to generate the income that is necessary to support a dynamic, large, technologically driven military. Thus, the logic of world politics requires nations to expand their economies, but this expansion comes at the expense of the environment. Domestic oil is devoured by the barrel, and coal is burned by the hopper. The use of fossil fuels increases greenhouse gasses that contribute to global warming and increases sulfur dioxide, which leads to acid rain. Inevitably, the consumption of the nation's mineral wealth drives nations toward natural resource imperialism and war. Indeed, many Americans believe that U.S. participation in the Gulf War was driven by its desire to secure reliable, inexpensive access to oil. Future wars will be fought by those nations of the world who, short on critical natural resources, are concerned with their national security. The anarchical international environment that places a premium on national security promotes the exploitation of the earth's resources and the corruption of the earth's environment.[58]

Feminists are concerned with other aspects of the realist's ecological arguments. The realists may claim that their philosophy is ecologically responsible and even progressive, given the importance of prudence and the need for natural resources in the future, but the reality is much different. The realists' appetitive view of human nature and their conception of a competitive, hostile international system require nations to arm themselves to the teeth. To do so, states attempt to manage a dynamic and growing domestic economy that provides the wealth that will allow them to so arm themselves to protect their national interests. Although a balance of power may temporarily suppress the desire to acquire power, realist principles suggest that there will inevitably be nations that will strive for world hegemony, and freedom-loving nations will be forced to increase their international base of power to prevent imperial nations from placing the world under boot and heel. All the nations of the world must exploit their natural and economic resources to protect themselves against nations with imperial plans. Thus, realism envisions a world political system that emphasizes the struggle for power and with that the continued exploitation of the earth's resources and the consequent pollution of the global environment. Feminists are also less likely to agree that common environmental problems such as global warming, tropical deforestation, the depletion of the ozone, and acid rain can be adequately addressed by nations that are continually faced with providing for their own national security. As long as nations live in an anarchic international environment, they will disregard the long-term effects of resource depletion and increased pollution of the world's environment and will instead concern themselves with their immediate needs for national security. Although this is most apparent for rich, industrialized nations jousting for great political power, less developed nations that are surrounded by hostile countries are driven to exploit natural resources in their search for national security. In sum, realism provides little hope of handling the environmental tragedies that are played daily on the world stage.[59]

As you will recall, the classical liberal believes that a capitalist world economy is the engine for economic development around the world. When nations—large or small, developed or undeveloped—apply liberal economic principles, economic growth and prosperity follow. Domestic economic growth creates new jobs for the jobless, generates more capital for continued economic development, provides a growing number of people with moderate incomes, promises an improved standard of living, and reduces population growth by convincing parents in countries with no social security systems that they will not need to have a large number of children that can care for them in their old age. The by-product of all this activity is pollution, but human life produces pollution under any form of economic organization that seeks to satisfy the needs of human beings. According to the liberal, the solution to domestic pollution does not rest with government's intrusive regulation of industry. Governmental action to solve the problem of pollution is justified only if the free market fails. Nobel prize-winning economist Milton Friedman believes that some minimal government intervention in economic life is necessary to limit pollution. He favors an effluent charge on businesses that pollute: the greater the pollution, the higher the tax. This tax would be passed from business to the consumer who buys the product or service. The cost of those products made by heavily polluting companies would be higher than those of a company that pollutes very little. To remain competitive, companies with the worst pollution records would be forced by the marketplace to pollute less or go out of business. Either way, the amount of pollution would be reduced by the marketplace with a minimum of governmental intervention.[60]

The spread of free-market economies in the world will help reduce pollution and help conserve natural resources. First, the universal application of effluent taxes in all capitalistic nations would have the effect of eliminating the sources of air and water pollution. International agreements between countries on establishing effluent standards and taxes would help reduce the amount of particulate matter, carbon dioxide, sulfur dioxide, and chlorofluorocarbons (CFCs) released into the air. Second, the mechanisms of the market—the price system and worldwide supply and demand—can be used to manage the problem of resource depletion. For example, as world oil use increases, the global supply of oil will decrease, which will drive up oil prices. Business, agriculture, and industry will adapt to the gradual increase in prices by developing and utilizing alternative sources of energy and by finding ways to conserve oil. This holds true for all nonrenewable natural resources. As they are depleted by increased demand, the subsequent rise in price will drive companies to conserve, and to find substitutes for, those resources. Third, capitalism utilizes natural resources more efficiently than any other economic system. Global competition drives producers to use natural resources in the most efficient ways so as to minimize waste and keep the cost of their products competitive. Allowing the free market to solve the twin problems of pollution and the depletion of natural resources is, to liberals, vastly preferable to having an international authority such as the United Nations impose and enforce environmental standards through economic sanctions, public pressure, and organized product boycotts. To impose environmental standards in this manner would violate the right to self-determination: the right of countries to manage their affairs in the way they see fit.[61]

The use of effluent taxes to address global pollution poses a political problem. One might ask, What international organ would determine the effluent tax on each nation or business: the United Nations or an international pollution control board? If such a tax were used, who would enforce the tax: the United Nations, or a group of nations that have agreed to coerce any signatory nation that fails to assess and enforce the tax? Or, would compliance by nations be voluntary? It would seem politically naive to believe that a powerful polluting nation would voluntarily enforce a tax on its effluents that would have the effect of making its goods less competitive in the global economy. To do so would be to commit domestic political suicide: no public official in a democracy would want to admit that he or she was responsible for increasing the unemployment that would result from lower domestic economic activity. It would seem that such a tax could be imposed and enforced only by some international political body that was given the authority to do so.

The liberal prefers market solutions to environmental problems. Yet is liberalism driven by its own logic to give some international body the authority to help solve pollution problems if the international market cannot do so? The argument for the effluent tax rests upon the assumption that the polluting industries can be identified, that the types of pollution each industry produces can be uncovered, and that a cost can be assigned to the amount of pollution that each industry emits. It is doubtful that this can be done. What is the alternative? Domestically, Friedman reluctantly argues that when the market fails and the action of one person or group does harm to others, who in turn have no way to compensate themselves for the injury, the government can step in to remedy the situation. Internationally, when pollution from one nation harms the well-being of other nations, it would seem that some form of international organization would be necessary to assist those negatively affected. Is this not the case with some forms of pollution like acid rain? If an agreement between the nations involved on both sides of an acid rain dispute could not be obtained, is there any recourse other than establishing an international body to settle the dispute? If one nation insists on polluting the air in a way that causes acid rain to limit the productivity of land in a nearby country, the only way to compensate that nation for its damage, or to prevent the polluter from continuing to pollute, would be to establish an international organization with the power to compel the polluting nation to compensate it for the damage that it has suffered. Thus, to handle transnational pollution, the economic liberal is driven to accept some form of international authority to solve pollution problems that cannot be handled by the international market or by voluntary international cooperation.

To many radicals, capitalism is the source of today's global environmental problems and disasters, not its solution. Liberal attitudes toward land, consumption, and economic growth drive capitalism toward the exploitation of nature and humans. For his part, John Locke believes that God gave the earth to humankind in common. As humans ventured forth into the world, they added the value of their labor to the natural environment. In so doing, humans gave value to the soil, and since that soil now included their work, that land became their property. In using the land, Locke believes that humans could farm as much land as they wanted, provided that the fruit of the land did not spoil. However, the development of money and trade permitted individuals to amass great amounts of land. Money could not "spoil," and trade allowed the fruit of the earth to be traded worldwide and not wasted.[62] Locke's theory of private property has parallels in the Disney film, *Pocahontas.* For Pocahontas, the land is alive and possesses an intrinsic value; it is by no means lifeless, devoid of value, and waiting to be exploited by humankind. She considers the British colonists to be appetitive, grasping people willing to take and destroy the land in their search for gold. There is nothing inherently valuable in nature for the British colonizers; to them, land exists to serve the greedy intentions of humankind. Land can be forced to produce the crops that humankind chooses to grow. Land can be ripped apart by shovel and pick to yield the resources that humans desire. Forests can be put to the axe to serve the housing and agricultural needs of humankind. The natural course of rivers can be dammed, channeled, and disciplined to produce power or recreation areas that serve the interests of humankind, not the well-being of all creation.[63]

Radical critics of capitalism concern themselves not only with private property and the attendant abuse of the earth, but with consumption patterns as well. Capitalism reshapes human nature and creates one of the basest inclinations in human beings: greed. Freed from any moral principles that restrain human appetites, capitalism stimulates the desire of entrepreneurs to make a profit and opens the opportunity for everyone to acquire wealth. Conspicuous consumption accompanies the increase in wealth, as people desire to display upscale goods as outward indications of wealth and success. Desirous of a life surrounded by material things, the consumer society creates a seemingly insatiable demand for Barbie and Ken dolls, deodorants, beers, cars, televisions, stereo systems, answering machines, designer clothing, and computer software. Shaped by slick Madison Avenue advertising, humans dutifully stand in endless checkout lines to purchase goods that will inevitably fall apart, forcing them once again to repeat the daily ritual of selecting another product and standing in line again. This consumer society is environmentally wasteful and destructive, and it gobbles up natural resources at alarming rates. With the boost in production comes more air, water, and agricultural pollution, which threatens the quality and longevity of human life.[64]

Finally, capitalism creates ever-greater economic growth, which is ecologically unsound. First, liberal economists argue that economic growth is the solution to many domestic problems such as poverty and unemployment. Economic growth opens up jobs for those at the bottom of the economic ladder and the promise of moving into the middle-class, consumer society. Second, an expanding economy whose growth exceeds the population growth of a nation promises all newly born babies a comfortable future. By comparison, a long-term no-growth or negative-growth economy is socially terrifying. By failing to create new job opportunities, a no-growth economy places limits on the ability of individuals to pull themselves out of poverty, and it dashes the hopes of the young and poor that a comfortable future awaits them. Radicals believe that economic growth is part of the environmental problems that face humankind. Fed by the consumer ethos and by the desire to use nature for comfort and profit, capitalism promotes growth at the expense of the environment. Economic growth, in turn, consumes energy and natural resources. Pollution, the mephitic breath of industry, increases. Greenhouse gasses blossom, bringing the potential of global warming and massive climatic change. Increased population growth sustained by continued economic growth places more demands on natural resources. Population growth also affects the availability of prime agricultural land, as growing populations require ever-increasing amounts of land for schools, housing, highways, and the like. With increased population, greater demand is placed on the diminishing supply of arable land. Only by turning the land into a chemical dump of pesticides, manufactured fertilizers, and herbicides can this land be forced to produce food for a growing population. At some point, this land will become so organically sterile that its agricultural production will decrease, threatening human existence. Thus, continued economic growth pushes humankind toward certain ecological collapse.

If this picture of malnutrition and starvation, natural resource depletion, overpopulation, and increased pollution is frightening to those who live in the industrialized, wealthy nations of the Northern Hemisphere, add to this the desire of the Southern Hemisphere's less developed nations to reach the same level of material prosperity. The continued spread and deepening of the world capitalist system would lead to even greater exploitation and destruction of the global environment as less developed countries modernize. In *Biosphere Politics,* Jeremy Rifkin argues that capitalism, starting in Europe, has slowly but surely spread around the earth, leading to widespread privitization of land, water, and other natural resources. Corporations have secured the right to log public lands, nations have claimed the right to exploit their continental shelves out to 200 miles from their shorelines, and MNCs have attempted to claim property rights to the genetic gene pools of some tropical plants. Through genetic manipulation, MNCs attempt to take "useless" plants and give them economic value. Recently, multinational corporations have been the primary instruments in privatizing or enclosing the global environment and spreading capitalism to less developed countries.[65] As described earlier, liberals have argued that the solution to population, pollution, starvation, and material deprivation problems rests in expanding the world capitalist system. However, radicals have pointed out that the spread of capitalism—and the economic growth that follows in its wake—will put more and more stress on the global environment.

The specter of 185 nations with a standard of living and culture similar to the United States is frightening. Earth from outer space appears tranquil and beautiful. Let us imagine a different world. One covered from north to south and east to west with cranes and shovels digging ever-deeper for the resources that are growing in shorter supply; of countless ships with aluminum tentacles reaching to the ocean floor, causing the sea to cough up the few remaining mineral nodules; of frenzied conveyor belts ceaselessly dumping the earth's resources into a cauldron of industrial fire and heat; of factories belching their black smoke and white steam into the air; of rivers and streams flowing with the deadly chemicals of industrial life; and of those who fish, endlessly casting, endlessly waiting, to capture fish that no longer exist.

According to some scholars, this vision of a global environmental tragedy may come to pass if economic growth is promoted at all costs and the global ecological system is pushed over its limits. Books like the Club of Rome's *Limits to Growth*, Robert Heilbroner's *Inquiry into the Human Prospect*, and William Ophuls and A. Stephen Boyan's *Ecology and the Politics of Scarcity Revisited* accept the fundamental principle that uncontrolled, continued economic growth will lead to an ecological catastrophe.[66] *Limits to Growth* was the first serious attempt to use computer technology and modeling to project what the future would hold if industrial output, population, and pollution increased and if greater pressure were to be placed on the soil and other natural resources. The vision, which the authors expect to come to pass within your lifetime, is as follows:

> The industrial capital stock grows to a level that requires an enormous input of resources. In the very process of that growth it depletes a large fraction of the resource reserves available. As resource prices rise and mines are depleted, more and more capital must be used for obtaining resources, leaving less to be invested for future growth. Finally investment cannot keep up with depreciation, and the industrial base collapses, taking with it the service and agricultural systems, which have become dependent on industrial inputs (such as fertilizers, pesticides, hospital laboratories, computers, and especially energy for mechanization). For a short time the situation is especially serious because population, with the delays inherent in the age structure and the process of social adjustment, keeps rising. Population finally decreases when the death rate is driven upward by the lack of food and health services.[67]

In short, with no limits placed on economic growth and assuming that technology does not come to the rescue, there will be a complete and utter collapse of industrial civilization as we know it today. The world will be turned into another Tara, where all the people of the earth will be like Scarlett O'Hara, frantically digging for food in a garden that promises little, and living in a darkening world largely devoid of hope.

Despite the despair that accompanies these dreary analyses of impending ecological catastrophe, human suffering, and death, many radicals believe that humankind can create a better world. Like William Ophuls and the authors of *Limits*, Murray Bookchin, author of *Remaking Society: Pathways to a Green Future*, believes that world economic growth needs to be stopped and replaced by an equilibrium-state, or steady-state. An equilibrium-state—a society in harmony with the natural environment—would place human economic activity within the limits provided by a healthy environment. Ophuls suggests that a profound cultural change needs to take place. Values focusing on community, respect for communal authority, elite rule, planned economies, stewardship of the environment, and modesty would replace today's values, which promote acquisitive individualism, individual freedom, democracy, capitalism, environmental exploitation, and human arrogance. The future world would be a patchwork of small communities encircling the globe. Largely self-sufficient, the communities would be united by a communications network.[68]

Ophuls envisions the dissolution of the nation-state into a myriad of smaller, independent communities, and he redefines the ends of human life on earth. After dissolving the state, humans, through a social contract, would create a government and elect those with the technical competence to manage the political and economic affairs of the community. The community would respect the natural and social ecosystems into which its members are born and in which they live and die. Rather than seeing nature as something to be mastered and conquered by human artifice, Ophuls envisions this community as seeking and finding ways to live according to the ecological laws of nature. Because every person will live within these laws, each individual will have to give up a large degree of "freedom." Presumably a person will no longer be free to pollute, produce as many children as he or she desires, engage in destructive "inorganic farming" practices, or manufacture whatever or as many products as he or she would like. In exchange for losing these freedoms, the citizen would develop a deeper spiritual life. The beauty and harmony of the natural environment would be mirrored in the soul of each citizen. Second, Ophuls reemphasizes the concept of respect for authority. He believes that each individual is tied holistically to the political and ecological communities of which he or she is a part. Since the well-being of one person is bound up with the well-being of others, all citizens would be required to respect the laws of the community that serve to orchestrate individual behavior so that the good of all citizens can be promoted. Third, Ophuls values modesty or humility. Ophuls believes that arrogance characterizes our current attitude toward nature and the environment. He also believes that the evolution of an environmental consciousness that places humans *in* nature rather than *above* it will lead people to live humbler, more modest lives. People will learn to live with fewer material possessions, and the desire for wealth will be replaced by the quest for personal fulfillment in artistic, cultural, spiritual, intellectual, and scientific pursuits. Far from limiting cultural and spiritual growth, Ophuls predicts that a steady-state would promote such growth. Because humans would live moderate lives within a political community respecting independence of human life and nature, humans would become stewards, not exploiters, of the environment—a fourth value. This means that human activity in the broader environment would be managed in a way that does no irreparable harm to it. Economically, enterprises would be small-scale, locally controlled businesses that fit into the environmental landscape. Production of material goods would be restricted by an ethos of frugality and the limited amount of available natural resources. As the entire community benefits from the contributions that each individual makes to it, each person would develop his or her talents in a way that satisfies the needs of the individual and those of the community. Thus, work would be given a greater, transcendental dignity. No longer would it be exercised for the narrow self-interest of the worker; instead, an individual's work would benefit the entire community.[69]

Ophuls does not develop a vision of world politics: he does not show how these individual communities would interact with one another on the world political stage. However, Murray Bookchin, whose outlook is in some ways similar to that of Ophuls, does develop such a vision. Ophuls's suggestion that each community would be largely autarkic or self-sufficient leads him to assume that the economic motives for conflict (e.g., the need for greater resources and markets) would evaporate. Self-sufficient, frugal, environmentally minded, no-growth states would not be inclined toward war. However, it is unclear how self-sufficient each state is, and one suspects that these states would be in need of some trade. Presumably these states exist in a state of international anarchy, and to the extent that the well-being of a nation depended on international trade, the possibility for conflict would arise. Bookchin, an eco-anarchist, believes that these communities will interact with one another. As a social ecologist, Bookchin thinks that communities and economic activity should be formed around the ecological regions in which they are organically located. Thus, the communities of different ecological regions would be producing goods that were in harmony with nature. Because it would be unlikely that any one community would be in a region that was so diverse that all the basic needs of the population were met, Bookchin supposes that all the communities of the world would coordinate their economic activities and trade in a way that would permit each community to satisfy the basic needs of its citizenry. As an anarchist, Bookchin believes that these small communities need not develop into states. He sees no need for a government with the power to coerce an individual or another community. Rather, the people in these communities would gather in open assemblies to formulate whatever social and economic policies were needed. The administration of these policies could be left to boards and commissions established and staffed by the people. However, he is unclear on exactly why human behavior will never require coercion. Finally, the economic activities of these communities would be united in increasingly larger confederated unions, until all the communities and peoples of the world would be united in one confederated organization within the earth's biosphere.[70]

To some ecologists, it is wrong to label realism, liberalism, and male-oriented theories of economics, life, and politics as the primary culprits of environmental damage; rather, they blame Christianity. Lynn White, in his essay "The Historical

Roots of Our Ecological Crisis," argues that Christianity destroyed the pagan view that nature was in some ways divine. In summarizing this point, Carolyn Merchant describes the many ways in which organic theories of nature put forth the idea that minerals, plants, animals, and humans were tied together in webs of interdependence. The life of each part of nature was grounded in the contribution that other parts gave to it, and it was often thought that the spirit of the gods permeated all things in the material and spiritual worlds. White believes that Judaism and Christianity have destroyed this organic view of the world: these religions have despiritualized nature and placed it under the domination of humankind. In despiritualizing nature, Christianity turned matter and nonhuman life into simple physical facts that could be exploited without any pangs of conscience. For example, the idea that trees are embodied spirits worthy of reverence and respect was replaced by the belief that trees were lower forms of life without any spiritual significance. They could be ruthlessly logged for sustenance and profit. In White's view, the belief that humans could use nature for their own ends has led to the human domination of nature.[71] Pointing to the book of Genesis, critics of Christianity argue that God created the earth for the benefit of humankind; then God gave all human beings domination over the earth and all life on it. After the Fall and the great Flood, God commanded Noah and his wife to be fruitful, to multiply, and to populate the earth. Thus, God clearly created the earth for the benefit of humankind, giving humans the power to dominate and use the earth for their own advantage.[72] And dominate and use it they did. Humans, with no conscience, made their way into the world, harnessed modern science and technology to force earth to bear the goods humans desire, relentlessly exploited nature's life and resources, and polluted the ecosphere with the by-products of human affluence and arrogance. Whereas the spirit of Christianity encouraged people to use nature for their benefits, liberals like John Locke used Christianity to justify economic theories that led to the exploitation of the earth's resources. Locke argues that the right to accumulate private property is derived from God, and this right justifies humankind's race to seize the earth's plants, animals, and resources for its own private use. Directly or indirectly, critics argue that Christianity is the fountainhead of humanity's domination of nature.

To the classicist, this is a superficial rendering of Christianity and the Scriptures. Pope John Paul II argues that all things in the natural world have value, that humankind represents the summit of creation, and that there is an inherent hierarchy, order, and harmony in all things in the created universe. First, John Paul II states that the human and natural worlds are filled with goodness and value. During the course of creation, God gave value and a function to the earth and all life on it. The natural world and all plant and animal life form a divinely inspired web, in which each part of nature serves some function. Ant and anteater, wolf and sheep, and soil and worm were created to perform valuable functions that help sustain the life of all creation. Thus, Christianity cannot be said to consider the realm of nature as a valueless, material world to be ruthlessly exploited by humans. Second, the pope takes the more orthodox view that there is a great chain of being: a hierarchy of goodness or perfection that is grounded in the world of matter; extends through the plant, animal, and human worlds; and reaches its summit in God. Thus, some things are simply more valuable than others in the universe, and on earth, humankind stands at the summit of creation. Though earthly creatures, humans are made in the image of God. All nonhuman things are valuable in themselves, but they also have a utilitarian value to humans. The organically connected world of nonhuman nature serves as a material foundation for the life of humankind on earth; without food, shelter, and clean air and water, human life would cease to exist. Thus, humankind was given the power to dominate nature to ensure its survival and to perpetuate the species; however, humans have the responsibility to use the natural world responsibly. Third, John Paul II believes that there is a natural ordering of the environment that permits all elements of it to interact harmoniously with one another. He suggests that in the creation, God ordered the entire universe in accordance with those natural, physical, moral, and biological laws that permit everything to exist in harmony with one another. As long as these laws of nature are not breached or violated, all life exists in a fundamental balance. Thus, the pope argues that critics who believe that Christianity views the natural world as without inherent value are misreading the inherent goodness that exists in all of creation.[73]

Although John Paul II insists that God gave humans domination over the natural world, this is better understood as a matter of stewardship than outright exploitive domination. Drawing on the book of Genesis, the pope argues that Adam and Eve were called to share in the unfolding of God's plan for the created world. They were given the duty of watching over the Garden of Eden and all its creatures. Because they were made in the image of God, they were the most perfect of God's worldly creation, endowed by God with the wisdom, love, and respect necessary to manage the created world. Human wisdom brought with it a knowledge of God's moral law and of those biological and physical laws that allowed all components of the universe to live in harmony. Humans, being subject to God's will, which requires them to respect all creatures in God's creation and to follow those laws that permit all creatures to live in universal harmony, are constrained in their use of God's creation. Thus, the pope argues that humans are not free to use and abuse the natural environment as they desire; rather, they are called by their Creator to use their God-given gifts in a way that satisfies their material and spiritual needs within greater moral, biological, and physical laws of nature that permit all to live in harmony with one another.[74]

When Adam and Eve chose to sin against God by eating the forbidden fruit, they were the first to break the harmony that exists between man and nature. Inasmuch as humankind turned away from God, humans no longer live their life within the laws of nature that would keep them in proper balance with it. Rather, humans have chosen to use their knowledge to gratify their passions at the expense of the natural world. In turning their backs on God's perfect order, an order governed by the moral and physical laws of nature, humankind's misuse of one part of the environment has inevitable repercussions in other areas. Thus, ecological order has given way to ecological disorder and ecological pathologies. Paying little respect to these natural laws and to the creatures of nature, humans have polluted the environment, exploited nonrenewable natural resources, harvested rain forests, depleted the ozone layer, and released toxic chemicals into the ecosphere. In language that reminds us that nature is "alive," the pope writes: "The land mourns and all who dwell in it languish, and also the beasts of the field and the birds of the air and even the fish of the sea are taken away."[75] Elsewhere he talks about the earth's "suffering," which has resulted from "a callous disregard for the hidden, yet perceivable requirements of the order and harmony which governs nature itself."[76] With the world witnessing increased cancer rates, global warming, and dying lakes and streams, the earth is "telling us" that there is an order in the universe that must be respected.[77]

John Paul II does not blame capitalism or socialism for the environmental problems that face mankind. Rather, he believes that the travail of nature is a moral problem that manifests itself economically, politically, and socially. There has been a loss of faith in God and in God's plan for human life. The loss of faith has meant that more and more humans no longer respect the inherent dignity of human life: a dignity that is grounded in the creation of man by God. This has led to a cultural crisis that values material over spiritual well-being. A consumer culture has arisen. On the one hand, Madison Avenue has reached into the soul of man and created an ever-increasing number of superfluous needs. On the other hand, the consumer—having lost his or her moral bearings by seeking "happiness" in a material world—drives the engines of industry to cough up more and more material goods. As a result, scarce or nonrenewable natural resources such as fossil fuels are unconscionably consumed with little regard for future generations, ozone-depleting substances are released into the atmosphere, and toxic wastes find their way into the food chain. In short, the ongoing exploitation of the environment menaces the very survival of the human race, and it threatens the natural order in which all living creatures are given a place to thrive.[78]

The pope sees the world as being in the grip of a cultural crisis, a crisis that has international implications for human ecology and the ecosphere. First, the pope fears that the worldwide spread of materialism and selfishness has led to a decrease in the respect accorded to individuals. He condemns international efforts to make abortion and artificial means of contraception available to less developed countries. In his view, abortion is an outright attack on the dignity of the individual. He believes that the solution to problems associated with pollution growth rests not in artificial means of contraception, but in expanding job opportunities, nurturing cultural development, and redistributing the world's wealth in a more equitable manner. Because population growth rates tend to decline with economic development, the pope favors a socioeconomic approach to curbing world population growth.[79] As respect for the dignity of the individual continues to decline worldwide, the pope fears that industry will find fewer reasons to offer a just wage and humane working conditions to workers in less developed countries. With nothing but the economic laws of the marketplace determining a worker's wage, the pope fears that labor will be exploited by management. Second, John Paul II condemns the selfish behavior that rich nations display toward poorer nations. Preoccupied with their own material well-being, rich northern nations limit the amount of economic aid that they provide poorer southern nations. Thus, the South languishes in poverty while the North wallows piggishly in material prosperity.[80] Third, he believes that world peace is not only threatened by the arms race, regional conflicts, and continued injustice among the nations of the world, but also by the plundering of natural resources and the decline in the global quality of life. The pope fears that nations that are unable to obtain natural resources or to maintain or improve their standard of living peacefully will resort to war. War, he notes, is often accompanied by serious environmental damage. Despite international agreements outlawing the practice, nations continue to create new and more destructive chemical agents and more virulent biological and bacteriological weapons. The effect of these weapons, the pope believes, could be as catastrophic as a global war.[81]

John Paul II is concerned with forces threatening the environment in less developed countries. In these nations, poverty, unregulated industrial development, and the international debt are the major culprits in the destruction of tropical ecosystems. Poverty-stricken farmers, after exhausting the productive capability of their land, are driven by economic necessity to log more of the forest in order to eke out a meager living. The logging destroys complex natural ecosystems and threatens some species with extinction. But the tropical rain forests are not cleared simply to provide food and employment to poor farmers. The rain forest is also logged to profit some industries, and this logging is supported by government policies aimed at opening up new job opportunities for growing populations. International economic pressures also threaten the environment. Many developing countries incur huge debts in an effort to promote national economic development. In an attempt to meet their loan payments, these cash-strapped nations may generate money by logging rain forests, growing cash crops on marginal lands, and strip-mining the earth's raw materials. Thus, international economic forces (which are part of the crisis of culture) are partly responsible for the world ecological crisis.[82]

The pope believes that the solution to global ecological problems lies in morality. The attitudes and values of the people in the industrialized nations of the world must return to an environmental ethic rooted in the Garden of Eden: humans must become stewards of the environment and learn to live within the moral, physical, and biological laws of nature that permit all of creation to live in balance and harmony. Fundamentally, all humans should honor and protect the value of human life. If humans do not value one another, it is doubtful that they will develop an environmental ethic that will honor and value the earth and all the creatures that rely on it for life. The lifestyles of people in developed nations will have to change. Crass materialism and consumption should be abandoned, and greater attention should be given spiritual dimensions of life that are most conducive to human happiness. Simplicity, moderation, discipline, and the spirit of sacrifice must become a part of a new environmental ethic. Second, each person, according to his or her role and social position in society, should seek to establish a new relationship with the environment, a relationship that will protect the environment's delicate balances. From the home, to the factory, to the corporate boardroom, to the government, all persons should commit themselves to environmentally sound practices.[83]

Internationally, attempts must be made to eliminate poverty, nations must commit themselves to respecting the natural environment, and new international agencies must be developed to handle environmental challenges that cannot be handled by existing organizations. First, developed nations should help eliminate poverty by committing a greater percentage of their wealth to less developed countries. The rich states must share responsibility with poor nations in solving the ecological crises that face humankind. Less developed countries cannot be expected to limit economic development to reduce natural resource consumption if the developed countries continue to live in comparative luxury. But poor nations are not morally free to repeat the errors of the industrialized world by polluting, harvesting the rain forests, and exploiting nonrenewable resources. Second, all nations of the world have a duty to defend and protect the environment from further defilement. Although the free market is remarkably efficient in using natural resources, it cannot adequately protect the environment. New scientific and technological advances should be evaluated to determine their potential impacts on the environment. States must take the lead in such efforts. Within states, families and religious organizations have an important part to play in propagating an environmental ethic that is grounded in the love of one's neighbor and the environment. Finally, new international agencies must be developed to handle global environmental problems that transcend a state's ability to do so. Setting worldwide pollution standards and enforcing them is the next step in helping to reestablish the ecological harmony of all of creation. This will require solidarity on the part of all nations to promote the international common good, which is so clearly reflected in the environmental challenges facing humankind.[84]

Whatever can be said of Pope John II's social thinking, he devotes little attention to a political theory of world politics; as we have seen, Pope John XXIII is more expansive on the subject. Pope John Paul II recognizes that global environmental problems need global solutions. However, his desire to create new international agencies to handle these problems and his suggestion that all nations unite in solidarity to solve them are perhaps somewhat naive. The fallen condition of humankind would seem to suggest that nations, like individuals, would pursue their own economic self-interests at the expense of the environment. Unlike Pope John XXIII, who believed that peace can be attained only when there is an international authority capable of maintaining peace between nations, Pope John Paul II does not discuss the possibility of a world government capable of developing and enforcing a common environmental policy. If any argument for a world government could be made, it would seem that there are environmental reasons to recommend it. First, the pope's belief that all parts of God's creation exist in a peaceful harmony, and that humankind should exercise its stewardship over the environment, suggests that an international body with the limited authority to reestablish the harmony of creation should be established. This international authority should be limited by the principle of subsidiarity: it should exercise only those powers necessary to reestablish human solidarity with nature. The nations of the world should retain all other power to wisely manage their environments. Second, if one accepts the assumption that humans are self-interested or sinful and that they will act in a way that ultimately does not serve their best interests, then one is driven to the unfortunate conclusion that nations may not be able to handle global environmental problems. Like nations that desire to consume the natural resources of other nations before they consume those at home, short-sighted and self-interested countries will burn the world around them only to be finally consumed by the fiery inferno that ever-so-slowly inches toward them. Only a supranational authority with the coercive power to force nations to live within the constraints imposed by a healthy environment would be able to bring self-interested nations to heel. Without doubt, a world government with the power to alter the lifestyle of environmentally errant nations would be frightening and awesome, and one wonders whether such an international government, without the support of major parts of the world's population, would be able to govern at all.

The other alternatives to solving global environmental problems are not without their own difficulties. On the one hand, many ecoradicals prefer a radically decentralized commune of virtuous and environmentally conscious citizens that would form a worldwide eco-economic web that lives within the bounds of nature. It is not clear that people in comfortable, industrialized parts of the world would submit peacefully to this vision. On the other hand, Lockean liberals believe that nations, motivated by enlightened self-interest, can agree on and implement global environmental regulations. Faced with serious climatic, environmental, and social problems stemming from the destruction of the environment, nations recognize that it is in their self-interest to hammer out international agreements to solve these problems. But will they? Despite twenty years of scientific evidence that human economic activity poses major threats to the environment, consumption of nonrenewable natural resources continues unabated, pollution continues to plague all nations, the world's population continues to increase, and international environmental agreements continue to ignore the cultural, economic, political, and religious determinants of global environmental decay. Thus, it is hard to see that traditional liberalism will be able to strike at the roots of global environmental problems.

Put down this book for a moment. How does your view of human nature, economics, politics, and religion help you think about the natural environment? What is your conception of nature? Are you inclined to see it as a breathing, living, integrated whole within which humans live? Or is it a dead, material world that can be bent to human purposes? Does it include the living and nonliving things that have been given to humans to use prudently for their benefit? Classical liberals tend to think that capitalism and the marketplace can solve most national and global environmental problems. Is this the case? Is liberalism part of the problem, not part of the solution? Does capitalism promote a consumer mentality that leads to growth, the depletion of natural resources, and increased pollution? Can the current world political system handle environmental problems effectively? Are nations capable of reaching and enforcing the environmental accords that are necessary to secure a healthy global environment? Is there a need for an international government to write and enforce international environmental law? If there were such a government, would it be able to handle global environmental issues any better than national governments have handled them up to our time? Does the balance of power promote environmental damage? Is religion, especially Christianity, the source of our environmental problems? If so, why are there environmental problems in non-Christian areas? Is patriarchy the source of environmental damage? If women are, as some feminists suggest, generally more caring and nurturing than men, would they also be more sensitive to the environment? Would bringing women into positions of world power lead to the adoption of sensible global environmental policies? Do our environmental problems stem from moral bankruptcy and not from capitalism? If so, can humans change their moral principles and lifestyles? If not, what can be done?

ON RIGHTS AND HUMAN RIGHTS

In recent years, television has carried many stories about ethnic cleansing, carnage resulting from mass murder, rape of women and children, political torture, starvation, and repression of democratic movements. Whereas worldwide television draws our attention to scenes of human brutality and abuse in Bosnia, China, Rwanda, and Chile, our response to human atrocities in these countries and others has been framed by a growing awareness of human rights. The United Nations Universal Declaration of Human Rights, the Convention on the Prevention and

Punishment of Genocide, and numerous statements on human rights by private organizations heighten our awareness of the rights that have been extended to the people of the world. These include the rights to one's culture; political participation; freedom of speech, press, religion, and assembly; freedom to organize unions; freedom from torture; and the satisfying of basic human needs (food, clean water, clothing, and shelter). Yet the notion of human rights raises many questions. What rights do humans have, if any? What is the source of these rights? Are rights truly universal? Who is responsible for enforcing human rights—the governments of individual countries, international public opinion, alliances, or the UN? Can a nation's national interest be jeopardized or advanced with a human rights policy? Finally, are human rights relative to the customs and traditions of each nation? To begin the discussion on human rights, let us turn to Islamic fundamentalism.

Abul A'la Maududi's conception of human rights differs from contemporary Western notions. First, Maududi views human rights within the context of a political theory that emphasizes the unity of God with the prophethood of Mohammed and the caliphate. God is the creator, sustainer, and master of the universe. Because of this tremendous power, God is sovereign. As far as the unity of mankind is concerned, God is sovereign over all humans; in fact, since all mankind has descended from Adam and Eve, all humans are related as brothers to one another. To some, nationality, class status, race, and language may distinguish one person from another, but these distinctions are purely accidental. According to Maududi, because Allah's law is the standard by which all the righteous are separated from the unrighteous, those who cleave to the word of Allah are the righteous and the most worthy of respect.[85] Second, God revealed the purposes and goals of human life through the teachings of the prophets and of Mohammed in particular. The Qur'an and the Sunna, both of which lay down those laws and the conduct of life expected of all Muslims, serve to direct all social, economic, political, cultural, and religious life within the Islamic community. Religion provides moral guidance in all dimensions of human life. Third, humans are God's representatives on earth, and God has given the Islamic community the authority to establish a social, economic, and political order in a way that leads all Muslims to a righteous life on earth. Equipped with that authority, the community should establish a government to promote a righteous life in accordance with the Shari'a: the law of Allah. By the command of Allah, all Muslims have the obligation to obey the Shari'a and those who exercise the authority of government.[86]

According to Maududi's political theory, there is no separation of "church and state," and the government has the responsibility of encouraging a virtuous life. Here Maududi parts company with mainstream, contemporary Western political thought. Many people in the Western world believe that individuals should be free to choose their own lifestyle and that governments should not promote one vision of the good or moral life. In their view, the government should give people the freedom and right to pursue their own view of the good life, and it should prevent people from interfering in others' pursuit of the good life. Maududi rages against this Western attitude by saying that there is but one form of the good life, and Allah has revealed it in divine law. The government's responsibility is to interpret and enforce that law. In so doing, the government must promote those moral laws, values, and virtues that enrich human life and eradicate those evils that defile human life. Beauty, purity, goodness, virtue, success, and prosperity should grow and flourish in the Islamic community.[87]

Against this philosophical and theological background, Maududi launches into his view of rights and duties. Maududi believes that rights are divided into human and civil rights, and one's rights must be viewed within the broader context of one's obligations to the community and Allah. Human rights are those rights that all humans possess as a result of being human. They have been granted to mankind by Allah and can be taken away only by Allah—not by any human agency. These rights, "which have been sanctioned by God are permanent, perpetual and eternal."[88] As these rights are given to man by Allah, and as humans by divine command are required to obey the commands of Allah, all humans have the responsibility to know and enforce them. These rights include the right to life, safety, chastity, a basic standard of living, freedom, justice, and equality before the law. People also possess the right to cooperate—or to refuse to cooperate—with others. As humans naturally form states to further the work of Allah, they possess certain civil rights—rights that are to be secured by the state. Among these rights are the right to secure one's life and property; to protect one's honor; to protect the sanctity and security of private life; to secure personal freedom; to protest tyranny; to exercise freedom of expression, freedom of association, and freedom of conscience and conviction; to protect one's religious sentiments; to be protected from arbitrary imprisonment; to possess the basic necessities of life; to enjoy equality before the law; to participate in the affairs of the state; and to avoid sin. Although some of these rights may seem particularly Western in orientation, it is important to recognize that these rights can be exercised only within what is permitted by the Shari'a, and that these rights have corresponding obligations or duties.[89]

As you will recall, Maududi's belief that human nature has material and spiritual dimensions frames his discussion of rights. The Islamic community, he believes, should conduct itself in a way that allows each person to flourish materially and spiritually. Because humans are material beings, with real needs that must be satisfied if they are to survive, Maududi argues that each individual has a right to property. Thus, a man has the right to start and own a business that will permit him to meet his family's daily needs. Although this is a right, it is also an obligation. All humans are commanded by Allah to provide for their basic needs, and each therefore has the responsibility to work. Maududi realizes that there are some who are less able than others to provide for their needs. There are differences in ability and some are naturally more successful than others. Additionally, all Muslims have the responsibility to support those who are unable to support themselves: the unemployed and the crippled, for example. Thus, the zakat, which is a tax on the wealthy, transfers wealth from the rich to the poor. In this way, everyone's right to the satisfaction of basic needs is met. The right to life and security is associated with the right to the satisfaction of human needs. Maududi believes that the most fundamental right is the right to human life. Thus, no human can take the life of another, including the life of the unborn. Only a court, guided by justice, has the right to take the life of one who has wantonly disregarded the respect for human life. Similarly, a person has the human right to personal safety. A person suffering from a disease, wound, or starvation has the right to be saved. This imposes an obligation on individuals and the community to do what is necessary to provide adequate medical care and nutrition.[90]

Maududi believes that humans have the right to spiritual development, and this spiritual development has implications for the rights extended to each person. Spiritual development means that individuals should avoid sin and cultivate a deeper understanding of Allah's laws. Individuals and the government have an obligation to promote the Islamic conception of a good life, and Maududi argues that it is right and proper that every citizen live in a polity that is inclined toward moral goodness. Thus, the government has the responsibility to enforce the Shari'a, and citizens have the obligation to obey those laws. The Muslim also has the right to avoid sin. Thus, all individuals, organizations, and the government have the responsibility of eliminating the exposure of Muslims to sin. Since drinking alcohol is a sin, the government should take steps to forbid the sale of alcohol. If the government does not take steps to enforce Islamic law, if it willfully commands Muslims to do what is in opposition to Islamic law, or if it does not act to eliminate sin, the citizen has the duty to change that government or to disobey unjust laws. The belief that all Muslims should live in a society inspired by Islamic law has implications for freedom of expression. Maududi believes that all individuals have the right to freedom of expression. But this should not be confused with Western notions of such freedom. Maududi thinks that freedom of expression is limited by Islamic law. Muslims have the right to express themselves as long as this freedom is used to promote Islamic virtue and truth. Freedom of expression cannot be used to promote what is contrary to virtue and truth: wickedness, evil, and falsehood. Although humans have the right to promote an Islamic way of life, they also have an obligation to do so. The Qur'an enjoins Muslims to do what is proper and forbids what is improper. Thus, Muslims have the obligation to reprimand and prevent another person from doing evil. Similarly, the right to association is a right that allows Muslims to organize themselves into groups. However, their group activities must be directed at promoting what is considered virtuous to Islamic culture. Finally, women have the right to have their chastity respected. Women worldwide have the right to be free from rape, whether in war or peace.

Furthermore, promiscuous sexual relationships—whether consensual or not—are strictly forbidden by divine law, which also prohibits adultery.[91]

Maududi believes that only a world state governed by Islamic law can guarantee all the people of the world their human and civil rights. The existing international system, while claiming to protect and promote the United Nations Universal Declaration of Human Rights, is ineffectual in doing so. The absence of an international power to enforce the declaration meant that enforcement was determined by the interests of states. States that choose to violate these rights out of political expediency could do so without fear of retribution. A universal state with the power to enforce human and civil rights is necessary to secure these rights for all God's people. Until such a state exists, Maududi suggests that Islamic nations make attempts to coordinate their foreign policies in a way that would make these rights real for Islamic peoples.[92]

The realist is skeptical of the Islamic conception of human rights. First, there is the question of whether human rights are universal and as such applied to peoples everywhere. Whereas Maududi believes that all human rights flow from God and apply to all humans everywhere, the reality is much different: human rights are in fact relative to each nation. The culture and beliefs that individuals of a nation hold develop in response to its unique geographical, social, economic, political, and historical milieu or environment. Each nation develops its own social, economic, political, and religious institutions and ideas. Thus, there is an incredible diversity of peoples and nations in the world. If a nation develops a conception of human or civil rights, it will most likely be in response to unique historical factors. Thus, some nations will develop one understanding of rights, and another country will develop a different conception. Although two countries may broadly agree that humans possess the right to life, freedom, and the satisfaction of basic needs, when one gets down to particulars, there is really no agreement on human and civil rights. Take freedom of speech. Although Americans and many Islamic fundamentalists would agree that humans possess the right to free speech, Americans could not stomach the Islamic idea that speech should be exercised to promote Islamic values. According to Maududi, speech that violates the moral teachings of Mohammed is clearly wrong, and he therefore prohibits it. Maududi also believes that human rights should be an important component of a nation's foreign policy. But for the realist, the pursuit of a human rights policy is tantamount to cultural imperialism, whereby one nation imposes its conception of the good life on another nation. A human rights policy directed at "civilizing" or "uplifting" the uncivilized world is likely to drag nations into crusades that may ill serve their ultimate interest in securing and extending their power in world politics. The nation's first foreign policy goal should be to protect and enhance the political power of the nation and not to promote human rights. It is especially imprudent for a country to campaign for human rights among nations that provide it with critical natural resources, that are important trading partners, that

lease naval and air bases to that country, or that have the ability to block vital ship-
ping lanes. Often, nations will retaliate against other states that attempt to impose
their own views of human rights and the good life on other nations. Those nations
that choose to pursue human rights policies at the expense of the national interest
may find themselves with fewer resources and friends at a time when they need
them the most.[93]

To this criticism, an Islamic fundamentalist might reply that rights are not
relative and that the exercise of political power must always be governed by divine law. First, human and civil rights flow from Allah and are knowable by people of reason who are enlightened by divine revelation. Once exposed to the
teachings of Mohammed, the world's people will recognize the truth of the Islamic idea of human rights, and it is for this reason that Muslims should promote
Islam in every country in which they live. The non-Islamic world lives in the
shadow of ignorance and cannot be expected to know the social, economic, and
political laws that flow from Allah and his Prophet, Mohammed. Realists, with
their minds darkened by ignorance, speak of the relativity of rights; an enlightened mind would understand that Allah brings universal human rights for all
peoples of the world. The fact that the world lives in a cloud of ignorance is no justification for adopting the position that all human rights are relative. Rather, it is a
call to all Muslims to work to spread the Truth of Allah and to generate worldwide
respect for the Islamic conception of human and civil rights. Second, all political
power should be exercised in accordance with the law of Allah, and this is true in
both domestic and world politics. The foreign policy of the state must be guided
by God's law, and Islamic states should take steps to use their power to promote
human rights abroad. Thus, the claim that states ought to pursue their national interest at the expense of the human rights of other people is a violation of the rights
Allah has given to all peoples.[94]

To the liberal, Maududi's conception of human rights is unreasonable. Human reason, not Allah, is the measure by which rights are understood. Humans
exercising their reason can come to know the fundamental rights that should be
secured to all humans, regardless of culture. Let us take freedom, for example. To
a liberal like Kant, all humans are naturally free, and this is something upon
which all rational humans can agree. But the freedom praised by the liberal is not
that advocated by Maududi. Maududi believes that freedom is the conscious
choice to will what is commanded by Allah and codified in the Shari'a. This is a
positive definition of freedom; that is to say, when one chooses, one decides to will
a moral law. The liberal more often than not has a negative definition of freedom
that is best expressed in Hobbes's view of liberty: liberty is the absence of external
impediments. Thus, people are free to the extent that nothing presents an impedi-
ment to their living their lives as they desire. To the extent that a person is coerced
by some other power to do something he or she does not want to do, or is prevented from doing something that he or she would like to do, that individual is

not free. In society, individuals should be given as much freedom as is appropriate in an ordered society, and they should be allowed to define and live the life they choose without undue interference from others and the state. To the liberal, the Islamic conception of liberty strains the bounds of reason. If reason suggests that humans should be free to pursue their own understanding of the good life, the Islamic conception of liberty does not measure up to that standard. In the name of freedom, Islam requires individuals to conform to a body of divine law and codes to which they might not wish to comply. A community that uses religion, social pressure, and the authority of the state to force an individual to live a life that he or she would prefer not to live can hardly be said to be free. Rather, the true measure of freedom is the extent to which one can think and act as one likes without incurring the wrath of those who disagree.[95]

Maududi believes that this understanding of liberty is a hallmark of a morally bankrupt civilization and one that will bring the loss of freedom. In his view, Western, liberal intellectuals are guilty of raising human reason to the level of divine reason: of turning humans into God. They have replaced God's law with human law. Living by their own laws and disregarding divine law, mankind has chosen a life of sin. Thus, Western societies are characterized by a freedom wherein each individual, freed from any higher moral authority and moral values, is given the right to pursue his or her own lifestyle even if it threatens the well-being of the community. In the worse case, if individuals reach the point that they can no longer agree on the ends of government, the door is opened to those who would use political power for their own benefit. Thus, the moral decay of society points in the direction of tyranny. Striding about the world in the boots of injustice, these tyrants would trample on all that is worthy of praise and glory. Rather than protecting liberty and human rights, these rulers would banish them from their states. Islam provides the best hope for freedom, because the community of believers encourages each individual to develop an understanding of those objective, universal moral values and laws that form the foundation of the Islamic view of the good life. Individuals who understand the truth and goodness of these laws and act accordingly are the freest of all people on earth. Rather than restricting freedom, Islam promotes, defends, and secures it.[96]

The classicists of the ancient and medieval worlds would not agree with Maududi's grant of human rights to individuals. In the strictest sense, these classicists did not believe that humans had rights; that idea is a product of the modern era. However, thinkers like Plato, Aristotle, Cicero, and Saint Thomas do have a conception of a natural and divine moral law. Flowing from God, this law can be known by reason, and it obliges all to follow it. Since all things in the universe are inclined to some good and since humans are inclined to self-preservation, the pursuit of self-preservation is a good that all should pursue. Individuals are required by natural law to pursue their self-preservation, and those in positions of political power are obliged to exercise that power in a way that permits individuals to preserve themselves. For this school of classicists, there are no individual rights; there are only obligations.[97] A right can be defined as a legal or moral claim that one person can exercise against other members of the community or the government of a community. To give people the right of self-preservation or freedom, as Maududi does, would bring society to the brink of disorder. Classicists might ask Maududi, "Does the right to self-preservation permit a homeowner to take the life of a person who is stealing bread from his or her kitchen? Does the right of self-preservation permit a person to steal from another to satisfy daily needs?" These classicists would be very uneasy granting people the right to self-preservation, because it would place the peace and order of the community in jeopardy.

Of course, Maududi believes that the strength of the Islamic conception of human rights is both similar and superior to the classicists' view of natural law. Maududi agrees with the classicist's argument that human reason is capable of knowing those laws that God gave to humankind to regulate their interactions. He also agrees with classicists when they argue that there are limits to the exercise of human reason, and that since humans do not possess the fullness of God's reason, humans are unable to divine some of the deeper recesses of God's mind. Therefore, Maududi believes that humans must not rely solely on their reason to understand divine law; they must also rely on that law revealed by God to mankind in the teachings of Mohammed. These teachings clearly point out those divine laws that Allah commands man to obey. The law of Allah, in Maududi's view, is knowable by reason and revealed by Mohammed; moreover, Allah has given all humans certain rights. Maududi believes that this granting of human rights is an improvement over the classicists' view of natural law. In the classicist's world, people have no recourse should their government wantonly take the lives of its citizens. Maududi believes that the extension of the right of self-preservation means that if a government violates that right, a citizen has a legal claim against the government. A government violating the rights of the people may be turned out and replaced with one that respects the rights of the people.

Both liberal feminists and radical feminists criticize the way in which Maududi interprets the rights of women. In their view, Maududi's philosophy is purely patriarchal, reinforcing the power of men over women. Maududi excludes women from Islamic politics for two reasons. First, he believes that males have an ability to govern that is not shared by women. For the well-being of society, men should rule over women in the public and private spheres. Second, Maududi takes Mohammed at his word when the Prophet says that nations ruled by women will certainly fall. Therefore, Maududi forbids women from holding political office; he does, however, permit them the right to vote. But Maududi's philosophy ensures that women will be restricted to the private sphere of the home, and that men will be able to use their positions in government and industry to reinforce their rule over women. Religion, according to the feminist viewpoint, is being used to buttress the power of men over women. Maududi believes that

Allah has given women certain rights, including the right to chastity. To feminists, female chastity is a patriarchal right, which makes certain that the son of the father is the one who will inherit the father's property. To feminists, the "rights" Maududi says have been granted to women in fact amplify the power that men have over women. By ascribing to women a specific function or position in Islamic society, Maududi's version of Islam denies women the opportunity to exercise their freedom in a way that men can. Lacking social and economic freedom and with no access to positions of power in religion, politics, and industry, women's oppression is particularly strong in Maududi's Islamic society. According to this feminist viewpoint, the liberation of women can take place only by destroying Islam; in destroying those laws that order or sanction the power of men over women, women would be liberated from men's patriarchal rule. Although Runyan and Peterson do not specifically address Maududi's patriarchal social and political theory, they believe that human rights should be broadened to include women's rights. They suggest that specific rights that promote and protect the rights and freedoms of women should be incorporated into the international inventory of human rights. However, the application of these rights can occur only with the cooperation of the countries involved, and this will require women to be in positions of political power.[98]

Maududi rejects the feminist criticism of the social position of women in Islamic society. In the face of what he perceives to be Western economic and cultural imperialism, Maududi desires to revive the traditional concept of Islamic society. He, like Ayatollah Khomeini, believes that Western cultural, economic, and political imperialism threatens traditional Islamic values. To his mind, the call to "liberate" women from the "shackles" of Islamic law and patriarchy is a blatant attempt by the West to tear asunder the fabric of the Islamic family. Attempts by the international women's movement to impose a Western conception of women's rights on traditional Islamic society amounts to cultural imperialism. If reason and the Shari'a lead Muslims to the conclusion that biological differences between men and women dictate differences in their roles and functions, then a just society will provide women with rights that give them a special and honored position in society. It is morally wrong—and culturally imperialistic—for non-Islamic nations to force their worldview on Islamic countries.[99]

Reflect for a moment about human rights. Would you agree with those classicists who believe that there are no human rights, only obligations to follow law? Do you agree with Maududi that human rights come from God and that corresponding obligations flow from those rights? Or would you agree with the liberal that there are indeed human and civil rights, which are products of human reason? Is the realist correct in asserting that there are no universal human rights short of those that develop in each country? If so, how do you explain the very broad support the United Nations Declaration of Human Rights enjoys in the world? To what extent should states pursue human rights in their relations with other states? Does the security of human rights for all peoples of the world hinge upon the development of a world state capable of enforcing them? Can the existing liberal international order adequately enforce human rights? How does one handle cases in which there is a conflict between human rights and national self-determination? As we have seen, a nation's right to manage its own affairs may come in conflict with the inalienable rights of humans. Can a nation or group of nations interfere with or intervene in the affairs of another country to press that government to respect human rights? On the one hand, the history of the last part of the twentieth century suggests that the community of nations is more willing to put aside the right to self-determination and to intervene where human rights have been put in jeopardy. With the support of many nations, international economic sanctions were placed on South Africa. Under international economic pressure and domestic political pressure, the South African government eliminated the policy of racial separation (apartheid) and admitted black Africans to the political system. On the other hand, there are numerous cases in which serious human rights abuses have occurred and nothing or little was done. Under the rule of Pol Pot in Kampuchea (Cambodia), an estimated one to two million people were killed in a brutal campaign to bring a "better" society into existence, but the international community did little to end the slaughter. Only the intervention of the Vietnamese was able to oust Pol Pot four years after he captured power. More recently, the nations of the world chose to intervene in Bosnia and Rwanda only after witnessing tens of thousands of men, women, and children shot, cudgeled, and hacked to death for political and tribal reasons. Given the sometimes conflicting principles of human rights and the right to national self-determination, human rights will remain one of the most divisive issues in world politics.

NOTES

1. Niccolò, Machiavelli, *The Prince and The Discourses,* intro. Max Lerner (New York: The Modern Library, 1950), 56.
2. Georg W. F. Hegel, *Lectures on the Philosophy of World History,* trans. H. B. Nisbet (Cambridge: Cambridge University Press, 1982), 69.
3. Hans J. Morgenthau, *Politics Among Nations,* 6th ed., rev. Kenneth W. Thompson (New York: Alfred A. Knopf, 1985), 32.
4. Edward C. Thaden, *Conservative Nationalism in Nineteenth Century Russia* (Seattle: University of Washington Press, 1964), 146–154.
5. Fyodor Dostoevsky, *The Diary of a Writer,* trans. Boris Brasol (New York: George Braziller, 1954), 387.
6. Ibid., 381.
7. Ibid., 575.
8. Ibid., 576–577, 979–980.

9. Jean-Jacques Rousseau, *The Social Contract and Discourses*, trans. G. D. H. Cole (London: J. M. Dent and Sons Ltd., 1973), 108–111; idem, *Rousseau on International Relations*, ed. Stanley Hoffmann and David P. Fidler (Oxford: Oxford University Press, 1991), 31, 36, 175–178.

10. J. Ann Tickner, *Gender in International Relations* (New York: Columbia University Press, 1992), 56, 74–76, 115–116.

11. John Locke, *Two Treatises of Government*, intro. Peter Laslett (New York: The New American Library, 1965), 374–376; Immanuel Kant, *Political Writings*, 2d ed., intro. Hans Reiss, trans. H. B. Nisbet (Cambridge: Cambridge University Press, 1991), 73–76.

12. Kant, *Political Writings*, 96.

13. Ibid., 132–133, 136–137, 164–165.

14. Ibid., 102–104, 105.

15. Thucydides. *The Peloponnesian War*, intro. T. E. Wick (New York: The Modern Library, 1982), 404.

16. Ibid., 193–201.

17. Immanuel Wallerstein, *The Politics of the World Economy* (Cambridge: Cambridge University Press, 1984), 4–6, 16, 33.

18. Ruhollah Khomeini, *Islam and Revolution* (London: K. P. I., 1981), 182.

19. Ibid., 197, 213–214.

20. Fred Bergsten, Thomas Horst, and Theodore H. Moran, *American Multinationals and American Interests* (Washington, D.C.: Brookings Institution, 1978), 3–41.

21. Pope Paul VI, "Populorum Progressio: On the Development of Peoples," *Catholic Social Thought*, ed. David J. O'Brien and Thomas A. Shannon (Maryknoll, N.Y.: Orbis Books, 1992), 245–246, 253–254; Pope John XXIII, "Pacem in Terris: Peace on Earth," *The Gospel of Peace and Justice*, ed. Joseph Gremillion (Maryknoll, N.Y.: Orbis Books, 1976), 220–221; Pope John Paul II, "Centesimus Annus: On the Hundredth Anniversary of Rerum Novarum," *Catholic Social Thought*, 445.

22. Michael Donelan, *Elements of International Relations Theory* (Oxford: Clarendon Press, 1992), 195–197.

23. Saint Thomas Aquinas, *The Political Ideas of St. Thomas Aquinas*, ed. Dino Bigongiari (New York: Hafner Press, 1953), 11–18, 175–177.

24. Pope John XXIII, "Pacem in Terris," 202–209.

25. Ibid., 222–223.

26. Ibid., 218–222, 226.

27. Heinrich A. Rommen, *The State in Catholic Thought* (St. Louis: B. Herder Book Co., 1945), 148, 185–186.

28. Ibid., 321–324.

29. Thucydides, *The Peloponnesian War*, 351.

30. Aristotle, *Politics*, trans. Ernest Baker (Oxford: Oxford University Press, 1958), 11–14.

31. Thomas Hobbes, *Leviathan*, ed. Michael Oakeshott (New York: Collier Books, 1962), 101.

32. Khomeini, *Islam and Revolution*, 195.

33. Ibid., 33, 127, 170, 239; Sayyed Abul A'la Maududi, *First Principles of the Islamic State*, trans. Khurshid Ahmad (Lahore: Islamic Publications, Ltd., 1960), 67–73; idem, *Human Rights in Islam* (Lahore: Islamic Publications, Ltd., 1977), 3–5; idem, *Selected Speeches and Writings of Maulana Maududi*, trans. S. Zakir Aijaz (Karachi: International Islamic Publishers, 1981), 151.

34. Morgenthau, *Politics Among Nations*, 71–77.

35. Ibid., 74.

36. Sayyed Abul A'la Maududi, *Unity of the Muslim World*, 4th ed. (Lahore: Islamic Publications, Ltd., 1979), 12–13.

37. Idem, *Political Theory of Islam*, 2d ed. (Delhi: Markazi Maktaba Jamaat-e-Islami Hind, 1973), 29; idem, *Selected Speeches*, 216, 240.

38. Khomeini, *Islam and Revolution*, 82.

39. Maududi, *Unity*, 11–12; idem, *Islamic Way of Life*, trans. Khurshid Ahmad (Lahore: Islamic Publications, Ltd., n.d.), 37.

40. Idem, *The Economic Problem of Man and Its Islamic Solution*, 3d ed. (Delhi: Markazi Maktaba Jamaat-e-Islami Hind, 1966), 8–23; Khomeini, *Islam and Revolution*, 170, 181–197, 237–240, 257–258.

41. Maududi, *Unity*, 4.

42. Farhang Rajaee, *Islamic Values and World View: Khomeyni on Man, the State and International Politics* (Lanham: University Press of America, 1983), 69–72, 82–83.

43. Maududi, *Jihad in Islam* (Lahore: Islamic Publications, Ltd., 1976), 18.

44. Ibid., 1–2, 5–9, 17–23.

45. Khomeini, *Islam and Revolution*, 27–28, 33–36, 127, 237, 239–240, 257–258, 286.

46. Ibid., 128, 131–132, 196, 234–235, 286–287, 323, 437, 439.

47. Morgenthau, *Politics Among Nations*, 32.

48. Ibid., 58–61, 67–77.

49. Nikolai I. Danilevski, *Russland und Europa* (Osnabruck: Otto Zeller, 1965), chaps. 9 and 10; Jacob W. Kipp, "The Zhirinovsky Threat," *Foreign Affairs* 73 (May/June 1994): 76–84.

50. J. S. Mill, "A Few Words on Non-Intervention," *Readings in World Politics*, ed. Robert A. Goldwin (New York: Oxford University Press, 1959), 324.

51. Khomeini, *Islam and Revolution*, 263–264; Youssef M. Choueiri, *Islamic Fundamentalism* (Boston: Twayne Publishers, 1990), 111.

52. Morgenthau, *Politics Among Nations*, 132–139, 397–398, 408–411.

53. Ibid., 143–145.

54. John J. Mearsheimer, "Why We Will Soon Miss the Cold War," *The Atlantic Monthly* (August 1990): 37.

55. Carolyn Merchant, *The Death of Nature* (San Francisco: Harper & Row Publishers, 1980), 103–104.

56. Ibid., 128.

57. Ibid., 156, 164, 192–193, 216–217, 234–235.

58. Tickner, *Gender in International Relations*, 100–111.

59. Ibid., 114–118.

60. Milton Friedman, *Capitalism and Freedom* (Chicago: University of Chicago Press, 1982), 27–31; Milton and Rose Friedman, *Free to Choose* (New York: Avon Books, 1980), 203–207.

61. Murray Wiedenbaum, "Leviathan in Rio," *National Review* 27 (April 1992): 45–56.

62. Locke, *Two Treatises*, 327–337.

63. *Pocahontas* (Burbank: Walt Disney Co., 1995).

64. For example, see Murray Bookchin, *Remaking Society: Pathways to a Green Future* (Boston: South End Press, 1990), 46, 93–94.

65. Jeremy Rifkin, *Biosphere Politics: A New Consciousness for a New Century* (New York: Crown Publishers, Inc., 1991), 39–77.

66. Donella H. Meadows and others, *The Limits to Growth*, 2d ed. (New York: Universe Books, 1989); Robert L. Heilbroner, *An Inquiry into the Human Prospect* (New York: W. W. Norton, 1991); William Ophuls and A. Stephen Boyan Jr., *Ecology and the Politics of Scarcity Revisited* (New York: W. H. Freeman and Co., 1992).

67. Meadows and others, *Limits to Growth*, 125.

68. Ophuls and Boyan, *Ecology and Politics*, 206–215, 290–304; Meadows and others, *Limits to Growth*, chap. V.

69. Ophuls and Boyan, *Ecology and Politics*, 285–304.

70. Bookchin, *Remaking Society*, 185–196.

71. Lynn White, "The Historical Roots of Our Ecological Crisis," *Western Man and Environmental Ethics*, ed. Ian Barbour (Reading, Mass.: Addison-Wesley Publishing Co., 1973), 25–28; Merchant, *The Death of Nature*, 1–31.

72. Genesis 1:26–30, 8:15–17.

73. Pope John Paul II, "Pope: Greed and Fight Against Poverty Threaten Tropical Rain Forests," *L'Osservatore Romano*, weekly ed., 28 May 1990, [4]; idem., "The Exploitation of the Environment Threatens the Entire Human Race," *L'Osservatore Romano*, weekly ed., 8 January 1990, [1]; idem, "Peace With All Creation," *Origins* 19 (1989): [5, 7, 9, 15].

74. Idem, "Peace," [3, 4]; idem, "On Social Concern," *Origins* 17 (1988): [29–30, 34].

75. Idem, "Peace," [5].

76. Ibid.

77. Ibid., [15].

78. Idem, "Exploitation," [2]; idem, "Centesimus Annus," *Origins* 21 (1991): [34, 36–37]; idem, "The Gospel of Life," *Inside the Vatican*, spec. suppl. (April 1995): [11–12, 18, 22–24].

79. Idem, "Gospel," [16, 91].

80. Ibid., [18].

81. Idem, "Peace," [1, 12].

82. Ibid., [11]; idem, "Greed," [3].

83. Idem, "Peace," [13, 15]; idem, "Environmental Ills Demand Political and Moral Answers," *L'Osservatore Romano*, weekly ed., 19 February 1990: [2].

84. Idem, "Centesimus Annus," [34–35, 40]; idem, "Peace," [9–10].

85. Maududi, *Unity*, 12–13; idem, *Human Rights*, 5.

86. Idem, *First Principles*, 3–5; idem, *Human Rights*, 3–8.
87. Idem, *Human Rights*, 3.
88. Ibid., 12.
89. Ibid., 14–32.
90. Ibid., 16–17, 31, 33.
91. Ibid., 14–16, 28–29.
92. Ibid., 11–12; idem, *Unity*, 29–33.
93. Donelan, *Elements*, 146–148.
94. Maududi, *Unity*, 31–33.
95. Rousseau, *Social Contract*, 165; Hobbes, *Leviathan*, 103.
96. Maududi, *Political Theory of Islam*, 2d ed. (Delhi: Markazi Maktaba Jamaat-e-Islami Hind, 1973), 15–18.
97. John Wild, *Plato's Modern Enemies and the Theory of Natural Law* (Chicago: University of Chicago Press, 1953), 151–153, 157–177.
98. Peterson and Runyan, *Global Gender Issues*, 159–160.
99. Maududi, *Selected Speeches*, 253, 258–262.

CHAPTER 5

THE BEST INTERNATIONAL POLITICAL ORDER

With the possible exception of war, nothing has occupied the thoughts of international political thinkers more than the question of what is the best international political order. And rightly so. What has been, what is, and what will be accomplished in world politics is limited or enhanced by the international political form. Political forms—whether characterized by a balance of power, a bipolar configuration of power, a world federalist system, an empire, or a liberal international economic and political order—effectively define and limit what can be accomplished by actors engaged in world politics. Compare, for a moment, today's political situation to that of the cold war era.

Some might argue the change in the international political order from the bipolar configuration that characterized the cold war to one dominated by the economic and political strength of the United States has helped spread democracy in the world. During the cold war, the United States and the Soviet Union clearly understood that Western Europe fell within an American sphere of influence, and that Eastern Europe fell within the Soviet sphere. Had the United States aggressively promoted Western-style democracy in Eastern Europe, Soviet hegemony in Eastern Europe would have been threatened. The Soviet Union may have responded to that threat by waging a conventional war, which may have escalated into a nuclear war. As a result, the United States and its Western allies did not attempt to intervene in the political matters of the Warsaw Pact nations. However, with the disintegration of the Soviet Union and the diminishing of Russian influence in Eastern Europe, those nations were free to adopt new political systems.

Many of them moved in the direction of appropriating Western liberal democratic institutions, at which point they received political and economic support from the United States and Western Europe. A change in the international political order enhanced the spread of democracy under the guiding hand of the United States and its democratic partners. In short, political change brought with it the promotion of a new set of values and institutions and a new political order.

Let us return to an earlier question that might help us begin to think about the best ordering of international affairs. If all forms of international authority and power (political and economic in particular) were to be abolished, what would characterize the relations between world political actors? Would they move to form some type of economic and political authority? Would these actors fall at each other's throats? In an ensuing war of all against all, would one hegemonic state rise to dominate other actors? Or would a concert of more powerful nations develop and order relations between themselves and lesser powers? Would these actors exist in some pristine anarchic condition, in which war and conflict have been abolished? Or would the actors organize a political system to promote their common interests and peacefully solve disputes? In the history of world political thought, there have been several stock answers to these questions. Most thinkers agree that the major actors in world politics would establish some way of organizing and exercising world political power. Historically, thinkers and practitioners of international relations have favored the balance of power, a universal monarchy or empire, a federal world government, and a liberal political and economic order as ways of managing political power on the world stage. Let us begin with the balance of power.

ON THE BALANCE OF POWER

He returns from the darkest recesses of the human soul: his eyes seared by sights too ghastly and horrible to comprehend, his face marked by terror, his mouth gaping with dismay, his body trembling with fear. He is witness to that part of human nature that turns dreams into nightmares, joyous life into violent death, hope into despair, comforting faith into disturbing doubt, and visions of heaven into spectacles of hell. He has seen the young killing the young; Gettysburg soldiers marching step-by-step into a battle that only souls escape; piles of skulls that seem to stare accusingly; monstrous cannibalism; piked heads; vicious rapes; cauldrons of ethnic and racial hate spitting death; and humans turning against humans for the sake of personal fortune or fame. A human is like a flagpole climber, whose goal is set beyond his or her ability to reach it. Slips down the pole are followed by ever-more laborious attempts to reach the top. The inner spiritual forces that the pole climber marshals to achieve his or her goal of reaching the top are defeated by the earthly force of gravity. So it is with our earthly nature: those spiritual forces leading us toward goodness or righteousness are forever struggling with and over-come by forces leading us into foulness and sin. For realists, the realities of human nature require them to think cautiously about the nature of politics, the motivations of humans, the purposes for which humans exercise power, and the ways the struggle for these purposes can be disciplined.

It is not surprising that this sordid depiction of human nature leads the realist to the conclusion that world politics resembles a Hobbesian state of nature; but such a condition is not without its benefits. States, like humans, are inclined to pursue their own (and often mutually exclusive) goals at the expense of others. States need power to achieve their goals, whether those goals are natural resources, international prestige, territory, agricultural products, peace, fair treatment in economic and political affairs, security from invasion, or power. But because states are essentially equal in power and inclined to pursue what they consider their own good at the expense of others, the international environment becomes inherently conflictual. Being equals in power, no one state has the capability of dominating another nation and bringing order to this chaos. Only through the exercise of power—and especially military power—can nations secure what they desire. And what a state desires most is to secure its own existence. Yet as strife-ridden as world politics is, it benefits nations in four ways. First, it allows states to exercise a large measure of freedom. Freedom, the absence of external impediments, characterizes this condition of international anarchy because there is no single world power capable of disciplining other states. Second, because there is no central authority to order the relations of states, political power is decentralized, or broadly shared among states. This prevents a central power from imposing its will on those states that wish to be independent of that power. Third, this condition of anarchy permits each state to develop its own national identity, culture, and political and economic system. In world politics, there are no ultimate standards for determining the just ordering of a nation's culture and life. Fourth, world politics calls on each state to rely on its own resources to defend, protect, and extend its interests without the help of others. This principle is called self-help, and it drives international politics.[1] However, conflict and war are the prices that nations must pay to secure these benefits. Are conflict and war worth the advantages that international anarchy brings with it? Is there a way of managing this struggle for power that gives nations a degree of security from the designs and machinations of other states?

For many realists, the answer is the balance of power. According to their perspective, the primary function of the balance of power is to preserve the independent existence of the state. It is not, as other realists might say, to prevent war; indeed, war may be necessary to protect the existence of a state. Whereas each state is interested in its own self-preservation, it is also interested in expanding its power to acquire what it desires in world politics. The state may covet natural resources, land, more markets for goods and services produced at home, or increased political prestige among the nations of the world. Thus, world politics is an arena in which states, in the process of pursuing their own interests, joust for power to maintain their existence as independent states. To the extent that nations desire to increase their power to protect and extend their existing power base, nations create a "security dilemma." For every incremental increase in the power that a nation pursues to increase its own security, other nations—fearing that their own security is threatened—take similar steps to increase their own power. This means that the security of the first nation will once again be in jeopardy. Hence the dilemma: the search for security results in increased insecurity.[2]

What drives the security dilemma is a nation's real fear that some other nation might acquire so much power that it would threaten the very existence of the weaker state. Even though realists cannot escape the security dilemma, they claim to be able to secure a nation's existence. If a balance of power between nations exists (that is to say, if no one nation or group of allied nations is superior in its power capabilities to other nations or groups of nations), no nation can politically dominate another nation. As a result, each nation—though always watchful of its power vis-à-vis other nations and always fearful that its existence would be threatened if another state's power surpassed its own—would have its existence as an independent state guaranteed. Take the analogy of two boxers of equal strength and talent fighting a fifteen-round match. They may emerge bruised and bloodied, but both would leave the fight "unconquered." However, when one nation amasses a preponderance of political power, the security of other states is placed in jeopardy. To prevent a nation with a preponderance of power from jeopardizing the security of a weaker state, the imbalance of power must be brought back into balance. As Sir Eyre Crowe, an early twentieth-century British politician, writes, the threats to the independence of states come from

> the momentary predominance of a neighboring State at once militarily powerful, economically efficient, and ambitious to extend its frontiers or spread its influence, the danger being directly proportional to the degree of its power and efficiency, and to the spontaneity or "inequitableness" of its ambitions. The only check on the abuse of political predominance derived from such a position has always consisted in the opposition of an equally formidable rival, or of a combination of several countries forming leagues of defense. The equilibrium established by such a grouping of forces is technically known as the balance of power.[3]

The balance of power may be used to prevent a state with a preponderance of power from subjugating neighboring states or expanding its territorial claims. Many methods may be employed to ensure that the balance of power is maintained. First, a state could increase its domestic power capabilities in such areas as population, industrial production and manufacturing, exploitation of natural

resources, agricultural production, size of the military, and military preparedness. For example, by increasing its industrial capacity, the state would become
more prosperous and would be in a better position to finance a larger and better-
equipped military force. Second, a threatened nation could form alliances with
like-minded nations. Alliances serve one important function: they aggregate the
power capabilities of the aligned states and thus can offset the political and military power capabilities of a preponderant state. By doing this, aligned nations can
increase the combined strength of their armed forces, share natural resources that
are vital to the national security of each nation, and strengthen trade relations that
would increase their domestic productive capacities and thus their ability to build
and maintain strong militaries. We could look to recent history to find an example
of nations forming an alliance to secure their common interest in survival. In the
face of Soviet expansion in Eastern Europe after World War II, the United States
and European nations created NATO; its primary goal was to aggregate the military capabilities of all the sponsoring nations to counter a military thrust into
Western Europe by the Soviet Union. Third, nations could engage in an arms race
to decrease a disparity in military power between two nations. For example, in the
early 1980s, President Ronald Reagan argued that the United States had fallen behind the Soviet Union in the nuclear arms race. He then proceeded to commit a
greater share of the nation's wealth to the upgrading of the nation's nuclear capability. His professed desire was to bring about a nuclear balance of power. Last,
war might provide one way of eliminating disparities in power. Recall the Peloponnesian War between Athens and Sparta. According to Thucydides, Sparta believed that war was necessary to prevent Athens from further increasing its power
to the point that it could overtake Sparta.[4] Thus, when one nation begins to act in
a way that increases its power relative to other nations, it may be prudent to go to
war to strip that nation of its ability to increase its power in the future. Nations
could do several things to achieve this objective. First, the conquering nations
might temporarily divide a nation among themselves. After World War II, Germany was divided into several sectors, each controlled by a major allied power.
The effect was to prevent Germany from uniting and once again pursuing its
plans for world domination. Second, conquering nations can "defang" a nation by
reducing its military capability. After the Gulf War in 1991, the United Nations
Special Commission was charged with monitoring the disposal of Iraq's weapons
of mass destruction, thus reducing Iraq's military power in the Middle East. These
and other techniques have been used to preserve the balance of power.[5]

What values do states operating within a balance of power system pursue?
Many realists argue that national self-preservation, power, political equality, and
freedom are the most fundamental values.[6] All nations organize for the purpose of
promoting the best life for their citizens, and their primary concerns on the international level are to protect their respective cultures, governments, economies, societies, and lifestyles. No nation wishes to change its lifestyle, and the only way of

protecting it is by accruing and wielding international political power. All this implies that the states in the international political system must also value political equality. That is to say, all nations should be roughly equal in power, equal in their ability to provide for their own self-defense, and equal in their capability to extend their interests abroad. Where political equality exists, no nation will be able to dominate other nations. On the other hand, political inequality can threaten the existence of some nations. To return to the boxing analogy, if one boxer is markedly stronger and more skilled than the other boxer, then the fight will most likely end with the stronger boxer knocking out the weaker one. Similarly, when one state amasses much more power than other nations, that nation has the ability to extend its domination over the others. This domination, often called imperialism, may be cultural, political, *or* economic, but in most cases imperialism is cultural, political, *and* economic. In cases of cultural imperialism, one nation may attempt to change the values and attitudes of another nation's citizens. Ayatollah Khomeini spoke fervently of the moral rot that the West had brought to Iran through its cultural, economic, and political presence. Citing economic imperialism, radical theorists criticize an international economic system that creates, perpetuates, and deepens economic inequalities that limit the ability of less developed countries to acquire sufficient political power to end their exploitation at the hands of rich and powerful developed countries. Thus, inequalities in political or economic power can threaten a state's existence and its ability to control its cultural identity and internal affairs. In addition to national security, power, and the equality of states, realists value the internal and external liberty of nations. Externally—in the absence of any international power to order the relations among states and enforce a common law or a common moral code—nations have great freedom to pursue their interests in world politics. They can choose to forge alliances with other nations and to break off these relations when it suits their national interest. Prudence—that knowledge that is necessary to achieve one's goals—is the primary virtue leaders use in choosing how to conduct international relations. If nations find it prudent to establish international norms, treaties, or laws to govern the relations among nations, these things should serve the self-interest of each. If a state believes that it is no longer in its best interest to follow these norms, treaties, or laws, that nation is free to cast them aside. Internally, states should be free to order their internal affairs as they desire, to create their own economic and political systems, and to implement those domestic policies that provide the state with sufficient power to secure its national interests.[7]

The nineteenth-century Russian nationalist and realist Nikolai Danilevski was particularly concerned with the balance of power between Europe and Russia. In his 1869 book *Russia and Europe*, Danilevski argues that history has produced ten great civilizations or cultural types, each with its own spiritual foundation. Looking back at history, he discerns a life cycle in all civilizations. The civilizations moved through the stages of birth, childhood, youth, maturity, old age, and death. European civilization had reached its height in the sixteenth and seventeenth centuries, but its power and influence were waning. Russian cultural life was heir to the Slavic civilization that was its youth. In Danilevski's view, the Russian people are the most culturally advanced of all Slavic peoples. Russians are the beneficiaries of the purest form of Christianity, which was embodied in the Russian Orthodox church. As Christians and people united in the peace of Christ, the Russian and other Slavic people were nonviolent and fit for political freedom. Freedom was possible for the Russian people because they lacked the lust for power and domination that served tyranny; obedient to the authority of the czar, they were capable of living freely within the laws of the state; and they had not succumbed to the greed of capitalism that drove European nations to the lawless pursuit of wealth.[8] Geographically, the Slavs lived in the Balkans, Eastern Europe, and Russia. They comprised peoples in Poland, Austria, Hungary, Ukraine, Slovakia, Serbia, Croatia, Slovenia, Albania, Bulgaria, Rumania, and Constantinople; however, they had not united into a single state or federation of states. In the Balkan region, they suffered repression under the scimitar of Turkey and under the gun of the Austro-Hungarian Empire. Indeed, Europe and Turkey feared that the union of the Slavs under Russian leadership would upset the balance of power between Europe and Russia. To prevent this union, Austria-Hungary actively worked to prevent the Slavic peoples from uniting with the Russians. As an emerging power and sitting at the east doorstep of Europe, Russia should not, according to Danilevski, involve itself in the political squabbles that took place between the European powers (France, England, Germany, and the Austro-Hungarian Empire) as they continually recalibrated their balance of power. The European nations agreed. The cultural, religious, and political dissimilarities between the Russian and European civilizations led European nations to exclude Russia from Europe's balance of power system. This led Danilevski to conclude that Europe's hostility to Russia forced Russia to become a military power in its own right and to use its military capabilities to protect itself. Only then were Russia's power and culture secure from European aggression.[9]

For Danilevski, the balance of power is not an artificial political construction built on diplomatic custom and usage. Rather, it is a natural, normal order of states in world politics. It supports the principle that each nation should develop its own culture and way of life, and it is a means of securing a nation's independent existence from attack by other states. Danilevski believes that Russia should unite her Slavic brothers of eastern and southeastern Europe into a Slavic federation. Only by uniting Slavs into a single cultural-political group could the Slavic cultural type free itself from the moral corruption of the Turks and Europe. Danilevski thinks that the union of Slavs under one roof would "inspire in all strata of society the feeling and the awareness of their ancestral and tribal kinship."[10] Only when Russia develops the political and military might to free the Slavs from the jaws of the European and Turkish powers could this Slavic federation be born. Danilevski sees this proposed federation as aggregating the power of all the Slavic nations in east and southeast Europe, thereby placing Russia in a better position to protect both itself and its fellow Slavs from Turkey and European powers. As long as an imbalance of power exists between the weaker Russia on one hand and the stronger European and Turkish powers on the other, Russia and its Slavic brothers would be unable to provide for their own national security. Thus, a Slavic federation provided one way for Russia and its allies to redress the imbalance of power that benefited Turkey and the European powers. However, Danilevski suspects that Russia and Europe would find themselves at war as Russia pushed to create a Slavic federation and moved to liberate the eastern and Balkan Slavs from European and Turkish hegemony.[11]

The liberal argues that realists are mistaken in their belief that nations have permanent and exclusive interests that result in conflict. World politics is not a zero-sum game: a "win" for one nation is not necessarily a "loss" for another. International relations are not always riddled by conflicting economic and political interests. The primary concern of nations is not necessarily the pursuit of power at all costs. Rather, there are broad common political and economic interests that all nations share that form a foundation for the high degree of international cooperation that occurs in international economics and politics. Cooperation, not conflict, is the rule of the day in world politics. Though a person can certainly find examples of the outright conflict and war between nations that the realist so vividly describes, these conflicts are dwarfed by a multitude of cooperative behaviors between nations. Take war. Most of the nations of the world are not at war today, nor will they be at war tomorrow. The leaders of most nations believe that peace is better than war, and that it is in their enlightened self-interest to resolve international disputes through negotiation rather than by war. War brings with it the disturbance of international trade and national prosperity, the destruction of human life and factories, and political problems for the national leaders that have to justify the human and financial costs to their constituents. Humans, rational by nature, are capable of sitting down at a table and sorting out differences in a peaceful way. The history of the world is marked by nations solving their problems through negotiation. Everyday negotiations take place to settle U.S. trade disputes with Japan or nuclear proliferation problems with the Democratic People's Republic of Korea (North Korea). Only rarely are interests so diametrically opposed that they can be solved only by armed conflict.[12]

Liberals disagree with the realists who believe that nations can easily pick and choose among the nations of the world to create alliances to prevent the rise of a hegemony in a balance of power system. Nations are not as free to break off old alliances and establish new ones as the realist believes. Nations are bound up in webs of political relationships and in a latticework of economic interdependence, all of which prevents them from ending and reforming alliances at will. Politically, it is unrealistic to think that nations that were at one time mortal enemies could easily form an alliance against a newly rising nation. In democracies—in which public opinion changes slowly and frames the parameters of what national leaders can and cannot do in foreign policy—the public tends to be slow to make friends with old enemies. Furthermore, nations are like birds of a feather: they flock together. Democratic nations tend to ally themselves with democratic nations in support of common values and foreign policy objectives. They are opposed to totalitarian and authoritarian political systems that challenge the fundamental values of liberty and equality so dear to their hearts. It stretches the imagination to believe that a democratic nation would ally itself with a totalitarian nation to preserve a balance of power. Alliances based on self-interest, like marriages of convenience, are built on shaky foundations and are easily broken. Furthermore, nations develop trading relationships with other nations, and they come to depend upon these trading partners to supply them with natural resources and/or to serve as outlets for manufactured goods. Nations would not be willing to put their economies in jeopardy by joining a different alliance that would make enemies of their trading partners.

The realist remains unfazed by these criticisms. First, the harmony of economic and political interests that the liberal believes exists between nations is an illusion. Nations are welded together simply by self-interest, and when a nation's self-interest is no longer served, it will break any agreement and start any conflict that does serve its interest. Whatever harmony exists in the world is the result of self-interested nations agreeing that their interests can best be served by working together. If at any time a nation is ill-served by its agreements or alliances, it will break them with the speed of light. The Greek dramatist Sophocles understood this well. In discussing the relationship between the cities of Thebes and Athens in *Oedipus at Colonus,* he wrote:

> Oh Theseus,
> dear friend, only the Gods can never age,
> the Gods can never die. All else in the world
> almighty Time obliterates, crushes all
> to nothing. The earth's strength wastes away,
> the strength of a man's body wastes and dies—
> faith dies, and bad faith comes to life,
> and the same wind of friendship cannot blow forever,
> holding steady and strong between two friends,
> much less between two cities.
> For some of us soon, for others later,
> joy turns to hate and back again to love
> and even if all is summer sunshine now
> between yourself and Thebes,
> infinite Time, sweeping through its rounds,

gives birth to infinite nights and days . . .
and a day will come when the treaties of an hour,
the pacts firmed with a handclasp will snap—
at the slightest word a spear will hurl them to the winds.[13]

Second, the birds of a feather argument is flawed. In opposing the ascension of a new power, nations of very different political persuasions are tied to one another out of simple self-interest. When the big bad wolf knocked at the door, the three little pigs did not quibble about what was the best house; they barred the door! Wise national leaders have the prudence and courage to break and create new alliances when a rising power threatens their national interests. When Saddam Hussein invaded Kuwait, his Arab brothers and sisters did not all rush to praise him for his leadership. With the exception of Jordan, Mideast Arab nations were shaking in their boots. If Saddam sat at their table, they knew they would be his next course! No, to secure their own independence, existence, and interests, nations will ally themselves with other concerned nations to prevent the rise of a hegemonic power. Third, a nation's preoccupation with its political existence is more important than the nations with whom it trades. Menaced by an ascendant power, nations will form the necessary alliances and will do what they can to remain as economically self-sufficient and independent of other nations as is possible. Prudent nations will not let themselves become economically dependent on other nations, nations that might at some future time become their enemies.

Classicists are concerned with the Arnold Schwarzenegger approach to the exercise of international power that realists display. Realists believe that there are no higher laws, norms, or moral principles that exist beyond and above human contrivance and world politics. Rather, the principles that guide the behavior of nations find their foundation in self-interest. Nations, living in an international environment filled with force, deceit, and fraud must live more prudentially, and they must always protect their own interests from the schemes of lesser states. Living prudentially involves adopting a course of action that permits them to achieve their international goals. If this involves breaking promises, assassinating political leaders, and violating the confidence of others, so be it. But classicists quiver at these suggestions. Nations form a society of nations. As a society, nations know and live by certain moral laws that serve to promote international justice. A nation, choosing to violate principles of international justice, will bring upon itself the weight of those nations committed to promoting justice in the world. As justice reigns in the breasts of humankind, it shall roll down like a mighty river, cleanse the land of wrongdoing, and seep into the soil, nurturing all life that grows upon it. Once again, no better example can be found than that of Saddam Hussein. In violating the fundamental right of Kuwait to exist as a nation, Saddam Hussein evoked moral outrage among the nations of the world. Most of these nations agreed to the economic sanctions that were levied against Iraq and many joined the international military effort to return Kuwait to its people. Nations also know that an international society is based upon honesty. If nations do not believe that other actors will keep their word, extended social action becomes impossible, bonds of solidarity relax, and strife increases. Thus, nations should always make agreements with the intention of upholding them and withdraw from them only with the consent of the other partner. Deceit and lying, so common in realist thought, do not serve the common effort of promoting international society. In fact, they hamper the efforts of nations attempting to act together to realize those things that are known broadly as the common good.

To the realist, the argument that nations form an international society motivated by sentiments of justice and honesty is an illusion. Rather, international society develops out of a concern to protect the interests of the state. Nations form alliances, conduct trade, and make international law simply because in so doing they benefit themselves in some way. In promoting their particular national interest, what is commonly called justice is often a salutary by-product. The desire of the United States for a secure and inexpensive source of oil led it and other like-minded nations to intervene in the Iraqi-Kuwaiti dispute and to restore the control of Kuwait to its rulers. By intervening, the nations vindicated the most fundamental principle of the balance of power: the right of each state to exist. Other than respecting the right of other nations to exist, countries are not bound by any transcendental moral code in their dealings with other countries. Rather, states base their foreign policies on prudence. In so doing, they take those actions necessary to ensure that their national interests are secured, even if this involves acting in a way that is often called "immoral" in domestic politics. The reality of international relations is that nations will employ whatever means are necessary within the realm of prudence to achieve their goals. In the arena of international politics, moral principles have no hold on the mind, and nations that act "morally" will become the certain victims of those nations whose policies are driven by less-than-moral motives. According to the realist, there is nothing inherently wrong with lying, deceiving, and breaking one's agreements in world politics. These things must be done for the good of the nation.[14]

Islamic fundamentalists and some Marxists argue that the balance of power is an outdated concept, because it presumes that nations are equal in power and assumes that nations will be able to protect their national interests. Historically, states may have been equal in power—that is to say, equal in the capabilities they possessed to achieve their goals on the world stage. This may have been true before the industrial revolution introduced huge disparities in economic and political power between developed and less developed nations; but it certainly is not true today. From the 1500s through the 1700s, European nations may have been fundamentally equal in their possession of world political power. Their political power rested on economies based on agriculture and commerce, and great gaps in economic and political power did not exist between them. But today, there are greater and lesser powers, and it is impossible to conceive that the power of Chad, Nicaragua, or Burma is comparable to that of the United States or of California, for that matter. For radicals like Wallerstein or Islamic fundamentalists like Ayatollah Khomeini, capitalism and industrialization have led to the rise of great concentrations of economic power in international relations. Nations that have not yet industrialized remain less politically powerful than nations that have successfully industrialized. These less developed nations do not have the capital, the variety of natural resources, the agricultural capability, the technical expertise, and the social solidarity to be major world powers. The United States, the "great Satan" for both Marxists and Islamic fundamentalists, ranks among the greatest powers in world politics. From 1945 to 1991, the so-called balance of power system may have ordered and balanced political relations between the United States and the Soviet Union and the blocs of nations that were associated with each. For the less developed world and the nonaligned world, the balance of power served to keep weaker nations in political and economic subordination to the more powerful and politically dominant nations. During the cold war, the world was carved up into capitalist, socialist, and nonaligned, developing nations. Developing nations that chose to remain within the capitalist sphere were exploited by multinational corporations and kept dependent on their senior partners. These nations were governed by elites that were educated in capitalist nations, and their traditional cultures were distorted by Western television programs that promoted Western values. Cultural and economic penetration reinforced the political domination of developing countries. For example, the Shah of Iran, a puppet of Western interests, was placed into power by the United States and Britain to secure their oil interests in Iran. For Islamic fundamentalists and Marxists, there is no equality of political power among the nations of the world, and the balance of power works to the advantage of the more powerful nations of the world and does not protect the interests of less powerful nations.[15]

This leads to a second criticism by Islamic fundamentalists: the right to self-determination and the independent existence of the state are not secured, but rather are subverted, by the balance of power. Regarding the right to self-determination, the balance of power has consistently led more powerful nations to intervene in the political affairs of the world's less powerful nations. This was certainly the case in Iran, where the Western powers installed the shah as their puppet.[16] However, the same is true in Western Europe. With the defeat of Germany after World War I, France and Britain imposed a peace settlement that denied Germany the right to manage its own military affairs. During the war in Vietnam, the Central Intelligence Agency (CIA) of the United States was implicated in the assassination of South Vietnam's president, Ngo Dinh Diem. To maintain a balance of power in Central Europe, Poland had been repeatedly partitioned by the great powers in the eighteenth and nineteenth centuries and made a buffer state between German princes and Russia. Thus, the reality of balance-of-power politics is that the self-determination and independent existence of states are not secured by that system. Rather, to maintain some balance of power, nations are carved and gobbled up to suit the great powers.

For the more radical feminists, one of the saddest commentaries on the balance of power is that it legitimizes war. Take the Gulf War of 1991. At what cost was this war conducted and concluded? It restored to power a patriarchal Kuwaiti government that does not recognize the rights of women and relegates them to a life of social inequality. The lives of women and children in Iraq and Kuwait were needlessly lost. Great sums of money were expended on a military adventure that could have been more profitably employed in addressing the global problems of malnutrition, starvation, and the denial of women's rights. Furthermore, a theory that permits war to balance power is fundamentally outdated. In an age of proliferating nuclear knowledge and technology, when nuclear weapons are still available and whose use could destroy civilization as we now know it, it makes little sense to place the fate of the world in the hands of those who believe that war is a justifiable tool in balancing the power of states. Ironically, the use of war to bring an asymmetrical system back into equilibrium could conceivably lead to a nuclear war that destroys the very nations the theory is intended to protect.

The realist responds that the inequality in world power, violation of a state's liberty, and the problem of war are not as problematic as the critics charge. There are inequalities in the distribution of power between nations in today's world, but that does not prevent the balance of power from functioning. First, a balance of power existed between the United States and the Soviet Union during the cold war. That balance of power protected the independence of those two powers. The balance of power also protected the existence of other nation-states. Under the policy of "containment," the United States entered into a number of alliances with free states around the world that wished to discourage the threat of a Soviet or communist thrust into their countries. After NATO was formed in Europe, no West European state lost its independence to the Soviet Union. The war in South Vietnam was fundamentally a war to protect a U.S. ally from an incursion from the north. Even though South Vietnam eventually fell to communist rule in 1975, had the war been prosecuted successfully, the territorial integrity of the country would have been preserved by the balance of power. Second, in the modern world the balance of power does not necessarily mean that nations are doomed to the master-slave relationship depicted by radicals and Islamic fundamentalists. There is nothing to prevent less developed nations from aggregating their power to confront developed nations. Indeed, the Islamic fundamentalist Maududi suggested that Islamic nations form an Islamic League of Nations to counter the overweening power of developed capitalist and communist states. The major oil-producing nations of the world formed OPEC to avoid economic exploitation by developed countries. Historically, OPEC has been successful in radically raising the price of oil sold to developed countries, and the organization secures to these nations a greater degree of independence from manipulation by industrially developed powers. Thus, the basic principles of the balance of power have survived historical change and are as applicable today as they were three hundred years ago, when they were developed.

The realist does not believe that the violation of a state's right to self-determination and the problem of war are serious criticisms of the balance of power. First, the fundamental goal of the balance of power is the preservation of the state. To that end, there may be times when the pursuit of the balance will lead to the intervention of some states in the affairs of other states. Because the balance of power is concerned with the preservation of states and not with the freedom of states to manage their internal affairs, the criticism that the balance of power fails to secure the right of self-determination cannot be justly made. There will be times when nations interfere in the internal affairs of other states. But this is the exception rather than the rule. Power is usually balanced by means other than interference in a nation's internal affairs. It may be regrettable that nations suffer from such interference, but it may be a necessary consequence of securing each state the right to exist. Second, although it is true that war is one way to redress an imbalance of power, a balance of power has the salutary effect of preventing war. Neither conventional nor nuclear war occurred between the United States and the Soviet Union and their European allies during the cold war. Strong arguments can be made that the balance of nuclear capabilities between the two superpowers (sometimes called the balance of terror) had the effect of preventing war between them. With a rough parity of nuclear capabilities and the capacity to unleash an unacceptable level of destruction on the other power, the United States and the Soviet Union avoided war between themselves and prevented it from breaking out in Europe. The same argument can be made for conventional war. When there is a balance of power between nations or alliances of nations, war is less likely. First, because equals in power have relatively equal chances of winning or losing a war, war is less likely. When one nation has a preponderance of power over another nation, that nation is more likely to go to war, because the probability of success is so great. Perhaps this was behind Saddam Hussein's desire to march into Kuwait. With the fourth-largest army in the world facing a puny Kuwaiti army, Hussein may have believed that war was the most expedient tool to increase his power capabilities in the Middle East by capturing Kuwait's lush oil reserves. Second, a war between equals tends to be more lethal, and it takes longer to conclude. Desiring not to become embroiled in a war that will last for many years, generate domestic political opposition, waste valuable national resources, and cost many lives, nations attempt to find diplomatic solutions to international problems.[17]

Finally, inherent in the feminist criticism of realism is the assumption that the balance of power is an androcentric, or male-centered, theory of world politics.

For the realist, the balance of power is not the result of centuries of social construction that has glorified the possession, use, and balancing of power by aggressive males. War is not a more serious form of masculine athletics involving the taking of life and territory, rather than the taking of medals. War is not for bigger boys with bigger toys. The desire for power, assertiveness, and a more comfortable life runs in the veins of all human beings, regardless of sex. The fundamental principles of the balance of power would be as valid under any form of sex-based rule: matriarchal, patriarchal, or androgynous (partaking of both male and female characteristics). Feminists delude themselves if they believe that they can eliminate war by eliminating patriarchy. To believe so neglects the fundamental political principles that are objectively rooted in human nature and evident to anyone who cares to pursue the political history of humankind. To base the foreign policy of a state on any other principles will risk the national well-being of that country.[18]

Sit back and reflect a minute on the balance of power and some of the objections that have been raised to it. Are the basic assumptions upon which the balance of power is built correct? Are humans and nations fundamentally egotistical, appetitive, and desirous of power? Do humans form nations for the purpose of satisfying their deepest desires for a comfortable life? Are nations primarily concerned with securing and exercising power? Can there be an ethical theory of international relations? Are there other values such as human rights, justice, or a more equal distribution of the world's wealth that are more important than power? Is the balance of power archaic, given the interdependent world in which the liberals say we live? Is the balance of power too dangerous? Does the balance of power legitimize war? Do asymmetrical power relationships between nations incline them to war or to peace? Does the balance of power lead to environmental destruction, as was suggested in the previous chapter? Does the balance of power make sense at all; do nations really attempt to balance the political power of other nations? Should world politics be ordered on other political principles? Some have argued that a world monarchy or empire is the best form of international organization. Let us now turn our attention to such world monarchies.

ON WORLD MONARCHY

In today's world, it may stretch the wondering process to make the argument that the best form of international political organization is a worldwide monarchical empire. In his own day, Dante Alighieri (1265–1321) was faced with the same problem: how to make an argument for a world monarchy in a day when people were beginning to organize themselves into more parochial nation-states. Dante wanted to discuss the "truth of the most beneficial yet most neglected of all these other beneficial but obscure truths [world monarchical government]" and "to draw it out of the shadows into the light."[19] His subsequent writing on the subject,

Monarchy, paints a picture of a world order ruled by one person. Dante's thoughts on monarchical world government are a panacea for those who have experienced the stress and emotional trauma of watching a world filled with domestic violence, terrorism, war, massive starvation, tyranny, human exploitation, divisive international politics, personal alienation, unmitigated social chaos, the yearning for a community of caring human beings, human brutality, and untold human sufferings. For those who value peace, unity, concord, justice, and freedom, Dante promises a glimpse of a much better world. In this context, Dante's thoughts are as relevant today as they were when he wrote them over six hundred years ago.

Dante, ever the classicist, holds an Aristotelian conception of human nature that he blends with Christian teaching. God created the universe and flooded it with that law that eternally orders all things. The physical laws of nature hold all parts of the universe together within a greater whole. These laws govern the movement of the stars and planets in the universe and keep them in their place. Just as there are natural laws that govern the physical world, so there are moral laws of nature that properly order the parts of the human soul and the relations between humans. The universe and all its laws are "naught else than a footprint of Divine goodness."[20] Humans are political animals whose imperishable soul and perishable body form an organic whole with the soul governing the body. Reason, which is unique to humans, is the property of the soul, and it is reason that has the ability to understand those universal, moral laws that direct humankind toward earthly and heavenly happiness. To the extent that reason directs the body to live in accordance with these divine laws, peace, unity, concord, and justice reign in the human soul. The body and soul are in union when the appetites of the body are directed toward goodness. However, this unity gives way to disunity when the body and soul pull each other in different directions: the soul toward divine goodness and the body toward earthly evil. When the soul and the body jointly move in the direction of following divine law, concord exists between body and soul. With the unity and concord of soul and body come the calmness and tranquillity of internal peace and justice. When individuals orient their bodies and souls toward living a life in accordance with divine law, they are just. Thus, a just person is one whose appetites are exercised according to God's moral law.[21] This notion that unity, peace, justice, and concord come with the right ordering of the body and soul should not surprise anyone. Take the case of music and studying. Although one may believe that some kinds of music (classical and new age music, for example) can put body and soul in a proper ordering that permits the mind to focus its attention on learning, one may also find that other kinds of music (heavy metal or rap, for example) agitate the body so that the mind finds it difficult to focus on studying. If the body and soul are properly ordered, the appetitive part of the body is quieted and does not generate passions that divert reason from its goal of studying. Similarly, a person passionately in love may find that the desires of the body are so strong that they put the rational capacity in bondage to the images of love. All the person can think about is his or her girlfriend or boyfriend, and this can make studying and the exercise of the rational capacity virtually impossible. Thus, only when the body and soul are properly ordered and in concord with one another can an individual successfully exercise reasoning ability.

Dante projects the notions of unity, concord, peace, and justice that exist in human nature into the sphere of domestic and world politics. Just as the soul and body compose an organic whole in which reason directs the appetites toward living a good life, a society is composed of related parts that work together to ensure that society seeks the good life. Each person has unique talents to contribute to the well-being of others in society. Unity among people results when carpenters, businesspersons, bakers, farmers, traders, and politicians contribute the fruits of their talents to society in a way that permits everyone to work for the well-being of the whole. From unity stems concord. In a society in which the people unite to pursue the good of all, concord results. Take the case of a driver who wishes to drive a team of horses and a load of wood across a bridge. When the driver identifies the goal toward which all work, when he or she uses his or her intellect and skill to direct the energy of each horse toward pulling the load of wood across the bridge, and when each horse pulls in the same direction, all elements work in concord or harmony to achieve their goal. In a society where all social parts are moving in harmony toward a common goal, all are at peace with one another, and peace brings civic tranquillity and calmness. As God intends all people in society to live in peace, unity, and concord with one another, He gives each person some talent that he or she can contribute to the good society, and He provides humankind with that moral law that should direct their activities in realizing a good society. Humans should aspire to live in a just society, one in which all people exercise their talents and do not interfere with others exercising theirs. Those capable of ruling should exercise their talents in governing, and those who are the finest bakers should stick to baking. A society is best governed if it is ruled by a monarch, because a monarchy is more likely than any other form of government to provide for a unity of purpose. A monarch embodies the common good of the entire nation and governs the nation in a way that all people find and contribute those talents that result in a unified, harmonious, and just society. This unity of purpose and function is not found in other forms of government. Democracies inevitably lead to division and dissension between parties striving for power; and unity, peace, concord, and justice give way to division, strife, contention, and injustice. A democracy might be likened to a society in which all people have their own watches set to their own times. With no common time, each holder of the watch fiercely defends to the death the calibration of his or her watch, and peace gives way to discord. With no common time, no work can be accomplished, because each person comes to and leaves work by his or her own watch, and this results in chaos. A monarch can establish the time by which all watches are calibrated and can bring a degree of unity, peace, and concord to the affairs of humankind.[22]

Extending these ideas to world politics, Dante argues that a monarchy is the best form of world government and goes to extraordinary lengths to justify his argument. Dante defines a world monarch as "a single Principality extending over all peoples in time, or in those things and over those things which are measured by time."[23] Thus, a world monarchy is one that is temporal or earthly: confined by both space and time. By space, Dante means that a world monarchy embraces many nations. By time, he means that the monarchy is limited to the life span of the prince or princes who exercise their authority over those nations. Dante bases his preference for monarchy upon the assumption that unity is good and multiplicity is bad. He justifies his preference for unity over multiplicity with a reference to the unity of God. God is the one source, governor, and sustainer of all things in the universe, and the "heartbeat" of God drives all things in the universe to their individual and collective destinies. Humans are made in the image of God, and humans should strive to be like God. To be like God is to unify all things under one rule and it is monarchy that achieves the greatest unity. Therefore, monarchy is the best form of government.[24] Dante also justifies world monarchy by suggesting that because the whole is governed by one person and the whole is comprised of parts, one person should rule over the parts. Thus, the nations of the world (the parts) should be subject to the rule of one person, the monarch, who rules over the whole of humanity. Dante also justifies world monarchy on the basis of justice. First, he argues that justice can rule in the world only when there is one person with the strength to pursue justice. A world monarch has the greatest amount of power at his disposal and justice is therefore more likely to be achieved. Second, a world monarch is less likely to be tempted by acts of injustice because as ruler of the world, there is nothing else in the world that he can desire. Therefore, a world monarch (lacking temptation) is least likely to be unjust. Another argument justifying monarchy centers on world concord. Because the unity of humankind is achieved under a monarch and concord or the harmony of humankind is grounded in that unity, a monarch is necessary for concord. Finally, Dante argues that a monarch promotes the greatest liberty for the people of the world. Freedom is willing according to the laws of God and of the monarch. A world monarch rules in the common good of all humanity. Freedom is one of those goods that humans enjoy because they are by nature free. Thus, a world monarchy secures the greatest amount of freedom for the people in the world.[25]

From the justification of world monarchy, Dante draws a picture of a world society in which peace, unity, justice, concord, and freedom reign. Although Dante is not altogether clear on what he specifically means by peace, it appears to be the calm and tranquil repose of a body. Whether it is the human body, the family, city, state, or world empire, all bodies are composed of parts. For peace to occur in these bodies, each part must be ordered so that it does not disturb the functioning of the whole body and it does make its unique contribution to the harmonious functioning of the whole. Peace results when all the parts order their activities to contribute to the well-being of the whole. Hence, peace for human beings rests in the tranquillity that results from the proper ordering of the parts of the soul and body; in a family, from the ordering of the man's authority over his wife, children, and servants; in the state, from the rule of a prince who rules in a way that harmonizes the social, economic, and political activities of his subjects and associations and thereby promotes the common good; and in a world empire, from the rule of the world monarch that harmonizes the relations of all nations in a way that permits all individuals to develop their moral and intellectual capacities as humans.[26] But peace cannot occur in the absence of unity, justice, concord, and freedom.

Unity is a fundamental condition for peace. In the absence of a monarch capable of ordering the world toward the common good of all peoples and nations, world politics is marked by nations divided against themselves. Motivated by the desire for worldly gain and power, nations march to and fro across the earth bringing war, suffering, death, and desolation. Never satisfied with the goods of this world, nations are driven into continual contention.[27] Having little care for the common good of all humankind, the strife of nations can only be ended when a single world monarch ascends to the head of an empire and descends into world politics with the sword of unity to bring peace, justice, and concord to the nations of the world. Only a world monarch can deliver the war-wearied world from its hell of sword, carnage, and fire. Armed with law and military might, the monarch can bring unity and peace to a world rent by discord. By following divine law, the monarch is able to bring to earth law capable of ordering the relations of nations. In so doing, the monarch can orchestrate the economic and political activities of each nation for the good of humankind.[28] Although divine law is one source of international law, it does not often deal with specific conditions; thus, the monarch is free to make other laws that are grounded in divine law but are also applicable to specific situations. On the one hand, as the human race exists in fundamental unity, the monarch is free to make law that applies to all peoples, in all places. This law, which emanates from the monarchy and may reach into the homes of all people on earth, should be enforced by the rulers of all nations. Examples of these laws concern marriage, slavery, military service, and promotions in military service.[29] On the other hand, Dante believes that nations and cities have differing social, economic, and political environments; and these political units need to be governed by laws that are peculiar to these peoples but always in conformity with divine law and the international common good.[30] Whereas the law of nations, legislated and enforced by a world monarch, brings unity to the nations and peoples of the earth, the world monarch also needs a judicial power to settle disputes between nations. Because nations occasionally pursue their own interests at the expense of others and fall into discord with one another, a third party, the world monarch, is necessary to render an authoritative judgment. Only this monarch, who has authority to render a judgment in international disputes and possesses the military power to enforce it, will bring a unity of purpose and peace to the nations of the world.[31] In summary, world peace can come only from the unity provided by a single monarch who lays down a binding law for the nations and peoples of the world, who has the power to enforce it, and who has the means to settle international disputes.

Although justice is another condition for peace in the state and the world, Dante devotes little attention to it. Dante agrees with Aristotle that a monarchy is the best form of government, because we are more likely to find one virtuous man to rule than a society of virtuous men capable of ruling well. Because the function of governing is to lead humans to a life of virtue, the rule of a monarch, rich in virtue, offers the best hope for achieving this end. One of the component parts of virtue is justice. A monarch, who is filled with the greatest virtue, will be the most just. It is his duty to see that the state is justly governed. The monarch must lay down law that serves to predispose the soul of each member of the state toward justice, and he should create a socially just state that harmonizes the activities of all people and associations in the state to promote the well-being of all. Justice leads to peace. By promoting justice in the individual, the monarch must order each person's body and soul so that each person may find a certain tranquillity and calmness in his or her life. By creating a socially just state, the monarch would orchestrate its economic and social activities so that all people have their basic needs met, have the opportunity to develop their moral characters, and have the wrongs committed against them requited. The triumph of justice will bring peace to society. A society that provides for the basic needs of all its citizens and provides an honored place in society where they can exercise their talents will not be riddled by class division, envy, and hatred caused by differences in wealth. Thus, the tranquillity produced by justice inevitably leads to peace in the state. Justice in the affairs of nations produces peace, as well.

Although Dante does not discuss justice in international relations in great detail, two things are evident in his writings. First, he believes that justice and peace can be attained only when international disputes are settled by a third party that has the power to enforce its decision. Nations go to war because of the injustices that they suffer at the hands of other nations, and the world monarch must therefore lay down and enforce those laws that prevent nations from unjustly taking advantage of one another. If one nation discards this law and falls at the throat of another nation, the feelings of injustice can be erased only when the aggressive state is brought to trial for its actions. In this case, the dispensation of justice seeks to heal the wounds of those who have suffered great injustices and to orient unjust nations toward justice by punishing their transgressions. Second, international peace requires social justice. A socially just world guarantees that the peoples of all nations are provided with adequate food, water, clothing, educational opportunities, moral development, and intellectual growth. Meeting the needs of the people of all nations requires a certain redistribution of the world's resources from rich to poor nations, so that all people in the world have the opportunity to develop their uniquely human capacities. If capital, natural resources, education, food, water, and shelter are spread across the world in a way that meets the needs of the people of each nation, there are fewer reasons for nations to go to war.[32]

Only a monarch promoting unity and justice can bring concord. Concord is the harmonious working of all parts of a body toward a common end. In world politics, concord is the working of all nations toward peace, justice, and freedom coordinated by the world monarch. International concord suggests that the good of one nation is tied to the good of other nations. Nations that are unified in their pursuit of justice for their own peoples and for the peoples of other nations have the power to cultivate justice in nations seething with hatred and injustice. By the same token, those nations and individuals that choose to live unjustly threaten the moral and material well-being of other nations. Take the case of Adolf Hitler, who managed to affect the life of virtually every person on earth. Morally, his philosophy of "Aryan" superiority twisted the minds of those who fell under its spell, and today, its legacy lurks in the minds of those involved in irrational, reactionary right-wing organizations. Materially, his march through Europe brought want, suffering, and death. The war, which brought down home, city, and cathedral, destroyed the aspirations, hopes, and dreams of millions of ordinary people who only wished to live in bonds of love, charity, justice, and friendship with those around them. To achieve concord in the world, then, Dante believes that a world monarch is necessary to orchestrate the actions of all nations toward achieving unity and justice.[33]

Finally, Dante argues that only a world monarch is capable of promoting the liberty of all people on earth. Once again, his writing is not very clear about this; however, it is possible to draw some conclusions from the comments that he makes about liberty and the other principles that form the foundation of his world political theory. Dante believes that freedom is the choice of obeying or disobeying the laws of God and of the world monarch. Liberty for states and human beings is possible only if the nations of the world obey international law laid down by the monarch and God. When there is no willing obedience to international law, anarchy results: a veritable Hobbesian war of every nation against every nation. In an anarchic international environment, the freedom of states and people is reduced. Independent states become more preoccupied with their existence because they lack the opportunity to work together to promote international justice and peace. Driven by the necessity to secure their independent existence, states find it necessary to repress the liberty of their subjects in the name of national security. They divert monies from domestic programs to defense budgets, leaving fewer resources for the material and moral development of their people. In the subsequent impoverishment of the nation, humans struggle to meet their basic human needs; thus, they do not have the freedom to leisurely pursue a life filled with all the spiritual goods that lead to happiness. Dante's conclusion is simply that only a world monarch has the ability to lay down that law that forms the foundation of international peace. Operating within that law, nations freely work with one another to promote the common good of all nations, and internally they promote the material and moral development of their citizens, development that will grant those citizens the greatest freedom.[34]

In summary, Dante's world political theory hinges on a world monarch with the power to promote peace in the world. All humans are brothers to one another and they organize in nations to promote the common good and their happiness. Because the peace and happiness of one nation are dependent on the peace and happiness of others, Dante places the princes of all nations under the rule of a world monarch. In bringing peace to the world, the monarch promotes the unity, justice, and concord of all people. The monarch concerns himself with managing a complex, international brotherhood of man that promotes the spiritual and material well-being of all. Working under the wise guidance and just laws of this world monarch, all the people and nations of the earth join in a common effort to bring peace, justice, concord, and unity into the daily lives of all peoples. For then all the people of the earth can rightly proclaim, "Peace on Earth, and Good Will to All."

The realist, awestruck by the argument for world monarchy, responds in the words of the fourteenth-century critic Pierre Dubois:

> No sane man could really believe that at this period . . . one individual could rule the world. . . . If a tendency in this direction did appear there would be wars and revolutions without end. No man could put them down because of the huge populations involved, the distance and diversity of the countries and the natural propensity of human beings to quarrel.[35]

However, Dante was writing in a time when a monarch would rule a much smaller world than ours. With a universal monarchy confined to the Mediterranean and Western Europe, a stronger argument could be made for monarchical rule. Today, monarchical rule is out of the question. Ruling our world would involve governing the affairs of some 185 countries, and many of those nations have vastly different cultures, customs, and traditions. It stretches the imagination to believe that these nations, so culturally different, would accept the governance of a monarch perpetuating a Western, Christian political tradition and culture. Moreover, a universal monarchy would not bring peace to the nations of the world. As Dubois points out, it is in the nature of people to quarrel, and even though a world monarch would employ a worldwide military force, the irascible nature of humans and states would eventually lead to war. Conflict will occur between nations that, by Dante's own admission, are culturally dissimilar and have opposing national interests. A world monarch might reduce the probability of war by limiting or abolishing the militaries in each nation. However, this raises the horrifying spectacle of a monarch ruling autocratically over the world with no check on his power. And finally, Dante believes that there is a fundamental brotherhood of man transcending national borders and that a world monarch is necessary to secure this unity. In point of fact, however, this unity does not exist, and nations will always strive to be free from imperial rule. The nations of the world are too culturally, economically, and politically diverse to permit the rule of a monarch capable of laying down a common law for all humankind. Peace, justice, concord, and unity are not the primary goals of nations; rather, nations desire to protect their independent existence. Fearing the rise of a hegemony that would subject them to a life not of their choosing, nations will go to war to protect their political independence and cultural uniqueness.

To a classicist following Dante, the problems associated with governing a world of 185 independent, culturally different nations are rather negligible. First, the cultural differences between nations are not a hindrance to establishing a world monarchy as realists claim. Because humans are created with a rational capacity and because there are moral laws discoverable by rational creatures that should guide the relations between individuals and nations, all humans, regardless of culture, have the ability to know these laws. Such laws might include the right for a nation to exist, the right of nations to conduct their international affairs within the laws prescribed by the monarch, and the right of nations to legislate in matters that do not directly affect the powers of the monarch. Thus, there is a body of law knowable by reason that transcends culture and history, which can form the basis of an international community. Second, realists argue that a world monarch will be unable to bring peace to the world because of the quarrelsome nature of humans. For a classicist, this argument is based upon a false assumption: humans are naturally selfish, egotistical beings who cannot make the individual sacrifices necessary to jointly promote the common good. Reason and history demonstrate that humans can and do work together to promote the common good. Reason tells us that individuals are naturally inclined to do good and avoid evil; no reasonable person believes that one should kill people for the enjoyment or thrill of it, for example. In world politics, nations desire to promote the common good, which includes peace and justice, and they desire to avoid evil, which includes war. History demonstrates that nations prefer peace to war; that is why peace is the ordinary condition of nations and why war is the exception. When peace breaks down, it is because a nation's leaders mistakenly conclude that war is a good in itself or that it is a means of achieving some important goods. Saddam Hussein thought that a war to acquire Kuwait was somehow good. In fact, there was nothing good about that war: he did not realize his objective of taking Kuwait, the Iraqi people have endured economic hardships as a result of the economic sanctions that have been levied against Iraq, and the lives of many Iraqi soldiers and civilians were lost in the war. When the leaders of nations conclude that their best interests are served by adherence to international law laid down by a monarch promoting the common good of all nations, and when they see that this law will be unhesitatingly enforced, war will disappear from the face of the earth.

Liberals fear international tyranny, and they see world monarchies as bringing tyranny, the loss of economic freedom, and war. Tyranny is the greatest threat that a universal monarch presents to the world. What is tyranny other than "the accumulation of all powers, legislative, executive and judiciary, in the same hands, whether of one, a few, or many."[36] With these words, the American political theorist (and later president) James Madison spells out the liberal's fear of centralizing all political power in the hands of a monarch. Unless world political power can be dispersed among various nations and other international actors, there is no conceivable way to check the singular and massive power of a universal monarch. Although humans are rational and capable of making decisions benefiting the whole of humankind, there are also those who would use absolute political power to benefit themselves. A world monarch would have a magnitude of power that dwarfs the most powerful nation in the world today. Having collected all the power the world has to offer, history shows that monarchs have desired yet more power, and with that comes a more thorough tyranny than any person has imagined to this day. As Lord Acton put it, "power tends to corrupt and absolute power corrupts absolutely," and a world monarch with the greatest power would be faced with the greatest temptations.[37] It is wrongheaded to assume that the absence of any land to conquer will quell the appetites of a world monarch. Humans will always have appetites—if not for territory, then for additional wealth, perhaps, or for greater social prestige. Once a monarch is left with nothing else to conquer, he or she will turn his or her appetites to some other object and establish a tyranny more thorough than anything we can possibly conceive. Second, the accretion of political power into the hands of a single monarch will lead to the loss of economic liberty. An economic system functions best when it is largely left to itself. The capitalist world economy produces a harmony of interests, which can benefit all nations and peoples of the world. Despite this, a person like Dante would permit a world monarch to manage the international economic system in a way that redistributes wealth and capital from richer to poorer parts of the world. This would inevitably result in the loss of the liberty and sovereignty that nations have in handling their own economic matters. Even if one were to attempt to manage the economic development of all the nations of the world, one would find out it would require an economic knowledge of the world and national economies that transcends human understanding. To do so for 185 nations would require an intellect so expansive and a command of the world economy that is so intrusive that one person or group of persons would be unable to understand and manage it, and if they did, the freedom of individuals and nations to manage their economic affairs would be extinguished. Finally, an international monarchy could be purchased only at the expense of war. Few if any nations would be willing to re-

linquish the internal and external sovereignty and freedom that they have to manage the domestic affairs of their peoples and their foreign policies. Should a
would-be monarch attempt by persuasion or force of arms to rob nations of that
sovereignty and freedom, the nations of the world would organize a military force
and resort to war. If world peace is an important goal, then the spread of representative governments worldwide is the best hope for humankind. If social justice
is the goal, a capitalist world economy is the best solution to the problems of economic development and poverty. If concord is the goal, representative governments are the answer, because they respect and foster the values that can permit
nations to live in harmony with one another. Representative governments respect
the differing cultures of other nations, respect the right of all nations to exist, and
respect the freedom that nations have to determine their own social, economic,
and political institutions.

To the classicist, the liberal's concerns about tyranny, the loss of economic
freedom, and the specter of war are unfounded. It is not true that absolute power
would lead to a tyranny for several reasons. First, if tyranny is the possession of all
political power in the hands of one person, this would not be the case under a
world monarch. The nations of the world would possess a share of the world's political power. Under a world monarch, countries would have a base of political
power for handling the economic, social, and political affairs that were not a concern of a world monarch. By definition, the world monarch could not lapse into
tyranny. Second, since nations would have a police or military force to enforce the
laws of the state, these nations could conceivably produce weapons and mass
their forces against a monarch who became a tyrant. Third, a monarch would
serve the common good if for no other reason than he can never escape the people
over whom he rules. Today, tyrants may flee from their own citizens by taking
refuge in another country. Under a world monarchy, a tyrant would find no sanc-
tuary on earth. Finally, as Dante believes the monarch would be one of the world's
most virtuous and righteous men, a good man would not be tempted by the
power of this world. Because the abuse of his power would bring such sin to his
soul and with it the threat of damnation and hellfire, a monarch would be inclined
to serve the common interest of the people of the world. Regarding the criticism
that economic freedom in domestic and world capitalist systems would be jeopardized, the liberal is wrong to think that economic freedom gives individuals,
multinational corporations, and powerful nations the right to run riot over the
world in pursuit of profit. The historical record of capitalism is one of the exploitation of labor at the hands of those who own the means of production. If
peace and solidarity between workers and capital are to be achieved on a world
level, they will require a power strong enough to manage those relations. Only a
world monarchy presents that hope. Finally, war—not peace—is the fate of nations and an international system that are not based upon the monarchical principle. Monarchy brings peace, unity, concord, and justice. Representative political

systems develop two or multiparty systems that lead to internal dissension, division, alienation, and the rule of the stronger party (often the majority) over the weaker. When nations are politically divided, leaders will find reasons to foment war to increase their public support at home, and when faced with a real or imaginary enemy, the people will bury their differences and rally behind the regime and their flag. The modern, independent state system does indeed bring war. And only a universal monarch can provide adequate remedies to the problems and injustices that characterize world politics.

For a political radical like Jean-Jacques Rousseau, world monarchy is not the solution to the two problems with which he is most concerned: war and freedom. In his view, peace and justice are only possible in an aboriginal society, in which the desire for property, wealth, social prestige, and narcissism has yet to take hold of the human soul. Modern industrial society has substituted egotism and political, social, and economic inequality for the peaceful, compassionate, natural person that Rousseau honors. He sees the modern desire for property, wealth, and political power as corrupting and distorting human relations. The pursuit of great wealth virtually extinguishes the compassion and justice that are written into the hearts of all persons. The pursuit of wealth drove the eighteenth-century industrialist to create the modern industrial sweatshop that exploits the laborer. The tyranny of the clock replaces the freedom that aborigines enjoy. To enforce their economic rule over the poor and exploited, the rich harness the power of the government to their burgeoning economic power. As a citizen of eighteenth-century France, Rousseau saw the corruption of, and the suffering brought on by, the French kings and members of the aristocracy. Monarchy, from his perspective, is the culmination of economic and political processes that raise the rich to the heights of political power. Internationally, balance of power politics creates forces that reinforce the exploitation of the people. The pursuit of power requires larger armies and added taxes on the already overtaxed poor. The pursuit of power means that nonindustrial nations have to industrialize if they are to produce the wealth necessary to equip and maintain armies, and the exploitation of the poor and weak is played out again in every nation that chooses to enter the game of international power politics. However, Rousseau believes that international political power is distributed too widely among nations of the world to permit the rise of a world monarch. If someone were to try to ascend a global throne, his efforts would be blocked by an alliance of other nations or by war. Thus, the social, economic, and political evolution of modern industrial societies leads to balance-of-power politics, the loss of liberty, and war. Rousseau believes that world peace and freedom are possible only with the proliferation of small, agrarian, economically self-sufficient direct democracies. He sees small democracies as promoting freedom: the obedience to self-prescribed law. According to Rousseau, people are free only when they actually assemble to make or prescribe the laws according to which they live. By his account, even the most virtuous world monarch stifles freedom, because he imposes laws—laws that were not made by the people themselves. Rousseau also asserts that only small, agrarian, self-sufficient, or autarchic democracies promote international peace. Rousseau believes that agricultural economies are not likely to produce nations of great wealth; thus, other nations are not tempted to acquire them by war. Self-sufficient nations will not, according to Rousseau, become involved in relations of economic interdependency with other nations. He believes that economic interdependency spawned by the modern world economy threatens peace, because nations, dependent for their well-being on other nations, are willing to go to war to ensure the supply of vital commodities such as oil. Therefore, peace and liberty are possible only with the proliferation of autarchic, direct democracies.[38]

For those favoring world monarchical government, the suggestion that peace and freedom can be obtained by the proliferation of small, agrarian direct democracies smacks of fantasy. First, the world is no longer built around small, agrarian, face-to-face societies molded on the tradition of the Greek city-state. Face-to-face societies have small populations; their people share a common culture and get to know one another intimately; and they can personally affect social, economic, and political life. Today's states are founded on an industrial, commercial, and informational economy. Their economic and political size dwarfs the largest face-to-face direct democracies that can be imagined. It is unimaginable, short of an extensive, worldwide transformation or collapse of the industrial world, that the world will ever revert to an agrarian way of life. Even if a world composed of direct democracies did arise, the people of these nations would not be free. Freedom is not obedience to self-prescribed law, but willing obedience to the law issued from divine and human authority. God's law and all human law derived from God's law are made for the purpose of directing humans to earthly happiness and eternal felicity. Humans are truly free if they acknowledge and obey those laws that allow them to live in peace, love, and charity with their neighbors. Only a world monarchy under the guidance of God's wise laws provides the foundation for this earthly life. Second, the history of ancient Greece is the history of warring city-states. Athens, perhaps the most democratic city-state of its day, and Sparta, a city-state with an agricultural economy, pulled the Aegean world into the Peloponnesian War. The squabbling of these city-states was ended when Alexander the Great invaded and conquered them and established a world monarchy. His empire, which stretched from the Aegean to India, was based on the principle of homonoia, the brotherhood of man, and his rule brought a degree of peace to the Greek city-states that was unknown in fifth-century Greece. Thus, if historical experience were to be our guide, a universal monarchy is more likely to promote peace than a system based upon fiercely independent city-states.

For feminists, world monarchy is world patriarchy, and Dante's worldview is based upon a conception of hierarchy that ultimately shackles women to a home as dark, dreary, and inhospitable as any medieval subterranean dungeon. This hierarchy can be found in Dante's order of creation. Everything has its allotted place in all of God's creation. In humans, it is the place of the soul to direct the body, of the husband to manage the household, of the monarch to rule the kingdom, of the world monarch to govern the world, and of God to rule the universe. As there is a ruling part in the structure of nature, so there are those who are to be ruled. The body should be subject to the soul, the wife dutifully obedient to her husband, male citizens subject to the monarch, all of humankind obedient to the world monarch, and the monarch faithfully obedient to God. Although this hierarchy places man a little lower than the angels, it puts women just above a slave. As long as power is conceived as "power over" someone or something; as long as men are considered to be competent and legitimate managers of the public world of business and politics; and as long as women are conceived to be the weaker, the more emotional, the less intelligent sex, men will exercise their power in the home, in business, and in politics in ways that will prevent women from exercising their minds, bodies, and talents in ways that will improve the condition of humanity. As long as men have substantial control over how a woman thinks about herself, her dreams of freedom and self-fulfillment will fade with each morning's sunrise only to reappear after the setting of the sun. In between, life is meaningless toil and perpetual bondage. The liberation of women and men lies in destroying the religious myth of hierarchy, and replacing it with a view of mutual autonomy. Properly exercised, power should not be conceived as an ability to control subordinates or limit human potential; rather, power should be liberating and empowering. All people should be "empowered" to pursue their aspirations and dreams in cooperation with others so that other individuals can realize their hopes and visions for a better life. Applied to world politics, the hierarchy of superpower over the powerless, core over periphery, and the haves over the have-nots must give way to a mutual cooperation of nations to realize the hopes and aspirations of all nations. The most practical way of doing this is by bringing more and more women into traditional centers of international power, for example, the World Bank; presidencies, prime ministries, and chancellorships of nations; multinational corporations; foreign policy bureaucracies; legislative bodies; political parties; the United Nations; and other international political actors that affect the horizon of freedom for all the earth's people. Because women tend to put a human face on power and use it to empower others, the inclusion of women in these traditional positions of power will permit women to remake how world political power is conceived and exercised. By empowering all peoples of the world, great strides can be made in ending world poverty; stopping war and genocide; eliminating racial, gender, and ethnic discrimination; freeing women and minorities from antiquated social structures; ending domestic violence; expanding discussions of international rights to address women's rights; and protecting the world's environment.

Dismiss the hierarchy of creation if one desires, retorts the classicist; but to do so is to cast creation into confusion. In the Disney film *The Lion King*, Simba chose to walk away from his kingly position as leader of Pride Rock. His wicked uncle, Scar, up-ended the "circle of life" by usurping the power of Mufasa, Simba's father. Scar, incapable of exercising right rule, brought an environmental catastrophe to Pride Rock. Only Simba's return prevented total devastation of plant and animal life. Simba was naturally fitted for ordering life at Pride Rock, and his wise rule permitted life to flourish once again. As it is with *The Lion King,* so it is with human life. There is a natural hierarchy in all social relations. The circle of life among men and women is complementary.[39] Whereas women are more inclined by nature toward nurturing and men toward managing the household, the family is best ordered when men and women fulfill their respective functions in the family. A happy household depends on concord: each part working for the well-being of the whole. Although women have the obligation to obey their husbands and children the obligation to obey their fathers, men have the duty to exercise their rule for the common good of the whole family. World politics must be naturally ordered, too. The one person with the greatest wisdom and the most political experience should rule over the rest of humanity. It is a mistake to believe that political governance is something that can be shared by those who are incapable of exercising that leadership. To "empower" those who are not knowledgeable about the wise exercise of political power will result in international strife and war. The more radical feminists do not understand that they are empowering the Scars of this world, and in so doing they will bring about their own demise at the hands of people with fewer scruples. There will always be Scars, people who are incapable of ruling in the common good of humankind, and the lot of humanity will come to know the suffering that these beasts can unleash. Therefore, let only those men with the best knowledge and the deepest political experience assume positions of power. Let them justly order the relations between and within nations. The peace of the world depends on their wise leadership.

Dante's theory of world politics has interesting implications for the global environment. As seen in the previous chapter, global environmental problems require global solutions. Two solutions involve either the centralization or the decentralization of political power. Many radicals favor decentralizing economic and political power. They would take the economic and political power of large corporations and the national government and redistribute that power to local communities. By placing this power in local communities, radical ecologists desire to integrate human economic and political activity into the surrounding natural environment. By working within the ecological bounds set by local ecosystems, humans are able to live in much more environmentally healthy communities. The other choice is to centralize political power into some international government that has the power to bring about a balance between human material needs and wants, the consumption of natural resources, and the regulation of pollutants and toxic wastes. Dante would certainly agree that a world monarchy is the best solution to global environmental problems. Dante believes that humans are part of a greater natural world that includes all creation. This creation—which includes stars, planets, the plant and animal worlds, and human society—is governed by laws of nature.[40] When properly ordered, all things in the universe are in a state of unity, concord, and harmony. Human beings should learn to live within this natural order; however, the fallen condition of all human beings inevitably leads humans to God's laws of nature. Turning from God and toward themselves, humans choose to pursue a lifestyle that interferes with the fundamental ecological cycles and balances. When humans overhunt, overfish, or overgraze, they upset the ecological balances that are controlled by natural laws. By overturning the natural order of things, all creation suffers. When nature is forced to wrestle with human desire, conceit, and arrogance, the peaceful ordering of nature gives way to a war between humans and nature. The harmony existing among all creatures fulfilling their unique roles in their ecosystem is replaced with discord and death. The violation of the laws of nature is not restricted to a few countries in the world but extends to all nations. Thus, only a universal monarchy capable of reordering human life within a broader, worldwide ecological perspective would provide the social ordering necessary to achieve ecological peace and harmony.

A world monarchical government may seem an anachronism today; however, the peace and hope for reconciliation with the environment brought by a world monarchy are appealing in times of great international instability and environmental destruction. When our personal lives are in turmoil, we seek the tranquil peace of the soul, and after much frenzied international political and military activity, the inclination among nations is to find an enduring world peace. This is no less true after the cold war, when the nations of the world are searching for a "new world order," than it was after World War II, when humankind created the United Nations in the hope of finally putting an end to war. It is not surprising that we often find monarchies or empires cropping up in times of great world turbulence. The rise of Alexander the Great and the Roman and Holy Roman empires followed periods of intense social, economic, religious, and political upheavals in the ancient Greek and Roman and early medieval worlds. There are false avenues to peace. After World War I, the United States sought peace through isolation. It wished to avoid the entanglements of world politics, especially European politics. This was in many ways an illusionary way to search for peace. The right-wing regimes of Germany, Italy, and Japan in the 1930s proved that the world's nations must work actively for peace. As Dante reminds us, peace is not just an absence of war but a positive condition of concord, unity, and justice. When there are warmongering states like Hitler's Germany, the nations of the world must actively work to promote peace. In an international environment with no ultimate authority to prevent war, the peace of the world hinges on peace-loving nations working together to promote justice, concord, and unity.

However, Dante's thoughts on a world monarchy raise many questions. What must people give up to ensure world peace or justice? Are they willing to allow their nation to relinquish some of its freedom and sovereignty to a universal monarch? Do people in all parts of the world want to transfer power to an international personage to regulate the world economy so that all the peoples of the world have their basic needs met and have a greater opportunity to live their lives the way they wish? Are people willing to grant an international monarch the unrestricted power to manage world affairs—a power restrained only by divine law? What other alternatives are there to a balance of power and world monarchy in managing world political power?

ON WORLD FEDERAL GOVERNMENT

Much can be said for organizing the world political power around the balance of power or a world monarchy; however, the problems raised by each lead some to argue that a world federal government is the best way to organize and exercise international political power. For realists, the balance of power provides one way of preserving the political existence of independent states in a world political environment wherein power, spread between the world's nations, is highly decentralized. However, the perpetual and restless desire for power that drives the realist's theory of world politics permits nations to go to war to protect their independent existence. With nuclear knowledge and capabilities proliferating throughout the world, one wonders whether the balance of power and war are perhaps outmoded as tools for managing the relations of nations. For those favoring world monarchy, the quest for peace is so overriding that the value of freedom is given secondary status. Political theorists who argue for a world federal system of government attempt to handle the problems that flow from Dante's and the realist's theories of managing world power. They attempt to find a way to purchase the benefits of world peace and order and at the same time guarantee the nations and individuals of the world the greatest amount of freedom within that order. In some ways, these theorists are trying to avoid the problems associated with highly decentralized and highly centralized methods of managing the relations of nations. They do so by arguing that international political power should be divided between nation-states and a representative, world federal government. A world constitution would secure certain powers to each state and give additional powers to the world federal government. The constitution would provide protections that states and the people in states would have against the federal government. In creating this form of government, the worst features of a universal monarchy—the centralization of world political power into the hands of one person—and of the balance of power—anarchy and war—would be avoided. Some international government representative of all the peoples of the world would organize world political power to promote peace, liberty, equality under the law, justice, order, and human rights.

People as diverse as the French author Abbé de Saint-Pierre, the German philosopher Immanuel Kant, and the American immigrant (and founder of Pennsylvania) William Penn favored a world federal government that would bring order to international relations. Humans have formed nations to secure human rights. Because nations are important guarantors of human rights and are the most fundamental political association of a group of people, the sovereignty of all nations should be protected. Liberals protect states by extending rights that all other nations should respect: the right to exist as an independent state, the right to self-determination, and the freedom to pursue foreign policies without endangering the freedom of other nations to do the same. To the extent that the nations of the world agree that there are some principles that ought to govern international relations, there is an international society of states. This society is built around a consensus on the values and principles that ought to govern the relations of nations and the relations of individuals to their respective governments. However, the existence of rogue nations—countries that prefer to cast aside these international rights—threatens the security of all law-abiding nations. The threats to all peace-loving states are so great that in the absence of an international government, the peace, justice, human rights, and freedom of all nations and of their peoples are placed in jeopardy. The only way to secure these rights is to form an international government that has the power to promote these values. As Abbé de Saint-Pierre has put it, the problem of a world government has less to do with human nature than it does with the arena of world politics: "No man can have thought long upon the means of bringing any government to perfection without realizing a host of difficulties and obstacles which flow less from its inherent nature than from its relation to its neighbors."[41] Therefore, creating a world authority would require humankind to deal with those world conditions that promote or detract from the project of establishing a world federal government. World government must rest on a body of shared moral, economic, and political principles.

The foundation of the argument for a world federal government is grounded in the belief that individuals are rational creatures and that humans can create or discover a universal code of values and law that would serve to guide an international government and the relations between nations. Some favoring a world federal system have argued that humans as a species have been given the fundamental rational capacity to know what is the good they and their fellows should pursue. Others, like Saint-Pierre, "see in my mind's eye all men joined in the bonds of love. I call before my thoughts a gentle and peaceful brotherhood, all living in unbroken harmony, all guided by the same principles, all finding their happiness in the happiness of all."[42] However, the proponents of a world federal government believe that there are some universal principles that unite all humankind. Knowable by reason, accepted on the basis of religious faith, or accessible to human intuition, these principles are real and living in each individual. As such, all humans on this planet are related to one another as brothers and sisters, and all are inspired by the common values of humanity. For Robert Maynard

Hutchins, a mid-twentieth-century proponent of a classical liberal education from the University of Chicago, the values of peace, justice, respect for human dignity, freedom, and the security of life form the foundation of the international society.[43] Indeed, there is a substantial consensus on these values that can be found in twentieth-century documents on human rights, such as the Universal Declaration of Human Rights, and in international discussions on shared principles that unite all humans. In parts of the world where such consensus does not exist, the conversation about these fundamental human values is beginning to take place. Today, the world's nations and peoples constitute a world society that largely recognizes the moral primacy of life, liberty, peace, justice, and the protection of human dignity. Because of this consensus on the universal goals of human life, the people and nations of the world are prepared to discuss and create a world federal government capable of pursuing these values.

The moral principles expressed in world society are supported by the spread of economic interdependence, which ties the material well-being of each person and nation with that of other nations and supports the values that form the core of international society. Economic interdependence breaks down parochial state boundaries that serve to shore up wealth in some countries and poverty in others. When nations are more autarchic and dependent on their own economic systems for maintaining and promoting their own standards of living, they tend to focus more on their own interests and problems. However, economic interdependence transcends the political and economic borders defined by the modern nation-state. When the fate of one nation's economic prosperity is dependent upon the economic performance of other national economies, the peoples of the world come to understand that the pursuit of universal economic prosperity benefits all humankind. Increasing world trade, world industrial capacity, and world markets ensures that prosperity will accrue to all peoples of the world. With increased material well-being in all the nations of the world, economic inequalities between nations can be reduced, and the basic needs of all the world's peoples can be fulfilled. Starvation, poverty, disease, and illiteracy can be eradicated as nations prosper economically. History has shown that the market system, moderated by governmental action to ensure that the benefits derived from a market economy are justly distributed, is the foundation upon which world prosperity can develop. Marxism and unregulated capitalism provide a false hope for the universal economic well-being for all the people of the earth. Indeed, there is a growing consensus that a democratic international political system would secure the rights of states and the rights of individuals within states. First, though the number of democracies or representative governments has ebbed and flowed since the time the idea was hatched 2,500 years ago in Greece, the overall trend has been to expand the number of democratic states throughout history. Second, representative governments are founded upon the principle that government is instituted and can continue only with the consent of the people. Governments are formed to protect the life, liberty, and human dignity of their people. Should a government transgress these rights, "it is the Right of the People to alter or to abolish it, and to institute [a] new Government, laying its foundation on such principles and organizing its powers in such form, as to them shall seem most likely to effect their Safety and Happiness."[44] Third, given the diversity of cultures in the world, a federal system that would give limited powers to the world federal government and reserve other powers to each nation-state would be the best way to centralize some power and to provide states with a degree of autonomy to manage their affairs as they see fit. With an increasing international consensus on the rights and values that ought to be secured to the states and peoples of the world, with the growing number of democracies in the world, and with a consensus that democracy is the form of government best suited to securing the rights of nations and peoples, it can be argued that the representative form of government is the best for the nations of the world.

For many who favor a world federal government, a social contract between the nations of the world would seem to be the best way to create it. Today, nations exist as sovereign, independent, and free states. As such, they are free from the arbitrary control of other states or from any international authority. These nations are free to the extent that they act within those laws that govern the conduct of states in the society of nations. By a joint act, these free nations can voluntarily agree to create a world federal government to secure the rights of the nations and peoples of the world. For individuals, these include the rights to life, liberty, property, and the dignity of the individual; for nations, these rights comprise the right to peace, justice, and freedom. In exchange for securing these rights, the contracting nations would bind themselves to observe the laws of the world federal government. In summary, the nations of the world, in making this contract or covenant, escape the vicissitudes of an international state of nature and place themselves under a world authority that will secure the rights of each nation and of the world's people.[45]

Given the growing consensus that a federal, representative form of government is the best international political form, it would be best to divide political power between the world federal government and the nations of the world, and to avoid the centralization of power in one person or body of states. Moreover, the powers of the federal government should be separated into legislative, executive, and judicial branches. Dividing world political power between a world government and the nations composing that government would have several advantages. First, it would prevent all political power from being placed in the hands of a world monarch or a single assembly. By spreading power out among 185 nations and a world federal government, these nations would possess a power base from which they could organize opposition to any federal government that attempted to deny these countries or their citizens their rights. Second, federalism is important in the culturally diverse world in which we live. In giving and reserving powers to each nation to manage its own affairs and make its own law within international law, nations of the world would be free to pursue policies and make laws that are culturally appropriate for their people. Third, world federalism would place some power in a world federal government that would attempt to solve the two problems that flow from international anarchy: the inconsistent manner in which human rights are enforced and war. This power would allow the federal government to enforce international law so that the people and the nations of the world would be secured their rights. An international government would use its executive power to enforce the human rights of all people and would promote peace by enforcing international law and by settling disputes between states in an international court of justice. In addition to the advantages that world federalism would bring to the nations and peoples of the world, the power of the international government would be separated between legislative, executive, and judicial branches. The separation of powers and functions would guard against tyranny by distributing power among three branches; as James Madison notes, the centralization of power into the hands of one person or body to make, execute, and adjudicate the law is the very definition of tyranny. The legislative branch would make international law to secure peace among nations, to protect human rights, and to provide for a just distribution of wealth among the people of the world. As all nations of the world would have an equal vote in this legislature, all states would be equally represented. The executive branch would have a multinational military force to enforce this law. The judiciary would have the ability to settle disputes in a just, equitable, and peaceful manner, thus preventing the resort to arms. Because all of these provisions would be enshrined in a world federal constitution that guaranteed rights to the peoples of the world and to the constituent states, this world federal government would be a limited government: limited to exercising only those powers delegated to it.[46]

Many advantages would accrue to a world federal government. First, with justice as primary goal, all nations and peoples of the world would be given their due. What is their due? Their due are those rights that nations and the people of the world should have protected and promoted. Nations would have the right to their independent existence and they would have the right to self-determination within the international law. The people of the world would be guaranteed their human rights: the right to life, liberty, and property; the right to have their basic needs met; the right to worship and believe as they please; the right to participate in national and international politics; and the freedom from torture and ethnic strife. Second, with justice secured to states and peoples of the world, peace between nations would rule the day. Third, peace would promote, not stifle, world trade. National resources that once were devoted to national security could be diverted to economic development or modernization of industry. Fourth, with world trade and economically just world capital investment strategies, economic prosperity would be more widely distributed. Fifth, the military expenses of nations would be reduced, because states would no longer need a standing army to protect themselves from their enemies. Sixth, a greater share of a nation's income could be devoted to addressing national issues and problems.[47] Thus, a world federal government would bring many social, economic, and political benefits that cannot be achieved in the current anarchic world political system.

To the Islamic fundamentalist, this scheme for world government is flawed in two ways. First, it presupposes a world society that does not exist, a society predicated upon the Western view of society and the international order. Although Western political theorists have concluded that there is a substantial agreement among the peoples of the earth on their vision of the good life, this is not the case. Islamic and many Eastern and African cultures have belief patterns that are fundamentally opposed to Western ones. Take one of the most important beliefs: the relation of the individual to the community. In Western political thought, the individual is the primary social unit: the individual has a value independent of his or her social, economic, or political stations in life. In Islamic thought, the community gives dignity to the individual. For example, according to Islamic fundamentalists, women, because of their unique abilities to bear and nurture children, occupy a unique niche in the Islamic social order and are accorded a special dignity. In the West, say these fundamentalists, women have been stripped by their societies of the worth and dignity associated with rearing children. According to this line of thinking, it presses reality to say that there is a world consensus on international values—cultures do differ. To the extent that Western values have come to dominate international thought and life, it has been a result of the West's imperial desire to make the rest of the world look like itself. Its nineteenth- and twentieth-century cultural, economic, and political imperialism has weakened the traditional and more humane non-Western cultures; however, the rise of Islamic fundamentalism has served to halt the West's march of cultural tyranny in the world. Therefore, argue Islamic fundamentalists, we cannot say that the world is moving toward a Western-inspired world society. It is in fact quite divided.[48] Second, the lack of commonly shared principles that form the foundation of world society has had important implications for human rights. Though the West would have the rest of the world believe that there is a single catalogue of human rights to which all nations and people of the world would subscribe, the reality is much different. Human rights are more fully revealed in Islamic political thought. The rights that have been extended to persons and societies by Islam are not fully appreciated by the West. Muslims possess the right to life, which means that they have a right to food, water, and medical care—rights that are not universally granted in the West. Muslim women have the right to their chastity, not a right found in a listing of Western rights. The screams, tears, and wailing of Islamic women being raped by Christian soldiers in Bosnia cry out as a testament to the West's lack of concern for the rights of women.[49] Finally, the right to avoid sin is found nowhere in the civil rights Western nations have granted to their citizens.

The people of the West are drowning in a torrential river of sin, and their governments have neither the moral sense to dam the river nor the ability to throw out life preservers to save the people. They merely collect and bury the dead bodies after they have washed ashore. The West has expunged all religious values from politics and economics. The political and economic marketplace seethes with sin. This can be seen in the West's unbridled fascination with sexuality and in its unremitting acts of violence that have cheapened the dignity of human life. In sum, it can hardly be said that there is a common core of rights or values that is shared currently among the world's peoples.[50]

In response to this Islamic critique, world federalists argue that Western society promotes many core values and human rights that are honored by all of the world's people, including Islamic fundamentalists. Beyond these core values, people may differ in what they believe, without threatening those core values that constitute the heart of world society. However, the core "Western" values and rights are not necessarily a function of cultural imperialism. Although the colonization of all non-European worlds (including the countries in North and South America, Africa, and Asia) did help spread Western culture, the respect for life, individual freedom, and the dignity of the individual is rooted in human nature. The introduction of Western culture, and with it these core values, in various parts of the world resonated in the souls of those who came in contact with it. In fact, all humans have the desire for freedom, justice, personal security, and respect; and Western culture awakened these values in these peoples. With the exception of some countries that attempt to repress the desire for freedom, justice, security, and respect, the world's appreciation of these values, which are at the heart of Western culture, has been expanding, especially in Asia. As the twenty-first century dawns, this core of values will seep ever deeper into the minds and hearts of the world's people. They do form the foundation of a world society upon which a world federal system of government can be built.[51]

To some realists, a world federal government pursuing justice would paradoxically sacrifice that justice, and in so doing freedom would perish. Federalists argue that by pursuing the goal of justice, each nation or individual will be given its due, and a degree of legal and economic equality will result. The poorer nations of the world deserve to have a share in the world's wealth so that they can provide for the material needs of their people. But to some realists, the condition of humankind is not one of equality but of inequality. Some nations, like some individuals, are superior in those qualities that make them more powerful: natural resources, military leadership, political savvy, industrial development, cultural and scientific enlightenment, and military capabilities. In world politics, the stronger nations will rise to the top and dominate those who are less powerful. To these powerful nations, justice is nothing but the advantage of the stronger, and the ideas and ideals of the stronger nations serve as the standard for judging what is just and unjust, lawful and illegal, right and wrong, and good and evil in world politics. By their effort, cunning, sacrifice, and strength, these stronger nations have accomplished more in world politics than other nations, and they deserve a greater share of the world's goods. World federalists have spun and perpetuated a myth that all nations and peoples of the world are in some way equal. In the name of justice, the federalists would try to prevent the stronger nations from achieving what is due to these stronger countries by using the power of a world federal government to prevent the strong from acquiring or keeping the material goods and political influence that are rightly theirs. By redistributing the wealth of great nations and giving it to less wealthy nations, world federalists violate true justice, which accords the strongest nations the greater share of world wealth and political power. The pursuit of justice by the world federalists also violates the freedom that nations should be accorded in international politics. The federalists would use the power of a world government to prevent truly exceptional nations from exercising their freedom to launch out into the world and make it their own. If the world federalists had their way in history, they would have prevented the rise of Athens and Rome—nations whose conquests laid the foundation for Western cultural and political life.

To other realists, the hope that peace will come with world federal government is utopian; in their view, even if a world government would bring peace in its wake, it would be at such great expense to liberty that peace would hardly be worth it. There are two reasons for this. First, the federalists fail to acknowledge the role that egotistical self-interest plays in the politics of nations. Nations live in a world wherein economic success, language, culture, history, previous injustices, and border disputes are the everyday facts of life. Just as a government cannot prevent thievery, so nations—unable to achieve their most precious goals within a federal system of government—would go to war to acquire them. No international force could be large enough to enforce the law of nations among so many states that have conflicting interests and would be willing to go to war to achieve them. But because a federal government would try to establish peace, it would have to resort to tactics that would infringe on the freedom of states and their people. Second, just as nations are not immune from civil war, a world government would not be immune from a war between it and its states or between states in the world federal system. If a federal system were established, it is probable that war would continue within the federation. Given the diversity of cultures and interests in world politics, the probability of war would increase with the government's inability to resolve disputes peacefully. Let us suppose a world federal government attempted to guarantee peace; liberty would then be extinguished. The long arm and sword of world government would reach down into the houses, neighborhoods, and cities of all nations in an effort to eradicate the sources of violence between nations. When traditional animosities threatened to ignite a war between two nations, freedom of speech and press would be curtailed so that incendiary language would not spark an incident that could escalate into war. It is hard to imagine that peace could be obtained without strengthening an international military force whose presence would be felt in every nation, on every street, and in every neighborhood of the world. Peace could only be purchased at the price of freedom.[52]

In response to the realist critique, world federalists are unapologetic in their support of a world federal government, which they see as the only way to bring about justice, freedom, and world peace. To the world federalist, justice is not simply the advantage of the stronger; rather, its foundation is written in the nature of every human being. All humans have a need for food, water, clothing, and shelter; they possess a free will; and they have a rational capacity. For humans to lead a truly human life, their basic needs should be satisfied, they should be extended freedom to conduct their lives as they desire within laws that assure the freedom of others, and they ought to be accorded an education and spiritual development that deepen their understanding of themselves and of those with whom they live. It is in their capacity as needful, free, and reasoning beings that people are equal to one another. Differences in wealth, social status, physical stature, skin color, and nationality are not inequalities that authorize people to be treated differently. Nations, if they are to be called such, have the right to existence, the right to be free from unjust interference in their affairs, and the freedom to conduct their economic and foreign affairs within the bounds of international law. Differences in wealth, power, international prestige, natural resources, and economic development are accidental characteristics of nations that are due not to nature but to history and geographical fortune. Consequently, a just international society is one in which fundamental rights are rendered to each individual and each state; and a just international order would prevent those nations that, by fortune or design, attempt to trample on the rights of humans under the pretense that the rule of the physically, economically, or politically strong is just and right. A just federal system should defend the rights of those who are threatened by a conquering state. The realist's conception of freedom also implies that people are free if they are free from the restraining influences of others. In fact, freedom can be granted only to those who are willing to restrict their activities in ways that permit others to exercise their freedom. The freedom of the realist is the freedom that tyrants apply in their nations: those with the power to do as they please are free to subject the rest of humankind to the shackles of slavery and oppression. A world federal government sets limits to the exercise of national power that would otherwise extinguish the freedom of others. In so doing, it promotes the greatest freedom for all nations. Finally, to the claim that a world federal government would bring neither peace nor freedom, the federalist responds that a world federal government is not utopian. It would do a better job of securing peace than would other mechanisms designed to manage world political power. It would do so by providing a common body of law, a political process to adjust conflicting national interests, a judicial process to settle disputes peacefully, and an executive power to implement the law of nations. By so doing, the world federation would virtually eliminate the causes of war: massive arms build-ups and the insecurity they bring to nations in an international state of nature; boundary disputes; international economic inequalities; and racial, religious, national, and ethnic animosities. Because a world government presupposes a worldwide consensus on values that ought to be promoted by all actors in the political system, such a consensus would incline nations and peoples to follow laws that guarantee the rights of humans and of nations. Consequently, there would be little need for the extensive, intrusive international force that threatens the liberties of the world's people.

To the extent that a world federal government supports a free enterprise system, the radical would argue that a world federal government is a creation of privileged economic interests, which find it useful in extending their control over world wealth. A federated government would secure the right to private property and thus protect the interests of those who would benefit most from the capitalist world economy. The spread of world capitalism would accelerate, and it would penetrate the lives of people in less developed countries more thoroughly than it has up to this time. Whereas the world federalist speaks of greater economic equality that would result from a more just distribution of the fruits of a world free-market system, the history of free-market countries with representative governments tells a different story. The bourgeoisie in so-called democratic countries uses its access to political power to reinforce its economic power over the laboring classes. A political elite with social, economic, and political ties to the rich uses the power of government to redistribute as little wealth as possible from the rich to the poor. In the name of social justice, welfare programs that defuse revolutionary fervor among members of the poverty-stricken underclass serve to perpetuate capitalism and the political rule of the bourgeoisie. A world federal government built upon and supporting a capitalist world economy would support the continued exploitation of the rich over the poor. As the bourgeoisie controls political power in capitalist core and periphery states and as it exercises overweening influence in the world economy by its control of international banking, finance, and multinational corporations, the bourgeoisie would be in a position to control a world legislative body. Members of the bourgeoisie would be able to control or influence the appointment or election of members to the federated legislature. They would also be able to use their vast economic resources to influence the world legislative process. By wielding power in the world's multinational corporations and through the political puppets of the largest capitalistic states, members of the international bourgeoisie would exercise more political power than would international labor organizations; socialistic states that had yet to succumb to capitalism; and other transnational actors such as the Catholic church, terrorist groups, and international social service agencies such as the Red Cross. Given the power of the international bourgeoisie, a significant redistribution of the world's wealth and capital from rich countries to poor ones would not occur. If anything, the bourgeoisie's hegemonic rule over less developed nations would be increased. Having gained access to positions of power in a world federated government, the bourgeoisie would use the political system to continue to exploit the laboring classes of the world more effectively because there would be no countervailing political power strong enough to prevent it from working its will in the world.

The world federalist would object to the proposition that a world federal government would ultimately serve the interests of the world's bourgeoisie. A truly just world economic order founded on the principle of distributive justice would not allow the economic inequalities that exist in today's developing and advanced capitalist nations. The deepening consciousness of the need for a more just distribution of international political power and wealth would bring an end to the excesses of contemporary capitalism. International labor unions, states, multinational corporations, the World Bank, international banks, churches, and other international organizations would strive to achieve a more economically just distribution of world capital and world income. Multinational corporations would abandon their practice of exploiting labor in less developed countries and would provide their workers with just wages. International labor unions would emphasize the responsibility to put in a fair day's labor for a fair wage. Loans to developing countries would be distributed not on the basis of whether the investment turns a profit, but whether it encourages agriculture and industry that will help satisfy the basic needs of the population. There would be movement toward greater world economic equality, through the diffusion of property ownership throughout the world, the provision of just wages, the extension of economic aid to nations in greatest need, and the deepening development of social consciousness among all those who are in the position to improve the quality of life in the world. Such actions will eliminate the traditional division between the bourgeoisie and proletariat and the rich and poor nations of the world. Thus, the criticism that an economically advantaged class would dominate the world's economic, social, and political life is unfounded in a socially just world. In fact, the lack of any effective political organization in world politics gives free rein to the stronger international economic and political interests.

In summary, the world federalist's argument raises many interesting issues. It attempts to solve some of the worst problems that are inherent to realism: war, the maldistribution of wealth, the hegemonic state, and the lack of commitment to human rights. First, world federalists pin their hope of preventing war on achieving a degree of social, economic, and political justice among nations that would diminish the possibility of war. To the extent that wars result from unresolved injustices that one people suffer at the hands of another, it would be no small accomplishment if the means could be found to authoritatively and justly settle disputes that would otherwise lead to war. World federalists would also establish a world government with the power to legislate international law, to enforce it, and to authoritatively resolve disputes between states. World federalism provides a program for creating and legitimizing a federal government in a way that would lessen the possibility of war between nations and would create an international military force with the power to maintain the peace. Second, federal world government promises to promote greater social justice. In a world in which the rich nations are literally getting richer and less developed nations poorer, world federalism promises a degree of social justice. An international authority with the ability to redistribute capital resources, technology, natural resources, and economic aid appears to be the only way of achieving a level of prosperity commensurate with the dignity of the individual. Third, world federalism provides an alternative to the politics of anarchy or the rise of a hegemonic state. By dividing political power between the nations of the world and a world federal government, it would permit a degree of cultural diversity among the nations of the world, and it would bring a degree of political and economic order that is necessary for world peace and prosperity. Finally, a world federal government would be better able to enforce the world's commitment to human rights. With an international body empowered to prevent the abuse of human rights, the world could practically bury the pictures of suffering, fright, horror, and terror that are etched in faces and souls of the persecuted in Rwanda, Bosnia, and Somalia. Despite this vision of a more just, free, and peaceful future, there are powerful forces arrayed against it. World federalism promises to shackle the more powerful nations to principles of international law and it would limit their ability to romp through the world as they choose. As the Athenians have shown us, powerful nations are not necessarily interested in pursuing justice. With the advent of modern communication systems, the people of rich, powerful, privileged nations can wag their heads at the poverty, suffering, and countless acts of brutality that occur in war-torn and less prosperous countries. But ultimately they can turn off their televisions and walk away from the whole sordid mess. The people of less powerful, struggling, underdeveloped nations cannot walk away from the television set; they are mired in the swamp of poverty, torture, and war. They can only hope that somewhere and sometime justice, freedom, and the respect for the dignity of the individual will light up their lives and lessen their burdens. If nationalism and ethnocentrism prevent nations from forming "a more perfect union," is it possible that a world society could develop if the remnants of communism (in China and North Korea) and fascism vanish from the world political scene?

ON A LIBERAL INTERNATIONAL POLITICAL AND ECONOMIC ORDER

In 1989, Francis Fukuyama proclaimed the end of history and with it the triumph of political and economic liberalism. Seeing postcommunist nations of Russia and Eastern Europe experimenting with representative forms of government and the free-market system, Fukuyama concludes that no ideology or worldview shares liberalism's current popularity. German and Italian versions of fascism, both of which provided an ideology and practical program for governing a nation and conducting international affairs, are no longer relevant to contemporary international thought and life. The crumbling edifice of communism in the Soviet Union and Eastern Europe raises doubts that communism could serve as a viable ideology around which the good society could be built. The revival of Jewish, Christian, and Islamic fundamentalism will be unable to articulate the hopes of a growing number of the world's people and provide a practical program to realize their dreams. Rather, the revival of religious fundamentalist movements is a response to the "impersonality and vacuity" of the modern consumer society. Without a practical, political program to solve the problems of a consumer society, religious fundamentalism is unlikely to displace the rising tide of Western liberalism. But Western liberalism has not won by default: that is, it has not won because other worldviews have failed. Rather, liberalism represents the ideological pinnacle of the evolution of the human mind. Throughout history, the human mind has striven to solve the riddle of the best form of social, economic, and political organization. Western liberalism, according to Fukuyama, is the solution of that riddle. Because we can find no better form of human organization other than that revealed in the Western liberal tradition, we are at the end of history. The rest of "history" will apply liberal ideas to societies that are currently nonliberal: China, Cuba, the Democratic People's Republic of Korea, and more traditional countries on the African and Asian continents.[53]

Fukuyama believes that the triumph of liberalism over other ideologies will bring greater opportunities for peace. As we have seen, many economic and political liberals believe that a zone of peace develops in geographic areas where liberal institutions exist. But in the short term, Fukuyama recognizes that there will be world conflict. After all, there are nations that are still "in history," nations that have not developed liberal social, economic, and political values and institutions that incline them toward peace. Because the states in history do not have such liberal economic and political institutions, in times of international crisis, these nations will more than likely resort to war. Thus, war is most likely to occur between states that are in history, and between states that are in history and those at the end of history. The conflict in the former Yugoslavia is an example of a conflict between nations that are in history that has managed to involve nations at the end of history as well.[54] Ancient political, religious, and ethnic feuds have spilled over into war, genocide, and ethnic cleansing. Thus, the immediate future will be characterized by peace and war; in the long term, however, Western economic and political liberalism will spread throughout the world and this will usher in worldwide peace.

As we have seen, liberalism comes in many different guises. As a school of thought, it advocates views on human nature, free-market economies, the ends of political action, the preferred form of government, international economics, and methods of managing world political power. Liberals perceive humans as reasonable and self-interested beings who have the intellectual wherewithal to create political societies that permit them to pursue their enlightened self-interest within the bounds of law. Humans understand that their particular well-being and success in life are inherently bound up with the well-being of others, and a harmony of interests arises among them. For example, humans know that it is in their self-interest to obey the law. Violating the law makes a comfortable, settled life more difficult to achieve and it diverts people's attention from activities that are individually or socially pleasing and rewarding. However, humans also realize that they are subject to the passions and appetites that incline them to become outlaws to their fellows, and they know that a government is needed to enforce the law and prescribe penalties against those who break it. Government would best be described as an unavoidable evil rather than a positive good.[55]

Second, the notion of a harmony of interests extends into classical liberal economics. As virtually all humans are capable of labor for the greater part of their lives and because each has unique talents and contributions that satisfy the demands of other human beings, the liberal believes that a free-enterprise system, which gives individuals the freedom to pursue their own "calling" in life free from virtually any degree of governmental regulation, is the best economic system. As we have seen, the process of working and providing for one's own and one's family's needs in turn satisfies the needs of other people. Governmental interference into this reciprocal relationship between producer and consumer upsets the process by which humans jointly satisfy their needs. By restricting a producer in the exercise of his or her talents and abilities, the government harms both the producer and consumer: the producer is denied the opportunity to produce a good or service, and the consumer is denied the opportunity to buy it. Therefore, governmental activity in the economy should be reduced to encouraging the development of a free-enterprise system: building roads to facilitate the flow of goods and services, erecting an educational system to support economic development, enforcing contracts, and establishing a banking system to provide for a common currency with which people can trade their goods and services.

Finally, liberals hold that a constitutional, representative government founded on liberal values is the best form of political organization. A constitutional government limits the activity of government to those necessary spheres of promoting the development of capitalism, establishing and enforcing the rule of law and contracts, and administering justice to those who would break the law. To further prevent the government from overstepping its bounds, the liberal argues that the separation of powers and a system of checks and balances are necessary to limit the possibility that government will fall into the hands of one person who would use that power to interfere in the private and economic lives of the people. Liberals typically prefer a representative form of government, because it limits the power of the government. Should the government overstep its bounds and interfere in private matters, the citizenry can protect itself by electing new legislators.

Finally, a limited, representative government should secure an individual's rights to life, liberty, and property. Protecting life is important not only because there is an inherent dignity in life that should be respected, but because without life the rights to liberty and property are meaningless. Humans need the economic liberty to exercise their talents in a way that allows them to support themselves and their families. They require the social liberty to be free to lead their lives as they desire within the bounds of the law, and they need to be free from all forms of prejudice that prevent humans from following those lifestyles that they believe lead to happiness. Democratic peoples require the political liberty to discuss and debate issues, to lobby their government, and to vote and hold public office if the government is to be kept responsive to them.[56]

Turning to the liberal view of international economics, the liberal favors a free-enterprise world economy, unrestricted flow of capital across national borders, and free trade. Governments should not interfere with the functioning of the world economy except to facilitate its growth and to enforce international agreements. A capitalistic world economy is superior to other forms of economic organization in creating national wealth and in providing individual nations with a means of satisfying their collective and individual needs. Operating under the principle of comparative advantage, each nation in the world can produce a limited number of goods or services that are superior in quality to the same goods or services that could be produced in other countries. Geography, access to natural resources, low labor costs, an educated and skilled workforce, and the capital to produce these goods or services at the lowest cost allow each nation to specialize in producing such products or services. By freely trading these products and services, each nation will prosper and raise its standard of living. A harmony of interests arises between nations because the producing nation benefits from the sale of its goods and the consuming nation benefits from low-cost, high-quality goods. Free trade is an essential component of the liberal view of international economics. It is only by allowing producing nations to market their goods on the same terms as others that the best and lowest priced product makes its way to the world's consumer. Liberals decry government intervention into the capitalist world economy. They therefore oppose tariffs imposed by one government on the goods of another nation for the purpose of protecting domestic industries. They also object to governmental subsidies to manufacturers that artificially lower the cost of the finished product. Liberals believe that capital, like trade, should freely flow across national borders because it is one way to stimulate world manufacturing, agricultural, and industrial production. The free flow of capital, in their view, raises standards of living in less developed countries, puts more money in the hands of the world's consumers, and helps to stimulate further demand for the world's goods. The best source of international capital, according to the liberal, is the multinational corporation. Some liberals will also make the argument that government foreign aid programs and intergovernmental organizations such as the World Bank should be sources of developmental funds and capital. Finally, the liberal believes that the world's governments should refrain from interfering with the capitalist world economy, because intervention may produce economic distortions that prevent nations from jointly enjoying the prosperity that derives from the free flow of goods, capital, and labor across national borders. Nations often find it necessary to establish some trading rules to order international trade, and they normally obey these rules because it is in their rational self-interest to do so. Only when international trade agreements are violated by nations that believe that the short-term benefits of such violations outweigh the long-term benefits to be gained by adhering to those agreements should the nations of the world intervene to enforce the rules of international trade.[57]

The German philosopher Immanuel Kant provides one vision of an international liberal political order. Kant believes that all political power, domestic or international, should be exercised in accordance with right or law. Domestically, Kant favors a constitutional government that seeks to secure liberty, equality before the law and equality of opportunity, independence (the right to participate in the political process), and justice. However, Kant gives priority to the value of liberty. Internationally, the relations between nations should be governed by international right or law, and international law seeks to secure the liberty and self-determination of nations, justice, and the equality of states before international law. The source of all domestic and international law is human reason, and "Every action which by itself or by its maxim enables the freedom of each individual's will to co-exist with the freedom of everyone else in accordance with a universal law is right."[58] In domestic politics, this means that the primary concern of government is to make that law that permits each person to freely pursue his or her own life in a way that allows others the freedom to do the same. This theory of law has corresponding referents in international affairs. Kant believes that international right or law is also a product of human reason and is established to protect the freedom of states. Kant guarantees each state two freedoms: external freedom and internal freedom. Externally, the state possesses the freedom to pursue its goals in world politics. However, this is not an unbridled freedom to act as they desire. Rather, nations are free to carry out their foreign policies as long as those policies do not restrict the freedom of other states. Internally, a state has the right to self-determination. Just as individuals exercise the freedom to choose a lifestyle that leads to personal happiness, so nations are free to order their social, economic, and political structures as they desire. Even in times of civil war, Kant believes that a nation should be free to solve its own internal political disputes and free from attempts of other nations to influence the political outcome. So committed is Kant to the principle of self-determination that he does not grant other states the right to intervene in the internal affairs of despotic states that violate the rights of their people.[59] In addition to the international law that secures the external and internal freedom of states, Kant believes that the international community creates laws that govern the relations of states in times of peace and war. First, Kant asserts that nations can declare war if the rights granted to them under international law are violated by another state and if the injured state has not gained satisfaction through international legal proceedings. Second, he holds that a state possesses the right to go to war if another state suddenly increases its international political power and military capabilities. Third, Kant prohibits nations from going to war simply to punish another nation for actions that are permissible under international law. Fourth, Kant prohibits nations from going to war to exterminate the population of another nation or to subject that nation to its rule, because such actions violate the right of a nation to exist. Fifth, Kant permits a nation to go to war to protect its property and territory from other nations that sought to unjustly seize them. Thus, Kant gives states the right to self-defense. Sixth, during the conduct of war, Kant denies nations the right to use methods that would make it difficult to establish peaceful relations after the war has been concluded. Thus he prohibits states from using political assassination, domestic spying, and lying (disinformation) to win the war. At the war's conclusion, Kant extends to the victors the right to specify the terms of the peace treaty so long as the treaty conforms to international law, and Kant holds that the vanquished states should retain their status as independent states. Kant grants what he calls rights of peace to the nations of the world: the right to remain neutral in a war, the right to maintain peace once a treaty of peace is concluded, and the right of states to form alliances for their common defense.[60]

Whereas Kant believes that the nations of the world know that obeying international law would lead to international cooperation, peace, and prosperity, he also believes that experience suggests that nations would violate these laws if they mistakenly thought to do so would serve their interests. He expects

> a hell of evils to overtake us, however civilized our condition, in that nature, by barbaric devastation, might perhaps again destroy this civilized state and all the cultural progress hitherto achieved [and that humans will find] perpetual peace in the vast grave where all the horrors of violence and those responsible for them would be buried.[61]

Like Hobbes suggested before him, Kant thinks that world politics, absent any international power to enforce international law, is doomed to a state of anarchy. In this anarchy, international right or laws exist. In many instances, nations acting in their own self-interest see reasons to obey them. However, Kant believes that states should observe these laws only to the extent that other nations obey them, too. If other nations throw international law to the wind, prudent leaders should abandon them also and "seek and use, all helps, and advantages of war," as Hobbes put it.[62] War and the threat of war place the security of the state in jeopardy. Without some type of international authority to enforce principles of international right, nations fear the loss of their political independence and the invasion of their homelands. Thus, international anarchy makes domestic life more oppressive. Standing armies soak up critical national resources that could be applied to the education and enlightenment of citizens. Taxes are raised to support military projects, and rulers, preoccupied with the pursuit of international power, turn a blind eye to the thousands of men who dutifully march into the field of battle at night, never to rise with the next dawn.[63]

Given this condition of international anarchy, how can the power of nations be put into service of international right? Kant favors the creation of a federation (better described as a confederation) of republican states. Though Kant's federation reminds one of the United Nations, he invests it with greater authority to enforce international law. Just as independent humans join forces to create a social contract to form a government to protect their rights, so Kant envisions the nations of Europe entering into a social contract to form a federation of free states. Because free states have the moral and legal capability to act in world politics, they possess the ability to form a federation of states or to leave it should they choose to do so. In forming this federation, states relinquish their right to war that exists in the state of nature and they agree to follow international law: the foundation of the freedom of states. This federation creates a permanent congress of states that is open to all member nations, and Kant supplies it with the means of adjudicating and resolving disputes between states, writing international law, and enforcing that law. Kant's federation of republican states sharply differs from the world federal state, and more closely resembles Bakunin's notion of a federation of nations. Kant's federation does not create a federal government that possesses the power to coerce states into obeying international law. On the one hand, Kant believes that reasonable nations, seeing the benefits of voluntarily obeying international law and respecting the freedom of other states, will follow international law. In this sense, international law is self-enforcing. On the other hand, if a member nation chooses to disobey international law, Kant gives other nations the authority to band together to enforce it.[64]

This raises the question of securing the peace through collective security. As we have seen, liberals typically pin their hopes for peace on the creation and use of international political institutions, the worldwide proliferation of republican or representative governments, and the expansion of world commerce that leads to economic interdependence and world economic prosperity. By creating and using international political institutions such as a world court and diplomatic processes to resolve international disputes, liberals believe that they can avoid war. However, if peaceful negotiations fail to resolve international problems, some liberals turn to collective security to secure world peace. Collective security is the joint use of international force by many nations to prevent one nation from attacking another nation. For example, if any one nation would give thought to invading another country, other member nations of the world community would collectively amass a preponderance of military force that would deter the renegade state from making good its intentions. The success of collective security involves eight assumptions. First, there exists a common body of international law commonly recognized by members of the federation. Second, member states find it in their interest to live by this law. Third, member states will band together to enforce that law. Fourth, nations possess the will to enforce the law. Fifth, all states are rational actors and they share a common knowledge about the distribution of power between the aggressor and the community of nations. Sixth, the combined power of the states of the world community is vastly superior to any single power in that community. Seventh, nations agree on who is the aggressor. Eighth, the potential aggressor will abandon its war plans in the face of a collective show of military force by members of the world community.[65] Collective security can work only if all these assumptions hold. Take the imperfect example of Saddam Hussein's invasion of Kuwait. In the sense of *preventing* the military invasion of Kuwait by Iraq in the fall of 1990, collective security did not work. Although naked aggression is prohibited by international law, apparently Saddam Hussein thought that he could take Kuwait without a fight. Perhaps the third assumption was violated: there was no group of nations committed to preventing Hussein from invading Kuwait. Without a collective international force to deter Iraq from taking Kuwait, Hussein may have believed that he could successfully seize Kuwait. Certainly collective security did not persuade Iraq to peacefully restore Kuwait to the Kuwaitis once an immense international military force of nearly thirty nations had settled into the Middle East. The United Nations demanded that Iraq leave Kuwait, and it authorized the use of force to drive Iraq from Kuwait. Politically isolated from any real military support, economically embargoed by the world community, and facing an international force spearheaded by the United States, the world's leading military power, Hussein still failed to quit Kuwait peacefully. Was the fifth assumption violated? Did Hussein misperceive the balance of power between the Kuwait and the UN-sanctioned international force? Did he mistakenly believe that he possessed the military capability to defeat the international force? Did Hussein underestimate the willingness of the world to enforce international law? In short, did he act rationally in making the decisions that he did? However one answers these questions, the Gulf War raises questions about the nature of collective security as a way of achieving world peace.

There is another path to peace for Kant. He believes that as more and more states choose republican political institutions, a zone of peace would settle in among them. Why would nations with republican governments be inclined toward peace? Kant defines republican states as nations that separate the power of the legislative and executive branches and whose legislators and leaders represent the interests of their constituents. A republican government encourages peace because the deputies (or representatives), subject to removal by their constituents, will not venture into a war unless that war has the support of the citizenry, most of whom, however, will be opposed to it. There are several reasons why people are opposed to war. They would do the fighting and dying; they would have to pay increased taxes to support the war effort; and they know that wars leave animosities that would require them to financially maintain a standing army for which they would prefer not to pay. Another brake on war, according to Kant, is the fact that republican states are built on the values of freedom, independence, tolerance, and equality before the law. These values spill over into the relations between republican states. Republican states recognize the independent existence of nations, safeguard their freedom to manage their internal and external affairs within international law, tolerate the differences that exist between nations, and hold all nations accountable to international law. Because members of the federation of republican states share these values and collectively enforce international laws, Kant believes that war is unlikely to break out.[66]

Peace could be promoted not only by a federation of states and by expanding the number of republican nations in the world, but by increasing international economic prosperity. Domestically, Kant argues that republican nations create greater economic prosperity than do other forms of government. Republican states protect the right of an individual to own property. Private, personal property in the form of tools, machinery, and land could be used by an entrepreneur to become wealthy. Because the state permits all people to own their own means of production and to profit, the productive capacity of the nation is expanded by the economic activity of a growing number of entrepreneurs. Internationally, greater economic prosperity at home would bring greater trade opportunities abroad. Surplus goods could be sold to other nations, and with time webs of economic interdependence between states would be established. As the economic success and well-being of one state depend on those of other nations, Kant believes that nations would go out of their way to avoid war. War, rather than encouraging economic prosperity, disrupts trade and in so doing, threatens the standard of living of the world's trading nations. Because people prefer a more comfortable life to a less comfortable one, nations avoid war. But there is a moral dimension to Kant's argument that international economic prosperity is a hedge against war. Hospitality, "the right of a stranger not to be treated with hostility when he arrives on someone else's territory," promotes trade.[67] Kant believes that commercial nations should act in the same hospitable manner evidenced by trading partners. When both trading partners are hospitable and open to trade, trade and economic prosperity flourish. Kant's comments on hospitality are a reaction to the inhospitable behavior of European commercial nations in Africa and Asia. He criticizes the West's use of slavery, oppression, war, famine, and treachery in promoting its commercial interests in the world's poor nations. Japan, he notes, had responded to the West's unscrupulous methods by restricting trade with Europe. He concludes that the exercise of hospitality promotes free trade, permits the nations of the world to develop a body of commercial law that facilitates international prosperity, and advances the cause of world peace. In sum, economic interdependence under a worldwide commercial law would generate such prosperity that nations would not want to jeopardize it by going to war.[68]

To the liberals' critics, the "end of history" theory and the liberal hope that the proliferation of representative democracies will usher in a reign of peace are illusions or dreams. How many dreams have turned to nightmares, and how many illusions have vanished at the hands of those who master the forces of reality? How many nations have turned swords into plowshares? How many leaders have sacrificed their own personal self-interest for the purpose of promoting the welfare of all humankind? How many nations rush to protect the weak nations of the world from the voracious appetites of the mighty? How often have the great liberal states coolly, calmly, and with little discomfort watched one nation savage, brutalize, strangle, murder, and slit the throats of another people and not lift a finger to bring it all to an end? No, we are not moving to an end of history when peace, prosperity, toleration, freedom, and obedience to law characterize the relations between states. Why? Because the liberal does not understand the dark side of humankind. Humans and nations are drowning in a sea of sin and self-interest from which only the extended arm of God, not liberal economics and politics, can save them. Liberalism places too much faith in the human ability to make the world a better place, and too little credence in the darkness that moves individuals and nations to commit atrocities and monstrosities too numerous to mention and too brutal to contemplate. There are other reasons to believe that we are not closing in on the end of history. Communism, certainly wounded by the collapse of the Soviet Union and its Eastern European client states, is not dead. China does not show evidence of becoming a Western-style representative democracy, and because nations in the phase of industrialization tend to become expansionary, China is a potential threat to international peace. Nationalism is another force likely to promote war. The liberal nations of the world may rejoice in the apparent movement of Russia toward a liberal democracy and a market economy. But it took the United States from 1776 to 1789 to establish a constitution that fit the character of the nation, and it may take many years for Russia to do so too. If Russia's dance with liberal political and economic theory and practice fails, Russia could quite possibly be lured into an expansionary, pan-Slavic nationalism that would drag it, the countries of Europe, and those of Asia into war. Russian sympathies for their Orthodox, Slavic brothers and sisters of the Balkan countries could bring them into conflict with the Islamic or European worlds. Even if Russia and China successfully reform and adopt liberal political and economic orders, there are other barriers to world peace. Peace rests on the democratization of other less developed countries, and the history of democratization in the twentieth century is one of ebb and flow. Some authoritarian nations become democracies, only to revert back to authoritarianism at a later date. This has certainly been true in Latin America, and if authoritarian regimes are more violent, as the liberal contends, the world's future will most likely be marked by war. In short, history will continue along its long journey. Nations will pursue their interests; war will result when conflicting national interests cannot be resolved; and the only hope for peace is for nations to pursue policies of realpolitik: power politics.[69]

For liberals, this is an overly pessimistic reading of human nature, history, and world politics. They see good reason to believe that the democratization of the planet is well underway and that the prospect of world peace lies ahead. First, communism and nationalism are forces that will not hamper the spread of democracy and peace in the world. Communist China is in the process of liberalizing its economic system and is adopting free-market policies, especially in the agricultural sector. The Communist Party has responded to the demand for increased access to consumer goods. Although China has a long way to go in becoming a market economy, it has made the first steps in that direction. Though liberal political reforms have been stifled, important segments of the intelligentsia are committed to political reform. As economic liberalization often precedes political liberalization, time is on the side of those who favor liberal democracy in China. The divisive force of nationalism is dwindling in world politics and is being replaced by nationalism with a liberal face. Centrifugal nationalistic forces in Eastern Europe and the Soviet Union have helped bring the Soviet Union to an end. In some Eastern European countries such as Poland and Hungary, the nationalistic desire for freedom will lead to the development of Western liberal democratic and economic systems. To the extent that nationalism can be put in the service of developing liberal economic and political institutions, nationalism will serve the cause of peace. Russia could indeed succumb to a form of pan-Slavic nationalism, but this threat is diminished by the relative success Russia has had in making the transition toward representative political institutions and in developing a market-based economy. Second, there has been a swelling in the number of democracies. From 1790 to today, the number of democracies in the world has risen from three to about seventy. Though the realist is correct in saying that there have been periods of time when democratic nations have succumbed to authoritarian rule, the fact remains that the tendency has been to increase the number of democratic regimes. Furthermore, these democracies have achieved a foothold on every continent, and they can serve as a beachhead for the continued proliferation of democratic regimes. The retreat of a divisive nationalism and communism coupled with the onward march of democracy bodes well for a future marked by international peace.[70]

For the Islamic fundamentalist, the end of history will not come with the domination of a liberal economic and political order; on the contrary, all brothers of Islam are called to put an end to the spread of world liberal economic and political institutions that have sought to destroy the message and unity of the Islamic community. All should fight in the way of Allah to convert non-Islamic nations to Islam. Between now and the universal rule of Islam, great wars will take place: first, wars between the oppressed and the oppressing nations of the world; and second, wars between good and evil in the souls of all humanity—wars to liberate their souls from false ideologies and to open them to a higher spiritual and communal life following the teachings of Mohammed and Allah. War between dar-al-Islam (the territory of Islam) and dar-al-harb (the territory of war) will mark the coming years in history. The Iranian Revolution signaled the revival of a spiritually and materially militant Islamic fundamentalism that seeks to recover control of Muslim nations that have been divided and exploited by Western powers. Muslim countries that have been tempted by the power and riches of the West to move away from the true teachings of Mohammed must return to the fundamental teachings of the Qur'an. Muslims in those countries should rise up against the reformist or Western-backed puppet Muslim governments, seize the reins of power, purge the society of all Western cultural, economic, and political influence, and bring to fruition a new government dedicated to uniting its people in the bonds of equality, brotherhood, and unity. As the darkest forces of Satan rule the soul of the most powerful Western nations, future wars with truly Islamic countries cannot be ruled out. Regardless of whether the transition to an Islamic world will be accomplished by a war with the West and/or achieved through a spiritual war that brings all people home to Allah, the people of the world will live in brotherhood and peace only when Islam reigns and only when Islam puts an end to history.

To the Islamic fundamentalist, Kant's understanding of the cooperation and conflict that characterize world society is wrongheaded. First, Kant believes that international law or right is based upon the agreement or consent of nations, not on Islamic law. Kant holds that international right is founded by rational human beings creating law that should secure the freedom of every state. In so doing, Kant throws away all the international law that flows from the mouth and international conduct of Mohammed. In place of Islamic international law that governs the nations of Islam and moves them toward the unity of mankind, Kant's international right justifies the division of mankind into a variety of nation-states. These nation-states reject the Islamic belief that God is sovereign in the world and that God is the legislator of the fundamental law that governs the relations between individuals and nations. For Kant, sovereignty rests with humans, and it is humans that are their own lawgivers, their own god. Nations are free to live as they choose as long as they do not infringe on other nations' right to live as they choose. This can lead only to war. Kant recognizes the right of each nation to choose its own form of government, and this includes a tyranny. If Kant is correct that tyrannies are one of the causes of war, then Kant's own world political theory accommodates war. Indeed, he uses international law to justify when and how states may go to war. In sum, to the Islamic fundamentalist, Kant's international political theory does not bring the people of the world into the fold of universal brotherhood and peace. Rather, it serves to cast up social, economic, political, and cultural walls that forever divide humans against themselves and against any hope of enjoying the peace, prosperity, unity, and brotherhood promised the people of the earth.

For a liberal such as Kant, this Islamic critique misses several important points that bear on the end of history and the nature of international political theory. First, the end of history will bring the spread of representative governments and of Western values. Some may believe that Iran's Islamic revolution has shed light on the sores of Western liberal and economic life, and that it will spark Muslims all over the world to build the bonfires of revolution. This cannot happen without the support of the Muslim people. In fact, fundamentalist movements in many Islamic nations are poorly supported by Muslims themselves. In Egypt, where there are active revolutionary organizations, the liberal sees little possibility that a traditional Islamic culture is what the people desire. Without the people's support, these organizations can remain little more than terrorist groups. Thus, the liberal sees little hope that a resurgent Islamic fundamentalism will bring an end to Western "cultural, economic, and political imperialism." Second, to argue that Islam will conduct and win a spiritual war with the West is unthinkable to the liberal. Western liberalism has gone beyond the more narrow-minded understanding of religion and morality provided by Islamic fundamentalism. The West is not without a moral foundation. People are free to choose to live by their own moral laws, and one great achievement of contemporary Western political theory is the recognition that the state promises to secure the right of all people to believe and worship as they desire. Domestically, this promotes toleration between people of different faiths; and internationally, it promotes toleration and peace between people and nations of the world—nations that have very different conceptions of the good life. The freedom and toleration that nations have and display toward one another are attractive alternatives to the imperial desire of Islamic fundamentalism to turn the world into a cauldron of war and then impose its peculiar moral code on those peoples who choose to differ with it. Third, the Islamic fundamentalist criticizes the Kantian liberal for rejecting the unity of humankind. Each nation possesses the right to live as it likes as long as it permits other nations to do the same. This creates a rich diversity of world cultures, rather than a unity forged by requiring the nations of the world to march in moral lockstep. To think with the Islamic fundamentalist that there is one moral law that will deliver the nations of the world into the kingdom of universal happiness and peace is misguided. Although there is much cultural diversity in the world, a degree of unity does exist. International life is characterized by a society of nations that has created and continues to honor principles of international law. With a federation of states to enforce international law, nations can unite behind international law and lead the world to freedom, peace, justice, and the equality of all nations before the law.[71]

To the Russian nationalist, the world's history will be written by the interaction of nations in the modern world, and Russia's cultural heritage can serve as a beacon for other nations seeking to free themselves from morally corrupt Western values and institutions. History demonstrates that civilizations have risen and fallen in history. Nations, which embody the values of those civilizations, are the actors that shape the political history of the world. Western civilization, and the nations that articulate its values, is in a state of spiritual decline. The Orthodox spiritual values of the brotherhood of man, of the love of one another in the person of Christ, and of individual freedom, do not guide the people and nations of the West. Liberty is no longer restrained and directed by higher moral values. In liberal societies, individuals do not normally use their everyday freedom to bring about a more just society that is committed to the union of all people in a brotherhood of man. Rather, freedom is used unscrupulously to pursue great personal wealth. In liberal societies, the accumulation of wealth is considered to be the crowning achievement of human activity, and when wealth is the goal, social justice and compassion for the poor are sacrificed on the altar of ambition and gain. The spiritual vacuity of the West and a free-market system that does not promote the norms of social justice can be no model for Russia. With the great economic and political upheavals that are taking place today, Russia should rely on its own Orthodox, social, economic, and political traditions that have served to unite the Russian people. In the final analysis, the influence and spread of liberal economic and political thought and institutions throughout the world will exhaust itself. The twenty-first century will witness the collapse, not the spread, of Western liberal economic institutions. Russia's revival should focus on creating a society that is capable of managing its own affairs, defending itself from the spiritual pollution that emanates from Western culture, and presenting mankind with an alternative vision of the good life. Russia's mission will be to renew the call to all people of the world to join in a universal brotherhood of man: "a brotherly accord of all nations abiding by the law of Christ's Gospel," as Dostoevsky understood it.[72]

However, there are other Russian nationalists who quibble with Kant's conception of world politics. World politics does not revolve around peaceful nations bound up in webs of economic interdependence and dedicated to pursuing their national goals within the constraints imposed by international law. Rather, the relations of nations are in a state of anarchy. With no power to guarantee the security of a nation, each must rely on itself to provide for its own national security. Today, Russia must recover its world political power in order to defend and promote its strategic national interests. To this end, Russia must turn away from the temptation to refashion itself in the image of a Western liberal state. Representative democracy and Western-style capitalism will not serve Russia's need to increase its world political power. An autocratic president with a supportive parliament is the only way to bring order to a society that exists so close to social and political chaos. Economically, the state should direct the reconstruction of the Russian

economy; under no condition should Russia move to a totally free-market economy. Rather, state-sponsored capitalism would permit Russia's leaders to place
the nation's few economic resources in those areas that can generate a rapidly expanding economy. State capitalism, not a free-market system, will permit Russia
to reclaim its position as a major world economic power. With an ordered nation,
a people politically united behind a strong president, and a growing economy that
can provide Russia with the military strength necessary to advance and protect its
interests, Russia will be in the position to reenter world politics. The great threat to
Russia comes from a unified Germany and a resurgent Islamic movement. To secure itself from the destabilizing effects of Islamic fundamentalism, Russia must
make a military thrust to the south to extend its control over Middle Eastern Islamic nations from Turkey, Iran, and Afghanistan to India. To counter the power of
a greater Germany, Russia should return to its 1900 western border and make an
attempt to solve the Balkan question. According to this view, Russia should take
control of Ukraine and Belarus; and central Europe should be carved up among
Germany, Poland, and Russia. In the Balkans, the Croats and Serbs (members of
Russia's Slavic families) should be given their own nations. In making these
changes on the political map of Europe and South Asia, Russia would be in a better position to protect its interests in a world where power is the arbiter of disputes in world politics.[73]

To the Kantian liberal, the authoritarian solution to reforming Russia's political and economic systems and Russia's desire to expand its empire once again
fails to take into consideration the new economic and political realities in world
politics. The success of capitalism and representative government in bringing
prosperity and peace to the world should be unquestioned. The authoritarian solution to Russia's political and economic transition to a modern state only points
to the international problems that it lets loose on the world. Because authoritarian
political systems place power and decision making at the top of the political system, the people exercise little influence over foreign policy. Thus, the people do
not serve as a brake on the ambitions of an authoritarian leader as they do in representative governments. For the safety of the people of Russia, Asia, and Europe,
Western liberal political institutions would best serve the Russian people. To
strengthen Russia's economic system, Russia should move to a free-market economy as quickly as possible. Free enterprise, with a minimum of state intervention
in the economy, provides the best hope of resuscitating the Russian economy, at-
tracting multinational corporations to help renew Russian industry and manufacturing, and expanding trade with the rest of the world. Building democratic
institutions linking Russia's people with their policymakers and creating a thriv-
ing free-market economy that is well integrated in the world capitalist system will
help guarantee peace in Europe and Asia and bring Russia into the community of
nations.

The end of history will arrive on the Day of Judgment for the classicist. Until that time, the obligation of all nations and peoples of the earth is to continue the struggle for justice and world peace. Even in a world that is often filled with injustice, conflict, and human brutality, the hope of building bridges across the divides of ethnic hatred, vain international ambition, and the lust for world domination is firmly rooted in the human conscience. As individuals and as nations, we have an innate sense of what is good and evil. The challenge for Christians is to grab hold of the good, to use it to banish as much evil as is possible in their souls, and then to work to bring the light of goodness and righteousness into a darkened, sinful world. As fallen creatures, humans will always be subject to the temptations that test their commitment to peace, justice, and the brotherhood of man. With the forces of good elevating human souls toward cooperation, justice, and peace and the forces of evil dragging them into reprehensible sin, individuals and nations, are forever suspended between good and evil, between heaven and hell, and between the eternal, blissful city of God and the temporary, conflictual city of man. As long as the leaders and peoples of the nations of the world choose to follow the path of injustice, selfishness, hatred, world domination, greed, avarice, and war, the earth will shriek and wail with the cries of the persecuted, the refugee, and the hungry. History will recount how successfully the nations of the earth pursued peace, justice, and the solidarity of humankind.

If the future relations of nations conform to the past, history will record the horrendous deeds that have been heaped on the peace-loving nations of the world. The liberal solution of collective security is inadequate to stand up to the task of bringing peace and justice into the world. For the classicist, some form of world government with the certain power to enforce international law and justice remains the best hope of humankind. Collective security promises peace by pooling the power of peace-loving nations to prevent a renegade state from unleashing its fury on another nation. Unfortunately, collective security is radically flawed. First, there is no guarantee that peace-loving nations will act to prevent a potential aggressor from attacking another country. Liberal theory suggests that republican nations believe that it is in their interest to preserve world peace. However, these nations will not want to risk a war to enforce international law. Because democratic nations are inclined to peace, political leaders are not inclined to stake their political fortunes on a war that could be unpopular. And because the liberal believes that a nation's economic prosperity inclines nations to peace, a war that brings with it the interruption of trade and economic prosperity would not find great support among the country's political leaders. This bias toward peace may prevent nations from displaying the power and resolve that are necessary to deter a potential aggressor. There is another dimension to the self-interest problem. When nations perceive they have no vested self-interest in a conflict, they are not inclined to risk blood, fire, and steel to prevent one nation from going to war with another. Second, although a nation may believe that making a stand against an aggressor is in its enlightened self-interest, it is not always clear that it will exercise the will to do so. For example, British Prime Minister Neville Chamberlain acquiesced to Hitler's seizure of the Sudetenland in Czechslovakia. Much attention has been given to the Balkan conflicts in the early 1990s. The world's nations (and particularly European nations) watched as Serbia supported Bosnian-Serb seizure of Bosnian land. Third, liberal international theory suggests that collective security is effective if the nations of the world can agree on the nation that is the aggressor. This is not always that clear. Aggressors are those without justice on their side; they have violated some fundamental principle of international law. In fact, all nations that are partners to a conflict call justice to their side, listing a long list of arguments to support their case. Sometimes, it is difficult to identify who is truly the aggressor, and the peaceful nations will be unable to exert their international power to prevent a war. Thus, collective security will fail. Clearly, the idea of collective security has serious flaws that do not make it the best way to bring peace to the world.

Responding to the classicist's criticisms of the end of history and collective security, the liberal argues that war will not be banished as long as there are nations "in history" and that collective security is not a perfect means to ensure world peace. As long as there remain states that are in history—states that have not adopted liberal social, economic, and political values and institutions—war will plague world politics. For example, war will occur between states in the Balkans, because people in those nations have a historical consciousness of the "wrongs" that each ethnic group has heaped upon the others. Many people of this region have not let go of ancient feuds and injustices, which therefore continue to fuel hatred and animosity. The memories of those feuds incline nations to war when irreconcilable differences arise between them. The liberal values of toleration and of respect for the dignity of differing cultures, values that enable liberal states to live peacefully among other nations despite their differences, have not, according to liberals, taken hold in the Balkans. Thus, war characterizes the relations between nations, like those in the Balkans, who are in history; however, peace characterizes those liberal nations that have reached the end of history. As the states that are in history modernize and develop liberal political and economic values and join the liberal international economic and political orders, world conflict will certainly diminish. Collective security is another matter. The classicist is correct in saying that nations do not always see that it is in their best interest to risk the possibility of war in order to prevent it. Had the world community made it clear to Hitler that it would not countenance the seizure of the Sudetenland, perhaps German imperial ambitions would have been squashed and World War II might not have taken place. In short, nations do not *always* do what is in their enlightened self-interest; but they normally act in ways that make collective security an effective way of maintaining world peace. Compared to the alternatives—world government or a balance of power—collective security is a reasonable solution to international conflict. Nations are not excited about the prospect of relinquishing part of their sovereignty to an international government that could enforce international law and ensure world peace, and the balance of power fails to prevent war.

But this leads us back to another liberal approach to peace. Kant is not so much a defender of collective security as he is a proponent of a federation of exclusively republican states. He believes that a federation that includes *only* republican states is the practical solution to the problem of war. In an international environment that recognizes the freedom and dignity of each republican nation, that applies international rights to all nations, that has international political institutions to dissipate and prevent international conflict from turning into war, and that ties economic interdependence to the economic prosperity of all nations, collective security is not needed to keep the peace. If world peace is to be achieved, Kant's liberal conception of an international political and economic order is superior to the idea of collective security.

Radicals and the more radical feminists do not believe that the end of history and peace have arrived. For radicals like Karl Marx and Vladimir Lenin, world peace is possible only after the contradictions inherent in the capitalist system have been resolved. Only after the oppression of the proletariat by the bourgeoisie is ended, only after the state that serves to protect the bourgeoisie and repress the proletariat is abolished, and only after the proletariat has captured the means of production and has harnessed it to create a kingdom of freedom and justice will humankind reach the end of history. Until that glorious day is reached and all humans can walk together in universal kinship, the nations of the world will be driven by the imperatives of capitalism to imperialism. But imperialism will inevitably lead to war, as nations continue to joust for markets, outlets for surplus capital, and natural resources. For feminists, the problem of war is not a function of the form of government as Kant maintains; rather, it is due to the state's patriarchal control. As long as men control positions of economic, political, social, religious, educational, and military power, and as long as they continue to use that power to perpetuate the idea that world politics is marked by international anarchy, war will continue to plague the peoples of the world. It makes no difference whether democratic, republican, monarchical, or tyrannical governments manage international relations: as long as the men who conduct foreign and military policy believe that human nature is tragically flawed, that nations have irreconcilable interests, that power is the only way to secure the safety of the state, and that war is justified in certain circumstances, war will afflict humankind. Patriarchy promotes a world culture of war, and until women find their way into the major power structures and destroy the culture of war, war will remain a scourge to humankind. Women's belief in the interdependence of all people; their ethos of care; and their commitment to greater social, economic, and political equality for all people promote peace and diffuse the causes of war. Take the interdependence of nations. Feminist perspectives on world politics can help avert war by promoting economic interdependence. Economic interdependence requires all nations of the world to promote common policies that maximize economic prosperity and to create international organizations to solve international economic disputes. For these feminists, the end of history is not at hand. As long as world politics is conducted by men whose vision is essentially conflictual, the world's political history will still be written in blood. Only the integration of women into positions of power can serve to reorient world politics in a way that will lessen the possibility of war.[74]

Does the spread of capitalism and representative forms of government incline nations to peace? Yes, argues the radical, but it is only temporary. The worldwide proliferation of representative government is a result of the spread of capitalism, and representative government is the highest form of political organization appropriate to countries with capitalistic systems. Through wealth, social position, and political influence, the bourgeoisie is capable of capturing the power of the state by using political parties and interest groups to elect politicians sympathetic to capitalism. The power of the state is used to secure the monied interests of the bourgeoisie as well as to ensure the docility of the worker. Though the worker may not be entirely happy with his or her condition, the level of prosperity achieved by capitalism provides workers with a standard of living that they do not wish to diminish. Realizing that war is a threat to that standard of living, the worker is inclined toward peace and this preference for peace reinforces the peaceful attitudes of those in elected governmental positions. The economic and political power exercised by the bourgeoisie creates a degree of domestic industrial and civil peace that facilitates economic growth. On the international level, the world bourgeoisie is able to culturally, economically, and politically penetrate less developed nations. This penetration sets up a dependent relationship between the rich, industrially advanced core countries on the one hand, and the poorer, less developed, peripheral nations on the other. To culturally reinforce its control over developing economies, the international bourgeoisie fosters the growth of liberal democratic values and institutions in the less developed nations. The exploitation of the proletariat by the bourgeoisie in purportedly "democratic" developing countries occurs under the watchful eye of the bourgeoisie whose economic success lies in using the power of the state to enforce civil peace among the proletariat. To ensure that a war that would threaten the well-being of the world capitalist system does not break out, the international bourgeoisie supports a liberal international political order. First, the most powerful capitalist nations give the world bourgeoisie a free hand in spreading and deepening the hold of capitalism on less developed nations. Second, they use their political power to support the spread of liberal democratic governments abroad. Third, they use their political influence to prevent any nation or anticapitalist movement from upsetting the world capitalist system. The net result is that the spread of capitalism and representative government throughout the world creates a "zone of peace" among those nations that are connected by the capitalist world economy. If war occurs, it is not between capitalist nations or between capitalist and dependent, less developed nations. Rather, war occurs between capitalist and socialist nations, between authoritarian countries, or between capitalist nations and authoritarian nations that seek greater political power in world politics. Ultimately, the capitalist world economy and the international political system upon which it rests will succumb to revolutionary social forces, and the transition from a capitalist world economy to a world socialist society will undoubtedly be accompanied by the last war between capitalist and socialist forces.

The liberal finds little reason to believe that the liberal international economic and political order will give way to the triumph of the Marxist or neo-Marxist view of the end of history. For the Marxists, their history ended with the fall of East European communist regimes and the earthshaking collapse of the colossal Soviet state. The practice of communism has been largely discredited, and serious questions have been raised about the theory upon which it rests. Without a credible theory to inspire a socialist vision of the future, there will be no significant alternative to the continued ascendance of liberalism. Indeed, most postcommunist states of Eastern Europe and of the former Soviet Union have chosen to experiment with representative forms of government and move toward a capitalist, free-market economy. Fukuyama doubts that the remaining communist states will survive much longer. Economic reforms and liberalizing measures taking place in China and Cuba will lead to the eventual fall of those governments. As Fukuyama points out, communist societies that promote economic liberalization will eventually become politically liberal. Because the economic well-being of a person is inherently bound up with a government's economic policy, individuals who take greater responsibility for their economic well-being will desire to exercise real political power. Liberal democracy is the best way to give individuals access to political power, because individuals have the opportunity to influence governmental officials through elections, political parties, interest groups, and the media. Thus, economic liberalization and reform will place great pressures on communist governments to revise their political structures or risk a revolution by those demanding greater access to the exercise of political power. In the long run, communism is dead.[75]

The liberal believes that the radical is correct in asserting that peace follows on the heels of the spread of capitalism and representative government. However, liberals do not agree with the radicals' explanation for why this occurs. According to the liberal, there are four faulty assumptions upon which the radical bases his or her case. First, the radical assumes that all governments serve the interests of the privileged classes and they use their power to control those who would challenge the capitalist system. Second, radicals believe that the bourgeoisie can frame the consciousness of the proletariat to support the cultural values of capitalism, even though it is not in their interest to do so. Third, radicals hold that representative democracy is a sham; that is to say, it represents the interests of capital but not the true interests of the laboring person. Fourth, radicals argue that the bourgeoisie benefits from world peace and is able to use its power to control the culture, minds, and political activity of nations with capitalist economies and that a zone of peace flows from the cooperation of so-called democratic capitalist nations.

There are, according to the liberal, cogent reasons to believe that the radical is wrong in making these assumptions. First, government is founded not to establish the tyranny of the rich over the poor but to secure those basic rights that all humans should be guaranteed so they can pursue happiness. When government fails to secure those rights, the people are free to remove their governors by the ballot box or through revolution. Because the people can change the government, the government is responsive to the needs of the people as a whole and not to the desires of a small economic elite. Second, the radical believes that the bourgeoisie has the ability to elicit working-class support for a capitalistic system that prevents workers from leading a happy life. In fact, humans are acquisitive beings who create economic systems to satisfy their basic needs. Free enterprise permits individuals to exericse their talents in a way that gives them material and spiritual satisfaction and this leads to happiness. Third, representative democracy is not a sham. As suggested by the first two arguments, representative government is controlled by the nation's electorate, which wishes to use its power to secure its rights to life, liberty, and the pursuit of happiness. Fourth, the radical suggests that because peace is in the interest of the bourgeoisie, the bourgeoisie takes what steps are necessary to secure it. In fact, the liberal recognizes that peace is in the interest of all the world's peoples, not just the bourgeoisie. There are tremendous cultural forces that dispose democratic capitalist nations toward peace. The desire for national prosperity, the knowledge that war brings higher taxation, and the wish to avoid the loss of life all predispose democratic nations toward peace. Elected officials do well to heed the call for peace among the people who place them in positions of public trust. The spread of liberal economic and political institutions worldwide is the best defense against war and the best hope for peace.

Put down your book and give some thought to whether or not the liberal vision of world politics is the best way to order international affairs. How does your view of human nature help you think about the liberal vision of international politics? Are humans as reasonable as liberals suggest? Are the leaders of nations inclined to promote the nation's enlightened self-interest? Can collective security serve as an instrument to prevent invasions of one country by another? Can human rights be secured for the world's people by a liberal international political order? Is there a potential conflict between the right to national self-determination and human rights in liberal political theory? Given real differences in wealth and environmental quality among the world's nations, does the liberal political order have sufficient power to handle these problems? Can the liberal vision of a capitalist world economy serve as an engine for economic growth and prosperity in less developed countries? Would such a system lead to more global environmental damage? Finally, there are questions about the future world order. Are we to believe with Fukuyama that we are at the end of history and that the spread of liberal democracy and capitalism will usher in a period of greater peace, freedom, justice, and economic prosperity? Will a malevolent form of nationalism and religious fundamentalism serve to limit the spread of a liberal political and economic order? Will some new theory for shaping the world order appear as an alternative to liberalism? How would the vision of world politics that you have been developing throughout this book help you think about the adequacy of a liberal political and economic order?

NOTES

1. Kenneth N. Waltz, *Theory of International Relations* (New York: Random House, 1979), 111.
2. Ibid., 186–187.
3. Warner Moss, "Britain and The Empire," *Contemporary World Politics*, ed. Francis J. Brown, Charles Hodges, and Joseph S. Roucek (New York: John Wiley & Sons, 1939), 130.
4. Thucydides, *The Peloponnesian War,* intro. T. E. Wick (New York: The Modern Library, 1982), 14.
5. David Hume, *Political Essays*, ed. Knud Haakonssen (Cambridge: Cambridge University Press, 1994), 154–160; James E. Dougherty and Robert L. Pfaltzgraff Jr., *Contending Theories of International Relations,* 2d ed. (New York: Harper & Row, 1981), 25; Hans Morgenthau, *Politics Among Nations*, rev. Kenneth W. Thompson, 6th ed. (New York: Alfred A. Knopf, 1985), chap. 9.
6. Friedrich von Gentz, "Chapter I, The True Acceptation of a Balance of Power," *The Theory of International Relations,* intro. and ed. M. G. Forsyth, H. M. A. Keens-Soper, and P. Savigear (London: George Allen and Unwin Ltd., 1970), 281–282.
7. Morgenthau, *Politics Among Nations,* chap. 5.
8. Nikolai I. Danilevski, *Russland und Europa* (Osnabruck: Otto Zeller, 1965), 291–300.
9. Ibid., 21–22, 191–193, 195, 213, 245–249, 265–266.
10. Ibid., 229–230.
11. Ibid., 213, 227–235.
12. Michael Donelan, *Elements of International Relations Theory* (Oxford: Clarendon Press, 1992), 163–168.
13. Sophocles, "Oedipus at Colonus," *The Three Theban Plays,* trans. Robert Fagles and intro. Bernard Knox (New York: Penguin Books, 1984), 322.

14. Morgenthau, *Politics Among Nations,* 5, 13; Niccolò Machiavelli, *The Prince and The Discourses,* intro. Max Lerner (New York: The Modern Library, 1950), 56.

15. Ruhollah Khomeini, *Islam and Revolution* (London: K. P. I., 1981), 181–182, 197, 237, 239–240, 257–258.

16. Ibid., 181–182, 257–258.

17. Morgenthau, *Politics Among Nations,* 198–200.

18. Ibid., 4–5.

19. Dante Alighieri, *Monarchy,* trans. Donald Nicholl (Westport, CT: Hyperion Press, 1947), 3–4.

20. Dante Alighieri, *The De Monarchia of Dante Alighieri,* trans. Aurelia Henry (Boston: Houghton Mifflin, 1904), 26.

21. Ibid., 9, 15, 20, 24, 28, 34, 54–59, 197–202.

22. Ibid., 9, 16, 24, 28, 34, 40–43, 54–59.

23. Ibid., 5.

24. Ibid., 25–27.

25. Ibid., 22–23, 27–29, 31–37, 40–45, 54–59.

26. Ibid., 30, 52; idem, *The Convivio of Dante Alighieri,* trans. Philip H. Wicksteed (London: J. M. Dent, 1940), 206.

27. Dante, *De Monarchia,* 21; idem, *Convivio,* 202.

28. Dante, *De Monarchia,* 27–28.

29. Dante, *Convivio,* 225.

30. Dante, *De Monarchia,* 51–52.

31. Ibid., 30.

32. Ibid., 9–16, 30.

33. Ibid., 54–59.

34. Ibid., 40–45.

35. F. H. Hinsley, *Power and the Pursuit of Peace* (Cambridge: Cambridge University Press, 1967), 14–15.

36. Alexander Hamilton, James Madison, and John Jay, *The Federalist Papers,* intro. Clinton Rossiter (New York: The New American Library, 1961), 301.

37. John Bartlett, *Familiar Quotations,* ed. Emily M. Beck, 14th ed. (Boston: Little, Brown, 1968), 750.

38. Jean-Jacques Rousseau, *The Social Contract and Discourses,* trans. G. D. H. Cole (London: J. M. Dent and Sons Ltd., 1973), 76, 79–80, 106–113, 177–178; idem, *Rousseau on International Relations,* ed. Stanley Hoffmann and David P. Fidler (Oxford: Oxford University Press, 1991), 19, 25, 92–93, 153–156, 175–179.

39. Don Hahn, *The Lion King* (Burbank: Walt Disney Co., 1994).

40. Dante, *De Monarchia,* 22–26.

41. Rousseau, *Rousseau on International Relations,* 54.

42. Ibid., 53–54.

43. Robert M. Hutchins, "World Government Now," *Readings in World Politics,* ed. Robert A. Goldwin (New York: Oxford University Press, 1959), 526–527.

44. "Declaration of Independence," *The Struggle for Democracy*, Edward S. Greenberg and Benjamin I. Page, 2d ed. (New York: HarperCollins College Publishers, 1995), A17.

45. See Abbé de Saint-Pierre's ideas as transcribed by Jean-Jacques Rousseau in Rousseau, *Rousseau on International Relations*, 69–70.

46. Ibid., 68–71, 81.

47. Ibid., 86–87.

48. Khomeini, *Islam and Revolution*, 263–264; Sayyed Abul A'la Maududi, *Unity of the Muslim World*, 4th ed. (Lahore: Islamic Publications Ltd., 1979), 1–3.

49. Sayyed Abul A'la Maududi, *Human Rights in Islam* (Lahore: Islamic Publications Ltd., 1977), 11–16.

50. Ibid., 33.

51. R. J. Vincent, *Human Rights and International Relations* (Cambridge: Cambridge University Press, 1986), chap. 3.

52. Inis L. Claude, *Power and International Relations* (New York: Random House, 1962), 210–242; Walter F. Berns, "The Case Against World Government," *Readings in World Politics*, ed. Robert A. Goldwin (New York: Oxford University Press, 1959), 536–540.

53. Francis Fukuyama, *The End of History and the Last Man* (New York: The Free Press, 1992), 13–38, 235–237; idem, "The End of History," *Taking Sides*, ed. John T. Rourke, 4th ed. (Guilford, CT: The Dushkin Publishing Group, 1992), 270, 275–281, 284–285.

54. Idem, "The End of History," 285–286.

55. John Locke, *Two Treatises of Government*, intro. Peter Laslett (New York: The New American Library, 1965), chaps. 2–3; Kant, *Political Writings*, 44–45.

56. Hamilton, Madison, and Jay, *Federalist Papers*, 300–313, 331–332; Locke, *Two Treatises*, 395–397.

57. Adam Smith, *Adam Smith's Moral and Political Philosophy*, ed. Herbert W. Schneider (New York: Harper & Row, 1948), 419–436; Milton Friedman, *Capitalism and Freedom* (Chicago: University of Chicago Press, 1982), 56–74; Milton and Rose Friedman, *Free to Choose* (New York: Avon Books, 1980), 30–46; Fukuyama, *Last Man*, 100–103.

58. Kant, *Political Writings*, 133.

59. Ibid., 96, 118.

60. Ibid., 164–170.

61. Ibid., 48, 105.

62. Ibid., 171; Thomas Hobbes, *Leviathan*, ed. Michael Oakeshott (New York: Collier Books, 1962), 104.

63. Kant, *Political Writings*, 90–92.

64. Ibid., 47–48, 102–105, 171–172.

65. Claude, *Power*, 106–115; A. F. K. Organski, *World Politics* (New York: Alfred A. Knopf, 1958), 373–384.

66. Kant, *Political Writings*, 99–102, 166–167.

67. Ibid., 105.

68. Ibid., 50–51, 105–108, 110–112.

69. Samuel Huntington, "No Exit: The Errors of Endism," *Taking Sides*, ed. John T. Rourke, 4th ed. (Guilford, CT: The Dushkin Publishing Group, 1992), 289–290, 293.

70. Fukuyama, *Last Man*, 39–51, 100–139, 266–284.

71. See Fouad Ajami, "The Summoning," *Foreign Affairs* 72 (September/October 1994): 2–9 for a treatment of the relevance of Islamic fundamentalism today.

72. Fyodor M. Dostoevsky, *The Diary of a Writer*, trans. Boris Brasol (New York: George Braziller, 1954), 980; Alexandr Solzhenitsyn, *Rebuilding Russia*, trans. Alexis Klimoff (New York: Farrar, Straus and Giroux, 1991), 45–50.

73. Jacob W. Kipp, "The Zhirinovsky Threat," *Foreign Affairs* 72 (May/June 1994): 76–84.

74. J. Ann Tickner, *Gender in International Relations* (New York: Columbia University Press, 1992), 133–136; V. Spike Peterson and Anne Sisson Runyan, *Global Gender Issues* (Boulder: Westview Press, 1993), 150–152.

75. Fukuyama, *Last Man*, 33–38.

BIBLIOGRAPHY

AbuSulayman, AbdulHamid A. 1987. *The Islamic Theory of International Relations.* Brentwood, Md.: International Graphics Printing Service.

Ahmad, Muhammad Aziz. 1975. *The Nature of Islamic Political Theory.* Ma'aref Limited.

Ajami, Fouad. 1993. "The Summoning." *Foreign Affairs* 72 (September/October): 2–9.

Aksakov, Konstantin S. 1966. "On the Internal State of Russia." *Russian Intellectual History.* Edited by Marc Raeff. New York: Harcourt, Brace and World, Inc.

Al-Ghunaimi, Mohammad Talaat. 1968. *The Muslim Conception of International Law and the Western Approach.* The Hague: Martinus Nijhoff.

Aksakov, Konstantin S. 1966. "On the Internal State of Russia." *Russian Intellectual History.* Edited by Marc Raeff. New York: Harcourt, Brace and World: 231–251.

Alighieri, Dante. 1940. *The Convivio of Dante Alighieri.* Translated by Philip H. Wicksteed. London: J. M. Dent.

———. 1904. *The De Monarchia of Dante Alighieri.* Translated by Aurelia Henry. Boston: Houghton Mifflin.

———. 1947. *Monarchy.* Translated by Donald Nicholl. Westport, Conn.: Hyperion Press, Inc.

Almond, Gabiel A., and Sidney Verba. 1963. *The Civic Culture.* Princeton: Princeton University Press.

Anderson, Thorton. 1967. *Russian Political Thought.* Ithaca: Cornell University Press.

Aquinas, Saint Thomas. 1953. *The Political Ideas of St. Thomas Aquinas.* Edited by Dino Bigongiari. New York: Hafner Press.

Aristotle. 1958. *Politics.* Translated by Ernest Barker. Oxford: Oxford University Press.

Augustine, Saint. 1890. *The City of God.* Translated by J. H. 2 vols. London: Griffith, Farran, Okeden, and Welsh.

————. 1958. *The City of God.* Translated by Gerald G. Walsh, Demetrius Zema, Grace Monahan, and Daniel J. Honan. Garden City: Image Books.

Bakunin, Mikhail. 1972. *Bakunin on Anarchy.* Edited and translated by Sam Dolgoff. New York: Alfred A. Knopf.

————. 1953. *The Political Philosophy of Bakunin.* Edited by G. P. Maximov. New York: The Free Press.

————. 1990. *Statism and Anarchy.* Translated by Marshall S. Shatz. Cambridge: Cambridge University Press.

Baran, Paul A., and Paul M. Sweezy. 1966. *Monopoly Capital.* New York: Modern Reader Paperbacks.

Bartelme, Jane, and Sarah Caplan. 1995. *Legends of the Fall.* Culver City: Columbia TriStar.

Bartlett, John. 1968. *Familiar Quotations.* Edited by Emily M. Beck. 14th ed. Boston: Little, Brown.

Beitz, Charles R. 1979. *Political Theory and International Relations.* Princeton: Princeton University Press.

Bergsten, C. Fred, Thomas Horst, and Theodore H. Moran. 1978. *American Multinationals and American Interests.* Washington, D.C.: Brookings Institution.

Berns, Walter F. 1959. "The Case Against World Government." *Readings in World Government.* Edited by Robert A. Goldwin. New York: Oxford University Press: 425–438.

Bodin, Jean. 1992. *On Sovereignty.* Edited and translated by Julian H. Franklin. Cambridge: Cambridge University Press.

Bondurant, Joan V. 1965. *Conquest of Violence.* Revised ed. Berkeley: University of California Press.

Bookchin, Murray. 1990. *Remaking Society: Pathways to a Green Future.* Boston: South End Press.

Boserup, Esther. 1986. *Women's Role in Economic Development.* Aldershot, England: Gower.

Brandt Commission. 1983. *Common Crisis.* Cambridge: M. I. T. Press.

Brock-Utne, Brigit. 1989. *Feminist Perspectives on Peace and Peace Education.* New York: Pergamon Press.

Brown, Wendy. 1988. *Manhood and Politics.* Totowa, N.J.: Rowman and Littlefield.

Capra, Fritjof, and Charlene Spretnak. 1984. *Green Politics.* New York: E. P. Dutton.

Carr, E. H. 1964. *The Twenty Years Crisis, 1919–1939: An Introduction to the Study of International Relations.* New York: Harper & Row.

Carter, Christine Jane. 1987. *Rousseau and the Problem of War.* New York: Garland Publishing.

Channing, W. E. 1849. "Discourse on War." *The Entire Works of W. E. Channing, D.D.* 2 vols. London: Simms and McIntyre. Vol. II: 156–169.

————. 1849. "Lecture on War." *The Entire Works of W. E. Channing, D.D.* 2 vols. London: Simms and McIntyre. Vol. II: 592–608.

Charlton, Sue Ellen M. 1984. *Women in Third World Development.* Boulder: Westview Press.

Childress, James. 1978. "Just War Theories." *Theological Studies* 39: 427–445.

Chimi, B. S. 1993. *International Law and World Order.* New Delhi: Sage Publications.

Choueiri, Youssef M. 1990. *Islamic Fundamentalism.* Boston: Twayne Publishers.

Cicero, Marcus Tullius. 1976. *On the Commonwealth.* Translated by George H. Sabine and Stanley Barney Smith. New York: Macmillan.

————. 1991. *On Duties.* Cambridge: Cambridge University Press.

Claude, Inis L. Jr. 1962. *Power and International Relations*. New York: Random House.

Connelly, Philip, and Robert Perlman. 1975. *The Politics of Scarcity: Resource Conflicts in International Relations*. New York: Oxford University Press.

Danilevski, Nikolai I. 1965. *Russland und Europa*. Osnabruck: Otto Zeller.

Deane, Herbert A. 1963. *The Political and Social Ideas of St. Augustine*. New York: Columbia University Press.

"Declaration of Independence." 1995. *The Struggle for Democracy*. Edward S. Greenberg and Benjamin I. Page. 2d ed. New York: HarperCollins College Publishers: A17–A19.

Di Stephano, Christine. 1983. "Masculinity as Ideology in Political Theory: Hobbesian Man Considered." *Woman's Studies International Forum* 6 (6):633–644.

Donelan, Michael. 1992. *Elements of International Relations Theory*. Oxford: Clarendon Press.

Dostoevsky, Fyodor M. 1880/1952. "The Brothers Karamazov." Translated by C. Garnett. *Great Books of the Western World*. 54 vols. Chicago: Encyclopedia Britannica. Vol. 52.

———. 1954. *The Diary of a Writer*. Translated by Boris Brasol. New York: George Braziller.

Dougherty, James E., and Robert L. Pfaltzgraff Jr. 1981. *Contending Theories of International Relations*. 2d ed. New York: Harper & Row.

Doyle, Michael. 1995. "Liberalism and World Politics Revisited." *Controversies in International Relations Theory*. Edited by Charles W. Kegley Jr. New York: Saint Martin's Press: 83–106.

Dubos, Rene J. 1972. *A God Within*. New York: Charles Scribner's Sons.

Dymond, Jonathan. 1971. "Self-Defence Incompatible With Christianity." *War and the Christian Conscience*. Edited by Albert Marrin. Chicago: Regnery Co.: 164–170.

———. n.d. *To That Small But Increasing Number Whether In This Country or Elsewhere, Who Maintain In Principle, and Illustrate By Their Practice, The Great Duty of Conforming To The Laws of Christian Morality Without Regard To Dangers Or Present Advantages, This Work Is Respectfully Dedicated*. New York: T. B. Smith.

Ehrlich, Paul, and others. 1984. *The Cold and the Dark*. New York: W. W. Norton.

Elfstrom, Gerald. 1990. *Ethics for a Shrinking World*. New York: St. Martin's Press.

Ellis, Anthony, ed. *Ethics and International Relations*. Manchester: Manchester University Press.

Elshtain, Jean Bethke. 1981. *Public Man, Private Woman*. Princeton: Princeton University Press.

———. 1987. *Women and War*. New York: Basic Books.

Elshtain, Jean Bethke, and Sheila Tobias. 1990. *Women, Militarism, and War*. Savage, Md.: Rowman and Littlefield.

Forsyth, M. G., and others. 1970. *The Theory of International Relations*. New York: Atherton Press.

Frank, Andre Gunder. 1981. *Reflections on the World Economic Crisis*. New York: Monthly Review Press.

Frant, Rebecca, and Kathleen Newland, eds. 1991. *Gender and International Relations*. Bloomington: Indiana University Press.

Fraser, Arvonne S. 1987. *The U.N. Decade for Women: Documents and Dialogue*. Boulder: Westview Press.

French, Marilyn. 1985. *Beyond Power: Women, Men and Morals*. New York: Summit.

———. 1992. *The War Against Women*. New York: Simon & Schuster.

Frieden, Jeffery A., and David A. Lake. 1995. *International Political Economy*. New York: St. Martin's Press.

Friedman, Milton. 1982. *Capitalism and Freedom*. Chicago: University of Chicago Press.

Friedman, Milton, and Rose Friedman. 1980. *Free to Choose*. New York: Avon Books.

Fukuyama, Francis. 1992. *The End of History and the Last Man*. New York: The Free Press.

———. 1992. "The End of History." *Taking Sides*. Edited by John T. Rourke. 4th ed. Guilford, Conn.: The Dushkin Publishing Group: 270–286.

Fyodorov, Yevgeny. 1973. "Against the Limits of Growth." *New Scientist* 57: 431–432.

Gandhi, Mahatma. 1968. *The Selected Works of Mahatma Gandhi*. Edited by Shriman Narayan. Ahmedabad: Navajivan Publishing House, Vols. IV and VI.

Gentz, Friedrich von. 1970. "Chapter I, The True Acceptation of a Balance of Power." *The Theory of International Relations*. Introduced and edited by M. G. Forsyth, H. M. A. Keens-Soper, and P. Savigear. London: George Allen and Unwin Ltd.: 281–287.

Gierke, Otto. 1957. *Natural Law and the Theory of Society*. Boston: Beacon Press.

Glahn, Gerhard von. 1992. *Law Among Nations*. New York: Macmillan.

Golding, William. 1954. *Lord of the Flies*. N. P.: Wideview/Perigee Books.

Goldsmith, M. M. 1966. *Hobbes's Science of Politics*. New York: Columbia University Press.

Goldwin, Robert A., ed. 1959. *Readings in World Politics*. New York: Oxford University Press.

Grimke, Sarah M. 1970. *Letters on the Equality of the Sexes and the Condition of Woman*. New York: Burt Franklin.

Grotius, Hugo. 1925. *The Law of War and Peace*. Translated by Francis W. Kelsey. Indianapolis: Bobbs-Merrill.

Haft, Steven, Tony Thomas, and Paul Junger Witt. 1989. *Dead Poets Society*. Burbank: Touchstone Pictures.

Hahn, Don. 1991. *Beauty and the Beast*. Burbank: Walt Disney Co.

———. 1994. *The Lion King*. Burbank: Walt Disney Co.

Hamilton, Alexander, James Madison, and John Jay. 1961. *The Federalist Papers*. Introduction by Clinton Rossiter. New York: New American Library.

Harding, James A. 1974. "Ecology as Ideology." *Alternatives* 3 (4):18–22.

Hare, J. E., and Carey B. Joynt. 1982. *Ethics and International Affairs*. New York: St. Martin's Press.

Hegel, Georg W. F. 1952. *Hegel's Philosophy of Right*. Translated by T. M. Knox. Oxford: Oxford University Press.

———. 1982. *Lectures on the Philosophy of World History*. Translated by H. B. Nisbet. Cambridge: Cambridge University Press.

Heilbroner, Robert L. 1991. *An Inquiry into the Human Prospect*. New York: W. W. Norton.

Hevener, Natalie Kaufman. 1983. *International Law and the Status of Women*. Boulder: Westview Press.

Hinsley, F. H. 1967. *Power and the Pursuit of Peace*. Cambridge: Cambridge University Press.

Hitler, Adolf. 1943. *Mein Kampf*. Translated by Ralph Manheim. Boston: Houghton Mifflin.

Hobbes, Thomas. 1962. *Leviathan*. Edited by Michael Oakeshott. New York: Collier Books.

Hobson, J. A. 1965. *Imperialism*. Ann Arbor: University of Michigan Press.

Hope, Marjorie, and James Young. 1994. "Islam and Ecology." *Cross Currents* 44 (Summer): 180–192.

Hume, David. 1994. *Political Essays*. Edited by Knud Haakonssen. Cambridge: Cambridge University Press.

Huntington, Samuel P. 1993. "The Clash of Civilizations." *Foreign Affairs* 72 (3):22–49.

———. 1992. "No Exit: The Errors of Endism." *Taking Sides*. Edited by John T. Rourke. Guilford, Conn.: The Dushkin Publishing Group: 287–294.

Hutchins, Robert M. 1959. "The Case Against World Government." *Readings in World Politics*. Edited by Robert A. Goldwin. New York: Oxford University Press: 411–424.

Inhelder, B., and J. Piaget. 1958. *The Growth of Logical Thinking*. New York: Basic Books.

Jaggar, Alison. 1983. *Feminist Politics and Human Nature*. Totowa, N.J.: Rowman and Allanheld.

Joekes, Susan P. comp. 1987. *Women in the World Economy*. New York: Oxford University Press.

Jones, Dorothy V. 1991. *Code of Peace: Ethics and Security in the World of the Warlord States*. Chicago: University of Chicago Press.

Kant, Immanuel. 1991. *Political Writings*. Introduction by Hans Reiss. Translated by H. B. Nisbet. 2d ed. Cambridge: Cambridge University Press.

Kegley, Charles W. 1995. *Controversies in International Relations Theory*. New York: St. Martin's Press.

Keohane, Robert O., and Joseph S. Nye. 1989. *Power and Interdependence*. 2nd ed. New York: HarperCollins.

Khadduri, Majid. 1955. *War and Peace in the Law of Islam*. Baltimore: Johns Hopkins University Press.

Khomeini, Ruhollah. 1981. *Islam and Revolution*. London: K.P.I.

Kipp, Jacob W. 1994. "The Zhirinovsky Threat." *Foreign Affairs* 72 (May/June):72–86.

Kireevski, Ivan. 1966. "On the Nature of European Culture and its Relation to the Culture of Russia." *Russian Intellectual History*. Edited by Marc Raeff. New York: Harcourt, Brace and World.

Knutsen, Torbjorn L. *A History of International Relations Theory*. Manchester: Manchester University Press.

Kotb, Sayed. 1970. *Social Justice in Islam*. Translated by John B. Hardie. New York: Octagon Books.

Lee, Donald C. 1982. "Toward a Marxian Ecological Ethic." *Environmental Ethics* 4 (4): 339–343.

Leiss, William. 1972. *The Domination of Nature*. New York: George Braziller.

Lenin, V. I. 1967. "Imperalism, the Highest Stage of Capitalism." *Selected Works*. 3 vols. New York: International Publishers, 1: 673–777.

Locke, John. 1965. *Two Treatises of Government*. Introduction by Peter Laslett. New York: The New American Library.

Lovelock, James. 1989. *The Ages of Gaia: A Biography of Our Living Earth*. New York: Oxford University Press.

Machiavelli, Niccolò. 1950. *The Prince and The Discourses*. Introduction by Max Lerner. New York: The Modern Library.

Mahubani, Kishore. 1993. "The Dangers of Decadence." *Foreign Affairs* 72 (4): 10–14.

Marrin, Albert, ed. 1971. *War and the Christian Conscience*. Chicago: Henry Regnery Co.

Marx, Karl, and Friedrich Engels. 1978. *The Marx-Engels Reader*. Edited by Robert Tucker. New York: W. W. Norton.

Maududi, Sayyed Abul A'la. 1966. *The Economic Problem of Man and Its Islamic Solution.* 3d ed. Delhi: Markazi Maktaba Jamaat-e-Islami Hind.

———. 1966. *The Ethical View-Point of Islam.* Translated by Mazhar-ud-Din Siddiqi. 3d ed. Delhi: Markazi Maktaba Jamaat-e-Islami Hind.

———. 1960. *First Principles of the Islamic State.* Translated by Khurshid Ahmad. Lahore: Islamic Publications Ltd.

———. 1977. *Human Rights in Islam.* Lahore: Islamic Publications Ltd.

———. n.d. *Islamic Way of Life.* Translated by Khurshid Ahmad. Lahore: Islamic Publications Ltd.

———. 1976. *Jihad in Islam.* Lahore: Islamic Publications Ltd.

———. 1972. *Purdah and the Status of Woman in Islam.* Translated by Al-Ash'ari. Lahore: Islamic Publications Ltd.

———. 1973. *Political Theory of Islam.* 2d ed. Delhi: Markazi Maktaba Jamaat-e-Islami Hind.

———. 1981. *Selected Speeches and Writings of Maulana Maududi.* Translated by S. Zakir Aijaz. Karachi: International Islamic Publishers Ltd.

———. 1979. *Unity of the Muslim World.* 4th ed. Lahore: Islamic Publications Ltd.

McGinn, Bernard. 1988. "St. Benedict as the Steward of Creation." *American Benedictine Review* 39 (2): 161–176.

Meadows, Donella H., and others. 1989. *The Limits to Growth.* 2d ed. New York: Universe Books.

Mearsheimer, John J. 1990. "Why We Will Soon Miss the Cold War." *The Atlantic Monthly* (August): 35–50.

Merchant, Carolyn. 1980. *The Death of Nature.* San Francisco: Harper & Row.

———. 1989. *Ecological Revolutions: Nature, Gender, and Science in New England.* Chapel Hill: University of North Carolina Press.

Mill, John Stuart. 1959. "A Few Words on Non-Intervention." *Readings in World Politics.* Edited by Robert A. Goldwin. New York: Oxford University Press: 317–330.

Mohammed, D. S. Mahathir bin. 1992. "Eco-Imperialism and Bio-Monopoly at the Earth Summit." *New Perspectives Quarterly* 9 (Summer): 56–58.

Montesquieu, Baron de. 1949. *The Spirit of the Laws.* Translated by Thomas Nugent. New York: Hafner Press.

Morgenthau, Hans J. 1985. *Politics Among Nations.* 6th ed. revised. Kenneth W. Thompson. New York: Alfred A. Knopf.

Moss, Warner. 1939. "Britain and The Empire." *Contemporary World Politics.* Edited by Francis J. Brown, Charles Hodges, and Joseph S. Roucek. New York: John Wiley & Sons.

National Conference of Catholic Bishops. 1983. *The Challenge of Peace: God's Promise and Our Response.* Washington, D.C.: United States Catholic Conference.

Niebuhr, Reinhold. 1944. *The Children of Lightness and the Children of Darkness.* New York: Charles Scribner's Sons.

———. 1960. *Moral Man and Immoral Society.* New York: Charles Scribner's Sons.

Nussbaum, Arthur. 1950. *A Concise History of the Law of Nations.* New York: Macmillan.

O'Brien, David J., and Thomas A. Shannon. 1992. *Catholic Social Thought.* Maryknoll, New York: Orbis Books.

Olson, William C., and A. J. R. Groom. 1991. *International Relations Then and Now.* New York: HarperCollins Academic.

Ophuls, William. 1977. *Ecology and the Politics of Scarcity.* San Francisco: W. H. Freeman.

Ophuls, William, and A. Stephen Boyan Jr. 1992. *Ecology and the Politics of Scarcity Revisited.* New York: W. H. Freeman.

Oppenheim, Felix. 1991. *The Place of Morality in Foreign Policy.* Lexington, Mass.: Lexington Books.

Organski, A. F. K. 1958. *World Politics.* New York: Alfred A. Knopf.

Orr, David W., and Marvin S. Soroos, eds. 1979. *The Global Predicament: Ecological Perspectives on World Order.* Chapel Hill: University of North Carolina Press.

Paehlke, Robert C. 1989. *Environmentalism and the Future of Progressive Politics.* New Haven: Yale University Press.

Palme Commission. 1982. *Common Security.* New York: Simon & Schuster.

———. 1983. *North-South: A Program for Survival.* Cambridge: M. I. T. Press.

Pateman, Carole, and Elizabeth Gross, eds. 1986. *Feminist Challenges: Social and Political Theory.* Boston: Northeastern University Press.

Peterson, V. Spike, ed. 1992. *Gendered States: Feminists (Re)Visions of International Relations Theory,* Boulder: Lynne Rienner Publishers.

Peterson, V. Spike, and Anne Sisson Runyan. 1993. *Global Gender Issues.* Boulder: Westview Press.

Pettman, Ralph. 1991. *International Politics: Balance of Power, Balance of Productivity, Balance of Ideologies.* Boulder: Lynne Rienner Publishers.

Piaget, Jean. 1972. "Intellectual Evolution from Adolescence to Adulthood." *Human Development* 15.

Piercy, Marge. 1976. *Woman on the Edge of Time.* New York: Fawcett Crest.

Pierson, Ruth Roach, ed. 1987. *Women and Peace: Theoretical, Historical, and Practical Perspectives.* London: Croom Helm.

Pipes, Daniel. 1983. *In the Path of God.* New York: Basic Books.

Pirages, Dennis. 1978. *Global Ecopolitics.* North Scituate, Mass.: Duxbury Press.

Pitkin, Hanna F. 1984. *Fortune Is a Woman: Gender and Politics in the Thought of Niccolò Machiavelli.* Berkeley: University of California Press.

Plato. 1983. *Gorgias.* Translated by Walter Hamilton. New York: Penguin.

———. 1973. "Republic." *The Collected Dialogues of Plato.* Edited by Edith Hamilton and Huntington Cairnes. Translated by Paul Shorey. Princeton: Princeton University Press: 575–844.

Pocahontas. 1995. Burbank: Walt Disney Co.

Pope John XXIII. 1976. "Pacem in Terris: Peace on Earth." *The Gospel of Peace and Justice.* Edited by Joseph Gremillion. Maryknoll, N.Y.: Orbis Books: 201–241.

Pope John Paul II. 1991. "Centesimus Annus: On the Hundredth Anniversary of Rerum Novarum." *Catholic Social Thought.* Edited by David J. O'Brien and Thomas A. Shannon. Maryknoll, N.Y.: Orbis Books: 437–488.

———. 1988. "On Social Concern." *Origins* 17 (38).

———. 1989. "Peace Will All Creation." *Origins* 19 (28): 465–468.

———. 1990. "Pope: Greed and Fight Against Poverty Threaten Tropical Rain Forests." *L'Osservatore Romano,* Weekly ed. 28 May 1990, 5.

———. 1990. "The Exploitation of the Environment Threatens the Entire Human Race." *L'Osservatore Romano,* Weekly ed. 8 January 1990, 9–10.

———. 1990. "Environmental Ills Demand Political and Moral Answers." *L'Osservatore Romano*, Weekly ed. 19 February 1990, 2.

———. 1995. "The Gospel of Life." *Inside the Vatican*. Spec. Suppl. April.

Pope Paul VI. 1992. "Populorum Progressio: On the Development of Peoples." *Catholic Social Thought*. Edited by David J. O'Brien and Thomas A. Shannon. Maryknoll, N.Y.: Orbis Books.

Prokopovich, Feofan. 1966. "Sermon on Royal Authority and Honor." *Russian Intellectual History*. Edited by Marc Raeff. New York: Harcourt, Brace and World: 14–30.

Raeff, Marc, ed. 1966. *Russian Intellectual History*. New York: Harcourt, Brace and World.

Rajaee, Farhang. 1983. *Islamic Values and World View: Khomeyni On Man, the State and International Politics*. Lanham: University Press of America.

Ramazani, R. K. 1983. "Khomayni's Islam in Iran's Foreign Policy." *Islam in Foreign Policy*. Edited by Adeed Dawisha. Cambridge: Cambridge University Press: 9–32.

Randall, Vicky. 1987. *Women and Politics: An International Perspective*. 2d ed. Chicago: University of Chicago Press.

Rifkin, Jeremy. 1991. *Biosphere Politics: A New Consciousness for a New Century*. New York: Crown Publishers.

Rodda, Annabel. 1991. *Women and the Environment*. London: Zed Books.

Rommen, Heinrich A. 1945. *The State in Catholic Thought*. St. Louis: B. Herder Book Co.

Rousseau, Jean-Jacques. 1991. *Rousseau on International Relations*. Edited by Stanley Hoffmann and David P. Fidler. Oxford: Oxford University Press.

———. 1973. *The Social Contract and Discourses*. Translated by G. D. H. Cole. London: J. M. Dent and Sons Ltd.

Routley, Val. 1981. "On Karl Marx as an Environmental Hero." *Environmental Ethics* 3: 237–244.

Runyan, Anne Sisson, and V. Spike Peterson. 1991. "The Radical Future of Realism: Feminists Subversions of IR Theory." *Alternatives* 16 (Winter): 67–106.

Russell, Bertrand. 1938. *Power*. New York: W. W. Norton & Co.

Russell, Frank M. 1936. *Theories of International Relations*. New York: D. Appleton-Century.

Santmire, H. Paul. 1985. *The Travail of Nature*. Philadelphia: Fortress Press.

Shiva, Vandana. 1988. *Staying Alive: Women, Ecology, and Development*, London: Zed Press.

Smith, Adam. 1948. *Adam Smith's Moral and Political Philosophy*. Edited by Herbert W. Schneider. New York: Harper & Row.

Smith, Fred. 1992. "Carnival of Dunces." *National Review* 44 (July 6, 1992): 30–32.

Solzhenitsyn, Alexandr. 1991. *Rebuilding Russia*. Translated by Alexis Klimoff. New York: Farrar, Straus and Giroux.

Sophocles. 1984. "Oedipus at Colonus." *The Three Theban Plays*. Translated by Robert Fagles and introduced by Bernard Knox. New York: Penguin Books.

Sprout, Harold, and Margaret Sprout. 1971. *Toward a Politics of the Planet Earth*. New York: Van Nostrand Reinhold.

Starhawk. 1982. *Dreaming the Dark*. Boston: Beacon Press.

Stone, Julius. 1984. *Visions of World Order*. Baltimore: Johns Hopkins University Press.

Synod of Bishops. "Justice in the World." *The Gospel of Peace and Justice*. Edited by Joseph Gremillion. Maryknoll, N.Y.: Orbis Books: 513–529.

Thaden, Edward C. 1964. *Conservative Nationalism in Nineteenth Century Russia*. Seattle: University of Washington Press.

The Holy Qur'an. 1946. Translated by A. Yusuf Ali. United States: McGregor and Werner, Inc.

Thucydides. 1982. *The Peloponnesian War.* Introduction by T. E. Wick. New York: The Modern Library.

Tickner, J. Ann. 1992. *Gender in International Relations.* New York: Columbia University Press.

———. 1988. "Hans Morgenthau's Principles of Political Realism: A Feminist Reformation." *Millennium* 17 (3): 429–440.

Tolstoy, Count Leo. 1905. "Patriotism and Government." *Letters and Essays.* Translated by Leo Wiener. Boston: Dana Estes and Co.: 143–166.

———. 1905. "The Soldiers' Memento." *Letters and Essays.* Translated by Leo Wiener. Boston: Dana Estes and Co.: 165–169.

Tong, Rosemarie. 1989. *Feminist Thought.* Boulder: Westview Press.

United Nations. 1949. *Universal Declaration of Human Rights.* Department of State. Washington, D.C.: GPO.

U.S. Catholic Bishops. 1986. "Economic Justice for All: Catholic Social Teaching and the U.S. Economy." *Origins,* 16.

Vasquez, John, ed. 1990. *Classics of International Relations.* 2d ed. Englewood Cliffs: Prentice Hall.

Vincent, R. J. 1986. *Human Rights and International Relations.* Cambridge: Cambridge University Press.

Vitoria, Francisco. 1991. *Political Writings.* Edited by Anthony Pagden and Jeremy Lawrence. Cambridge: Cambridge University Press.

Vys, Jamie. 1980. *The Gods Must Be Crazy.* N. P.: Mimosa.

Wallerstein, Immanuel. 1974. *The Modern World System.* New York: Academic Press.

———. 1984. *The Politics of the World Economy.* Cambridge: Cambridge University Press.

Waltz, Kenneth. 1959. *Man, the State and War.* New York: Columbia University Press.

———. 1979. *Theory of International Relations.* New York: Random House.

Ware, Timothy. 1993. *The Orthodox Church.* Revised. New York: Penguin Books.

White, Lynn. 1973. "The Historical Roots of Our Ecological Crisis." *Western Man and Environmental Ethics.* Edited by Ian Barbour. Reading, Mass.: Addison-Wesley.

Whiteside, Kerry H. 1994. "Hanna Arendt and Ecological Politics." *Environmental Ethics* 16 (Winter): 339–358.

Wiedenbaum, Murray. 1992. "Leviathan in Rio." *National Review* 27 (April 1992).

Wild, John. 1953. *Plato's Modern Enemies and the Theory of Natural Law.* Chicago: University of Chicago Press.

Williams, Michael C. "Rousseau, Realism, and Realpolitik." *Millennium: Journal of International Studies* 18 (2):185–203.

Worster, Donald. 1985. *Nature's Economy: History of Ecological Ideas.* New York: Cambridge University Press.

Zacher, Mark W., and Richard A. Matthew. 1995. "Liberal International Theory: Common Threads, Divergent Strands." *Controversies in International Relations Theory.* Edited by Charles W. Kegley Jr. New York: St. Martin's Press: 107–150.

Zernov, Nicholas. 1961. *Eastern Christendom.* New York: G.P. Putnam's Sons.

Zile, Zigurds L. 1911. "Lenin's Contribution to Law: The Case of Protection and Preservation of the Natural Environment." *Lenin and Leninism.* Edited by Bernard W. Eissenstat. Lexington, Mass.: Lexington Books: 83–100.

INDEX